T0290222

STUDYING HUNGER JOURNALS

Bernadette Mayer

Station Hill
of Barrytown

Published by Station Hill Press, Inc., 124 Station Hill Road, Barrytown, NY 12507
www.stationhill.org

Station Hill of Barrytown literary publication is a project of The Institute for Publishing Arts, Inc., a not-for-profit, Federally tax-exempt organization (501(c)(3)) in Barrytown, New York.

Cover design by Sherry Williams, Oxygen Design Group. Interior design by Kathryn Weinstein and Sherry Williams.
Interior photograph of Bernadette Mayer (circa 1975) by Ed Bowes.
Cover and interior artworks by Bernadette Mayer, copied from original manuscripts of *Studying Hunger Journals* at the University of California, San Diego. All rights reserved. Reprinted with permission.

The author and publisher wish to thank the following whose generous efforts have made this book possible. Michael Ruby originated the idea of the project, worked with the author on the introduction, proofread and served as adviser on the book. David Brinks chose and scanned the images from the original journals. Miles Champion retyped the original typescript into digital form.

The author wishes to thank Bill Berkson, the first publisher of the journals in the abridged version *Studying Hunger* (Adventures in Poetry/Big Sky: New York, New York and Bolinas, California: 1975).

Library of Congress Cataloging-in-Publication Data

Mayer, Bernadette.
Studying hunger journals / Bernadette Mayer.
p. cm.
ISBN 978-1-58177-120-6
I. Title.
PS3563.A952S74 2011
811'.54—dc22
2010045286

CONTENTS

INTRODUCTION TO STUDYING HUNGER JOURNALS

I kept these journals while seeing a psychiatrist. I'd gone to see him because I thought I might be crazy, after my work on memory, shooting 36 pictures a day & keeping a detailed journal having driven me to the brink. But I thought why not go over that brink & see what's there. On the other hand I didn't want to wind up in a mental hospital, tied to some bed or chair.

In my experience people didn't expect a woman to be intelligent so they thought I was weird and/or crazy. There were no female nerds then. One mistake I made was thinking linearly, that knowledge led somewhere from which you can go somewhere else, but you'll have to forgive me, I grew up & lived in western society.

David, the psychiatrist, gave me two journals to write in, so that he could always keep one to read, though he had said at the beginning of our work that he didn't want to be inundated with written material. I wrote in the books with colored pens because I hoped I would hit upon a way to color-code emotions, which I never did, & in imitation of Hannah Weiner, a close friend. It was also a reflection of my own synaesthesia—I saw letters as colors; I was hoping the colors of the pens would help me see emotions.

I was asked to do two readings during that time, at the Paula Cooper Gallery & at RISD. Wanting to read what I was currently working on, I made two works, which I considered to be lectures for the readings. These were published by Adventures In Poetry/Big Sky as STUDYING HUNGER. I loved gerunds because they signify the present. Bill

Berkson, the editor, told me later that if he had known there was more he would have published all of it. But I wasn't finished yet.

Both MEMORY & STUDYING HUNGER were published in the same year, 1975. The latter began with this explanation:

Listen

I began all this in April, 1972. I wanted to try to record, like a diary, in writing, states of consciousness, my states of consciousness, as fully as I could, every day, for one month. A month always seems like a likely time-span, if there is one, for an experiment. A month gives you enough time to feel free to skip a day, but not so much time that you wind up fucking off completely.

I had an idea before this that if a human, a writer, could come up with a workable code, or shorthand, for the transcription of every event, every motion, every transition of his or her own mind, & could perform this process of translation on himself, using the code, for a 24-hour period, he or we or someone could come up with a great piece of language/information.

Anyway

When I began to attempt the month-long experiment with states of consciousness, I wrote down a list of intentions. It went like this: First, to record special states of consciousness. Special: change, sudden change, high, low, food, levels of attention

And, how intentions change

And, to do this as an emotional science, as though: I have taken a month-drug, I work as observer of self in process

And, to do the opposite of "accumulate data," oppose MEMORIES, DIARIES, find structures

And, a language should be used that stays on the observation/notes/leaps side of language border which seems to separate, just barely, observation & analysis. But if the language must resort to analysis to "keep going," then let it be closer to that than to "accumulate data." Keep going *is a pose; accumulate data is a pose.*

Also, to use this to find a structure for MEMORY & you, you will find out what memory is, you already know what moving is

And, to do this without remembering

The "hunger" in the title comes from regular hunger which I felt in the extreme because my parents had died young (there was nobody to feed me) & from a concept delineated in a line from a poem I wrote then: *eating the colors of a lineup of words.* You know how people say they "devoured" a book? The synaesthesia I experienced made the letters & words seem as edible as paintings.

One of the symptoms I experienced was that I couldn't swallow, perhaps as in "I couldn't swallow it." For more about this phenomenon, read Freud's case of Anna O. David & I did traditional analysis but he was not a traditional analyst. We went out together in his Mercedes-Benz, kissed & once we came close to making love. He had married one of his patients who was Elaine May. He had had a lot of 'famous' patients including Alger Hiss whom I'd see in the waiting room where we'd discuss the way we read the New York Times. I didn't pay David; in fact he would give me money because I traveled with so little. A friend of mine recently sued her psychiatrist & was able to buy a summer retreat.

The journals include some drawings, some of which are used here. When I made the journals into a text, I changed all the names, so eventually David becomes Belial, one of the biblical devils. Unfortunately I threw the list of name changes away.

It may seem odd that both books, MEMORY & STUDYING HUNGER, were published in the same year or that I embarked on STUDYING HUNGER right after doing MEMORY but I was in a great hurry. I figured I'd die like my father did, at age 49. I did have a cerebral hemorrhage at that age just like him but I didn't die, I had brain surgery & lived to eat more oysters.

February 2009

● BOOK I

Dear David,

I'm having dinner in a restaurant, alone, before the poetry reading. It's a restaurant where they know me, you know, in case anything happens. I've decided to keep this journal at least for tonight, maybe for our information, maybe as a companion. It's not a letter though of course I was tempted to make it a love letter. In a way I'll write as little as possible. I thought this afternoon at least I'm not an infant but it didn't last. Tired, hungry and scared: it's hard to chew leaves. I've taken a quarter of a valium and had a beer, the power of the imagination. What's the difference between a grownup and a child? First day of summer. I don't have to eat this dinner. The salad appeals to me more, the real food seems forbidding. I ate an olive, that's hopeful. Never eaten one before. I guess I'm refusing to eat. All of this seems very clear, I'm not at all confused about it, but I'm wondering what's going to happen.

I can see the helpless infant and all its fits, what I can't see is this: how does this happen, this pattern or transference or whatever it is. I want to know how, neurologically and every other way. It seems a lot different from anything I know. I'm chewing just like a baby as though solid food's too much for me. Something interesting happened before, I felt businesslike. I haven't eaten much but I got some energy. She turned down the baby food and ate the salad without teeth. It's interesting to know no matter how little you eat, the food serves you. Spend the night alone, o.k. I'll try. And did I start writing as a companion to myself? Who cares? Well, right at this moment, everything's urgent, everything's new. I wanted to eat for energy, I knew I didn't have to eat but I wanted to be able to drink without getting drunk so I eat. The secret is to eat in front of friends.

How strange, from a baby's point of view, my relationship with you is. Water, wine, tea and strength. And salad. I'm getting an enormous sense of humor like a hard-on. Tea weak tea Tetley tea my favorite kind of commercial tea. The work I did today, mimeographing posters, I did a terrific job and they're being really terrific in my restaurant but will I have the energy, the walking legs, to go out to a bar later, say, at two or three a.m. Only in defense of a kernel of corn, I wish I were that. A soul can't be hurt by tea. Today I saw the man I was supposed to marry when I was seventeen. I acted like a mother, I can guess, ought to act. Like a blotter, I didn't get involved. I feel like the wife of the owner. No I don't but she is getting spooked by my behavior, sitting before my expensive dinner and only writing in my book. Is behavior a puzzle with a solution or not?

So I keep wanting to say I love you, please accept this as only an element in the pattern is complex. I don't mean to give you a hard time. Laughter cures what I might say next, I'm so sorry. I'll get a Guinness Stout for the reading, more support for a mother, sure not as brave, brave as Jack Kerouac, what do we do to ourselves? Do our best? I feel freer in this area of feeding than in the dreaded empty home. I love Max, I know you don't believe me, I spent a lot of money today, I'm being very careful. I feel my way around like a baby, fear of adults. For David the myth of poetry exists like a canal.

And now I'm exhausted, why don't they feed me when I'm hungry, and the ink's too black. I keep trying to feel the way I would feel if Max or who were here. The reading's gone on too long, I panic but and I seem to be totally what. What I mean is these people don't make me nervous they make me bored. I'm exhausted and it's a struggle to concentrate. I'm home. Max called right away and I didn't want to talk but I did and so I did and then I realized that I must assure you again that I do love him. I've laid out all the pills next to the bed and the t.v.'s on, now that sounds like it, but it's valium and antibiotics. The window's open but I haven't crept out onto the fire escape yet. The walk out here, it is a long loft, wasn't as bad as it sometimes is. I leave all my clothes on as it's safer. I switch to a brown pen as black was too oppressive and thick-pointed. I'm alone here yes. I can only eat little bits again. This is very interesting, I mean that. Distance and the phone call are terrifying, ending, this is an ordeal, no reason for it either, my memory of the past, mother, father, what difference does it make, here I am in the act of my own conception, like a drug without the pre-selling acid of something you get, fear, I walked outside, there's a certain point at which you get dizzy if you want to, I do and don't. I'm too tired to weed out all these thoughts for you. I won't be dramatic but this is traumatic, now if I say that I distance myself, I'll have to pay or suffer. Max is so interesting I'm speeding. Proud of myself and afraid of dying. I'd call you on the phone but what I'd say wouldn't be to the point, a big quiet laugh will do. I went outside to see if the door was locked. So I've drunk a small glass of Amontillado behind the bricks and I won't take the antibiotic because I haven't eaten. I still say to myself when I see I can be alone for a while, humans can adapt to anything. A moment of hopefulness. I feel like I'm risking my life. These notes are censored now. Once I wanted to do something whereby a person, by means of a complicated code, would record his every thought and mind movement for a short while. I wanted to set it up. I feel that these are all clues and you must solve the puzzle. Not abstractly but hesitatingly, I also feel ashamed. I have thought, the thought popped up, so many times of you being "inundated" with written material and of course I want to please you.

And my next thought always is: Do I know you? Goddammit, it drives me crazy. I know I'm not crazy. Can I give this to you? And then I feel desire and then I feel cold. I'm leaving everything open.

Thursday 5 p.m.

I bought a lot of nuts, I can eat them without thinking. Teresa's coming by, I tried to convince her not to, I dread talking about the past. I made the bed so things wouldn't seem too grim to me. When I'm alone here the loft, which is actually very beautiful in the light, looks dark and grim and bare-bulbish. Since I first came to see you I've continued to be nervous in this house alone even for the shortest times, with only one exception, the times when the guys are outside playing ball.

Billie Holiday and all black music. I'm working, I'm working well with, as usual, all the black music. Eating leaves cheese and nuts continuously. Max's mother on the phone: "Are you eating?" And another call from Max, I was afraid then for fear if I felt optimistic, he'd die. If I'm suffering I'm sure he'll survive (till he gets back). I'm alone here yes. An almond. Maybe I'm too good (to survive). A bottle, switch to coke. This rubber cement is making me high, have I eaten anything today? The noises seem barren here and I'm planning another excursion into the world tomorrow, all day and night. Packed a bag, it's only 12:20. Called Andy, he's not home. Now I'm continuously eating and drinking. Now I've typed the piece of writing addressed to my mother that begins, "You sleep..." I'll try to concentrate on more work. My chest is tight and my nose is tense as if I'm pushing it down.

2:40 a.m.

I made a tape for Bartholomew, partly to explain all this. I owe him a letter and now I think I may have gone too far. Feel awful.

4 a.m.

I just got up and devoured a pretty old piece of cake and milk. There's nothing wrong with me. I'd forgotten again. Another quarter valium makes you hungry. She saw she had been secretly hungry. The t.v. set just scared me out of my wits, it isn't even on.

Friday

Woke up speeding, I'm in a cab to the church where I have work to do. Stayed in bed till the last minute so I'd have to rush out of the house out of my mind but it's o.k. I keep thinking, don't blow it, it's almost over. I keep thinking perhaps people find me disgusting because I never eat. Just enough to stay alive till Max gets home. And then I think to add, to add a morsel extra to keep Max from standing for a mother until someone else comes along in my day I can relax with, what a word. I mean relax.

Later

Fern fixed me a dinner which I ate. So, David, I'm writing small. Now much later things have got really out of control and I don't know what's going to happen but in a way I'm in control, at least I'm driving. Someone had asked me to read at a benefit reading and tonight I certainly felt like it so I did and now I'm in a car with friend Grace and Francisco, a black poet who wants to stay… And at that point I'm interrupted by Francisco who gets back in the car and says he wants to sleep with me. I say no.

Saturday 4 p.m.

Max isn't back yet, I feel pretty easy, now I laugh at you, he should be back today but I don't know when yet. I slept with Francisco. I'll try to just list my thoughts: I didn't want to sleep with him unless he somehow knew all about me, or at least about the last few days of my life. So, I'm in a daze. Maybe I found out something, maybe that guy was really you. Well I remember one specific Monet I saw with water lilies, I mean one specific moment when he was, all night I was concentrating hard, the reading four hours long, it's a good thing I had food from Fern, and when I saw what was inevitably going to happen, I kept concentrating. We were in a bar for a while, I drank real slow. The meal I had, sleeping with Francisco, that was not a meal, I'm sure I really wanted to do all that, but with this reservation and this is only as far as I can say in my daze: the reservation: since I knew Grace was staying over too, I knew I had a choice or it would be easier to have a cohort's choice about fucking. But, and there's a big but, my instinct was not to do it, though I like Francisco and he turns me on and so on but it's you I couldn't resist. Showing off. Add this: everybody's coming on to me lately even the fucking butcher's coming on to me and they're tormenting me about you. And when Francisco said "I want to sleep with you" I started laughing hysterically because I know he's not the butcher and I can't resist a friend, a real friend, not now. Add too that it seems to me to be a somehow dazzling and dazing climax to these four days alone and what I feel I found out is this: I felt this enormous tenderness for him and it was really for him and not him as you, though for a moment when I touched his face, I wished it was your face. So then so what I won't go on with this but there's a seemingly perfect parallel here to me and you: a person who is a symbol to a doctor who is a receptacle. You may think it's much simpler than this and you may be right. Thank you very much.

10 p.m.

Now Max won't be back till tomorrow night, so here we are again. I'm tired, tired of drinking, tired of wondering whether to take some pill or smoke or be tired. I slept three hours last night and was coasting toward the finish and the kind of real despair I've been avoiding by covering up with sheer nervousness is showing up now. So I started spending the day just doing things to the house for Max and now I feel angry, no knowing he'll be home tomorrow night either or the next night. I eat all the soft foods, I find myself thinking I'll never see you again too. Everything goes on as usual, I can't believe it, the t.v. It should be all news about me, instead it's very hip, I'm watching whatever comes up on channel 2. And then I think it's possible this Max doesn't even exist, now that's a fine example for "want to be crazy." Last night I asked Grace, I begged her not to get drunk so we could talk. She got so drunk she couldn't stand up when we got home. Is this way of feeling what people mean when they say they're bored? I just had this fantasy: Andy calls and I tell him I'm not feeling too good cause Max was supposed to be back and he isn't. Andy doesn't think that's such a big thing so I yell at him, this time for sure, hang up and vent my rage on this chest I wish didn't exist. Is the bravest thing I could do go out for a walk? Fuck this scene. And fuck Bartholomew pretentiously learning to draw among his servants. But making a mess with some pastels makes me feel better, I've got my clean adult clothes all dirty. All fuck channel 2, channel 2 really must think I'm a maniac. Is it me or is it them that always wants to fuck? Talked angrily to Max, not at him, wrote angrily to this Bart shit and what do I do now! Fuck! I will write in my book till pen falls from hand. Goodbye, I hate this shit. Sorry, David, but you get the picture.

Sunday Noon

Dream of an odyssey, another one, alone or was Bartholomew there. The t.v.'s been awake all night. Funny taste in mouth, as if infection's curing, my tongue is a month of Sundays. Did I tell you about the muscle I pulled to give me a focus for real pain, it's all these heavy boxes I've been lifting. Whether Bart was in the dream or not, I don't want to admit it, I was alone. I flash on Sunday mornings as a child, Mass, what're they like for Jewish kids, are they like this particular Sunday? I eat breakfast: a notebook, coffee and an egg. Fern seems to be leaving for South America today. And hide nor hair of Andy as they say. So I slept in my clothes again and this morning I wouldn't change them because they're so full of colors from the pastels I was dreaming with "like a child in a condition of neglect." Ha ha.

A ha ha is a breather, ah! Like, this is all very interesting but ha ha, I have the answer, no dream will tell it so far. Friday when Fern was fixing me and a thousand other people dinner, but I thought it was just me, she left the refrigerator door open at one point. I stared unconsciously into it, hers, and she surprised me when she said, "Is there something you want from the refrigerator?" Oh Fern, I do adore you.

6 p.m.

Knock knock that must be her at the door, no it's no one. I know I'll go from rags to riches, if that's how it goes, before the sun comes out again like it did today, that one was on me. I keep discouraging people from coming over, John and Edmund, there are others I wouldn't discourage… Cleaned and rearranged the house again, rearrangement a tradition with us or with me, I made some "improvements." Max does come on the 11:30 p.m. plane. I hope. He said to me: "You can stop feeling bad now." I felt some small resentment and one more thing, or so: in the last few days ideas come to me with such suddenness and when they come I am absolutely sure of them, maybe it's not so new but it's new for me to recognize it this way. So I sat on the fire escape in the intermittent sun and made up a few sad songs that I could weep to if I would.

Hannah's coming over, finally a visitor I don't mind having.

Monday Noon

And Max home and before that I went out with Hannah and ate a fish. So, thank you very much. I dream an extravagant dream, a genealogical show, and something else begins. I can stand on the brown and green ground.

I wasn't going to write any more to you but I feel an incredible anger now as though I've been cheated today, Max is at Hilly's, and it's not any different from before, just as hard going, blah blah, but the anger, maybe it's because our idyllic relationship, yours and mine, is over. This being home is a let-down, you understand how I mean that and there's a distance I've created between me and the Max I don't want to deal with at all and I feel neglected and that's all. One more thing, why don't the sun come out and now I'll stop for sure, that's all.

Bernadette Mayer, 74 Grand Street, New York City 10013. I'm coming in the door, there's gonna be water there. Saturday or Sunday, mescaline's on the route. The counterculture is baby girls, it's homeostasis. You see I've gotta stop and make magic, I get out of the code beyond the secret code which would have worked, it would have worked anyway but since I am you, now, a part of the supposed fusing, the confusion of possible yous, I will milk, impose, I will come out of hiding in impossible daily language about food and it's time, I've already begun anyway which is why my knife drills into you... Defend the states of consciousness, spend gold and silver paper routes and yes, that's the trap door to America under the rug and Jack Kerouac and I go down there and giggle a lot all the time. You can't realize, I mean relate, tell recount remember, but you can address, love, vision, vision of any kind, vision your house on a street, Jack and David is your penname SHUT and who are you and we are equals coming in the door when we encounter culture in the name of baby girls. Something about a cockpit on the moon, the sun shines, begin. It's March or April, it's a man with a peace sign for a mouth, it's Max he bows and Bernadette, Max has big blue arms and purple legs and Bernadette long pink hair and a green signal for a face, or eyes race, it's April, I know it.

April 1

I dream a piece of pie for ninety cents, custard cream yellow pie, remember the placement of events in a dream, what was happening was happening on the left side of the screen, Max says: "What benefits do you want from your employer?"

I have my intentions: to record states of consciousness, special involving change and sudden change, high and low food, levels of attention and how intentions change. And to do this as an emotional science as though, I have taken a month-drug and work as observer of self in process, to do the opposite of "accumulate data" (Memory). Yes, no. A language should be used that stays on the observation/notes/leaps side of the language border between observation and analysis (just barely), but closer I guess to analysis than "accumulate data." To use this to find a structure for Memory and to do this without remembering, what's the danger? What states of consciousness and patterns of them are new to language? What is the language for them. Answer "all" upside down. What is the relation of things that stand out, things that seem interesting like a sentence from the tape: "The food of the mother is better than the food of the fatter father;" like poem titles and poem ideas, to the rest? To develop moments, to see and feel consciousness like anyone does, as "standing out" like language does, ideas do. A portrait by Gina of a man on a camelopard with one house in the distance and another a profile, the man in a dunce cap, a portrait by me of two men playing cards at a table, a light above their caps, a portrait by Neil of a woman with eyes and teeth.

April 2

You wait. I dream two boys and in trunks and closets and I feed them. There's a shot through the bar sign which is a guillotine, zooming in. And three men are pushing me on the streets, one is John who's gone to the Ranger game. And everyone's being guillotined, especially someone like Holly. We all drink wine in a bar, we travel all over. At 12:20 I wake up in the bed by the window, it's 3001. Parents are in but parents are out. I set two watches last night at the head of the bed to check on them. Review: one, two, three, four, you're a jerk I'm a whore; about intentions, add, to be an enchantress; about sentences, add, the chest of chicken, that's how Big Max refers to the breast, and, "How long have you been head of this business?"

At 3:35 a.m. I record I ate too much food. Food weight is family food; I take in, I take over power, money.

April 3

The massacre of the house. Bill Berkson's rooms and Frank O'Hara's book are destroyed. Gerard is the queen of the parade. Instead, they follow me, I lose my knife. The man in the room takes his corset off. Bill's rooms are at the top of the house: there are warm spots and cold spots and books, it's a kind of paradise. When they follow me I'm on a motorcycle, like a fool to be followed. The man in the room has breasts but he could still be a man because: "He developed them."

In the morning stillness of the house I think what do I want to be doing, I upend the records and put on one. Visiting Pierre seems like a good idea, entering the P-phase of existence, phase with many rules I have to even think to remember: you can be hungry at Pierre's but you can eat! And when Pierre tells us about being sick and a fear unlike, lucky strike, my own, I sink into that state for a Monet of water lilies again, for a moment I drink coffee will my heart stop beating right then from it and there's the damp air: a slice of your own head, you can't cart anything away from Pierre's for free without the sun going down on your conversation, I stare at lights behind the heads I'm looking at, it's the head and neck of a man with all the parts of his brain quite clearly coming to an animal-like center of control at the base of the whole thing.

April 4

Hashish at the basketball practice with cheering cherries and group readings and performances. There's a little nun outside the door. I am waking up and going back to sleep starting at eight a.m. in a delirium remembering the alarm, remembering dreams: I think of a word, like, hashish, like group: the word brings back one scene of a dream when I am awake, one center of a fantasy but what predominates is was this: it's Tuesday the day I get up at ten. What am I hiding? Is was this and is was morning. It's one o'clock now. This: I'd like to be a basketball player, one of the players, I include no description of their movements; left out of the group reading, I fantasize in dream around the periphery, control those feelings in dream again of refusing to admit to the denial of being left out, I create a paced and rapid movement in around and about that event, event of being left out, I synthesize a dance that is for me alone, that is I'm active I'm looking through windows, I don't speak I preserve the sheet surface clean white sheet of my presence in the room when I get out of bed, I move I don't want to move to the instant where details and foods accumulate later in the day, are the foods I ate late last night digested are they gone am I this clean surface or does all the work come later like practice, you've seen it, you've seen the other team play now so... I calculate people and their diseases as numbers to come up with a figure and do all the work later for corrective calculation on my own body today. Again Père Pierre was sick. Again Max will never die. Outside the performance area I exist. Outside the process the arena of real activity a space for existing, I might float around, or, am I going too far. But no it makes sense. In this way from the outside I put everything in, take in everything, I must spew it all out, what prevents me what seizes me gently when I try to emerge is that nun outside the door, she has a purpose, I put her there: let nothing myself get out of this room, let no judgments be made, let no law and order exist except this: nothing escapes from here. I gladly stay inside to observe, what? To melt with love over...you'll never know.

Maybe to be in a prison like this is to refuse a guide, to refuse a direction, a person who has used the word human as a lie without levels and that one might say I'd rather be in prison where I am different. My responses I want them to be automatic, my physical movements, indifferent, undifferentiated, uncalculated, cool, almost unnoticed, calm must be calm for this activity, inner motion, emotion, design. Yes it's a surface, you can draw on, out from it, anything, everything, I know what's going on.

It's not the whole story I've left out the psychology of it the motives the history and memory of myself the parts that have direction, I've left them out because in that way I could be pinned down, possibly tortured.

3 a.m.

When all the colors are available I don't spend much time thinking about them, I just use them all. …in your normal voice and with your small hand just write small, write this. And this writing or this diary throws me off or away and I have no advice to give, nothing wise to say, I'm writing a history is all. I try, I tried to move slower in around a review: Harris: backtracking on the phone, Sjöwall: existential, Paul: "Do you wanna play cards?" Max: "Was that what you wanted to do?" I don't know what I'm thinking about, got a lot of food in the house but I doubt it. And vitamins too.

Pleasure in time or in order: coffee, a pile-up of words, I sit at table, Max sweep bed, mice. Pictures, walk streets looking up, breathe, predictions, fruit and vegetable, Knicks game, wine and Harris poem, Max looks rhubarb sex strange, read and tea and subject (this).

And pain: coffee, Vito influence, Paul malaise, Barbara and Neil, Max is high, why, someone pretends she doesn't know where to go, I scream "What?" People just talking. L: "I always keep my promises." And stupid Stanislaus. And politics and some real feelings are pain. People want to talk, just arrange, just plan, just not go at all in the end. So choice and chance.

Sentence: David moves in my room—"emergency." Is it of interest?

Note: No color little color in this yet.

Definition: <u>analyze</u>—to separate whole into parts to find nature size function and relationship; to examine parts, analysis a loosing. Up—loose, throughout—loose analysis. <u>Inductive</u>—from particulars to a general conclusion and inducing, lead-in. <u>Deductive</u>—from a known to an unknown, from general to specific, lead away.

Detective deductive. High stakes of consciousness: thoughts feelings impressions and the whole, plus, hilarious elated drunk and intoxicated, or, knowing and feeling that something is or was happening or existing. As, pleasure, poem, healthy high and hollow, point, then to write is wrong, this is basic English, humor ice and idea, or, digestion direction discovery. A yellow wash or a yellow mountainside.

April 5

The mountainside is yellow. Hitler is in Notre Dame. "The movies were a good hiding place." "Will you be sitting here during the intermission? Will you watch our coats? Do you want some coffee? Vous-êtes juif?" Marlene Dietrich sings Lily Marlene.

Colors of a black and white movie 4 1/2 hours long, a light from the projection booth falls on my seat I cast a diagonal shadow, it's the yellow mountainside, a suggestion of hair tumbling down it. And of the street when we emerge, look at those red lights, red lights are bright late slanted rays, cloud hovers over color, holding it in, bright as blue pants green sweater. And of Fanelli's yellow light yellow beer yellow Max in clothes that place him in a yellow parched field, I feel. And of Clark's reading: language demands its form maybe language demands its form, in bed head down muscles arched color of readers plotting the outline sound of a language yet unmarked, not controlling it, forget any substance or substantive of (too noun) many meanings and get it gradually paler. And of loft spot-lit inside out. And of "Secret of the Incas" too, advance red green and blue of gold.

Note: I can hear the log before it falls or is it still falling when it hits and I hear it hitting, seeing sound vibrations in sleep closed eyes, a sound is a lamp hanging, it lowers and disappears. Another shaft of light on the side of a screen, another yellow mountainside. Red and gray complements.

April 6

Up in the morning for no reason, where's your sense of humor (of interest) a bracket of folding chairs.

12:30 p.m. breakfast work quiet work quiet Chris alone, that's description, this is this: I try to predict something: I try to remember if I will be tired if I get up now, so 45 minutes goes by fast and all this still has to do with remembering, later. Now: reflection all around. What do I mean by this: a sound an image there are no real reflections but I am reflecting and it's painful without, the presence, of other, people, thus the "all around" and this boundary between reflection and surrounding. "A peninsula is a body of land almost completely surrounded by water," I said. She said, "There's no such thing as 'almost completely.'"

Analysis of abstraction and the system for a process distract me. They move and reflect the needs, the needs arise out of information much more toward motion, the need to do something and the emotion like of singing down a lane in effect but needs arise and we fill them out since everyone knows everything, remember, and feel free and this is called you're having no excuses today and excuse is as much an object as meat of course but why not but why. It's the same thing for everyone, a level rest or a level nest but please perhaps a chance a choice, let there be no levels no plural levels you are bleeding right on Freud, I take that back, enter. I mean, come in.

Review: is a disguise: this end up, no mail. What's the danger? Anyway you wa-a-a-ant me well tha-a-at's how I will be-e-e, I will be-e-e. A big brown window.

April 8

Max dreams he realizes I experiment in "garbage." Ha ha, he's right. I have to get to the bank by three: but I dream a guard outside my house in Ridgewood, I ask to see his identification, people rarely do that, I think he falls down. And now it's getting later, hands on a clock quarter of then ten to it's just the bank on Canal Street I've deposited six thousand dollars (six thousand hours of (cinema?) memory in bank?) in the bank and we need cash realization, I can see I have seen the actual bank statement in my dream. At some point, I haven't gone to the bank to announce the banns of marriage yet, David comes and tells us we have to turn all our bodies (selves) superimposed on paintings on the wall to face in, we must look into the wall, genitals face the wall. And will we someday have to look out, out the paintings? out the windows? everything turned to the inside? Something about a pool.

Review: "You had a hard day." "The car broke down and someone threw an egg at me." "I have a dog and I work at Gimbel's." And so the next day, John Cage calls. Drug use and health foods.

April 9

Music play, accept dissonance relationships, I keep thinking where's the danger in an experiment: non-negative lack of sleep makes me laugh and projects make me busy: to find a mate.

Notes: anarchy isn't anarchy, it's only in relation as learning is to imitation. Sun's out.

April 10

I get a check for $27,000. Ed is dealing with a woman in red fur for money.

Notes: be 27. Two dealers. In Memory, the same dry spell, July 10-11.

Observation: I expect something to happen, daze, and fear, mother exception, end of people having children but what happens too much is twice as easy.

April 11

I dream the history of all people in the world, good and evil. I zoom in on a familiar cat-face. The next part of the dream says to me this part is about you personally.

Ann-Margret, that's me (so history comes first, what about you personally, Gertrude?) is arrested for accidentally killing a guy she kisses. She kisses everyone especially a (golf) boy she doesn't know at all named Clancy, that's you Max. She makes scenes about people not wanting to get involved and her two children are with her, all the way from Texas. Now that gets complicated. And before that: a crowd scene here, everybody brought someone. Card playing just before we found some more money and Grace brought back a book that was a deck of cards and the money was in it and just before Max and I lie down on the bed a section of the loft wall isn't there and somehow we look over, inches away, on Dick and his wife also lying down and I talk with him through the wall. He comes out where the "World Works" poster really is and later I can't stand the crowds again and I think they'll take our money, put away like Horace put away film, no they don't want money, I see that now. Scene on the streets, I run and come back and they go.

Oh heavy boxes, teach me a dance! To get out of this mess of names.

April 12

Why all these slices and pieces? A big cake is brought and cut and eaten. The cake gets eaten before it is shown. There aren't many pieces left to go on a tray so they are eaten without a presentation. What came along with the cake was a bin, a display, a wall of slices of lime and grapefruit and fruit is no desire but these fruits are bitter and we live high on the top floor. There's a religious Mass of some kind with science experiments and undressing, all is edible. A nun or a whore is temporarily in search of something, this old project. She's just temporarily. They say they'll send me to a doctor. I say no, anything but that, that's as bad as what Phil Jackson or Jack Marin would do to me. There's two sides to every question. Before that a museum.

This is the dream answer, the dream summary, but not the dance, not cool. Sweet eats make a sour show, is that what I did or is that what they do? I think color is sour. A science system is what is prescribed or planned again, what have I got to show, what's anyone? A nun is surely covered, what would they do to me? They punched each other in the nose. Jack-Jack. A museum is as old as a clock or a cock, Doc.

April 13

Can't focus, it's no wonder. I'm playing basketball, I dunk a box of cookies. Where's the net? A little offense? A little man by a stream or sewer might get caught and we talk about streams or sewers, that little man is a desperate floater. Even these minor old cookies are still wrapped. Sweet sewer systems, sewer grate, net system, sissy. Sight is motion. I esteem you an elation.

Subjects: fame/culture, handwriting, leave out/put in, do/not do (things (every)), feel.

And, I miss the seven- and eight-year-olds' trip around the world, it costs $121.

And, mountain of chaos, I'm climbing up an almost vertical mountain, Max I'm counting on you. "If Max can't do it I could try but the momentum'd be lost." This mountain is in the picture. And, the payments on the car must be lowered by two dollars a month to keep Max out of jail, have I put you fear I put you in prison love? That would lengthen them to 35 weeks like a boat or a jeep but when we try, it turns out we're all paid up anyway. And I see Carolyn Cornelia in here and later she tries to commit suicide. I give up.

April 20

It's 4:30 a.m. and this is an unusual green, I feel the earth move, what does Hemingway have to do with this? I gave up the original project. And, mental anguish is middle English, listen is implicit. And fools feel fear, fear fools feelings, feel fear fool, feel fool fear, fear feel fool, or fool fear's feeling.

And, there's an answer in dreams but there isn't any question: Divine David "lets me out" at nine, an hour early, and Chris Max and Curtis Perry need a place to stay, I think Curtis Perry is somehow sad or pitiful. Old Bob is Gore Vidal in back of a convertible, he's been hiding this secret identity and as his face changes before us, he begins to look slick. All this is on a bridge, back to the idyll: I return to David's and wait with crazy people and friends on a country road, I try to rush in. And I go shopping with Justine in a box, when she gets up powder and smoke come out of her mouth, like an inactive volcano. We've climbed over a refrigerator but it's only a display of tasteless food we've reached. "Don't buy that it's awful." So we go back to our box to breathe smoke.

And, David and I are in a booth, I give him lots of room. He's writing down a time: 10:37, no 10:53, anyway it's seven extra minutes.

And one word, Jim Dine.

And, Rico is on health foods, we eat giant hamburgers fried in the subway and hot dogs for two. I have to sleep in a bed with a woman who is having young boys painted.

And the dream also says fuck Oscar Robertson as a letter of the alphabet.

The weekend of May 6

And surrounding positions and pictures: Max goes to Sweden, traveling with David: I refuse to zip up wombs: there's a house in Bermuda, a stone castle and fields: "I have decided that a single book is the key to your life": art convention fair and Bridget Bardot's brother threatens me with a gold bullet, his thumb: everyone has to go to Vietnam, mines in harbor: there's art to convince them: What's B.B. doing cowering over there.

This weekend I traveled all over. Ed loses his white coat because we have to make a run for it in the passport-like office. The only way he can make it is if we push him, me, over the sides of stairways and we know these stairways well. So we make the commercial, Holly plays the maid or dog. A little uncoordinated, we walk on land across the water.

The ship is moving away from the harbor so low in the water I thought it was sinking. We eat and drink inside, outside a ceremony celebrating my basketball career in pictures.

May 19-20

I live with an Italian family, there's a lot of cheese to eat but some of it turns out to be stomach (tripe) or skin (derma) or maybe fat. Teresa calls for $5000 for a loft like the man in the street undressing in Gordon's piece. She says something like, "You were deep." A group of people are on this floor, headed towards the hotel, one of them is "someone who knows you well from the past." I say to them "Go home!" The two Annes of Berlin? Who are they? In the loft, poetry is in the spotlight. I go to the vegetable stand but too many relatives have come over. There are some kidneys roasting. The guy wraps and delivers one to a customer. I take one, it wraps around my hand. One of the kidneys starts to walk away, it grows a neck and head. I say to the guy, "I always think I want em but I don't." Back behind the stand are some wilted vegetables, the real food.

Nap: a whole scene on a boat with Bartholomew. It's somehow his trip. I sneak on. A leave-taking. Smaller boats go to shore. Before that many meetings. Max is Andy. The boat he leaves on goes to shore. He is being paged by his mother. I see him standing up alone in the boat, looking mythical, "the little man in the boat." The boat I get into is crowded with women. I say no but I am in it. I think, "In case of a disaster there's very little room here." I imagine clinging to the side of the boat and being pushed down. A woman, a gym teacher, pulls the motor. Another woman, her match or twin, steers. That is all there is of that.

But next, I'm in bed asleep when some people bring in a sick girl, Nina I think, nearly green. But no, it's ---a, from 42nd Street. These people are strange, they sit and wait, they have infinite patience. Am I supposed to take care of this girl?

So we do Chinese acrobatic feats to become one person joined head to feet, we make the mental leap. We haven't been in training. The one, arms swinging, is made of many people. We can leap over states and giant-step united states in one to California. George McGovern gets his hair cut just like Jane Fonda and wears a black silk scarf like Nathaniel Tarn (not his real name). I guess it's my father for president (Nathaniel and Theodore both mean "gift of god" one in Greek and one in Hebrew and Tarn is wiry but too romantic).

All women are spies, I'm suffocating like a young boy in them. Down the dark cellar stairs there is everything and nothing to fear: it's dark. Fern carries all kinds of reams of colored paper, she drops it, she's suffocating too. One black sweater (Fern wore it and with teeth she gave me food) and one thing: don't speak. You'll just waste time. Until you grow up there's nothing to say, there's nothing you can be sure of. Hospital or dormitory, it's all the same to me. Terror you threaten me with, we're on a boat again and women engulf me.

I have a date to meet someone at three for fucking. "Someone wants you." I watch the clock, I'm at a lecture. My whole (dead) family's there. I get approval, wear a skirt, fly in the streets. At three I go upstairs, it's David B. but you are lying drunk in the corner. Where's David? "He's in the corner."

I am on a moving island where everyone is stuck in a hole. With great effort we get out of them, extricate ourselves, so we can swim in refreshing waters. Those of us who get out first, I am second, feel guilty that the others will be too discouraged to try because we've moved so expertly and so fast. The water is very deep. On an edge of the island they give out presents which we unwrap, arrange on boards. Some things don't stand up.

June 7

Dennis turns into a moth.

Harris and I sit by a sewer system.

Thomas decides to climb up the rope ladder and fly away.

Horace and Hollis look at a white mound to the left.

I kiss Bartholomew in back and white, he walks down the hall smiling with Andy. "You get a lot of rest," he says, "Max is coming." David calls, "It's I."

New men, menu.

Look up excuse: n. 1, a plea or explanation given in defense of one's conduct, an apology. 2, a release from obligation, duty. 3, something that frees a person from blame; extenuating or justifying circumstances. 4, a pretended reason for conduct; pretext.

I have a pretext to weave before disguise, I have a false reason or motive to be happy; to be happy you need an excuse to hide the real one. I have another person in the room. It's the U.S. It's the book with the writing as a pattern so that only the names of colors emerge so that one page reading green actually makes red and it's too much writing for the west coast. Those long swinging suspended bridges, some without sides, some submerged in the water. We get to the house of the sewing girl and the books start to fall. I try to help by removing Stefan Themerson from the shelf. Willoughby's storehouse of food is all corn, I cook a pot by submerging it in water.

June 19

We look for a California beach, they're all numbered, I have a portfolio. Mal de Primitives or "as bad as they come." We get to make the movie without having to pay for paper. Larry and Bill take away our-creative control, stubbornly they wait at the door. Joe kills Bartholomew for being young.

Swell and neat it's the heat and I don't need that much to eat and so on: Bartholomew's going away party, we put off the pleasure of touching him, then he's gone. The dangerous room of the men in the subway but, we get to touch first in the dream. There's another party of rare red meat given by Holly for dinner all over, she gives me a pink fur piece too. Then a turquoise insomnia after the symptoms of not breathing disappear, I envy Jack Kerouac not afraid to be alone on Desolation mountain at the cost of a vision. It's wet but it's been wet for weeks rain no sun the rain's a relief a week of surface a week of rain, I plead with the man at the railing in the dream, please come forward come out of the shadows, show yourself, show me who you are, I need some basis for a new dance, I battle those demons you already halfway know, mixing colors, I'm trying to remember something it involves a buzz and an explosion and three sentences. I don't. Now I see it now. This information is chronological and that explains unwelcome and tedious guests, the dreams. But what else after memory, put together all too quickly as a framework to do this and to do more of this all at once. To write it in one moment, when you are ready. The fiction. Change names. Max.

More than a personal space is here. But no more information than what's here to start with. Ice isolate cold, review: I could write it now: "I had to stop. I had to stop and begin again slowly…

Because I (act as if I (children)) shouldn't be left alone. And why child again (I was already one). So I am afraid because other women die. And then I painted my toenails red and wondered about just general pain and did I really believe what was written on the page and what else could be threatened but my health or sanity and what is it about being imagined alone with no one to make existence firm but not dead I suppose not dead, is someone thinking of you and must you meet someone, are you in transit, is forgotten the word, are you found, discovered and loved all of a sudden, is the thesis "Unless there is somebody watching you you are dead" and certainly when they go away I think they are dead and when they go to sleep there's a heartbeat next to me and I'm an animal, I don't like to listen to my own, go to bed, why sleep.

A trace of a half-moon, a blue spot in memory. These diaries are for David, I want to make love to him.

Sex and generals are all alike, I throw a stone to you. Fucking wow it's as simple as that, hot shit, Francisco's cute and the Chinese man on the t.v.'s cute and it's getting warmer out, that's so masculine, everything takes time. There's no competition between the me on the streets and the me in bed. I can't move fast enough, I pulled my shoulder muscle, I'll probably save the round world but not as Gertrude Stein, you see I've read her secret journals at a talent hunt and we won. So what is all this shitwork I have to do as the page is filthy with ordeal, holy cow hot shit jesus christ suck cock or maybe make me well and then maybe come and see me. I saw this movie before and what I mean by that is baby I actually sat through it and you're not the one to tell me who you are, you're the director giving me a hard time, jesus christ. You're always trying to find me but when I creep around corners to meet you then you change your mind. Up our ass we turned the tables on ourselves, you prick think back, don't worry that's a line from some poem called memory and what I wanna know is how far can I go with you for a dad. Ha ha you win, your head makes me feel skinny.

Dear Agnes, Lamb of God, you make me sick, I wouldn't drink milk in a moment, you sink the same old ships again, flooding America's flames. Married buried, three drive to get the wedding ring. Gold and silver paper routes and yes, that's the trap door to America under the rug and Jack Kerouac and I go down there and giggle a lot.

June 27

First dream I remember in weeks, sleep in hammock, nap, and I'm sitting on the bed watching a movie and suddenly there's two black people sitting next to me and I say I'm sorry I was so engrossed in that movie I didn't even see you come in and they brought two half-cakes and I eat a piece of the cream and someone else eats a piece of the other and that's the one that's got tuna fish in it.

Free and ritualistic, eh? Moralistic and righteous too? And so on, so is it all forbidden pleasure? It's not or it can't be so you must believe we're doing business, I'd like to mention so-and-so but I won't and I hope we haven't offended anyone so far, or, specifically, so-an-so, though I wasn't really listening again, I was thinking about something completely different then.

I couldn't live just anywhere but I'm tired of rearranging things here: what you do, who you barrage, what you garage and shit. How does Andy keep his papers in order. And you can't relate (tell recount remember) but you can address (love) vision. Vision your house on a street, Jack and David is your pen name SHUT and what am I beginning now a work that goes off into a distance I've created, it was so easy, from now on I'll start to say nothing, I've hidden too much already. I need more to amuse and Saturday will be the moon July 1.

July 11

Near noon on the night of the morning before, leave near noon, not the total eclipse not the sun and the moon (I can't write it, Poe is right), not the menstrual rush, not certain and like a doe and a lamb I concert my escape, mechanic effort lamb and dove that I am I flew not overlooking you, can you and men America come quite hard they don't record it, it's a waste of time, why do I think that, hello I'm jealous, I tingle, not enough hands and try to get to the black forest, melt one like sons the method tried, serve deserve rest work to melt code and risk die, tie the same something nothing, meet me, it works, you come, I move in, you move over way back, what is it? Memory design, when you go I'll meet you and melt, I next a mushroom embrace, service health center edges yes I do I repeat over and over, you do need space and design time, the blood wine you concentrate need, you must it's a design you see people moving in time, you conglomerate align you move you sink you are like wine, you want someone to be coming in you're swell, well-liked and cunning, short and giant in fact, you could list them as associates in cunning drift desire, they know how, as you do like Jack and you are not distant or dead, that is, you don't make time you swing the dials around, you're over your head mink coats and dashing cars, why not, you exit dance you South America, dazzling design that's not my eye, I'm straight as a mask in seven circles, dash and devastate you mix yourself a punch and I send you in and we're free, we each make up words, don't use the old ones keep it down, hush it up, you empty you full, you're still giant and this is an awful stand to take nationally, it's all a trick, got any gum on you dick, the mast of this darling ship is pointing south-divine and so we sink, it's a win for you, for me how long and longer each can this go on, well, Shakespeare says a neater yes to it and nods in something smites consumption, says it's smaller than a wink in lime, a sauce, a notion towards learning the right gesture for I'm learning I'll call, you ask me now when I can't stop, design design, he's young, you're young we wing it and crows like those we fly by, roofs of starling city draughts of heavy drifting, our refusing edging sister country by is mother, a nation derivation come from where, the start the stars of sea she melts, she works she rests too when will the rest begin.

And punctuation, ask for that. Demand it. We need time. We edge around a code, must break it out. I know you don't name time, the coke deciphers this in some last hour, an innocent silly painter's view, you see the view, it's grasped, they blew hard and harder for it, lost a

Shakespeare's crow he flew with us we fly right by and signal gesture, stew's in the pot, we unctuate and clobber these designs, they're passes at you, see the simple drift of that. Why suffer through the code, it's a path, I'm on it, you get it. You get it? Caught in this design these ropes I'm exhausted, I'm wide awake I'm looking for a language that will carry you to this place: this place is isolated: it is here and this, this here: if you would knock on the door a few hundred feet away, I would answer it and let you in. The opening of the door would excite me and the gesture you would make of our novelty. I would understand that it was strange that you were here and that movement our movement in our sphere, sphere of action and of motion and feeling, all this is constricted and that it is hard to move and agree with feelings, hard to move and be staid and satisfied be excited not be denied. You and I would know this as you came in the door. I would answer it. You would make some gesture. You would move me. I would wait expectantly for the door to close behind you but that motion would seem longer to me than to you. To you I would appear nervous. You would wait for some sign. Seeing this I would do something dramatic something to satisfy a dream. Perhaps you would go outside again and repeat your entrance, only this time the door would be open and I would be sitting, my back to it, on the bed in some dream room. As it is here the bed is so far from the door that it cannot be a part of the stage for your entrance. It doesn't matter. Let's say that as you enter, you come in the door for the second time, let's say you come in noiselessly. I'm not expecting you, I have my back to you, perhaps you even walk across the room and just as you extend your arms to take me by the shoulders I turn to see you, I had heard you coming in a moment before, we could say I had suspected you, had faith in you, it's all the same, that question of movement comes in here again, you understand this way of talking about movement, it's in a certain context, like, you say you're keeping busy, you can't stand to sit still, you don't really mean this, you want me, but all this is irrelevant to this design which isn't meant to be real this entrance your entrance is a clear fantasy this moment an entry merely in a notebook or other recording device, maybe something quicker, more attractive, electronic, blue, like you. I speak into the tape recorder. I say: there is a knock at the door, it is you. But before I can answer it you come in, the door is open. I am still sitting turned toward the door. You are seeking me. You can't resist, even though... but that's an element that figures later. In fact you are asleep now I'm sure. You're an escapist. You deride the facts, sink into the pillows currents and wake refreshed. Let me tell you this one thing: it's something I've never told you: I seize on you: you illustrate me, your sons design need, you are a fake and the you in oceans makes me two, you know it and can't speak. Sleep doesn't refresh me as it does you, you design cool shaking you make me angry, we're cut short so we won't walk in together, I'm always sure there's more. I must begin to address myself now to my hunger since you've left me, haven't dared, and how could you outside all context, you could investigate but you're stuck, there's a knock on the door. I know it's you.

Another hour goes by the wind, resist it, I'll try to resist the wind, the wind comes in as a joke, mothers and fathers the same, I live in caves where they meet me, there are no other children. We flew, four corners. We resisted each other, we were stupid we missed our chance now we are crows, meet air there are colors on your chest you lie down, I lie on top of you, we speak correctly to each other, "There, not there," "Be careful" and "Watch out, you know what I mean." You don't want me to lie on your penis, you are afraid. But why then am I sleeping with you? Your clothes are fresh I remember your smell we are in a small hotel room, a room named after a tree the cherry or magnolia room and in the adjoining room, there's a common bathroom between, your wife and my sister are asleep in the same bed. Do you want me? I'm used to sleeping with my head on your stomach, I'm not afraid. There's a knock on the door, you come in, I'm a woman, the script's changed, you're surprised at first, my presence is insistent, what happened then.

How child like my parents were: and flies light on thing and flies light and milk tastes butter and sinks a ship as usual yes she had to suffer through her style her heavy style to get somewhere to touch and bury the dead, to seek to touch and bury the dead, you must investigate the dead remember to seek out the touch of and bury them do it yourself, and big flies light longer in the long slow (months) moon of investigation dash don't know where you're going, don't know with a long sky towards morning, cooked uncooked and a direction shown sure it's the four corners of the world and you identify yourself so far out to those four corners go the children of parents riding, you know this, you already know this, you've heard it, it seems to work right now.

Mothers and fathers a grain to fill you and the movement (motion) of things you do in the dark, some natural like firestorms some too quick you are human, you relinquish your right to tell me this I spy on you so please watch me now, I'm innocent too, sleep. No of course not is the answer to the secret question you ask, yes, no, now you barrage me with questions and if they keep coming then I'll know where you are so you better watch out, count to hundred in your state translation moon quick a match, it's pretty sure that I saw you seeing separate a chance I saw you, keep to this code you made me and this is why, to me, nothing in a normal history is worth recording. States. You bent over and you and you are one. States of image. A door. Touch them. If they die, with them die. Don't avoid this. And now a wide of work opens and closes but I'm not ready yet. I'm still with you. But you you seem to stop and start, come back. Seek out wide windows, I win, I've got your body yours it's core and coil of cave and shelter showing this secret code communicates state wide world wide you're in some state they'll all agree I'm not so sure it's you at stake and in control yes touch the molecule of ocean broth a feast you bring me like cannibal mother moon a feast your density your state suggests.

Through the moist warm atmosphere of the room whose envelope unglues in calliope madness as each night precedes three hours of the day work week of hayrides crosstown in the buses nudes are driving when sudden like sun slivers, ice glass severs men, women not nude now flying flying now barely floating hanging on air, where's the ceiling of this room, hanging there say or hovering, fair air blue-ribbon legs and spans eggs hatch on the bridge all the eggs and moon covers, it's cause of moon and sweat covers, it's cause of sweat millions systems throws, throws out severs, feeds milling seeking mixtures him and her and catches throws it back headlong, catches sex of system catcher mother father milk and all head and all headlong over zoom and over clean over precipice come and long ancestor rolling balls come and room room pending around boom the long one spirits mistral bath simoon directions and natural nautical sea heaps natural crevices nautical loom weave sell swell women diving sprite of loom spill weather driving mist on fishback smell currents drawing ten knots of a spill sky, meets sex of systems moment merchants wife currents mother father caves melts compass points down where sons (blue) and daughters (brown) rode there and stand reverse, met, rode mix rode horse soundless and more demons scatter pieces, slask a sky diamonds eye make out a second, listen to this.

●

Totally fucked the train is going, there's no more sweetness in ever going, moving a pace or a space on the board. Claws dig in to a nervous spot. You can't even make out what's being written in moving states like this, they aren't states at all. A big book a giant book roots you in the moving train, what's the use of it? Dull and heavy, I shouldn't have told him so many stories I didn't want to hear myself. Dear David the thing is if I write to you well it distracts me, it's not the end of the world not by a long shot, where am I. The cool information you give me, the fucking hot train, it's my duty to fake it. A girl like me is sitting on the train. I wish I were unconscious now, I wish I were you, cool, and for my third choice I'll take being richer. What's the thing to having a talent, is it like having a television, don't let it go to waste, you paid good money for it. Existence, just plain, why not, I'm sick, I dive into the water and down to touch the bottom of the pool, it's a talent pool. No doubt about rising but I wish it was funnier, I wish it was work. Anyway it's there, Times Square. I'm sick. Yes I know the next stop and the next one, paisley pants, black girl, no hair but a knot on her head, express leaves, local stays, it's fucking hot. The man to my right is holding a paper open to the editorial page, the heading reads, "Over to you, David." I look over. A man who looks like John Cassavetes and a couple of fat men. You remind me of you. I'm sick I'm full of it. I don't want anything more to happen. It's wearing off, I'm sweating, it's getting dimmer, it's dim protection, I wasn't orphaned in a war, I don't wanna hear about it. I'm only writing to keep moving, as protection to get there, it's hot. Hot shit, lean

Scandinavians, purple crosses in the war, how many do I get, nothing new. Bags and papers, 66 Street. Watches and leaning, dry cleaning, I suppose I'm getting there. Another base, a man with the Times, I'd like to be there or off somewhere. Max doesn't have to account for himself today, he'll be drinking beer right now. See that? 79 Street, Goodbye forever, I'm almost there. You won't make me laugh today.

Home see what words I write I want to see: it's the end: you want to see how minds work: It's mine it's simple: I'll tell you: Andy's getting dressed, that's all I can think to tell you, I like red plants it's no mystery, you're no charlatan, just the impossible, just between us, failing. So I gotta make a spectacle, special you. Mercedes-Benz. I'm not destructive. You're crazy about me. You'll be distracted. The mayor has suggested that it's a very delicate subject. There are various ways of announcing things and so they have no need to speak: I have a new Asian connection, he's the mayor of Chinatown and we are Chinese individuals, words cannot describe at least in one language, we have many, what I want to say to you. What is the decision of my desperation: I'll tell you this much it's the only thing I can do to only love you to force you into looking for a hotel, it's August 23, 1972. You have some shortcomings, shall I name them? You'll do anything I want, you know too much you know too little, that's not very good, I must be able to do better than that, sure I can manipulate language and charm but never thought is never charmed magic, we need a medium, something in between, there's nothing between us, half the time. I'm not desperate, I'm desperate for a move, think about it, how can I impress you that on you something so monstrous is coming over from me and I don't want anything bad to happen to you, that's not it at all, that's all biased and bared. Wanna come to a party?

●

I will write in the big book again with the colored pens, no color seems right except this spring green and further real green, forest green and what they call bottle green, green of bottles a rich green I will write in forest green, greens change they develop. Scared of the good signs of green the green of earth with feet in it the green of stars seen from the earth, once again I don't know enough words. You have the reasons for it. It was a beautiful afternoon. (I think of Les Levine who said that's a pretty cheerful view of things and meant you don't show the bad side the side to the side I guess he meant, in speaking of my memory, I think of Bartholomew who doesn't know what being drunk is, who is protective by design.)

So much time's gone by. Some child, a picture of her, she punctuates the book. If you wanted to be mean, if you wanted to you could be very good at it, you could be mean. I am an expert. I am not mean. There is someone I love, then I don't say much. I can sleep here sleep peacefully I'm almost in the sun, the sun's on the floor, red, next to me, I am somewhat free. We are making a proposal, we are making a careful vow, we are not knowing, we are knowing everything. We are not weeding out we are full of desire, we are pending. Scared of being so careful I'll write in orange, in earth brown, orange seems to be brown brown seems to be orange you look like me we are making mischief: hold onto me. A wind a rain are the details important, do you want them? So much time's gone by, the record is endless and none of it recorded, who needs it? Something else begins, sure, I think I'm sure, I'm still drinking your bottle of wine but I can't say that cause the language is mine and so I did, missing you. Miss, so I'll be you, miss, I am not married but I don't escape your notice, in fact, it was me who came to see you, a clear memory that we exchange notes on, we can change, I'm home, you don't escape my house, a glance the eyes the hands, what a catch we've accomplished, what we've done you see and hear, his ear his hair what we perceive you are aware of, a mixing up and you know us by now by our perceptions, alike perceptions storing, perceive moving, perception motion that's the order I speak of through you, I find it intricate, I find it hard, don't overlook this, the words fight among themselves, don't let it go by, there's a finer point, a black translucent picture, black a power you are fine, no escape or avoiding, some forgetting yet to do in the middle of so much concrete, I'll keep you, you are present at my birthday party, sections of it, this one, again the concrete one I am revealing you the conscious one still conscious now of a day of birth. Absence or loss, one by one. I've spent all my money and I don't need some. I am tuned to your absence: there's no one here, a lingering. I am not sure, not sure

I want my watch back, the one that was stolen, I'll let you know, we'll play it by ear. Form of a human part is aware. Is here. There's no telling you point to wanting, we haven't missed at all not wide but designed to the mark, if any, if design is free, he is. I hit you, I meet you, I see you, we were both scared in such a bravery way, it's summer and running open, what? Begin? I sleep I am asleep I had a baby, it's close. I could go on forever this way but you in the confusion of yous for you I must make magic, I must stop and get out of the code beyond the secret code which would have worked it would have worked anyway but since I am you, now, a part of the fusing, the confusion of possible yous, I will milk, impose, I will come out of hiding, it's time, I've already begun.

I'm out, look around, it's blue. That blue is me wanting to fade away to fade back into your body to fill you. That's why it's blue, a blue of not existing, a sudden blue, I hear the word boy, yes, that's what I am, it's surprising as blue is green, a certain day of the month, a certain year, recorded. It's certain the wind blows unsteady, we are secure, you are my base, you are full. I milk you. I needed this time. I am not absent. I am knowing you, you have special feelings, special designs, maybe you are present here now just for an instant in the color I saw first like a light between my legs, a glance, the eyes, the hands. I try to grow. I try too hard to grow. Growing is instant. I see it instantly. You are coming, you're feeling good, you're thinking how easy it is, how hard, I'm too big, it feels good. I was careful, wasn't I? I would've died for you, you warm. You want me. I'm lost where am I, I want to make you just to be sure. But you have bigger plans for me, you feed me. Later I will be your mother. I am sinking. You make me dizzy you make me well. What a blast of power I feel just for an instant, then you are gone, or is it: when you are gone, but it's awful, a curse, how does the wind get in here, here that should be, here that ought to be sealed, how does it enter, can I do that, or is that me, is it me, I am sensitive the wind a knot of it has pushed me too hard I am hurt, pushed into you where I belong, I am keeping a secret, I am not speaking, I am hurting, I am stoned, I am a bubble, I am seen, so many winds, some of them in knots, such sinking motion, always sinking, in my mind, I am high, now that I'm sure you're near, how sure can I be how near you are, you are excited, I can feel it, it's not like the wind, do you know as much as me, when are you born, when are you coming, what a map for the streets of cities I could design. What I could show you, meet me, I'll show you my instinct to show you is still, a desire: you are mine and I know your insides I know you better than myself, I've survived it even though I would've died for love, given up easily, so you could go on, your presence reminds me, the wind that blows between us close, you made my love, first thing I feel and I am sinking again too soon I want you back. I have you. You emerge, vision, tones of brown in warm rounds, a sucking person, like me. The same sex the same motion perceive the kiss as my identity with you. I am on you. What a look you give me, in secret, what a tone, in silence, silence your mere presence stretches out like long form not quite golden light. I have a message for you: I am ugly, compared to you. I am not quite distorted in the center of your star, I am proud, you spring back, you are resilient, know me. You are brown, I am on you. The sun seems to take care of us, we're warm. It's rude.

Impending disaster, impending doom, unending impending, a reorganization of the employment of faculties, a pigeon flies by the window, the subject frames, see, just, so, much, who are you and how did I come by you? I'm anger, my anger is sense, drills into you, I am set in this piece, this, a move, you, little man doll, fall down, little woman doll moves closer, is wounded, you get up again, a miracle, we mate, like two watch faces on the same wrist band, water proof, I hope. Set them. Set them back a few hours to noon. Back a few hours to noon. Inked. Your move, in a certain number of hours-moves-hours. Like you mentioned before, as a reorganization of the one who was mentioned before, to the one my presence here speaks to, I shoot the moon men all at once, and then I've got all this time left to twiddle my thumbs. I've got to get a watch face and start needing it. There's no two ways about it, it's like pissing on the most analytical version of all the stars, it's like breathing, breathe the smoke of your own fucking brand. So I smoke yours. Kools. You renegade, why not admit it and set me free. I hate sets, chess sets. I hate power, except the power I have to show you something. I resign, so you can't move. There are some motherfuckers I would like to show the stars to, stars climbing up in the sky. Not you David. I don't mean you. Stars climbing up, what a trick, for a trick you get money, see the ones in front of the sun, of course you can, lunatic, for a trick you get money, for a match you gotta win, I want evens, with you. Who am I speaking to? The market place. No deferrals, we do not cash checks, what a lioness she's tempting to be bitter, what a lion is, are you, that is, hungry? Eat meat. Pay at the store. Only thing is, you can't walk out, my legs won't hold you. Better transactions go on in the south, at the pole, at random, you wanna know why? The pole at the north, it can't be seen from there, it can't even be dreamed of. Opposites attract a couple hard lines of defense stinks money. Child loves patterns of any kind. Where am I going, I'm going out. I'm mad I'm playing, feinting, fainting mad, I'm always playing, I'm going out to play, I'll play with a few hims and hers, I'll say to one of them, I'll find a chance, and I'll say, you stink, you stink and then, I'll laugh, you feel so bad, you want me to devour you? Then? Sure, O.K., whatever you say, you say goes, David says goes, what a mess, a great mess, stinking again, I'm no princess to end the day with a start sweetheart, wanna roller skate, I'm faster than you, wanna race, my time is race, I'm sinking ship, noble captains of which are covered with shit. My infection's a rage at the hospital, the doctors are covered with blood. Honor would spit, I just chew naturally, a full count, higher than ever, what a bloody tundra on the pitcher's mound. I curve a fast knuckle spit-one and spew it all round the bend to the monkey-moon, far fucking out, what a gas explosion that was, the crowd's still steaming, all energy is loose, and a little gnu says, new systems can be found on any field or fields. It's unreal, scared shitless who is. Fuck.

What a sport. A few of the hers and I will mosey down to Mexico to suck cock, dribble the cream on our blouses, prostrate at the nunnery, invested into the order without oil on our heads, bare heads, new order of the all-of-the-saints cocksuckers, all-stars, south of the border, all the way down, no time for a snooze, it's the rising sun, so pay attention, I forgot to include the fee in this prospectus, coincident with the new day—you dont pay, we levitate, like elevators, sentient beings glow with the auras of saints, their very cells, amazing blue light, about two fade away, you'll never see us again, motherfuckers, you, a new race of blacks and us a visitation on your absence of color. We are close, we got this image from the church that made us angels in the red, a vicious lay. Sex slain is sex slayer. Now that we know this, we make the relic institution pay, shell out through its fucking teeth and eyes and nose and asshole, the well-hung robbers of our sex ingest themselves before our eyes, as we get up to go. We go over the preceding was a play. Now let's eat dinner, watch the tube, love design.

Hey stop that and put your feet on the ground, there were no blacks in the restaurant where we ate breakfast today, that's because the owner of the place comes from the place where I was born, shell out shocks and from last night we bury stone white culture with you two or three families who say, what is a family group. I find comfort in the insistent San Francisco smells of growing up, I like the bugs and flies in the uncut grass sticking over green on a blue field, no spots. I like downy little girls, the little girls who ask me for a light, real pretty and mysterious, I like them, the beautiful one and her gangster brother, twelve years old, the man whose wife won't listen to his story anymore, that man, his wife, his electrical information, he wants a breast to suck, she gave me two boys, what else can I expect from her and Walt Whitman expects you in his dressing room, he wants you in the sun today, he sinks into the uncut grass and pulls you down on top of him, the girl who was reading The Junkie Priest, I'll make a picture for you, I'll break a glass: the counter culture of emotional homeostasis: two or more seasons in the same field. I change. I absorb blue ink and it outlines it dyes my organs of delivery of delivering blue and fading fast emergency baby girls who need to eat. It outlines it dyes it marks or maps out a certain space for you a certain future a possibility. There's nothing in this, who is Madeleine La Rue? I go to a training school for allied spies at 13 Rue de Madeleine. I marry John in Topeka or Poland. I make roux at the Reader's Digest chateaux.

If I've left anything out it's because I don't know where it belongs. Then again some things just seem to be contributing to a pile-up of the same old emotion when they are abandoned to chronology so I abbreviate those for the sake of a rhythm.

At first we are sleeping in a new room, it will be my study. Then the two-headed dog pokes its fingers into the back of my head. We keep moving looking for a place to sleep. There are other people and a cut-up of beautiful fish. I am no longer Max but he reassures me when I wake up terrified in dream. The girl I'm with is trying to make deals and investments with the invaders. I cannot invest in an R-rated movie, she has her income tax. I don't know who these people are, a Chinese couple burned in a fire, the man has cloven feet, we try to sleep outdoors where vagrants sleep. The deals: "Maybe when George and Christophe get themselves together they could give us the fish heads to eat." I say, "As if I wanted to eat pieces of dead bodies at this point and who are all these people?" I'm afraid, if this is a dream, I want to wake up and write it down but it might be real. It's our loft strewn with garbage, the loft keeps changing to blue, blue grass and real grass, "Be nice." A man is making love to the girl in black satin, they laugh. Max went to sleep outside. My papers are taking up the whole bed. Now I'm afraid to look around. Old bureaus, no room for my desk either.

Dear David, the wind is blowing hard. I'm afraid I'm reading "Experiences of Awe in Childhood," I'm afraid to be like you, I will race to the movies tonight in the rain that's coming. Navigate. I know that this interim confidence, my ally, will soon disappear. I really don't know what will replace it to explore. It's hard to seduce you since I don't want to hide. You appear. Hide in words. Blow away. We struggle to find a new magic for language like the Indians open in woods in forests in words, do you see my image, her image. Comedy. A flash. I forget that I'm already smoking, breathing smoke. Smoke on top of mountain where I place us I can place us. An image, your image, tissue, the green of woods, tissue, drops of water, waxed, the tissue they wrap plants in, cut plants, I bought flowers, orange weeds, grown and cut, they were for me, and one blue flower, a complement, a gift. The blue flower, a giant flower named "majestic daisy." It's not here, for no reason. Here I am. Right here. Rocking back and forth. I look up the word "work" in the dictionary because it's the work we want to do that separates us. The roots of the word ally work to organ from the Greek ergon, work. I get stuck on several meanings of the verb form to work, I get stuck on "to perform its function" and then, laughing, the nautical usage "to strain so, as in a storm, that the fastenings become slack, said of a ship," and "to bring into a specified condition, as by repeated movement; as, they worked it loose." And still laughing, laughing more "to provoke, rouse: as, she worked herself into a rage" or fever. I'm tempted to say David, let's shoot the works (supreme). Ant. Rest, play.

I get lost in the transference where I'm supposed to be but I find myself again. Desire. I look up want. They think I'm destitute or impoverished, they think I am lacking! Wander and Wandering Jew catch my eye, the eyes, a glance, the hands, a magic wand is flexible, a string of white beads, a trade. What is lacking in me, my want, what can't be educated or brought up, my want, it grows luxuriantly, is extravagant, it swells, runs riot, playful wandering rivers, senseless rivers, an excess of rivers and vegetation, an excess of plants, luxuriant plants, a language, nonsense, of plants, careless plants, their immoral pleasures, growing all over, recklessly rooting, love-making, with no upbringing, a criminal waste, needless, headlong, indiscriminate, the luxurious excess of a sensitive love, sensitive pleasures.

If only you hadn't had your car stolen so that I could think you might be cruising around the city somewhere and you might see me. If only you could enter my blouse, see my desk and my chair. O.K. I'll stop.

Monday. Talk self to sleep (Massachusetts), wake up at dawn, ravenous, thinking the two mosquito bites are the two locations of different stories (histories). Studying hunger, studying to be like you. Paul et Virginie. Give people what self wants.

Men who have rejected my sexual advances: my father, my uncle, Michael Layton, John Hefferle, Peter Lupario, Charlie Entwissle, Steven Casey. Dream: from then on, I knew how to jump and run but even more, when I ran, I was thinking. House or body in pain or danger. I was also furious that you couldn't force yourself on a man, couldn't rape him.

Ocean: John invents a balloon, the theory is if you let air out in bursts, you can fly. I try it from 100 feet up, it slows the fall but it doesn't work. I'm sleeping in a poets' co-op, I take a shower in the streets. Gregory and Raphael want to sleep with me but I sleep with Dick, Max gets under the bed.

I dream Gerard Malanga and the delicious Oriental soup with hunks of pork and pineapple in it. I had to climb over so many fire escapes, drops and cul de sacs, I had to to wind up in this restaurant and there was Gerard big as life with two girls. "What are you doing with them?" He was pissed off at me for not coming through with the sex-video show, the t.v. show, the one you can look up in the phone book, it meets on the 7th of every month, I had been there twice and not gotten a chance to go on, so why go back? For the money? Besides, it was a trick of Edmund's to get me to fuck with him in public, I wouldn't have known what to do anyway.

I dream free marinated fruits. I can feel the blood rushing into my hands and head. The grilled cheeses are burning. Max says, "I've eaten all your breakfast, you have three places to look." I answer, "I shouldn't be living in Ridgewood anymore, I should get another apartment, it would be dull, no woodwork." Childhood fantasies of having a refrigerator next to my bed and a machine that cooked small chickens by turning them on a spit.

●

The cool mother distance of her died, she was a color. A third and secret death will hover corners, secret: lucid yellows emerge from black so deep, the deepest edges meet behind it, melt. Hide him. Protect him. His secret sleep. I confess the murders. Eat now eat. My father's dead, purple ladybug down my brown leg, protector. Father's dead, mine I swim heavily in the current, night air. Father's dead, 1/2-hour to go. An urgent message to my father ends: approach me.

Friday

The girl having to wait and the contractor for occupied cars having to fence. "I figure pretty soon the heavenly bodies are going to disappear with the _____ right between them." I was in a room with Mary Riser. You're in the corner.

And why are the sentences dreams will give me the totally dried-up, no-feeling, denial of feeling, code-word stuff. Don't the dreams think I can face the rest? Unspoken. Design and texture of dots, now a mist. I want to fuck, I am a queer, I mistrust myself. In high school the rumor was "homos" wore green on Thursday, our high-school uniforms were green.

Saturday

It's a set shot. I keep hearing people calling my name, the noises outside. Using the etymological dictionary, studying. At the same moment: I finish reading the introduction to The Scarlet Letter, thunder and lightning strike, the phone works again. Electricity I am blue and Nathaniel is wracking the heavens for me, I cry with awe. I decide to masturbate hoping you'll call, the phone rings, it's Andy, "Did you fuck him?" I masturbate, the phone rings, it's Edmund. Dear David, I think I stole your car, in order to leave you helpless and without a future.

I dream the primary beat, the murders: I hold back the man who is going to shoot by pretending I want to fuck. I turn him towards the gun. A black mushroom is growing under my breast. Agnew is murdered and they never mention it again. Max doesn't wanna see two halves of a movie that he'd have to put together. "It's pretty weird not to have to try not to think about those things." Sharing an orange and fanning it with my hands. "I guess it would be very good to call and tell you what color they are."

Sunday

Kathleen's a martyr, sleeping outside with the kids. A man with stripes in his hat folds his coat under us, "Don't let him near us!" We eat fish for dinner. Max's mother goes to visit Andy in the hospital. "I can't marry a man."

Later, the stove's on fire. Edmund and Kathy live next door. "I think something must be wrong, you are jeopardizing me." Then I see the stove's on fire, a wood stove, we take out the block of wood that's left, it becomes a man. The dance piece is extremely difficult, acrobatic, higher and higher from bar to bar, turn around, higher... "And now that I have done that I'll never have to do it again."

●

They are meek the meek
their soldiers chart the deep
I am alright to speak
speak a century ago
deep and drifts the snow
the sea the builders laugh

Laugh and melt drifts her laugh
my laugh I'm her her blues are meek
and the snow blows it blows snow
the snow's deep
a week ago you, you and I long ago
you teach me how to speak

Speak my baby you are alright to speak
some spaces open I can spill and laugh
and laugh like centuries ago when centuries ago
the silent same the silent suns were coming light
were coming meek

Eyes look for entry at your doorstep we are deep
Snows deep design its layers, wait for snow

My father's dead, when will it snow
my father's dead it is sweet to speak
to you. My secret beginnings deep
Deep luminous, spill over into laugh, we can laugh
You bend around and poke your elbow into mine, boy-meek
Like eyes like eyes like mine my eyes are come to you
        from centuries ago

Time goes I could go, you. Listen long ago
I saw a merciful cage of snow
spill up from ground ground meek
as me. You, sky, it fell without, for once
        you are dumb
and I speak: You enter and laugh
the designs of earth are deep
But you know them, here you know them,
        earth anger deep
but you know it, you know long ago
what silence passed, is gone, is over, laughs
please laugh with me, you do, in the snow
sky again speaks, I learn to speak
at first I mumble: a past that made me meek

Sleep with me meek my arms are deep
Love me to speak loved long ago
I give you the snow from the sky, sky laughs,
        gentle and laugh

6 a.m. Democratic Convention

I dream the book I am writing about my life, I must tell you, I'm up to the dangerous part, who's gonna stay. The two volumes in the middle like a clump of trees seem important. I was having another dream, charting snakes, I don't want to admit it, but I knew it would be light soon, even in the dream. An unarmed shooting gallery. All the cities we've ever been.

Sweet, a man of kind 4 kind of sweeps the sweet out the door. Mill, Whitman kneels. Ghost of gold of the hall filters through air, he's getting old he's from Mexico, brought a cache of air there, he milks a goat hanging over the convention sky. Erect pussies can't come in. No trees. Wear medals. Mean and women they come, break twigs off trees, settle the difference from white through gray. Hey hey oeey, they eat a man. Think eat a man, man copy, gorgeous puzzles. Pink-rimmed: a person moves agile toward a vacation, a trip without thinking, maybe he's smoking, he gets on a bus, plane, even train, plain train, he carries Roget's Thesaurus for this: Vermont, New Hampshire…fleeting, flying. Abortion, homosexuals walk the plank, defeated a motion to gang the plank and platforms suffer. Edgy noise reverse rehearse, the spirituals render a version, refuse to liberate vice, the men were gay when McGovern amounted the women rehearse in skirts. Cool dry ink day. Come in. First names please. I'm outside that's a door. Bar and bolt it, we'll go out the back way, the sex-security guards will show you the rhythm, do you need to smoke. Thousands of people are here of four different kinds. One kind eats while it goes down. I cover a press on there, here where there were more of those than any other besides. So don't get caught, developed differently in more of a rim glow than expected. An edge on it like old times, kind three. Kind two moves an agile merry rim. I'll block it for you. Square air. Sunny fair and monkey moon. White and blue refrigerator ice. Getting back to the crater rims here: orange a fjord felt feeling national unpeeling it: you watch the whole thing? You dig it, finger stuck into the top and glove spurting citric acid all over kind three in the hallway. Electric study the docket. Docket advance. It's interminable. Edge tide corrupt tide milk tide, there's mothers here, each eat. Fennellosa. That fell open, picked it up. Wednesday, Tuesday morning and cute hair. A round bubble. Free the man, elect the few, who read? Even swell and research float a reel of swim on the ocean floor's clean and swept, your notes have grown over the mescaline arms, they grow long go over the streets and feel the heavy traffic move there. It's sweet.

Circle line, cheerful America, no danger, rivers no flow. Dream Patti Smith again and before I even realize sleep awake there are possibilities for dream. No strip poker, we snowball it, we sail through the coast, do we sail right through the heavy coast, its line, we're out of line, we're sweating cold snow, the heat, no, no coast, bows and arrows the Hottentots of Africa, the Jivaro of Mexico, Rhonda Fleming of Maine in a white satin slip.

I am working for someone, I aim to shoot someone down, no first I go in to where it is dangerous, a dangerous place, the foot of the castle wall, I run stop aim and shoot, I shoot at the footman the guard, he leans against the castle wall, a volley of our arrows, he leans against the machine, I realize I can't hit him but I can shoot so fast I'll keep him "off guard." He can't hit me then, I run to get inside, this is the mission I've been sent on, I'm working for someone, another guard at the top of the wall, defending the top, his bow and arrow, I must keep running so he can't shoot me, I know I can't shoot him, how did I get into this, how do I smell, the primary colors, running the eyes a glance the hands. Home they don't know what I've been into, they expect me for dinner, they set a place for me, the light's on, off, I go upstairs, I don't come down for dinner, I am working for someone, they, the two of them eating, they talk about me, my empty place, my husband and another man, man who lives with us, they eat, it's perfectly normal I'm not there. I am at the door, Nora, my bag is packed, I'm leaving, the danger, my work at the castle, I'm working for someone, they don't understand it, I'm leaving, I'm going away, cut.

I'm having a baby and so is K and so is M and so is T. But T is the one with her stomach slit open, a dull-edged knife stuck in while she bides her time, it's not time for the rest of us, it's too early, the hospital's cheap, no doctors, but I'm at work at 8 a.m. dreaming the specialized dream, dreaming the dream that he put in an order for, dreaming so the work can go on, dreaming I wish I could have the baby, my stomach hurts so, baby's pushing down, the nuns make us sign a waiver, if they miff it or muff it or if it's a variation of baby, they will not assume the cost, the expenses, you got me to the hospital but I wouldn't lie down, I stood there in the doorway signing handwritten waivers handed to me by pigsty nuns, then I split for a ride in A's car, top down, a lot of junk on the dash, my belly's distended but I'm still small, there's lots of room in my jeans from the side as I measure at least three widths of me could fit in easily to the belly of one real carrying mother, her eyes a glance why are her pupils so small in this dim light, why don't they widen, why is her eye like a flower why isn't she sleeping why isn't she awake, it would be so easy.

Dull browns and filthy blacks to the bright and hell color of A's sports car, lucid slide shades lined in thin black, a whole drug, a whole pot of tea's my last outpost before I give in completely to this design. Open it, it's closed. And you, I'll tell you what I think about you, great dreams-for-you monster, I think I am saving you, I don't mean rescue or preserve, if you knew you'd know that I'm only an intermediate swimmer, but saving you, a laying by or laying up or maybe I'm hoarding you for later, no I'm not I'm treating you carefully, no I'm not cause we play every day, sink ships, blow them up, they've added a strip of canvas to my sails to help me catch the wind. The tie-in isn't quite perfect yet, my overalls are still falling down, my pinafore's too small to catch all the money it rains, I'm sinking the bank's upside down, leave it, I'm coasting to safe, I'm bound to get somewhere strapped in this chair, give me a push, the ocean's electric, let me out, leave me alone, my head is buzzing and I've bitten all the plants, they can't help but be influenced by me. Sea cow harbor seal butted to shore in the shape of a feather that writes. I've got sea legs and sea room, feathers in the season for taking risks. So I'm drinking down the sea I came out of, back with the ones who eat their own heads.

I want to make it bright and brighter so a light can fall through, he stirs on the bed. The chair moves an arm. People see through. The plant stands. Electric burns right electric burns left in a circle through. Knee. He turns over. Blue in relief. Relief I am as far into the wall. Suck on the screen. The frame blows. Window walks on all fours. He walks out. Sneezes. The bats of Sumatra, the dreams of the Malaysians. He picks up his bow and arrow but will not shoot. A method for shooting the helpless by intuition. Helpless in ice, helpless in winter water, helpless in trap. Out of season. Unnatural. He's going for a piece of cake. All right. Door legs complain again, can't walk, the window walks around. There's room for it. I didn't go with him. O.K. Will he come back. Is he hungry for cake what a lion is, the door speaks in another vein, alone, spills it. I haven't made my entry yet, the telltales are blowing for rain, rain, backs of leaves showing, I'm hungry too, one more, two more, three more hours to show your cards, he says to me, I've only got aces, I say, and even those I keep concealed, what hard work it is, sooner everyone's noticed the aces are missing, no aces left in the deck or ever was one. I tighten up. I've bet moderately not to show. I'll fold. Everyone's suspicious. I don't mind another hand. They deal me, they deal me the aces again, all five. I could really sweep up. I don't have to, door walks over to me and smiles. There's been an emergency you must race over in your car and cannibalize the surroundings, these people are poorer, they will be purer if you eat. The biggest details go first, I swallow them whole. Look I'm not trying to make a mystery of it, I just want to go on.

It seems to go on forever, it could, a man with padding between me and him picks me up, I'm a baby, and sucks me right in. You age the toys, you should've left them young, little bows and trumpets, cords and all brass plumbing play sets hugging the mid-winter frozen late summers mud pies. I feel so lazy, I feel so tossed, eat them go ahead, eat the splinters too, they're succulent and they won't enter into the bloodstream, don't worry, eat the snapping turtle in the yard and the bachelor buttons growing, I know a bachelor, he lives upstairs, he's my mother's kid brother, he likes to eat the wash line with me tied in knots on it, eat the fence and their lilac trees, swallow the thorns of the bushes whole, thorns of uncle's special rose bushes whole, special sprays may poison you, swallow the uncle, he's scared, he poses for a picture fists tightly closed, fists made tight, it was more than a fist fight, you've been missing us, swallow the feathers I'm made of raw kernels of corn. The strawberries get flooded growing low, the ditch goes to China, the whole yard never ends, it has no edges, I'm squatting down, I'm floating in the snow as tall as you high, I haven't sent the memo yet, I'm waiting, it's stiff, I'm near to the end, I'm taller than you, the confusion is dreamlike the boys are on their boys bikes, I wish I knew. Memo there are phantoms and ghosts at the door, you scared? Memo you open the door there's a lion and a savage, you scared? Memo you open the door there's a lobster, scared? Door opens, there's nothing there, then the bell rings, are you scared yet? the shadow of my hand is blue does that scare you? You take your first step towards…do you remember being scared, where are you falling endlessly into, falling, a man is a woman, women are men, aren't you scared? I'm not me I'm someone else, are you scared, it's too dark to tell and I'm screwing up my face making faces, faces of an attack on your bed on your person, I'm not me, I'm someone else, there's a hole in the wall goes into eternity, the faucets and drains are connected for millions of miles, there are alligators living in the sewers, spiders fall from the ceiling into your bed, there's a poisonous snake caught in the drain pipe, his head peeps up, there's someone laughing under the bed, his hand grabs your leg, there's a thousand-legged on you, there's a man two men in the cellar, you can't get in to the light in time, you step on a beetle, it cracks, there's a face at the window, devil's face, he's coming in, you must walk through the cellar in the dark, I dare you, your bed is grabbing at you, erupting, a hand reaches up, you may fall out the window, the doorknobs fall off, you get a shock, a cord blows up, you go out you come back, someone's missing, he can't be found, you never see him, you are forced into something, you are hiding, you can't be found.

Snap and sudden the screen memory of a calendar with photographs and dates like memory from a really old tree. Like Sherlock Holmes, we feel like cats and are wide awake. Like we get used to this feeling of never sleeping, we might get on top of things soon. And now with the pointer I point to the times which are screens when I was somewhat free. There was and is that time I was walking down the street free and someone stopped me. We slipped on our black rubbers and beat each other up with our garden of the flowers hose, the wet newspapers of the war, what a picture. There's hardly any room to maneuver myself inside this tiny frame, I want to be in a position to enjoy this victim, I want to be in position for several straight plays in this narrow time slot. The legs of the picture go walking the streets. You turn over and lower the t.v. I point to another date on the chart, another picture. Design memory design what design it is. It's just a question of analysis this screen says to me, we want to get somewhere, we fight the amount of time that's past, we want to work out through which, which is why I'd like to scare you, which is why you frighten me which is why my knife drills into you which is why bears and lions are at the door now which is why rivers listen which is why everything slows becomes hazy is clouded which is why I faint and lighter blue which is why the walls have eyes the walls have ears merely listen to something, it's haunting, a space that's not spoken of, edge on the pattern one mere point in the silly rearrangement of my removal from time and philosophy, it makes me laugh. I think it. Down the street and free. Torture of it, rare red steaks of ice cold meat slab stones of my sawdust country, I ate that and something else. I'm trying to get to it in between here and there.

She was given a little boy's muscles and tried to make them work. They work fine but don't grow. No definition but a strong resilience and soft to touch. Something moving. I'm trying to get away with it. She had a red dot on her arm, a little too soft and cool, pushing in. His presence made things alive. I begged her to get married again but she wouldn't. They were protecting us against rape. I had a new sister my mother. Real sister she ceased to exist, her friends wrestle. I read at the yellow kitchen table in bright fluorescent light with the telephone till 3 a.m. every morning. Slept four hours and went to school. Slept on the trains. Worked till 6, took naps and ate veal and seven sandwiches a day. No dates but the Red Cross, they sent me, and one I attacked like a stone on the stoop. And Peter who loved me, folk music, and got jealous of Bob who I secretly hated. A messenger. I cut my hair. Her wounds were fierce purple lions in the limelight room. She called the police. I agreed it was a stranger coming in but were we as helpless as that? She screamed in her sleep. She wept, she asked me questions, she didn't live, she asked me to be alone with her, I expected a miracle, it was a secret, I washed her hair and skinny back, I read all books in a chair facing the rounder windows and when O the priest came I was watching and went to the door with candle and hat to answer. O was the one I pleaded to for sex much later. Am I allowed to kiss him on his birthday? And who was the one who used to take you out in taxis? And where is your diary written in stenography, secret codes for what parts and my father's love poems to you? You wink at me, don't bring her here, she won't understand. Morphine. And something black, maybe the disease itself, your mouth is open. I kill my aunts at your funeral and put on your clothes. You were one of the survivors like they say in the papers, now you've made me a hero. They send me to the Red Cross to have an affair. I have one with a man who can't pronounce it. I wish to drop him dead or flat so I leave him at the gate and realize you're not with me. I redelegate all authority and power over me to myself. I become my own curtain. I become my own design. Except for uncle. Him I try to scare tear into being my lover as he suggested, but he has no passion. He's just a room in the house upstairs. I go up there. He's militant and orderly I'm curious, he makes me move in with him, he tells me who I don't love. He is forbidding me. He meets me at the movies in Manhattan, Ben Hur. He takes my arm and we eat sandwiches at Toffenetti's where he goes on his dates with M. who is a woman mentioned of means, she owns her own house. Across the street. I watch her blinds. He used to love a woman whose name was the same as his mother's but she died and his mother died and beautiful jealous Ted and Marie die and then he died but first he stood at the foot of my bed with his laundry and asked me what were my plans and how long did I expect to sleep. I set up a place to fuck in the basement but we didn't use it. Grandfather moaned all night in the bed through the wall next to me. I moved mine over. I wondered about his prick about both their pricks never fucking and his magazines they were all in order. He wrote me letters about money and promised me his desk. He had beautiful hands and wrists blue eyes, he was milking me, he sent me to college, he felt me out I fainted for him, he announced me but where could we go? He said I didn't love him. It was while I was ironing. He was right. I stopped coming home. I couldn't understand how one hour of the day was more sexual than another. We eat out on Sundays and take long walks, he visits the cemetery, he takes me with him, it makes no sense, he is alive, he fights with his father, he loves the Giants, I meddle with him, he pays me money for being so smart, we make bets with each other, he brings blouses from Manhattan and beautiful bolts of cloth, he astonishes me, leather gloves. We talk about taste. My father's flannel shirts and gray suits with pink shirts and black and pink ties tied. I want a pink and purple convertible, I have a sky-blue-pink dress and one red velvet with a white lace collar. To imitate him I dress in pink and gray, he imitates me. We look alike. We go to City Hall and the botanical gardens. We sleep in the same bed in a room resembling a tree. I'm in a flower dress. I love my jeans but it's Sunday. I love to pack my bags for vacation, turquoise shorts, I'm in the back seat, I yell stop and he does, it's lemon ice. On my mother's birthday I refuse to get out of the car, I am sick. We play horseshoes. I'm as good as he is, with uncle I play catch, they don't get along. I watch him work with wood. I do the sandpapering and hand him things. We work in the garden growing corn. I get hot. We order the seeds. Tea roses fir tree hydrangea bushes bachelor buttons, our part of the garden, look how far I've gotten.

●

I had to stop. I had to stop and begin again slowly. A buzz, a confluence of noise sound all correcting and weaving, weaving to call my name. Bernadette. I stopped. Papers and books smoldering, black edges of them too close to the flame, flame leaping easing itself out the cracks the edges the lines in the construction of a normal stove, an oven, oven like the one in our loft, mine and Ed's, Ed is a man like electric light, a human nature, suffer the flames, the fire came from its source a simple block of wood in the broiler, the source of the flame, the block of wood black at the edges, source of fire, black and its rectangular shape interfered with, cut off at an edge on one side where it had burned, a burning wedge a block an edge burned off, a slice disappeared it burned a slice maybe in the shape of a triangle, that slice that edge off the block of wood the wood about two by four, the block of wood that was the origin of the flame the fire in the stove that was threatening everyone, jeopardizing their lives, something was wrong the fire started. I was used to it. I am the leopard. I am the bear. We found the source of the flame and took it out of the oven. It was a man, laid out. A dead man. It was an image of my father and his father and wood.

Gradually then I began again. It was time for my piece, in an auditorium full of friends. No more paper and no flame. I would execute this difficult dance and the secret, the resume, the explication would remain hidden until the end. I had rehearsed. I had driven myself from one moving bar or pole, attached to the wall, hinged there at one end, so that they could swing open and closed like a door. I had driven myself through rehearsals over these posts these outposts these locations of histories of individual ghosts, ghosts that were not only haunting me but had ceased to be real. They had come alive but were really dead. These points of focus were like swinging doors. Only the most acrobatic feats could control their random motion. Only a master of equilibrium could navigate the surface of one, much less all at once. I had rehearsed. I had worked. Unsure of myself still, I set my performance off to the side like a sideshow, like a simple element in a complex pattern, a homage to its variety "and all living things." The performance was extremely difficult, difficult, she wore black, she had no contact with the ground, she rose and descended executing the relationships between the horizontal posts which were secured at many levels. To get from one to the next, and its chronology was clear, she would make use of a turn in air, an impossibility, her arms must have had the strength...an impossible strength, her feet could never touch the ground, a short performance, in tight black clothes, she must make use of every muscle, every muscle is tense, every second has been dreamed of many times before. The performance is over, she is on the ground. And now its crux, its central point, its purpose: her declaration. And she has kept this secret: it was not a real performance, not a process, not a show. The feat, the feats of movement, this exhibition of strength of study and agility—all this was a lead-in so that I could speak, so that I could say and I say, listen: now that I have done that, now that I have done it, I will never have to do it again.

It's over and in this recounting I want to be clear, clear about its purpose, about the reason for the existence of this peculiar performance in space, and that reason is this simple statement: I had to do it so that I would never have to do it again. And to those who accept a rose from me, I add this: I am sorry to cover my feelings with images out of fear, but please believe me there are things you cannot write. I had to sop. I had to stop and begin again slowly.

●

On the moon. Muddy water, and we find an old shoe to eat. I went to all the different police stations looking for you, hitching rides in the backs of trucks, risking my life. At David's house, his wife and kids are black and invisible. David is there somewhere with one of his sons who is no longer black. I begin to play this game: alternately, we draw lines with a thick felt marker, the texture of the line and its style indicate our desire for "a certain person." David goes down in a glass elevator like a shower with a bunch of flowers, I'm jealous. Then a voice says, "You must begin to pay for your own food." I look in the mirror at all the colors of my skin in two different lights. Different spatial relations...Paterson. I swallow something whole.

●

One two three four the door slams from the wind, there aren't enough colors to put it off anymore, the light's on me, I'm so tired, the wind blew my breath right flat, I'm breathing, you'll live so much longer right now, you are mountainous, your breath is cool, you are the source of my saying you know everything, you are sweating you are eating, the light set on me, you set the sun, the strongest wind every driven bends a call to that plant's branches, the one that's right there, that one, it drinks all the water you give it but can't say anything, clouds were pink, now an only-in-sky color like you require more description than I can drink but I can't say anything, you read me a color you read me an only-in-sky color, what a dreamed-of dance where the monster you spoke of, the one that you wanted, the monster you talked to for hundreds of years, giant love monster, he befriends the earth and how can I tell you what he knows, he has secret powers, he mixes things up like my name where no syllable has an accent, he makes old things cool and boil like the elixir you stand in the light of the moon till its coolness is natural or innate, opaque, it becomes something else, say it, say my name, become more than a mixture, the elements, correct, I've forgotten them in gathering you, you are all over all of the spaces and times, give me things, things that I can design space with and place only in the sky, that kind of motion, I am cloudy I am moving, I am colors that can't be described without too many words, beams you can stand on and rain that high up it beats on us, it misses us, we look through, we look at distance, you say in words my words are muscles, then what's the silence you put me through today, silence where I talked all messages sent, so much mischief in the reception, I never think about bad things do you? You are enormous you have many parts, you are not a warning, two hours go by. Circle lapse and tender buttons yells immerse yourself in milk, I do, he's on his way here, some yells, a switch a curse a house and a secretary I envy you and your housekeepers and all your lovers, I mix mine with yours, secret separate entity, entice design midnight midnight with you monster and maker and play knows how to play, play everything, know how much I didn't know how much I'd be afraid to write down, the background of my finding out how could I know how much I was beginning to be afraid to write down what you know, or do you, I know you know, it's so simple, you are a genius, but that's not it. Factory works and no one's startled but my edge on the sky that's never ending edge on the sky. Please beat me up. That's a false request, this is your final chance to send me back home where I came from. Now you belong to me in many colors, brown and silver, gray and yellow, blue and orange, silver and gray, yellow and it's not monstrous, you've seen my feet. It's nine o'clock, I've singled to first you're the only one on. It's a problem. I can't read the weather for all this desire to storm the doors. I'll never sleep again. I saw a cat who simply died, what can't I influence, the own body is as mix with you. Are you waiting, is it time, I open my mouth, soon I'm starving, I love grapefruit and cheese, fish, strawberries, asparagus and cream, nuts, snowpeas, potatoes and cream, leaves, corn, squash, mushrooms, scallops, onions, coffee and tea I've eaten enormously brandy and bed, I love fall, who else eats this much, who else is served such sauces separately. Every night I make my head spin, that's after I swim with the monster we met in the field, they only spoke to me cause you were there, spin after I work out with them, try to con them with a fast pitch and see what happens. Thank you for your influence with these men and women. But, you, listen to this: every night at the edge of the spin, there's no describing it, there you are, or is it me, I shouldn't leave myself out to get away with a simple spin.

Dream: Punch—jail—jump out the window—rescue—sick. Julia Child and Alice Toklas come. They were always too busy to come before. What is he doing here, why is he interested in staying, he has so much serious work to do. He just felt like staying this time, because of me. He points out that she spends so much serious energy at it. Yes but she's not doing anything, her work is silly, it doesn't lead anywhere, but she does it. Now he's butting in trying to listen to our private talk, we're lying face to face. Who is he, I can't figure it out. Climbing up a stairs in a store, structuralist levels, a center stairs, a stairs with nothing on either side of it.

●

My legs are bare the covers fall off them
I must come just thinking about it extending
If I can come just thinking about it
It's the trick of having a cock
It's coming on ten per cent
The chance of rain on Monday
He turns over
His dream-masked man says to me
I'm not interested in your coming on ten per cent
If you're interested I'm not interested in your proving…
He leaves off
That was what I wanted to do and I did it
In the green woods she is compliant
The light's on in the factory
The covers fall off my legs
His arm is around my waist
But he can't hold me from carrying out this experiment
Test coming from beforehand
Before I went to sleep I was high
I was aching to do this

●

The Olympic dream team: one living as two. Study the adjournment position, the avoidance position. My father calls, he says to me, "Where've you been?"

What am I learning baby I am learning you. The plant stands up I'm scared to stop, I might choke on my food I can't find the paints. I'm eating my food like a baby, how do they survive it? Not talking I mean. I've earned a place on your floor. I am painting a mural of my satisfaction from left to right I am going to go swimming in it, words may be cut short or extended, words may grow differently, inside something, inside it. One lives as two one lives as two one is two one is opening one is loose, closed, now two now two can close, I don't have the right pens, I don't have any materials, the bums play ball, watch the ball, I conduct a review, I explain the paint, I say to the paint secret rituals weird rites certain burials of dead bodies which are under the ground, someone is curious about incest, I am no longer sick with the flu, I ain't got the flu, it's psycholinguistics, deeper structures than you find in the alligator mouths below Canal Street, they're eating their dinner, you press too hard on the pencil, you flirt with production, you flirt with death too, I didn't know you were already drinking brandy, invite me to join you, invite me to speak the smallest words in the room that's all, give him some head and become senseless, I play with the permanent ending of all life, I got to the permanent ending of the novel I was reading and sneaked a look at the beginning, a plant dies, a red-topped plant loses its color, becomes a skeleton in a black robe holding a scythe in a state of murder and bloodshed pestilence, a plant can't sustain it, sustain the upright condition of being without water, too much water. There gonna be water there. I leave that out. Mothers and fathers come to the hurricane, indoors hurricane wept in waters, the plants murder the aunts and uncles especially of women, like the Black Muslims, dirty or clean. The food is all over the place. You don't talk like you should. What's the visual you're on, you got on, are you on one. Strike zone's an empty visual for language, no good, I'm out in the country, images don't collide. I'm back here old and new, what's the story, I'll inch toward it, I'll come to it through mud. I want you to think I'm suffering more so I won't get cold or old, to keep you keep, pen always writes without me, dress always falls again like a glance to the floor. Games over in here. What a collision and thank you very much. I am not violating in system any of the rules of coordinates. I'm out to systematically violate the rules in succession one after one and add a extra any. Swallow now. This is compelling. Neat flow. She sure was kind. She sure was well taken of. She sure worked her fucking arm off. He sure fucking well didn't give a shit. Create something endless in little designs like a million babies, fat babies. What do you need? What's the right lingo for a successful succession secession from the seat of power and righteousness down on the floor with everyone and birds crows fantasies beginnings of words small syllables giant letters image continuous green and black leaves. All leaves are successive and boring. I refuse to make the connection, no image supply room, concentration ideal. Defend the states of consciousness, run for your life. You eat too much you drive too fast, it was time not distance that amazed him and so he bought a watch. Thirteen watches at the store and devoted self to avoiding empty messages, the clocks the fine Swiss tower is as sandwich earls and manors, deer shot in Bavaria then the sinking ship. I've fooled you. No focus is as fool as focus is. It's a rip-off, they trade bits of brand new checks no cash. A song. A miracle, cynical imbecile miracle. Largesse veteran's beverage. Big sign. No sky. Empty mirrors make. Her mix is to imitate and mind she's confused tonight. Refuse garbage. A signed matador. A metal detector and fire prevention for exit's escape, you clear the door, the door's too tall, it sounds letters specious sounds, the softball team in their yellows, bear up on legs, all fours, perching mischief on a beam of language light. You let yourself get away with it.

If you need a piece of cloth and you're still holding it wrong and you want to go faster and faster and if you need a piece of cloth for some design you go get it, it's as simple as that. First try dry run, you run for your life shake down the street, get money have money, pimp it, test out your friends, more information, friends end, did you kill em? He bounces the ball he is all thought and loving gentle fucking asshole, he is near perfect he is swelling he is near purple, he is yelling fucking keep it to yourself. You got the worst fucking something, I got the piece of cloth, the newspaper rides around the floor, hovers and covers the ground, how do you move that's you, you, in a schedule in a regular routine, there's no past here, it's all past, I'm so pissed off I'm spitting the endlessly permanent blood on the pavement that fell from the war where they stimulate the guts of your stomach, men only, for pay. They pay me not to. Give me all your money. How sweet can you be? In pennies. That's a three-bills deal, it aches, I give up. Thank you Catholic churches very much, you were right, I love ironing and changing into clean white clothes. Why can't I say what you mean, you and I and a couple other yous and seven graven images taken stoned in a tableau with their names in aces in the yard. Centuries ago when the moon something and militant staid armies selected you I ate the poisonous berries, same yard, drew the wrong card, pirate ships and all all this time staying on as a woman in the fine big household the earth supplies. What a region of terror, that space by the fire, like dogs home exhausted from their work in the circus, following masters, sleep, fall down, piss and eat. I used to hate stone. I ate stone. It's far from direct. It's crooked and senseless and just goes on. I'm putting you on. Of course you enjoy it. Nature puddles, western saddles, hurricane derision, final entrance, mixing armor, cell and block, wall of China, message sumptuous message old, no sound wizened sound, poets of China arts, pimps at the wall, black and bitten, shaking the pumpkin, an actual an actual the feat of becoming one across the states across divisions american national american puddles american fucking american fingers american blanks american monsters Emily Dickinson cock crows murders hangings to gospel music. God can't spell, you seem to always be well dear, god is not too natural and all of my fathers fucked jesus at the altar of my friend inspirational Patti. God stipulates that he is constrained, he is stained, well old grandfathers don't do too good, just sit around and peer at the mean motherfucking round the sweet bonfire of the shit white culture where we each came from and we hope to emerge re-merge without Vikings and Washingtons and columbines can climb the trees and colors rearranged and many men sink ships anyway, we don't need ships please, eat this much of me and you will see I would like to draw you without any background. Ships from Europe were full of people. The ocean is full of food. People have a wide range of emotions. In writing, it is interesting to work in a kind of continuous present. I am sitting on you. You are each of you a pear. A human steel. In x is inherent y. Make me feel good. Philosophical flying. American amperes west. See me?

Section two. The meld. I am a space I am keeping pace with you, exciting. Unending beginning the permanent showing of all life in humans and plants, in plants animals in animals humans in humans animals in plants humans in animals plants, every eye. Eye pushed out a current of air with its breathing in of vision. Concentric ranges tending in, extending in. Circle encloses itself, whirls in vortex, down and re-compels gravity to notice a fault in the ocean's mountain range. De fault in de ocean its mountainous range I'm sweatin bout it tis due to de heavy man's striations made in de excellent ground dat wuz laid there one day in May. Say hey how you doin my baby you sweet and you lovin I love it to make it with you anytime, human beans they borrow matches but with you nodding next to me nobody don't have to learn to make love like as we do like as we don't sure as shit I have to say. I make my play. You give an inch, you inchin towards me what a baby say and it's more than I can take or stand, men and women all inchin round. Mud and money and a sexual existence makes you feel richer, I feel richer when I'm a switcher. But back to that picture, it's then I feel more mix with you and all the own bodies, just a minute of the poor black whites assembling for the own meaning, meant an act of meat and potatoes means whole trees in motion after storms are mourning cause somebody dies. I feel the wind on the face of the leaves. I can't walk, I'm sick enough to flirt with the wind that stops my progress, lost the vision, I paint a new structural wind that is bound to the tree, cannot move. My motion as wind is resembling me, it resembles me more. I can do anything, I can do nothing, come from nowhere, I am damaging, I am slight, sick, white, uprooted, clear and divine, divine by vision lost, divine by total false and magic, divine by instinct for death, damage of death is slight, instinctual, evanescent, clear, clear and fading, an immigration, new uprooted, no progress is my progression as if I were sleeping in a work fit, a fit of work for one single special levitation one mystical throwback, like football players, stupid and thoughtless and at best speechless. I wish I were. I try to throw, no catch, no moment, only the damage without clarity, emergency reroots me, I resist, they clear the rubble, it's down, I'm fainting with the desire to destroy more, as far inland, I will go as far inland as I can to damage everything, there's no more sex, there's nothing alluring, no connections between things and nothing mapped, your experience of me is rare, it's no coincidence it isn't planned, it isn't anger and no joy, you do not experience this, you do, I fuck you up, I turn you around, everything's in reverse and resembles me and if I have a motive or energy that's it, the damage is awful, spread wide. Accept the chaos if it's a trick, receive it, I've done it, you must, you must not, please notice this fine chaos, men and women, what can you make of it, women and men, with nothing open. Laughing at you, you taste of me, hate your selves, destroy all life I mix with you, you are only seven years old. A space where motion grows and something changes. Still, you can't identify me and you are too extremely simple, everything, your eyes. I greet you.

●

Strawberry Tree

Come over here
A fake sends lie a new book
Bake it with currents
Bands play around your head
I ache hate for you I message you
You enter and are caught message ends
You think back you cannot
Hate poems relentlessness
The pestering sisters made you at once
I arranged it a match made of evils
And significant designs you fool
Of genius and even habits and sense to fool
I dish you out a disaster a lobster
Full red and green living death of lobster
An anchor for your sails you'll wind up floundering
You'll try to make them fly in a sky
That flies away from you and leaves
Leaving you and your relations fooled
Alone and open to attack,
Without senses.

●

Heads of women who laugh: It's a puzzle, it's not a puzzle, it is. Write in the dark or speak out loud. Little family disappears, don't mourn the objects of your desire, find a source of pleasure, their heads pop up again. At first I'm coasting through but then loss is guaranteed so I have unreal pains, I collapse, I recover but I'm not getting what I need, I don't get married though, I meet Max, we live the high life, that ends and begins again, I begin to write, I flirt with physical motion by crossing the country, the country makes me laugh, a few tremors, I find it hard to walk the streets for fear I'll collapse, the work gets done but eventually I will not move, I try to solve the problem psychologically, I have sporadic allies but something's wrong, I need to take a chance, what chance, maybe the chance is this: I will actively love you: "In a rich woman's house…in blue…"

I've got to elaborate on the principal message of the saints' murals, murals in churches that sink and are shadows, murals that fade, the unfinished statue with horns that shatter, shatter themselves and shatter you, you are no longer a shadow in the grove of monsters, you and me we provided the monsters and nurtured them and made them grow. Give me something else. Those monsters speak, they step up, they rush, in the door, they watch the doors, they don't get caught in the rush, they don't get spooked by the crowd, they just keep coming, coming and going. I am amazing. I've stopped where you are. I am at your opening even though I myself am always beginning again, still I'm right there, present for the trade, we make it. Mourning and grief and anger summer here, maybe only as words, expectant and full. Full yellow is the predominant color, color in so much. Times Square. Step back a little more. The doors open. Looks at watch. What I started to say here, the image I saw was the one of us moving, moving in relation to each other through a door, we are so similar, we are so alike. I wish it. I can't bring anyone else in and so the saviours all simpletons in a nice way, they save me and bring me a whole new regiment of new monsters only this time they come alive, like it worked, the experiment, and new regimen, new routine: you eat this you eat that. Get out, the image, get it out of there, out of here, don't waste your words because people…hello. A green stone. Prisoners say hello. People save their money. Why were you sleeping in my sister's room, why do you encourage me to think about leaving, why I want to encourage you to, some people are so well-dressed and inter-connected we've suspected them forever, this continues right on just as expected, the earth is green and brown. We live in town where it's a struggle to hide in the grass. It's nothing is the secret I'm showing you how to do, it's ordinary and usual. I can do it, can you? I get off at the next stop or maybe the next one. I can't remember what a beautiful finger I had, to sliver the pad and slice into tendons too fine to recover without growing and back into their design.

The plant's getting darker in color, the pens won't write as usual, I won't admit anyone but you to this here, they come in anyway, everyone comes in anyway and when I begin, now no matter what, everything comes right in and seems to fit and sit down and by fit I mean stretch out, distract and leave openings to find and play with. You're fine. You are going to tell me I don't love you again. You are going to tell me, no you are not saying anything, you've decided not to say it. I'm out here all alone, I don't want to confound what's already unending. I want to plead with you, we are all right for a while. Yes, no, I've been here the whole time and it's been awful. I'm holding out for the next storm. I'm despicable for not coming over to you, you turn over. What a chance I'm taking what a face I'm making, connections allow. Seven slices of lemon meringue, we ate the whole thing on waxed paper, he liked it too, did it contribute to his death, did he throw something away, what's the search for now? It's much more fragmented here and now that living people have invaded once again this hell-hole. You hate that word but it's better than design which is flattered and insistent, reassembled and wise-ass, gnomes in a sideshow, keeping time. You still awake? You sleeping yet? I'm cold I go outside to be where you'll soon be. I'm hungry I'm fantasy, evil circles, homes of evil changes, evil prose, a sentence destroys, you could destroy a tree a plant a definition a space, I keep wanting to draw in those other people and then push away. There, we all love them. They send us notes sometimes, we must answer them all. I'm making too much of this, it would be interesting then to go back to the past, you'll know what to do. My ice cream's fallen, whole scoop of it, out of the cone.

●

I think I'll miss you more, hand in the pen hand on the streets I'm walking what shall I buy him what shall I get him, it's awful hot in here and colors. Sense is stimulation, oceans meet dry they never dry, a tip of ocean's smaller than a pin's head where they meet. I'd like to be there. That's black music, he the music lives back in his ancient mother's cottage, not a prayer, cottage far away what a word. Way down below the ocean where I wanna be she may be. Drift below any drift, add a extra sense with drift. Potato. Loaves. I keep thinking my father puts me on a train. No stops except stopping, what a spectacle I must make. I always make the train by a second on my way home. Scared? Yes but fighter-writers inch along along the way from left to right you let me get away with so much, you let me coast on through, once you're on the train it's going to take you there dead or alive. My question always is: can I get off? Can I make it to the door? Can I swerve with the crumbling train crumbling without crumbling apart, it's awful hot in here. Your car. Painted fingernails on a white dress. I am below you in the station, it's a long ride underground. One way for you and one way for me, way back, in time. It's real fast, it's real emotion, no. The closet opens and it's everything in one, peaches and pears, colors of pastels, times square folding people in their robes, ancient writers editing equipment, a fine t.v. that works and magical film develops magically, you leave this wonderful box in the attic, I open it but I remember you were looking for your pastels right after you moved. What I want to know is this: how have you changed position exactly and where have you moved to: can I still get in touch with you. I have high standards, I could become a person who was always only running: "She's the one who runs." I'm worried about this: are you still there? Anyway because I'm always naked they're committing me. You say, get to the point, anyway when I'm always naked I mean if I'm always naked in my dreams, going around, even working, without any clothes on, if I do this, I am committed, if I do it, it's only because I'm committed to revelation, committed to show you. She committed suicide when she realized he understood how she had manipulated his love for someone else into his love for her. I'm almost there but I get a dispensation, I get the go-ahead, I get the trust: it's written out in designs of the scientific lines the heart and other organs make, the brain waves are explicated, pretty pictures drawn on them in colors, brain waves illuminated illustrated by an official priest. He is giving me the signal, all systems go, in the corridor, secret, beyond where the real work, real meetings are being held. I don't need those, I am independent, I am going.

Times passes breasts exposed, write heights with a new pen, the dictionary has words for it, I speed you toward and forward, showing off. I wait for the local.

Pedestals. Fine. Emerge. Naming nails, naming bolsters and struts, waiting. Monday. Haven't seen you in two days. I just missed the train. Waiting. Time flies, I'm exposed, I'm empty I'm full it takes a long time, time signs falsified, just missed it, no paper no space. What are you thinking, it takes five minutes for the train to get here. I want to kill you. Knife drills into you. You tired of that? When the train comes it's not interesting. It's interesting for me to admit you know your own mother, you know mine, I admit it, admit you to the absence of image you think you can turn a profit on, your head is on my breast exposed, left to right. Far? Shortened, grooves, serrations, those are difficult names, what's to distinguish between them when people talk. I expose my breasts. Baby II and Boy II.

Cue to begin, let you go. There's a lot here, it's coasting, shut down the engines to the setting allure. Want you. Beginning. Float and try everything. More ice and more words and the rhythm which is air of the radio waves, stopping and starting in waves, it's simple. I'll pick up some food, be good. Who do I know? She used an abacus real fast, leaned to the right when the north train came to a stop naturally so body could wave bye-bye in a whisper. That's right. Comes into focus: my eyes have been bullied into blurring the image after I see it, the Palisades are blurred, I can't see them in the dark in the sky. Afterwards, it's clear it presses itself on you, like I do, even in the dark, the railroad goes by more often than we expect. We go out. Electric currents explode. No one's interested though—you violate the code—they, the ones who weren't alive, explode now but don't make the connection either to being free. Look up and look around, music sat down, is being read off a page, heading towards somewhere, as usual, definition like me, no moment its everywhere, this guy's engrossed in it in America for sure, we do what we want on the trains no matter how race or courtship we are, I smile when her silver pocketbook strap falls on me as instantaneous as any connection I see she is sorry, her watch reads ten to three. I'm late. I used to say the words I was sorry and am with a gulp, I took a drug to do it, what day was it, how many children do you have, it's simple and clear, is the day set straight in your mind, no matter what, strong, I'm speeding toward you, I don't know what language you speak, if mine is too free well it comes along very much that way with me to you, up and down just anyway, white spots on a light gray field, an ermine trimming for anarchist robes that judges all can afford while they float naked in the stream like you do and anyway a body is on to something new. There's drifts I will allow to seep in. They like my reserve, it's a beautiful day.

Floating, it's appropriate to come to the end here's a false ending based on trumped up charges and comes to you in phony code words like holy cow, the best dressed man I ever knew flew higher than you, dawn on a sunny day, the first generous empty day of the perfect work week. She's cheating, she's not feeling anything, she's feeling swell, it must be worked on, it must be realigned, she's there for no reason, that's her teaching of lonesome floating, she's keeping it from you, she's not keeping anything for you really. She's taken her clothes off again. I've taken my clothes off pictures. Hungry. Hot. Dense and speed boats speeding on the canal, why things look different through glass, she says through glass you can't see, it's really a mess, full of speed boats. He and I have a memory of horses. When we play with each other, it ought to be a scene, recorded indoors, a book is being written, a book is brought out: some pages are just fabric of pattern and design, some pages shake, like continuous therapy or Wittgenstein, like an even running along through on the side and over, stopping and starting through it, very even is moon, clear light and unnecessary for warmth. Change, think of all the other people who've studied acting, independent and acting and impostor, he gets the break, brings out the dancing bears. Someone knows all about it, someone can hear breath carried on waves through air in existing communications, the thermometer-binocular, look through it, it shows you the prisms of a face a very small space broken up and kept together in the center of the field through glass, look how different things look through glass, look, I am waiting and even running through stopping and starting an even running long through on the side, train that came came too fast and is stopping, making us wait and shiver in the heat we steal and get our just beautiful long red robes, jewel and ermine throat cut low in a v. so we can hear more, it helps us to see, see comes different, stop long at vertical stops, right through to the finish, it just goes right on, well past where I get off, isn't the finish, not by a long shot, not by design, a head that never aches is dyed, is covered with blue hair dye, I dye yours, black woman, fine, blue enough and blue clear through, very even, very much in time and waiting at full speed boats that stop on a dime, the floor's swept it's clean, what's it waiting for full of tension is iron, is swept irresistible underground painting the memory running of horses running, we want to ride them, we've swept up the code.

You're full of colors, why things look so different through glass and marbles, an eye tinted blue and hair tinted blue of black women, the black woman in you stop. You are black or lately everything is. Laugh but don't get me wrong, independent cause black is new and invisible, real new. Everything is backwards and upside down. I did it. You make real love with your clothes on like prostitutes and when we fake it, that's when we take off our clothes, it's all talk and radial mikes, come on, something's changing, now you've pushed me over here where I like it, like to get away with things, child wife. I'm here.

●

You people across the street painting and sanding and erecting struts, you don't know what I'm doing, I hardly know myself, you know. FBI agents continue to surround the bank. Call me if anything comes up. Andy's thinking of going to the summer Olympics in Munich. New books to buy. What's Max doing? You said they're dead, up till now you haven't believed that, I took it to mean, now they'll never visit me again. We're talking about here, parents who are missed why miss them they were jerks they just stood there or sat there or put on an exhibition of love just for me, in the water of a black black lake. They had terrific workshops conducting the business of making things with wood, electronic connections, I want to come back to you and make a scene, hello, workshops for making wine and plants grow, magic pastels and interior of a house design, florid ferns and flowers in colors on walls, walls they never got built, a sense of style, making it in the thirties, if you can write that as a socialist then I can write it as a trade-unionist, United Electrical Workers of the world read Frankenstein and Dracula in their spare time, collect spare parts to recreate what. He studied at night school, radio and t.v., that's after designing failed. Do you know what you made me do? You made me see an afterimage of the sun when I was only in my room in the dark. I close my eyes, I see things, everyone does but I see too much, you made me do it, now you lose faith in me and I giggle because what else can I do now that I'm here, I'm alone but I'm not and what's the difference, lots of people are stopped up for centuries, this stuff, maybe, maybe not, sure I can pose real strong, I can write: I may go out tomorrow if I can borrow a coat to wear. Three dream that each two is one. One interferes with work that only two should do.

●

End of the primary red book. Mixed up. Dear David, A whole picture history in hieroglyph on the Saints-Day walls from left through right, emerging. At first on the left is a stick man in profile facing right his penis erect making a perfect right angle, extended, you guessed it, to the length of the mural, design resembling a mural, imposed, penis points to the continuing pattern, introduces it, lays it all out, I've really mangled the page while framing it, it's a history, next come the military and authorities, the police, asking for money, asking for a wall, tips, how have they helped us? There are so many of them we must give them something, a bribe to make them leave, leave us, we don't want them in crowds sitting at our table, we give them just more than half of what they expect, 6 out of 11, like the number 51, the age, a perfect number, there's a man who will live to be a hundred because he is now 51, a number of presence of rounding it's pictured like the half moon but with the visible outline of the rest of the sphere, the implied sphere. This is significant, it connotes absence which isn't pictured. 49. Moving further right, next, the cleaning up, the rearrangement, many figures moving some are working, some are casting spells, they are speaking, we can't see their words, their words picture a history and have shapes only in the space between you, the observer, and the continuous mural, flat against the wall emerging. Words take shape in between. It could be anywhere. There's a sudden change. Perhaps a vertical line is drawn between what came before and this, the next: figures of women in nightgowns are changing into their street clothes, I'm really eating up the page with this machine, it's in ribbons, in nightgowns are changing into their street clothes, they were caught in the daylight in sleep, they were walking and playing all night, now they must change, they ransack the clothes closets and drawers, an intimacy with my own sister or your own, look for the right outfits and put them on, put you on. You are looking. A rich man is sleeping in the corner, he's you, you're almost unnoticed except that I recognize you, he's almost unnoticed, just a little element and he is covered. Then another man, he isn't marked, not identified. There could be many men in the end. Finally this scene: a woman alone with a man. The man is speaking to her. They are standing, isolated, in fresh clothes, no, only the woman is changed, the man has been fully dressed all along, in fact, carefully dressed, he is well turned out, well turned around, he is asking her a question, it's the one that's been asked before by the expression on her face which is tired, smiling, nervous. The question refers to a continuing process of thought, no that's too general and evasive, but maybe not, cause the question, while it seems superficial, is more full of significance than its language conveys. He is asking her if she has been thinking, he doesn't say for how long, if she has been thinking recently I guess about doing something he wants her to do, has she been thinking of it at all. The something is something like leaving, perhaps it is leaving her home and coming to stay with him for a while or maybe just leaving, abandoning everything that now surrounds her with the implication that she could then do whatever she wants. They want each other but are tied down or tied into these questions. But why is he asking her, he must have some connection to her and to what came before, some desire even to spend more time with her himself, or at least to find her romantic, so he encourages her to leave, without words. Maybe he is asking just to find out and leaving it open for her to visit him for a while, stay with him. Or it could be just an objective investigation, he is very sociable and polite, maybe he is just making conversation, he won't commit himself, but he has taken her off to the side, to the edge of the painting, to ask this question. Then it ends. I didn't design this mural, someone else entered my dream and set up the plan and I described it as I painted it as you would eventually describe a circle with your finger in the air. You.

Songs of evil: I want to leave this place I want to get out of here I want to move into an eternal space the right space I want to design it have you freed me to addict myself to take this risk, escape no longer draws me in, just kill the pain, take my wrists in your hands, I can't find anything on the floor, we have no regular game, no drama, in the dark everything's a mess. There's no end to it in a space as big as this no walls and I hate myself for keeping on going as if the production of something out of nothing out of here where there is nothing were worthwhile, preserve my sainthood. You help to preserve it, perpetrating the finest evil that was ever devised, a false glamour on the surface of simple veins bulging, their blood bursts back into the needle, and then flows through back through the veins, southest asia, infusion, injection, replacement, maze, there was a fog all through the city before my eyes, I was sweating, what's the verdict of sleep: I can't find out: observe me as I trance myself beyond death: write it down a written record dead poet flying crows.

A trace, a stronger texture impossible to tear, I still imitate I still review, the fog goes on, there's a name for it: surface of the eyes pervert senses, clouding heavy sky, diffusion in all directions, pose and empty, the idea that I would do anything for him has become a joke. Tomorrow the joke's perverted and I mean it again. What is it? That he would do anything for me is clearer, is accepted, is loved. Sure the love is inherent in murder and the closeness designs a wish for death, the death of someone is the death of all. Reminded. Can you still see? A small dark and trembling tree is able to reassemble the qualities of wind within its leaves, by means of them. The tree, its image, is a trick, come out of nowhere, committed. Committed to an institution, you must stay there, committed to a man or woman, you must leave them free, committed a sin, a crime, you must commit another and maybe commit another person to your crime. You cannot be alone, you cannot escape. Bulbous images in dark, balloons, lustrous growths of them emerge from under your arms from your groin from whatever's beneath your feet, I can't imagine. Insects bite you, bite your feet, lay eggs on them, hatch and grow even larger than the haze of your eyes can conceal. You are eating.

Begin again, you leave traces, I don't mean anything, cut short, let go: and merging complete unexpected cells of design, saint a feint for message hood and monk's disclosed the edge of the circle the mix is as the own body is as mix with you as lion is hungry as coarse and shooting confines in cells and caves mothers and fathers at their stations, the rest riding four horses in directions to poles. We're children, where else can we go, go out to, we eventually describe all possibilities as you would describe a circle tangent to a point extending indefinitely, you could do it simply, with your finger in the air. You're happy with that, I won't be satisfied, it can't be seen. Something funnier is going to happen. I'm committed to it like fuck jesus, phrases that ring in your ear when I'm sleeping you pause. It's too simple. Insects beyond calculus are at my disposal, magic isn't subject to elegance, magic's not an art and neither is sleeping, remembering the past backwards, power without senses, immersion, submersion in the fluids of the own body, how great that is the idea of the own the own body without motive the own body just a presence and a note—I made this present, in a way, to you, any way I can.

Sensual power greatest evil without design her rule, the impossible, and pose the finite as a trick. Don't light on me. I'm patient I am cruel, I possess your trance. Excess ownership, deacons of the church, metals drift on the sea. Anything. Pores. Surcharges. Sunspots. Masterpieces. Growth peppers edge entrance exit peer. Like owl his murder tickles the ground and spills out black ink, knife drills into you you are down, live the night? in dark? And if you move the movements of branches cracking, branches speak attack, someone is holding them, bears down on you, threatens, curses, face down you have no power, flooded, you can't find out, you were warned of secrets you were told they were necessary, luminous yellow on a field of black, glows. Crosses for darkness, parallels for light. What trees are around you, which ones are living, can you move, hold your eyes open, do battle, bend down. This ground is the real ground that circles and stratas to core, it boils, the only ground, crawling, nothing between you. Banging and crashing. A flame.

●

You are destroyed in the fire, you are black ash, you are stone, charred, fertile, a bed for hundreds of years of black work emerging. Your soul rejuvenates the soul, blood-red flower, an element of the mix, aces your grave. Now I'm present, I'm there. When you see my face white and design you are fixed to it, repulsed, by its effort to love. We mix. Young and live forever my blackness seeks the moment of your death without communication. The legs of the flower, bending, screens in rest. Hide us. All night. Poisoning, extracting the drugs of the flower. You are lost. I choose loss. Waves and shores, oceans of loss, separate, meeting, destroy. No one can get there.

Ha ha it's so simple and dead, I'm nearly dead, if anyone sees me tell me and please have energy I'm cold, go away, you see me? I look like christ, you each got your chores.

Breath, you should be me you should see me duty bound to create a state to begin again. Let me stop picking at things. I saw this coming. This that I can't decide. I run I hide baby what you want me to do. In the sun. I was worn out and sweating in the back of my head where I've gone sun's hot. Twist off. Don't make no mystery of it, don't wanna stop but don't wanna not, can't decide, well I create the news well I could stop the news easy I could drop it I could watch it sing wow space of a feeling that exists where it does in my head is mine all mine like that woman's stream, she owned it and wouldn't let us swim there, period.

Streams are running through things, it's not my fault I'm wet all soaking soaking wet, you shouldn't ruin, wet before I go in, makes me the guilty one. This book by now is a classic safe, too heavy to carry, too small to protect, no, too heavy to carry, too small to be noticed at all, that's not it, too small to carry, but too heavy to move. A safe can't be small, no, it can be small but it has to be heavy, too heavy to move, too small for the money.

Mixed up. I knew I'd knock it over. And let this exist in only one place: I am my own father, there are many different kinds of bread, some of the bread is dough folded over and containing higher protein food like cheese or meat, I tell my wife to look, look over there, while we're standing in front of the open refrigerator, the room's been rearranged. I tell her to look, we see a movie of the future and we see our two sons who are also our only daughters and they are our lovers, my lovers, we see them walking down towards us, and I say to my wife, look they're grown up, they need us. And as lovers they are coming back from the war and I think to myself since this is a movie, what if only one of them gets back. But then I'm myself again, studying in the dark before the open windows of every house I've ever lived in, the books are spread out and the writing, I'm working and I wonder what can get me back to this work, a cup of coffee? a thought? It's dark and I think to myself, if I'm going to get back to the work, I'll get back to it. Anyway, it's there.

BOOK II

FREUD FREUND FRIEND FREEZING

END for yourself FRIGID J'ai froix J'aime les fra
roses

rosemary - sea dew

You are King Lear / oh no.
Cordelia is I cant say it.
+ Goneril + Regan's venereal disease
+ Edgar + Edmund are Ed for short
[illegible] 2 B a madman + saves the day
Did I know all this? I know more.
You are each message in the water I drink
Tomorrow will be a hard day
Cause the kingdom is a cause made up of
families collapse + who is the subject
of the king?

Dear Lear Goliath how many are you + am I
to fit into you, there's no mother there
SHAKES BEAR
+ Shapes bear
Shakes beer - it explodes
the wine field
the juices
Someone once told me that frozen juices ex
if you let them get warm
+ I said "everything anticipates as much
as it's past"
+ I imagine myself in a loft with the ceiling beam
from them with a perf
sed + many plants hanging
eep them grow + Ed leaves / I am alone I am al
ou are free to visit me whenever you please, a

1

I had my Amazons shoot you, my dress is on the piano, it's too small for me, orange with a white neck-ruff.

Train running train nearly naked on the train, to show you, it's too revealing for me to shoot you down and kill you, it's still so hot on the train, there are spaces of my body to be stared at, navel and ribs, the space between my breasts, a strong breastbone, you keep making me come uptown without making me, w.o. (medical abbreviation).

I create an illusion, an illusion which points out what you're leaving out, you're always skirting the issue, playing with my dresses, carving to see what you get, no plan, no Moses in the statue, and so there are endless revisions, endless repeating as part of revision. Is it funny that movie you're watching? I'm pretty persistently illustrated. August 30th the day you resume persisting with water and take your daughter for a look at a great elephant, you create her irresistible image. Six days ago: minutes make something happen: I'm at Penn Station. Shoppers come in, I can't conceive of shopping, how can they shop for anything but food? How can you bear, I create, my pretensions, like no punctuation. Food, even that's impossible. Allen was arrested and Edmund was too, my shoe's falling off just like it did ten years ago.

Something to stare at and avoid, I want to be clear, I wrote my name in the subway, a big B. You cracked the puzzle yet, by the way? Times Square ends the same city in a circle, go around, go around together, how can you go alone, men on the subway attempt to look down at my breasts which are covered with hair, I won't go too far below the line, but they can't really see anything which perhaps is worse after all I'm no dummy, 59th Street, I'm getting to the point, I sneeze and a woman, I sneeze and a woman moves over. Poetry's simple and clear, step lively please.

2

The same is true for you for us, no plan, step out step lively my mind is full of tricks and junk. How can you expect me to get to broadway, we're just a sweet city island. Why don't you come out and tell me all that you know so that I don't fear your derision, you're someone else. Real suffering is one thing, the exhaustion of a fool getting nowhere is something else.

3

We go to City island, just to place this in time. Just in time, I find a moment to tell you I love you and tell you to make sure in the restaurant with the giant seafood dinner and the waiters staring at this May-December couple holding hands discussing structuralism just before you die. Forgive me.

4

How can I be alone here now when I've been with you half an hour ago, I'm afraid I must fill you with doubts about my character and its nature, a word one should never use, ha ha words elude me, you elusion of...when I pull out the money for our hotel room, do you want to see some credentials too, I have experience. Draw a card, draw one by one, coffee together, the cream, it's hard to ship out, it's even harder to stay at home.

Moon just rising equals the same as four hours of time waiting and not with no one on either end, why the code it sucks, you're waiting and I'm always waiting, you're doing something I'm not, yes I am, I'll be a little clearer: couldn't we go long and far, I know the rain would fall on us and seem like the beach with just ordinary people, they do it, and they do it as well as anyone in the universe, they make love in a universe aware of their fear too, but in universe, as though, some two, make love, one to the other, and all the beach thoughts speak to them in memory, same as me and you, beach rolls around, I won't list them, I can't remember that way, crowds of much more than that asserts importance, above all lists and beyond any past or anybody's, I'm going too far and take you higher, you aren't scared like no one I've met recently. My speech isn't listed in the books as some kind, read it to me, I make the language fly and it's hot, two crows black crows fly, black sky, they deal with what's there, they learn to love the haze more than that, a crow any bird speaks to the haze in incredible motion, towers and level, not standing, they are.

5

I make these divisions unconscious like cutting a pie, there's a whole history involved with it. What was the dream and why I would kill you, is same so much equals the same why I wouldn't cause you, romance of the universe I saw, visible once in a beam of light off the highway and visible once lying in bed, I'm a child, I lie on purpose on my back, legs spread and arms spread so that no limbs are touching, the center of my body the torso is the receiver, I lie there, summer night real late, visible once, I receive what's there I leave myself open, another reason remembers that night, what's probable? No covers I am careful to keep limbs from touching I am floating, like floating on waves, recreation from the sound, remember swimming plans for this but more than that, I'm receiving differently, it's night, shadows, and I think to do this, the own body, and I'm full of a feeling from a nothing that I know is something, special, what you bring, and it's nothing, it's all visible once, I am proving I'm in awe like reversing your existence from seeing to what is seen: I am the shadows lights make at night in the back of the moving car, going home, mesmerize me and cars passing like the surf there's no end to it do you see? You! Don't worry I'm glad I said myself to you or I would have died or I would have survived you like everything, single out structures only for time, either to make time for something later or to deny it, we do we don't exist therein, a funny place for us, I need to make speeches, you ravish the objects with a word at a time.

6

A single word, or invective against length, a choice is in love with you. Let me ask you a question: you let me.

7

Exhausted dizzy but can't sleep. This is so small. Think more think back. Are words more in code? The red rose doesn't the rose is red does. Make a sentence reverse. Is swinging mix as several are ones as much or more than I am waiting for you. And you for me but not that simple sentence question mark. If it was in a movie and not allowed to dream, real slow, much English the language and one sight, one sight at a time would show, a course planned ahead, that this was true or that was there leading somewhere (at the least, out) but spelling continuous like I do, it draws you in and makes you swear at drama, dreams they don't stop at me, can't even plan die no more, that black woman was you. I dyed your hair and than man my son's an escape from dangerous love. All true. Let me die for you. You won't let me. They want to go to the barn, which barn, what's a barn all barns belong to me for a while, after while I won't need em, everything, even the storehouse of food you taught me how to keep: shells hard shells edible shells shells can be boiled cracked, your watch, crabmeat, soft shells, I am lying on the couch what cough? Watching my party, they want to eat, go to the barn, storehouse of food, she even gave me away, my dress is reduced, my dress is too small, it's on the piano, I'm a piano player like her, need cello accompaniment, I want a piano to fiddle around with, it's on the piano, the dress like a knick-knack, orange with a white ruff, reduced to the size of doll's clothes, a dress, I thought of buying a dress and high heels, I can think I can't think, watch out for your brains, remember what expansion of the head feels like on waking like a slab, now that I'm moving within this system sure I can move but I sure can't fly I'm stuck, wings legs thighs and breasts and need to break out to see in, let me in.

8

So I sent them. I sent my Amazons to shoot you because I'm amazing, left breasts exposed, one day, one day and more. I'm afraid to tell a lie so I should tell one: here, I'm greedy no I'm not. Or here's one, someone is raping me, or this: the pennies flew in armchairs on Monday or else: the fire is colder than mauve is a color I don't know the nature of. I wink and you are unleashed.

I know why I keep trying to crack the code: poetry is unethical, you shouldn't do it, it's bad, it's filth, it screws you around till you wind up up a trail toward a mountain or whole mountain itself, all by yourself without (w.o.) a house.

We live in a mound, there's a hole in the top, there's a whole in myself I'm a head taller but pink from the struggle to extricate you from the stone. I resort to "you." I need a plow. The moon is even why not mine. What am I saying here. State. Lie down. Bubbles. Giraffes. Holy shit. Reduced to fertile silt on the bank swimming as the Nile I'm the longest river in the other wrong sphere, hemisphere, wrong one. Open the altar gates, send men in, helicopter them in comfort but when they get here, it's a gruesome scene edges of war, "who's dead?" in a whisper in an ear, stone eyes, grammar of the states awake, I know you. Signal me. Strangest gunfire like cats goes on till I drop, fall down on the docks cause forever keeps itself asleep sleep keeping something moving in alarm, a magic happening, the only one we know any more, food.

9

It's a relief, someone's coming, to remember what, I forget, if I told him someone's coming, if I told him I trusted and I did, then he came. Closed. It's my father, he's not saying anything small, I say: I'm tired of you just hanging around, do something. I don't care, do something dead. He laughs at me, cause I can see he's thinking she's a fool she thinks backwards she thinks in reverse and the dead can come alive or even come and so they do. But you even looked at my eyes of the owl with your eyes of the owl. Some gift. Thanks. Some generation. You can have it. I can't even hide it anymore. No you can't. But whaddayou got? You got any proof any references pictures or jealousy?

It's a labor of love you prick don't take it out on fucking me. I'm nearly bankrupt too, remember? You fool around and imply a mother. Well listen she's far away she's a mound I can go in to sleep well there and you know more about it than I do you prick. Think back to when I said without even thinking in a nursery rhyme, catch this one you crook: the food of the mother is better than the food of the fatter father.

Journeys and oceans away, just more seas, more. Don't need em just for food. Keep em. Crack up if you want. Slide down the simple-minded banisters and crack your fucking ass, highly polished, real wood. Your turn. I done enough aches for you guys plenty and the secrets all mine. Here I thought all this time you were storing it for me. I shouldn't even talk to you. Why bother, what's in it for me? A dense bolt of material for a brand new dress tufted dress will the dress get me to fly like a bird, no! and you guys quit it, you stand there looking like grim mother reapers at me all the time, don't you ever smile you want a drink? Lose something? Loosen up a little?

10

Listen. This is it. You either stay or go. If you wanna stay and by the way you never were real independent, if you stay these are the terms: you gotta fade right into the walls, I don't wanna hear a peep outta you and don't expect regular meals or attention when you freak out cause I'm too busy, I got work to do and giant famous mouths to feed enormous appetites here and if you wanna know the truth I'll be straight with you I'd rather see you go, a few things about that, before you split come over here cause I have to touch you all over both of you and that other guy lurking around behind you, thought I didn't notice him, hell you mr. hall bedroom, that and this: a peculiar thing's happened. You see there's this guy I know who took it on himself to be you for art's sake or science's, shut up and wait till I finish, so he got to be you, yes all of you, I made it real easy for him, well not exactly but anyway, the thing is he's not you even spinning like a top and now he and I have got to the point, o.k. o.k. so you hate the way I talk you want a real blast for your imaginations, I'm sick of you guys in the guise I disguise for you hanging around like hanged men fucking things upside down inside out and treading on me, I mean you're always peering at us around corners and freaking me out, it's getting so I can't even think straight, I mean nobody ever did that to you did they? So lay off I mean I got some power too, used so much of it writing public paeans to you, you oughtta give me some room, besides he feels like a heel cause all the yous I so innocently and dutifully threw back laid on him or in him or whatever the fuck it is are making me suffer so much. You don't like him eh? Well that's explainable wanna hear about it? Ha ha, so fuck off and stop breaking my fucking back. I do love you all a lot but if you breathe down my neck like that once more I'll kill you, get out the mob. Goodbye.

11

The moon is moving. Look, you wanna know what you did for me: my body's all disorganized, I feel like a baby, cramps in my stomach, everybody's somebody else, dizzy all the time, my legs won't hold me, I can't even walk down the street sometimes, my chest hurts, the things in my head that go on beat everything, I can't swallow food half the time, aches and pains all over, I get all itchy sometimes and sneeze, even banged my own hand till it hurt.

12

You're supposed to exist on the moon, you're supposed to resist the moon. Fuschia and orange moon, it's purplish-red but really yellowish-green, time in between: Helen dies, dreams change, I kill more people, I am phony, I act, I change my sex, I perform, I drink milk, I'm put away, I'm special, singled out: a special grounded crow, sink back, Max brings the thing to completion, ends the thought, it is almost completely surrounded by water, peninsula, there's no such things as the toys you give me and they cannot fly, sink ships, he lines them up, he has power, he is brave, the finish runs, it's almost completely dry, can't wait can't stop, can't bedriven all over and giving everything away to any one. Needle park's right up your alley under ground my way to you, our turf, pay phones. I recommend it: drive the rain right into the lightning, two wheels won't crash in the dark, for two dollars I'll watch, for one I'll set the alarm, who's out there? Who needs to be covered and warmed and tired and worn out, needle tracks up through the arms winding path dirt road through the woods is green. I brought the real green in. I drifted the floating wood to shore. I ate thedrifting food that reddens the sea. I'm almost done this mix: when the scooter was stopped by the rain in the dark I said we'd have to stay here for a while, grounded, rubber, a light plugged in, can't fall into the ocean the fish are in danger, you learn the rules, water is a conductor, rubber is a ground, this vehicle is wired negative earth, will a deer cross the path, will engines get wet start up again, is it water or oil, did I break the ground rules, is my mouth dry, can anyone's mother die, no and she dies on, the reverse: once was a man who was never satisfied but once was. Then he ate the food of the father, daring. Three, he gave it all up looking newer, find reform. But no one could surround the mother, even for blackmail: she was perfect: divorced, living alone in her cave. She did nothing.

●

Helen Winston

The moon, the Red Lion-like inn. Your hand on my arm, "Do you mind?"

"All I mind is your asking 'Do you mind?'"

"Your lover, I don't like his body."

"Are you just trying to be mean or have I mistaken your intention?"

"Yes" (mean).

"Fuck yourself."

Down a long sloping green hill, a man with a cut-off tail. We finally eat there. John has ten dollars, Max has ten. Or maybe we should go see how many White Castles we can eat, they are serving them with feta cheese.

Danger of arrest: "If they try to put me in jail again, I'll have to call David." Max and the others have found a way to operate the (butcher's) money machine while the store's closed but can they exchange the stamps for real money? Arrest? What did we steal?

A beautiful carnival walk looking for Mulberry Street and all the streets with decorative names, we get caught up in another (family) group. One of them drinks from my bottle in doorways. (Two old people in front of us force us to walk slow.) There's a design or a pattern on my front tooth.

Like islands, like the Hudson, we were already in the woods. Clouds move past the moon. I wait for an opening. As bright as possible, I want the moon to be as bright as it can be for once. Rest clouds like a bed of just texture, deep blue and muted gold cloud halos when the brightest light finds a rest for its reflection at an angle, clouds mounting up. Phases. Oceans right and left of dense clouds will cover moon whichever way the wind blows. This dream catches up with me as I'm on my way. Seconds escape a full moon on the train.

I'm pretending to feel much less than I feel, what else can I do, Helen died. She races, she erases, controls memory of her. All I think is, can think is I still do what I want anyway. Time passes real slow. Let's just get there. Be strong, don't be silly. One day and the next day, is it me? Am I guilty, there's no telling what today, papers that can be torn out in the new book, will be like yesterday and when you will take me in the storm to our island we mischievously set up the rain for it, my feet are wet my arms are wet my legs the legs of my pants are wet, the train speeds all over, it has a point. You a book for poetry, you a close resemblance to my song, it's an ache now I take the public transportation by a choice you threw at me. I'm tempted to relate Max heard the news about Helen late last night and though he didn't tell me when we went out for a late dinner, my stomach became swollen as hers did before she died. The details of her contact with me, why bother, and trust in touching close with a ceremony not to annihilate or exorcise or even free, but a ceremony to focus, what can I do? What's the present, I think about it, I don't think about it, sudden rain, no one's prepared for it, a life raft is displayed in front of the store, it attracts us like the idea of a permanent home in the brightest green colors, yellow and blue, here I am and I may get there, I make the move, slip and fall, in danger of slipping in the rain, why not, my feet are wet and I'm wearing rubber shoes, drenched and grounded by the power of localized mind. I am scared, what does it mean what's all this paraphernalia I'm carrying with me, it's a connection, a draw, a drawing in to life, like a shock, I withdraw and think about it. Max said, say something. I predict I know. I said what he told me to say, I'm almost there, it's a stone's throw away, I'm so sorry, how could she leave us, sudden leaving, she represents herself to me as a mother in words before she goes: "If you want I will always tell you where I am and you can reach me." She says she is psychic, Max is experiencing a first throw, close toward death and its penetration of his mind. I'll take my time. I'll penetrate loose, I'll pry into it and go through the motions of extreme focus but I won't lie down with her, not this time. She tempts me, she draws me in, a man across the way is involved in a crossword. Sentences form. Images are endless yet they're all the same. He likes what it makes him think, at random. He takes a chance. The street. Non-stop.

●

Cover to hide, surface to lean on straight, everything will start beginning now, running sooner, sooner than I thought, an experiment, no, a piece of clothing, no colors, no, pencils and organs of the body, I own a sea of white a sea direct, I can write direct to you today cause death is more important, its dues. She did her own time in flashing color, I mold things together, whether they hold or don't, like you.

Come on in Barry, that's me, take a bow, for not eating all week cause you had no money, it fits right in all of it from where I can sleep on the moon, a deadly fuchsia pale iris and the color of lilies, no one likes us and all around us even our old friends let us down because they abstain too, vegetable carts and die. Given given where you come from and say your name is beyond that. Given taken slash received, which is which, it's the same even size even though it looked smaller and grayer and fragile and even day. It poured blue lines across my ribs, the light is sneaking in like water, anger can't be real as water, who said so, ribs are flat and curved, you swim all night, a whole night swimming, you remind me that you're not me, who said so, that's why I can't leave, predict for me, if you weren't so interested you would, you're waiting to see what happens, I want to hurt you momentarily and leave and come back with a suntan, Max wakes up suddenly like branches cracking, a twig snaps, the phone rings to remind me I'm scared, never was no sun scare like this one, all dry and creeping in between your arms and eyes a drink I guess, poison, no fear of fish, of disruption of chaos, I know it pretty well to do with choice like a button that bends, sleep ends sooner than it should, it never began. Never to have done this before is dangerous when you leave me alone. Did you give me an iris warning, or a fear it would destroy me open full of pieces of shells crack a warning and I die. It's simple. Where? Sky or shy away from where. No time. Fuck the energy it takes, how shall I describe it, you should always carry a spare in good condition, you should eat meat on Friday, you should take a chance, buy one? You should never sweeten a well you use, the sugar's like ice to your heart and you fall, keel over and imagery die, like hell, I could go on forever. Babies fed through tubes, the works. Right now sex seems boring compared to nothing, aches like the next unexpected sensible line, I've got a line, I'll try it on you: track me through the woods and shoot me through the eyes. Tender, a reflex wink and stare as I race I absorb wind, there's anything in it. I wasn't fooled by your call, you had equipment to breach the code. To reorganize, to panic, Barry's glass falls in circles, drawings of fear, black man with dirty feet is three black faces in the dark, hello. Three men big enormous, I want to include everything, this is a clean-up, this is like the old review: rules of all fair chase are existing conditions: any animal taken under any of the following circumstances shall not beconsidered taken under the rules of fair chase are conditions that exist and grow: helpless in or because of deep snow, helpless in water, helpless on ice, helpless in trap, while confined behind fences as on game farms, in defiance of game laws or out of season, our season, by "jack lighting" or shining at night a shining light, from power vehicle or power boat, or a bear says, property is theft, I don't need sources anymore, Blackula.

●

Taking the cure at the magic mountain of unsatisfactory air, verging on unhealthy, I've got the whole view of the dream, the moon is a boat, I'm under the waves. The sign lights are on and glowing and spectacular mists run through the air set up for me, space for light, a little gets in. I've put myself out I might get sunburned. The plant's here. The dead man, the hanged man, the man on stilts, the man on struts, the aching men the wild man the beginning man the eating man, he blew through a tube and wrote mystic lines in the dark, leave him alone, you can move faster than that. Chronology is a piece, like babies, itching all over and cannot sleep. Very sweet and beginning a rich shore tempts more to excess gold a showing a place, to find a cool place delight in the cold. Someone dies is a vacation for angry pieces. A long ride in a car at night with one person. You could do a lot with a car. Meet, melt anger, perverse, sections in the back of my mind revolted by yellow and piercing right through the hammering message, wide windows a light on the shore, portholes, teaching floating awake. Kind like bottle. Not one single word but a battery that endures for fifty cassettes. You don't understand, you understand nothing, you're perverse, some son. It's easy to see in the dark, it's easy to get eidetic iceboats to row themselves home, a little igloo in the crack in the ice world where you curl up and go to sleep, precious stones pile up under the snow we can't get at them, leave them.

Turn off the street lights what's making the light, what's flashing over my head. Are you there? You finally succeeded you can keep it, it leaves me alone. Tonight I'm an airplane disturbed by the plane crashes flashing around, please succeed me so I can grieve you too. There's nothing in it, the ice melts a grace. Room for how many? Its angles are practical as the dead ones condense themselves and sell us the space. Just some business. You crack the whip. Wasn't ruthless, was grave and all this time to second the moment, sorry, milk confounds the puddle. What'll I dream out here, something far out, it isn't good, I keep seeing things, my head itches, nothing issues to fine the language and pink spots appear, many unusual dreams, they bring in a man died in the revolution, dead is deed always, a space man killing and shooting with gas, a dead politician he is god the father excreting art but not on the streets and a dead father he did it, jerked his head over and died, his death, name the name, to keep something from you like poetry itches it's too cloudy for the moon, she submarines it and I'm out here, all done, what's done is done the creatures past are furious and they stink like a cold bottle of cream warm. Enter in here will you and tell me what is the lead-in to disaster and what colors should I expect to see and would you be with me…I think you are distant and cool, I make messages, is it white birds flying that flashing, make noise, you interest me, this is like junk. Which is which, send me mix-up, it lasts forever, Helen of Troy who keeps coming in mixes a paste like the race in the judging, mix-up I said, a whole other story, Venus or Paris or some other Underdonk Avenue morning gets picked up on and blended in, you should only fold, with cream, the cream I want. Anyway, you, in the middle of this fucked up fast distance we did like John Donne and speckled birds are the ones make the mist glow above me, I've figured it, there's too much to do so what do I do? Lights on, the church, I'm out, I'm really far away, just for myself, mysteries solved if only, forget it, sink back into the pillows currents, I'll get you a boat too and three mounds, middle distance, of hay. Smoke rises vertically, I'm still in the race, without you don't wanna finish don't wanna stay. If you're angry she said there must be some…and I said I've been swell, border angry helicopter, times before. So eat me, it's my own creation. Plenty of depth in the street lights you hit with a bottle to make them go out, one field. Seen it all before. Same aches too. Somebody knows how to do it right: you disconnect the fuse and are feeling free. Free of light, are you threatening me? Eat shit. There's plenty more, sky's white, never was before, moon is surfaced and monkeys around. Above the church, above the ground, see it, a vacation from the subways, a regular patch, no good. I'm ending. Moon cover, aching light, a light for aching, get away, go I don't want to see you any more, the moon says so too.

Fire escape sleep: How did we get there or how did we wind up there, cars coming from Cleveland and St. Louis the predominant color was royal blue and silent people driving, not looking where they're going. I ask to sit in the back, everybody moves to the back. Mary Sue Diver and Lewis Warsh. Fern's the first one there, she's checking everything out as if it were a warehouse, or shit Bill was there too, maybe it was his house that he would open up if we all came to live there, a giant estate, we would be taken care of, I say I refuse to have a maid.

When we get there then finally a lot of people start coming in, poets, the place fills up I'm out here on my mattress, my arms and back hurt, I realize something's wrong, something suspicious is going on, I go round looking, everyone's funny or drugged or ear-plugged, a man's going around plugging up ears all ears, he tries to do mine, he gets the left one but I manage to close up the right with my finger before he can get to it, just like Max's bad ears.

His ear-plugging (three white pigeons blow by) is irreversible. Then I begin to investigate. I find a room with three men sitting, a meeting, one of them is reading a paper, "The Chinese Conservative." I realize they're planning to murder us all. I look around, everyone's still drugged, then I see two people moving determinedly down a hall. I follow them because I realize they're not drugged and trying to get out, maybe they know a way out. We get to a double door, push it open, it was locked so no one could get in but there must be a guard here, there is one. He lassoes one of the others with a long scarf, a giant necktie. I'm caught by it too but get free but the other one is close to being strangled. Should I run and leave her or get her free and maybe get caught. I untie her and we get away.

●

A man is killed in the revolution, we want his body. We go to the church for it: he is hung by two heads: "He didn't want to die like that." We try to get him out of the church, the coffin's too heavy, no handles, we're caught.

●

A space man shoots down with a gas gun all the people in a fenced-in playground, except one guy who keeps coming at him. The police come and the two pretend to be pals and walk real slow out of the park. (Bartholomew has been home since Thursday, he's got my favorite food in the grill, cooked it, but didn't eat it, watching for me in "the School Town." We're waiting for Max.)

●

The t.v.'s pink, it's dark. David falls asleep on the couch, his head falls to the side. We're watching pink t.v. and eating life-savers, a session. Max wants to wake him up but I say no, there's more I can tell Max. I eat green life-savers out of a bag. The three of us are in the loft, I'm in the hammock trying to record dreams in the dark but all the blue paper is filled with Max's figurings (numbers) and even when I find some room I write one line and then the next above it so it's no good, it's out of order, the three of us going about our business, we're trying to live together I guess, one of them stands behind the hammock, I can't tell if it's Max or David, to see what I'm doing, the wall is already filled with the windows we want, but I've put curtains outside them, yellow and gingham, why? As a gesture, David goes out and brings back some food, what is it, he says: "Wait till you see, something special." We've already got a house full of food but David wanted to show he liked being here, wanted to stay. Every time I think I've written my dream it turns out I haven't. All I have to do is dream.

There's a memory wall painted blue with brick exposed, the white paint below. Nobody would miss one of these windows, is it my room? And then I could go? And then I'd be free? Breaking down a wall, I need some more room, breaking through, some brick exposed, inside is outside, the code to break is memory, and outside on the brick wall, someone's job is to write the daily headlines like billboards and today's is "God (the) Father McGovern Seeks to Keep Art Money from Art in the Streets." Biblical David.

August 27, 1972

The Olympics are on, there's a bum in the hall with dirty feet, hello. The police come and spend hours looking for prowlers.

I'm stuck on Canal Street, battered ram, in a taxi drinking beer. Max is doing the laundry at Sun Yat's and now I'm reduced to writing recording in case of instant death, even when I'm speeding faster than in the sunny subway. What do I do if pen runs out completely, my head is blasted my moment's fear but what could even happen anyway? Well for one thing it's Monday, it's the usual thing, I'm too terrified to move, this idea to focus, I've gone further than you will and that's only natural since it's my crutches falling and my open window, turning inside out and outside, in, topsy-turvy and so on. When I go in a taxi, soon as we get on the highway I open the window wide for a blast that hurts my face and I think to myself, other people have gone further than this. I borrowed the cab driver's pencil, my beer is between my legs, further into where? It's not the same place at all, that's the thing about it, every human being creates a different one, different what a cool dry wooden word for what I mean: every human being is intent on being a unique one, the space intensifies, is drawn, but only if the human chooses to design it and then it designs itself in all directions, sown and left to drift and some, the subtler, continue. Soon as I begin to write I feel living again like I do when I tap dance on a table we built to test its solidity which I already know by instinct is for sure, built-in. Fear submerged, re-emergesanyway, it's not the fear of being alone, complicated, but a further fear that co-existence with humans only eventually intensifies, it's forced out in the open. What a great blast of wind on my face finally, the river smells. I'm here, I may be here, I'm shaking. A leaf blows into the cab. I let the wasp out. I take Elaine out and examine her. Jerry says, "I've only known you three or four times and look how I'm acting." John Ryan leaves on a trip with a 16 mm camera. Bird in tree identifies with me, I'm no different from anybody else. He or she sees me admiring the spring tree and lights in it, this is my only power.

That's all now over and dread curtain roar the B-train. To Grand Street and over curtain back-ache I'm fear swallow gut and gumption not gum but yellow and green life-savers, David got the red and orange one in the pack, I need a speech by you. You have to stand right, you have to sit right by Easter morning on the train whatever could happen, you play with it, you need with each to wait a time and blown over, climb it a calm mountain in the dark, center edges align, you right like that a new train, the walk was unending, not like open, not like before, bugs books and this one goes to Grand Street, get out the cudgels I got meat cleavers in there. We all wait. Buzz. You talk too loud. Doors open again. Waiting I'll get there. I don't remember that one. I didn't look at you enough. I did fill myself with your look and your face enough, I was afraid your back might hurt too. Help me up the stairs, don't dwell on it, soon it will be over, I put my feet up on the seat as a gesture of revolt, a gesture of despair I'm on the train, I wet the pen with my tongue and this is all I'm gonna do and it writes more for a while, it must last, it must hold out, everybody's doing it, you can't get sick, you can't not be there, sure I thought you were dead at one point, sure I thought you were distant and cold. It's predictable. It's all those aspects of habit I abhor. Ha ha did mother overdraw her account again, ha, the family who was funny and continued to be when no one else was, let the pen dry out, they laugh at me, they wonder what I'm doing up to "I can't see, hell." I'll make it simple and clear: I'm drawing a butterfly all over, I'm drawing a butterfly on the train, repeating gives you time to keep the present flowing and repeating, continuing, repeating is necessary but when you race against time all the time anyway and can't conceive of enough pens it even becomes a problem you can still repeat but you must abbreviate to save X, which is time and to save X U go on & write short and brief be be briefer still the B-train is speed and short sever it I'd dared it ever again. Vrybody's readin their paper and stoppin short or jus sittin like crows on fence wire shortage circuit cut and blew out, what next? All them crows will get sum new ones us younguns speak in kindergarten, les people are purple than pink and green is grand, the nex stop, is at whut e sd. Hey! You over there, I'm a mix, I'm doin it fer you, speak easy and take care a me cause I don't come easy while you and you do, eek! A bird in my eye, closer to home is blockin my vision and tackles a bigger and stronger opponent than me. Touch water. There gonna be water there. B'way and Lafayette two ancient of names like the biblical David. Just passin the time till eye gets where it relaxes and see, I can't see, Hell.

●

Crazy cab driver, ancient weather turned to stone, he stops he starts and when he gets his own car he's going to paint it yellow he says, drive carefully.

Hand hurts and pencils aching the calendar's clear September is bright blue, blue wipe open spaces again, what should I do in September, I cross the street, I sneeze, blue stop, you etch your patience in which never left you, it will return to take up my time as yours. I need to blow my nose. Movies are made all over us. It's only a quarter to five, I sneak around in the pink island lake or land light where I sobbed anger as a bright yellow summer boat, there's something green about fire in this light.

I want seconds. Remember the movie about faces and clenched fists and blue earth moves over and makes a clean white space on the moon for us to lie down and drift and play with our clear glass tables with nothing else to do. I wrote my name on the train. I dare you. It's easy, somebody's watching, the guys across the street are still working, clenched fists clenched teeth, a stopper for the drain, a cinch for your waist a clasp, a clipper for the faucet where it connects with the hose and then I laid down my...and then I got up again and then I laid myself down and then I ate some sleep, I storing up for winter I go by year by year. Cracking branches out of nowhere. Film cartridge in a gun shoots ballets and samovars shrieking at their heads, cut off or Samothrace or Saracen blades of salamander creeps the final word beginning with...something's glowing, bounce, something's reflecting the light drawn out, who are the men in Japan who commit harikari and draw out their entrails for view and like westerns write novels to cut off their heads. As usual there's only one. Sees a movie. Circus in town. Hens resolve. Code for the country where leaves commit a gruesome act of vision whatever state they're in, look at them, no draw on their culture, no nature for a judge or penance given, you me noises spin, spring up, terror of false beginnings and rumors, there's no telling we're singular and piece by piece we each choose to leave a piece behind, study the "adjourn" position, I hate that game. Milk is better or custard. Frozen pies. Whipped cream left on a plate. Bread soaked in butter and cream and ice metal and suck on styrofoam like Kathleen did in memory and chew and mental alert on friend Kathleen, worry, paint pictures, imagine or fear, then sway, some gin or rigging for a boat of nerves, float fine on a sea of edges, watch out for the shore, you may want to be there but the ocean below brought you out, that's where it's deep, sink, a bottle does, the hatch is open and all that stuff, portholes, you an illegitimate look on your face, all at sea, back out of our element exhausted, stones with no air in them to sing tunes and roam around bloody.

It's only ten after, salty foods and everything's eidetically green after seeing so much pink, even the cross on the wall runs out to meet eyes: hair brown, medium height, he sinks ships. Became a convert to messages at age 11, when I fell down the stairs with my toys. I gave that up, saw stars, was warned, got pink a lot from the struggle to extricate…, got kidded, the imp, imp's skinny rib-cage, boney all bones, beady eyes, all eyes, brewing all the potions I could blackmail from the shadows, they let me in to dream tigers, I'm an Indian boy and all I want is feathers in my hair, headdress and free feet and to be brown and have nothing in between the own body and the laid-in possibility of getting to the pavement, even if it's just dry old dust on the surface, even if it's war, you pitch tents real low on a historic battlefield and take root in the fertile blood-red flowers, they spring up, you mix a potion with that.

I'm safe: while my mother was in the hospital I swallow a bobby-pin, my father has to deliver it. When you call I'm already on the phone with you, do we have another line? I see my parents too, they didn't think I'd come back so soon, are there any maddening genitals to touch in America? "You've got to remember the real substance of the dream, not just the part about yourself."

August 31

Stranded here with the bugs and the flies leaning on the garbage can in the filthy air eating: you laugh, a virginia ham sandwich with lettuce and mayonnaise on whole wheat soul bread, all the men, I say all the men look at me, why? Because though you may say I'm beautiful all the other men have pricks too, nothing sacred about that, it's all too wholesome and true, even smart black Peter who works in Screw and Specialty Co., nearly too intelligent for eyes, smart black Peter has a United Parcel Service penis, when he looks at you he says to you it's all right as long as you get by with it, O.K. I leave you with your work there Bernadette, it was very pleasant talking with you. Someone throws a kiss at me like Mary had a little lamb fleece was white as snow, that's racist poetry, Peter says I wish I had a life like you. He catches my yearnings, I mean my eye, he's smart, I'm on the street or the steps, locked out, locked in where are you? Small. It don't look like poetry, is wheat at all. I like being locked out when Peter's sitting out here next to me, I think to say, you know the building on the corner's for sale, just a regular bird flies by on through. The Lucky Apparel Company is here too, I ate my sandwich like a good eel, a conger eel who... Watch out! Whales are swimming in the ocean of the street all too close to the much more electric radar tower, guardian of southern Manhattan's skies and a big fish wearing pince-nez is swimming straight towards the sky like an arrow where birds with beaks and very hot suns are. There may be a moon in the water but also my own reflection. Danger!

●

Meretrix, prostitute. Mere, a boundary, an arm of the sea. Massachusetts, at the big hill. ana (greek), at once together with, at the same time with. Emos, my mine. Emeteros, our. Emeros, tame, gentle. Emera, day. Better—ameinon. Bitter—pikros. Meros, part. Mesos, middle: blastomere, mesoblast. Maia, mamma. A, non-.

Mother (original sense uncertain). Hysterical passion, womb, a mother-fit; mouldiness, mud or mire; the dregs, mother of wine; MUD. A book is FAKE BEECH TREE, MY NAME IS MUD. Merge plunge under water, DIP. Emerge rise from the sea. Verge, a wand a rod a yard (of land). Edge, limit of jurisdiction, a pliant twig. Mountain at the big hill to remind you of faces to remind you of black warmth.

I'm so tired, I'm so tired, I'm so tired, I'm not a teacher, I'm so tired, I'm so tired, taxi onto the highway again, I'm so tired, I'm so tired, stopped for the light, I'm so tired, I'm so tired, I'm so tired, watch to see how fast he goes, I'm so tired, I'm so tired, save my money, spend it, I'm so tired, I'm so tired, don't wanna see anybody, I'm so tired, around the curve, I'm so tired, air, I'm so tired, I'm so tired, I'm so tired, I'm so tired, where do I live? I'm so tired, I'm thinking, I'm so tired, I lost my dream, I'm so tired, I lost it, I'm so tired, I'm so tired, I'm so tired, will I find it? Tired, I'm so tired, so tired, find me? Tired, I'm so tired, white ship in the river, tired, leave a piece behind, I'm so tired, ah.

Sure I know I know I know a long separation then haze, I'm riding in a taxi, speak easy the boats are slow, it takes a long time to, that's my favorite line too, awake I award you the medal of excellence, I award it to you I do it's difficult, it's spent it's drowning I like the wind to hit me to take over on the sunshine drive, the light I like to see is morning light the morning I make of the afternoon, never enough time and in winter it gets dark before I ever get up and grow up too fast too slow, I'm pretty low in the river pretty low on the ground, I look familiar to you, I direct traffic, I hate holidays, I wear out my jeans, I give more than adequate directions more than clues, I throw something out the window, if they paid me three dollars a page it would be worth it to always ride in a taxi. It's never better than to always break a rule even if it only stretches at the seams, it will break, pull, you can break it, even if the fabric's a brand new image with a fabulous design: a griffin sucking at the core of a corn cob your teeth left blood on, a wafer floating like a halo above the head of a wild animal springbok and wildebeest or giraffe who will only be seen again in a child's book or a zoo, lean neck around one's life is a threatening angle and then I bought Pasternak's poems and then I ate them and wrote poetry and cut a square corner into a piece of pie laid out on the table, invasion. Your table is terrific, the tree smokes like a cigar as you sit in it with a pile of leaves burning beneath the samovar, you'll smoke them you'll inhale their smoke, their charcoal air you need a list to keep track of who you are when I call you so many different names.

This is distraction, this is out of focus, this is no decision, what will protect me the plant? What will signify me the shirt of an Indian?

If I had navigation I would sail clear direct toward the furthest point in the middle of nowhere and begin to snow there like a natural event. Max can't hear me his ears clogged and stuffed and plugged, his ears clamped. Max out of nowhere or should I begin to say you, "you," so you can make ice-cold percepts out of my epileptic-eidetic stone-cold confusion. Everything's white. Aces met inactive in a store. What are you trying to play, thing? What woman represents three men? Before the judge and pleads for them like a stone splintering? Three or several stones on a slab create sparks. We did that at the beach, you can't hear me, you hear me but you can't find out anything, you're too silly or too young, you hate me and you know everything and can't do anything, why distinguish between the dents that have been made in my enclosure and spaces that open up seeming yellow, black background in a field of yellow secrets is a fake, fools you and closes in on itself for the sake of physical fitness and decorum and rightness or any climb—you're all so fucking careful—off the ladder to where millions of anarchists fly in the sky in red bandannas sinking ships, what else could I be? Why don't you join me instead of you're always expecting babies or something like that. Why don't you fly like you're supposed to, it's not me merging up out of the sea anymore, it's all you hand-picked expecting babies, waiting around, storms. Signal me mask me I don't want you back unless you fathom the code. Unless you screw into the rigging the save-all for wind, speak up, she blows acrobats out to sea.

I almost made you laugh, you pygmy me. It's just a squall. She burnt off her right breast her mother taught her, give the men back to their fathers or mutilate them, to throw the javelin better, like Keats studying Lempriere's, all the studying, all the water towers, all the time. Red doors all over the place, red peaks, seams in the doors, cracks, meet currents flow around, you get full moon, you get quarter, you half. Just the spoils of victory, bums carry packages, they don't eat meat. The evening weather changes, the earth is whole. What a grand entrance you make, sink back, covers fall off elephants tremble like trucks, inside kids carry sleeping bags they don't pay rent, they aren't scared of parents or holes in the ground.

You scared me into paying rent. My face is scarred, fatigues for the jungle, a Latin name if you're bored. Signify me. Antedate me by many years. Wear your protection plate and don't go cheerfully out the door when you think it's not burning. Make a spectacle of your revolutionary bath and piss in it if you will, I'll draw up a lend-lease agreement and you'll look down from the fire escape and not say a word. I should but I won't buy you some groceries, you're hungry and have no money. I should lend you a lamp that runs on batteries, a pretty clear light why did it go out, yes the batteries are rare, you can only get them in some Long Island City, I should educate you to make better milk to produce closer to shore or home so your expenses will be cut down, I should commit you to current nonsense so you can be free, I should take your hand and put money in it once a week, I should give you books about time and information with quizzes at the end, I should suffocate you and crack your bones, lay eggs on your body to grow into monsters to rule the world, I should enervate you and make you weaken, fall down and die, I should fall for you, fall down on top of you, what else could I do, I should make you mix things up, I should make you come in upside down and rectify you only to turn you around again, I should go around corners like sound and keep to myself like driven light, I should crack your spectacles into a million pieces and give you only one, a splinter, to refill the prescription for the lens, I should extricate you from all your suffering and make a danger you never saw before for you, never could see and then wear you on my sleeve, I have no sleeve, the ones I have I'm cutting off tonight, I need an excuse to find you, what time is it? Do you like the streets, are they roomy enough for you or do you think I should have more children? I see visions, do you? We hear the same sirens, no reason you don't see the visions except you're blind, oh cover me up and I'll hand you one vision out from under the covers. That should hold you fast to it for a while. Dear radar equipment, I designed myself and put on the telephone building to guard the south, I'll never tell you what to do but there's a crack in you. So watch out. Watch out the other way and remember to feed back one plane into the other or the dizziness in the sky will haze you out, your antennae begin to speak instead of listen, your whole mold made of the strongest alloys starts to melt and it's not the sun and you don't destroy but just real slow you disappear, outmoded, paced out, faced out, spaced out, machinery not sensitive enough, time's up, phased out, let the planes fly free and let them crash or drop their weapons, you'll never know, you're not a part of it, simplex mechanism, temporary storehouse, very receptive but not a ribbon of it left. You're on your own, you're full of lies, but least well as the skies will ever be, be you there warning or not. Come out to show them, come out to show you, come out to show them, come out to show you, come to show you clouds how proud clouds will be smoking a five-cent cigar, just out of the blue and nothing to show for it, frees you and you and you. What a relief, I wish that could be a pleasure, mean.

A BLUE FLOWER is trying to devour us, flower turned on its side, blue leaves timely stems and blossom, invisible crosshair transparent filaments are the part that kills, my instinct about the flower was danger, an old woman is responsible for the elegant flower, we leave the blue room and return to it, in the interim: the danger, the killing was in a small apartment, we want to move back in, "We want to move back in." I always intended to, "I was always intending to."

I've really switched to that level where I don't need to record events like: Max has fallen asleep on my bed: "Billions for defense, not one cent for tribute" and Max nearly fell asleep in the tub, those maniacs they nearly got me high and the ice cream couldn't get hard, soft enough, Max kept singing cause I only have eyes for you and another song like I love you only and secret stores of work to be done on midnight, Labor Day, will I be able to navigate now that I've staked the ground, I mean taken my stand: "I'll get by as long as I have you." Max's mind caved in and when are you coming over as if I couldn't but when will I be normal again and write good.

It was simple, it was really simple and fair, everybody giving me a lot of room, coffee like mud gives room to work, spaces I realize I sink in the mud, someone thinks there's nothing to do, two people think there's nothing to do, how could they, how could he, how could they eat ice cream soft ice cream, I watch through the window the whole business, she tries to cut his hair with the scissors, he's black, the scissors she's brought to cut the paper that comes sliding, hangs out the cash register machine in green neon and purple contact, he pulls her long hair, I'd like to be there, once when they were nearly ready, neither Max would sing a song so they ordered it to be closed.

Unique me. I saw the flat extending desert and warm pink light play and I saw I could blackmail anyone who leaves with this: don't expect anything of me, tell the men to have their own babies and then I saw in a crossword of pure nonsense that I felt I had to serve, you take care of you all you you come back like you come back up out of sleep and mourning every day, as you come back you see me seeing this: I swim in the ocean and assume my motion is sinking you or at least that I'm so pushed forward, thrust into you that the blow of myself against you, it's the wave that's pushing me, is sure to destroy you no I mean devour your hour by my hour you go by getting thinner and weaker, I've learned to rely on you I've cooped you up for myself alone, I enjoy you I am powerless to leave on my own but you sit up suddenly and independently suddenly and make a speech in your sleep in the middle of the night that amazes me, how can you sleep? And you say: Men built out of oranges will be sweet and take care of you. I'm going. I'm a shark but you've pinned me down. That's what I've always been afraid of, part of a mistake to swear on nothing. I am not autonomous. I am not you. Did you make some laws for me to go by? I am specialized. Other custom. I am ousted, outside, blue and not blue, radical blue. I am not the same equal or like, I am not like the same like equal as like, I tear the tears from my eyes. It makes me think of everything. You are thinking of anything. It can't be denied. Deny it is false. False is a beech tree, tree is a book, book is attack on you, I step on a tack, full into my foot, your foot could write a boot about you, nothing but you, you is a boat, boat is a country, country designs the shape of the signs you can grow out of, country designs the patterns you see on the floor, floor is a mosaic, mosaic continues to construe, you're a mix-up, deliberate, bernadette, desperado, the end of the play is not and so on, on own's won and give me another one, one and one and one and I've gone off somewhere, where without hope where without yes discipline, costly where, whatsisname, come home one to the other and find four or more there, how do you do, do you ache somewhere? Go to the moon won't you sing a song I'm a cliff dweller and I hide I steal paint to paint: the bar is on the drink, I rest on the ceiling at night and steal a scene from the floor for later I wear plates in my hair and fly through them I eat meat from bananas and peanuts from flesh, I limp I reach south as I go north and drown in the city, I melt under snow, you're catching on. What a great sensible plant we've made, what an ancient race of heated pebbles to put in the stew, I could take to you, I couldn't take you to, hide. No travel. No light. Revolution.

The shades the blinds close your eyes, the reverse the outline, the figure draws you in, it's a plane, it's empty, words appear, you don't make compromise you entice them they come in, enter from ahead, drawn around a body like ocean to the other, right and left it's all mixed up it's true, like lightning lightening a picture of a tree, ladies and gentlemen will you mix with me, tear my tears apart for me and load them heavy into the truck for storage for years I won't need them, till I do, the strange and heavy tiles of an antiseptic house you live in, you can't live in, how many images do you need before I mobilize you, how many vultures have to pick at something and threaten and so on, how many methods of attack to get you far off etcetera. What's the instant of this time space addition melting secret distributed special after sameness sensate division of my self from you, elves and imps are into mischief they don't miss a trick to turn you on turn you upside down, you write the dialogue, I fill in—lemon ice, stop! You do. Stop! Lemon ice. Seconds. Not any, explore. Curtain. Miss or Mrs. beggars and thieves, willows and reeves, entymology, birds, sandpipers ruffs saskatchewan places even sublime, the scarlet tanagers court me country sunday and yellow, a stop a sludge a mess a mire a father, a week, secret denial, sensible drift, circus aplenty ages mixed-up, the average American, the circus applause the entity drifting the different applause, the meekness the window, why come to it why fly, the edges go on forever, you could create them anew, I mean over and over again I mean edging over every day I mean much more than every day I mean mixing without completion I mean courting without design, see what happens, play, the structure, the structure we discover is a playground, with handlebars you could lift it and replace it new. Cover it over cover it up, every body emerge from it dip in, why continue why what I'm getting at, I'm getting ahead of myself there's not enough vicious alarm in the sound of my voice to entice to read on till the murder's committed, I'd rather be thorough and dead, I'm way ahead now, I'm drifting, what am I doing here where am I and soon, what's the difference now how pale words are synchronous endings golden foldings into my head which is flesh my flesh which is already gold, passed through the colors before the right colors in the right order in the right mix as no more right than wrong were present to simply fuse the same with song.

A song's a blend. Signify me. It's morning I'm able to day. I tear the lights off, there's not enough room, there's more room and you're trapped. What I want to get to is this: Leisure to listen. I know I'm an act of removal right now. I have hope in the sum. If only I could be subject of same system same rules same observing as thought can remove me from space for a while, then I could see you and more brightly me, get me. Stop and think is an impossibility. Be alone where you can think is a toy. I'm in the mix to complicate and yet to be more right about it, I'm not coming I'm not thinking from out of anywhere come out of there if you're there, I know you're in there. So desperado, outside the law, to free them they put them in prison for begging for it without crime was the crime. A special treatment. Locate yourself. Specialized in a new note of noise. A distinguished signal dips dangerously into the sea and pops right up again bobbing around.

Just more before I can unend. Something on a shelf. Someone wants you out there so you want to go out. Something seems impossible, ordinary motion. Something is too long, you don't think it, you never expected it, you run like the stream, you unearth rocks just by accident by going alone, please create me, I am already there some part of me and some part heading in thatdirection and so unending in never knowing but knowing some part of all that unending can never get there, so all the force of it so all the energy, just there, in different spots, if you can call them that, you can catch it, you can go along with it, please forgive me and no don't, I have so much time, I'm in advance of it.

8:30 a.m.

Freezing cold morning. Bobby Drivas changes his act, he lies on my breasts and tells me they're terrific, I won't go back to the institution, I won't go back, the storms are up, they'll take care of us, parents take care in storms parents are there in storms, fear of the elements themselves, they'll send up to the kosher coast, we'll memorize the script, kosher is comfortable and warm and plenty to eat and care, the turtles turned upside down, the toilet's removed from its facility, its facility is a source of water, this is instruction, and then, the brown and white checked/striped space: like taking your time in the dream, and seeing things through, what an unusual idea for me, what a tablecover. And now I'm condemned to write something new, about a taxi who gets cursed at about a plumb line that falls, some fellows are stupid at driving but I'm arriving anyway as usual and soon a day will come I won't come, so why make a note of it on your pad cause how I'm driving, as the usual Tuesday comes after the frequent first Monday in yellow and green September and it's neat as can be, makes me a despicable monarch who lives in a tree to be higher and closer to annual rings, he keeps asking questions of me, I'm a ring yes it is true, and a field open field, educated guesses ring better than true, I've lost sight of it all, crosstown crossed up today I've missed all my appointments I've gone down in style, hate constantly fighting and never giving up, I give up, it makes me laugh, I'm almost there.

The stone wall shook when I sat on it, my situation gets worse and worse but I can't leave that as the last thing there so I'll eat it and swallow it whole. All this started with a simple note to myself about my mother being in focus that began you sleep and that ended you make me dizzy you make me well. Go to hell. A threat, I can't swallow, I can't swallow the threat I can't eat meat I eat it, someone's looking, a spider's on my shoe, how can he board a plane alone, animals live alone insects alone in the old world elephants alone, everything's changing and so on blah blah.

Why am I experiencing things this way instead of some other way, if, sense telling me to want to be someone else, the wall shakes when the bus goes by and the skin of my face trembles. Moon september june trembles earthquakes monsoons simooms storm shelter. The coast. Till the sun went in, till the haze burned off, stared into space, what's next? Sure.

I'd like to go to Mexico I'd like to go to France, I'd like to let my feet just walk as if they're in a trance, I'd like to be south of where I am and forget that south is north I'd like to go inside it's cold, I'd like to make a trip just travel freely the while. I think all the time: what if the world ended now, I couldn't handle it, I'd go mad, a great disaster, I'd be a cripple, years ago I'd have been adam and eve, if the house burned down or something like that that wouldn't be so bad, what they call a personal disaster now that's just fine, I'm used to that, but a great world disaster encompassing in its fury hundreds of thousands of people regardless of their race, that would be embarrassing right now, I'd make a fool of myself, I'd fall flat on my face, like being caught on the subway waiting, it'd be almost that bad.

Coding and decoding, that's my job. Messages received, it's a race with the other world, what world. Yeah the other world has a keen sense of humor and drinking beer all the time to keep going nice and fat. Other world. Please come in. I pretend to come in. But I stay out. I'm deciphering messages, no milk thank you but a roast voodoo pig. I'm careful about what I eat. I lapse for a few seconds.

●

A plenary indulgence, peace at home. The absence of incense is mistrust like icicles hanging in a cave, someone's favorite word is stalagmite, and stalactite, we move off the moon in traffic, the repeat of a feeling stops traffic, the ice is nice of your love of my love, a desperado is better at comedy than an eccentric, you walk out the door, there's a car waiting.

That is that isn't a sign, just a human everyone as a fraction ready to be multiplied and crossed. Many quanta are more difficult many quanta are more fine and more exact, more multiplied, my quanta overflows into the case of please applaud. Ancient babies live with their eyes, my ears, my nose and throat all involved with a new master. I've got a lot of money and the wind blows read hard through the window, so why not take me out again. We could go out at night in the winter, moving fast on some giant road into perspective but something's missing. We start a search for it together, that's the best part. If I wink at the sky something crashes to the floor. I like to mention the month of September as much as I can, I like to relight my 5¢ cigar, thank you very much for it, I'll move around the room all the more for it.

Dream in the middle of a boat David's bored with the movie of a psychoanalyst being funny. Prisoners show their wounds but outside the window are well-healed scars. The queen goes to the tile palace in the black servants' colony. I get called in to be a good administrator. There's a murder. I'm Ted Thompson being measured for a hat at a school in Vermont. They say to me, "Bend out on it, honey."

It's not really very much but I'm concerned with the sizes of things here. Entropy and quantity and nothing's ever finished. I'm prim about it, limousines are long, lots of room for your feet but still scared in traffic, take the easy way out, a beautiful big blue flower like eating bachelor buttons looms over the river like what. I'm scared of house painters and floored at a whole new schedule a whole new routine, I'm always looking for completion like a movie mogul's deals. Windows on the wall, their numbers take hours to open and the haze waits itself out for a trip to the air of the country, what's the difference, smells drift cleaner and a brighter and much earlier morning with nothing between you and the windows and what's out there which is final if you dig deep enough as the way it was born and always was, stayed that way. The people of the household move off air, air around each other, they move air as if they'd faint without it, move some air over here, of the three or ten of us, now I need it, now you do, we're humans being human, fair, that's air enough. You see it this way, every way, the way it is buzzes enough. It takes me twelve minutes to get here and I'm speculating I'm excited on whether there's nothing or anything I have to laugh to show you as amiable or as soon as a simmons mattress, I mean a simoom or monsoon routine sets itself up for even a day or two, I'm relieved, I'm twice relieved and hoping everyone's happy, I got here on no drugs today and hardly any waiting seems like waiting at all. The driver a terrific skinny father-man who swerved and drove too fast but made eclipse of adequate energy and nerves that inspire me to be the same, direct and zooming, he knows what he's doing his voice is too high for the lines on his face. When I saw your face standing like captains on the boat I was worried about you, after all you were standing and all you might fall in, a movie in transit, an intimate movie, intimacy shown, should I face the sun like I usually do or ignore it, I could eat and take a bath if I wanted to. It's surprising that nobody cares as much as I do how secret I've grown and taken their time away that way. Yes they do. Those two and green apples and pears, never eat them, a black humor poem, it says you'll die if you eat them, it mentions death, how dare they or she or he or it or us, no not us:

A little peach in the orchard grew
A little peach of emerald hue
Warmed by the sun and wet by the dew
It grew
One day passing the orchard through
Came Johnny Jones and his sister Sue
Those two.

The rest of the story went: they ate the green peach and died. We memorized it and elocuted it and then it electrocuted us or at least me. Research this. All the sixth graders are 27 now and icy cold housewives putting their babies in a bath or worn-down torn-down struggling men hate to come home old linoleum and tiles and plastic eats, only one architect among them and a few phony teachers, they dream let's slap the kids around and steal their clothes and send them home for good and maybe a few good priests and nuns visions of suds in the air, it's not fair of me, whose blouse is clean, whose blouse is cleanest, before your own eyes, squirrel digs up a nut in shell and runs wrong way away, no memory of it. Come clean. I'd like to see his storehouse. I'm drawing a picture of mine.

●

Pat Nixon and the street gangs, complete gangs to come home to, I live in the white house I residue the lawn every morning and take out the crap that diplomats accumulate behind their tails and drop on the cushions and rugs like dolphins, they don't need to bother to control, with muscles, the movements of their bowels and urinary tracts, they just shit and piss all over whenever they please, in the morning at night at dinners of state, in state rooms, in cubicles for secret meetings, in rooms larger than a whale's stomach, in the tiniest dishes and plates and on the most enormous of platters, left on the floor, in front of uniformed guards and ticklish generals, on the serpentine lawn, in the closet hanging coats, under the ashtrays just laid out, and in the spittoon, on the president's best cigars, in his humidor, in his presence, all over his residence, by accident, some piss up on his portrait as it flies by on the wall.

●

And now I consider them precious, nice weather we're having, isn't it? I panicked again, I love you to fit it all in we could sink back into the pillows forever and ever, take me down to the next corner where I will try and get a present for Max, this has just occurred to me: your thoughts must be just as clustered and dare I say it fond and confusing as mine except that you explorer have access to either dynamite or magic, a verge, a magic wand or rod, to measure the land and lonely move around in there, weather, a fair amount freely of fear than me, amount of difference and concern, differential entropy of Fern, you're right, signs and signals all along the noisy way, I was mad when I left you today, present for Max, panicked, cool taxi cool enough to bring tears to stinging eyes but not removed enough from the driver who's also black and it's nice to be close to him anyway, though I'd like to be far away, throw that away, home clean. Now what do I do with those two. It's mud it's a muddle it's a mystery (sic) St. Thomas Aquinas was robbed by the angel-driver, he liked it, robbed of his fears, robbed tears, he considered his penis a distraction and threw it all away, tore up, you can lean on me, I change my size too, this might turn out to be the worst day of all in fall, mixed something up, lost it, who's to exchange them surrounded by men who guard them with their lifelines left loose on purpose to be free somehow, I don't feel nothing, I don't feel same, I don't worry anymore I won't forget nothing I won't ever feel same except when I feel the same something so how do you song forget your troubles, laugh richer, you might find something in the store, you say the simplest thing-thought you got and see what happens you say: who here wants to go to the store to search for something, you say you didn't expect me so soon, so neither did I neither say it nor don't like the great philosopher Pleistocene who entered Quattrocento quite right in the flowing so fast sometimes waters of the pretty dictionary. Dirty underwear, we don't seem to wear none no more, let the dirt drift on out and in, it's coming in, the well the better to survive it, the stream's beneath the traffic, well it's always always been there no matter what they do, street and clear running like a test tube experiment that no birds flying in the lab can ever shit in or sit in. Preserve it just the same. Hey Max walk me to the store. Which store? I feel it's my duty to go to the store and get food. Three sweet potatoes one short and fat two long and fat three ears of corn two cold slabs of liver and honey I mean onions cold onions sweet sleep defines defined and one wonders as two: I never told you I can't swallow pills I have to chew them up, we move around real carefully so we always make mistakes in rhythm and then they let you know how we feel, the stakes that we drive in. Splinter in. Time flies I'm not the center of things though I'm a master of mistakes, drive in the equilibrium band comes to play hey not right there on our doorstep while my self's put out to catch flies on my knees rolled up to go fishing all alone, dinner is ready you fucked me up, ha ha upside down again, applause for the little weekend sink back and she does, yeah I think so, you wink at me, streamline the work you do and Saturdays are just the same days even though we change the wet sheets, black sheep, thoughts never ending winding our way down south to make our escape within the same landform without any passports, come in free, you could see a lot else there besides what you see me do, do you see.

Worse yet is the threat, area, loss, lands along the beautiful river explores explode, let's keep let's preserve, hear hear, do we have a fall, do we have liftoff, do we have currency, stick in your place, mental alert, run home, a well-run home, you're on your own, what's a hero come clean, the perfect human wants to know, will be very pissed off if I'm wrong, she walks away, athletes in the hands of far-speakers, guerillas, who's that you want information, I got some sprawled on the bed, you read any good books lately, I'm busy and so are you but someone watching's got nothing to do and I don't think I'll ever go outta the house again, discretely hung up, loose the terrorist phone and buried the dead ones who were attacked in high security who were bespoken severely cut off from even the furthest from perfect humans, who's this your brother? Your father your mother your color-corrected eye lens glasses sweet cream desperadoes living underground, wait a minute, it's eccentric, are they, does living there I mean little baby deer full of innocent cheer, doe-eyed and sophisticated, spindly-legged and invited to eat dinner for free. It's too much for me. I give up. But in caves? Did I say caves? Or mounds or nests or just under a tree, yes, shit, I give up again too much for later.

●

Water in the sprite, an expensive repair. I come to tell you David, in white sequined evening gown and an undershirt but you're at an "affair."

Don't this window open in air? I'm driving on up and swing open low and people move around in their cars, one hand for pen one for cigarette, no hand to cover my sunlight, it's nice weather for the weekend, yes it looks that way but oh how does it look that way or stretch or suck now anyhow how drift so is as is, so drift towards you like this. Madam I'm as Adam as you are. Sprite gremlin, people worried about their health, the haze, how do we get there becalmed, sea's a lot of footage to shoot, you can count on a big big movie. When I told you, when I told you, you believe this, when I told you I'm so tired oh go slow but please go fast I'm driving, blink for a second then come right through, aggravate the loss, excite it. Pins me down.

Pins me down I said, separate separate separate through, pins on the highway, pins on the floor, pins in the currency they sell in the store my store, psychoanalysis is a mere river feather that's got bent, I'll make a diary to you, I'll make a diary through you, please come in the doors open, please come in I'm fine and high as the sky is blowing, high just enough to get by as a cloud writes as rain as the meaning says generating, can't help itself, your name, by chance. What a topography we also are. Study. No study has ever been done on the mind of a man who, as a colonel, eats corn and spits half of it out when he talks in the sun, play with yourself, we could drive up with you in the dark except for divisions of labor and colonels of corn each word does a million works and sets itself up as knowledge for boring into like any of several insects that bore in maize, how's the traffic today and what part of the city do you like best? What part do you live in and what do you hear, a century's noted now and then, an ace turns up a few centuries more, which is older and hides the facts, I make my plans, I swim in the human whaddayou callit, whatever else the fuck I do too.

As soon as my babies get back I can eat sleep and breathe again free. Looks good for the weekend he said, one two three four, I was so scared when I got home why senectute senechdoche seneca and all the rest I've a classical black background in the heady slip-yourself-in and slide the worst women-haters of them all the men the priests, they temptation you to death, saint or not, suffering metonymies endlessly, sayings they say em all and run and jump in the fields by yourself long as you separate, long as you keep apart don't desecrate the vessel is a sacrilege like hitting god right smack in the face with a nickel bag when he asks for me, I mean more, just like you, just like me, just like the rest of us flying free right out of our habits, hands and wrists come first and nestle on all the forbidden parts, pretty comfortable there, arms and breasts legs and thighs and all different kinds of genitals, all the kinds, touched. Screams on the streets, anathema sits there stoned on belladonna, out of its mind, right on the white line, waiting for cars, and laughing its head off for you and for me, anathema's dick. Crunched in the teeth of the comic strip zone and drooled out the ears of a masculine legs-meet bucktooth nothing, nothing's there, the metonymy's a little man peering out his head and everyone sings in a chorus line: out of nothing! Out of nowhere! Out of educated guesses, no hands! Which one are you what can you do, what can I do that you can't do, what we do is the same, what's your last name, how does it ring in your ear, how does it echo your fear and stone, your forbidden faults, is what the wall's made out of, that's all, come over here, you got the right one, sings all over and does it all over again, he's a master, he's perfect, he's out of his mind balancing a miracle, pure gold in a circle, can you stretch it out to there, a winning prize, oh shit—they were talking when they played the national anathema and just showing off their gold like cocks, what a disgrace for the nation's cursed talisman, what a disgrace on the penises turning gold all gold and silver on the lamb.

●

Country starts begin to swing heading sweetly almost on the Taconic fantasy parkway as if I've said it before, armored with habits a bag full of cigarettes and pills and a new country only nothing to say. Black black air of summer, summer's forty degrees at night somewhere and in South America it's backwards, the space is small but it's unique, ignore the lines, late night all night all talk in the safe with Max in car and images will appear before my very now own the own eyes.

I slept merry with guilt, I left another guilt home and dream merry-go-rounds and racks and rows of blouses, blouses without skirts, tied, I mean blouses for breasts and breasts in blouses, some pulled tight so you could see the shapes of the bodies of thought of the women who own them and plan to wear them and wore them before, see-through, and tied in back, yes breasts, you don't write around the words, you don't really write around them, period. I'll remember that one, it's not a dream, it's a whole body of work I reviewed (with you), there is no way to forget it. Saké. Record saké.

In the Hancock morning I record I'm afraid of losing something as it's far away or in with the trees, warm bread. Synergy. Example, example of blood continuously flowing but the sun is with you. Some thing in a dream about paying for something or everything here, reminds me of change of being transferred of being brought out of being illumined, we have lotsa money, of being taught and trained of being inclining towards something, the grass and leaves are almost invisible the windows if the house won't open they are closed, everything about here reminds me of some part of myself and of terrible pain and the pleasure of denial, everything about here reminds me of some fault in interest or hobbies about here about me, swells of being someone else, how easy it's been. Bees and sun a weak wreckage, storms never rage when you need them, I see the point of never raging anger being at the sharp of one as victim and one as cloth. Energy destroys it, energy warmth as pain and drift, I ignore the new words I hear for a moment and fight them, they aren't you, I'm using you, you pass by, you pass through here, you've got my name wrong, my name is like ice the winter weather, these words can now can finally be thrown away. Clark eats away at the pronoun I and I eat Susan's warm bread and strong sense, did I enter them here to discard them to allow you to discard them in any season in every season like protection from bees.

Something is reliable, nothing much lives in caves, everything generates fear and destroys it, anything destroys it, pestilence was once a thing that was opened, doubt and hesitation like I deny you is crusty, planned that way and whole windows fenestration balustrade, empty mountain underground deep even here trip of time, untime, you get away with nothing anything and so on, it eats up time, time is dissatisfied with the way things are, what things are, what is a question, someone will explain it, it's unconvinceable, conceivable it cannot be convinced, I have to use it, it corrects stands up and the weight is on your back at the small, don't care, stain the rock with reddest blood what a thing once more to get away with a presence, what one to be denied as if it once more was is something or isn't sure of, negative space, an empty stone or drone or drome. I insist on continuing continuing country whatever writes itself in the air. I am sure you are there in the house. I am sure you are there in the cave and will come out, it is impossible to get away from anyone it is impossible to use leaves as you show them, it is impossible to locate space and anyway surround it. Even almost completely a slow progress of revelation I decide to ask the rearranging question, is it why wait, you are so patient, you are so dream once or twice a year and I am...I guess there's hardly any way to finish it, it's time to wake Max and us and go to our cave deaths for sure, aren't we manufacturers of swim. Blood are storing are in our bodies in our ear even and sweeter ear known is as known for sure to be sweet, to obfuscate more besides bedsides where identities are shown, almost completely exhibited, almost completely shore and wait for more, I'll never take one again to show a lot of iron feldspar and tin slowly flowing like rivers from the mouth of the cave that will eat you, find a spot and tense and tenser words between them, why are they eating why are they waiting so long what's the difference between what they say and what they drew in pictures at night that we couldn't see.

They're ready to describe them, they leave some things out walking down the woods is what you notice some things get pointed out, eyes tuned to dream all over the dream space extends forever if you look, there's no end in it, eye space tuned to dream, eyes tuned to woods, all eye space accommodates movement, directs toward it movement is an endless surround an endless depict, the trouble with style, come out come out wherever you are, it's time to go to the cave there are scared white-haired slaves hiding there and my picture of you is a drift one that bleeds, accomplished revisions, drew crowds and was changed ever since like once you wince and I leave that out, I wish I could break out and curtains around the code and notify me as soon as you wake, ate, sentries enter and order the floor, this one is quaking this one is bent, summer measure is over if you drift north to see the foliage it's fine and crispy and ready to change. Change means fall off. You get in. You are moved from the surface, everyone's the same, sound of wind, pincers moving a murdered prospect design engineer no fear no image so must be fear, I tried to stay here longer but the rock I am sitting on grew and burst in red flames underneath me, made a kind of sac or hole in its own matter, a new texture for gray, feldspar and granite, a pure slate rock. Of course that was me. Two mountain ranges in space: something is in the clouds, something is not in the hose, you are the clouds. You are not the hose, patent leather expensive patents, everyone's designs are bleeding fear and no one can mention it for fear of the trailers hooked up, long lines, back of the single energy word. What a supposition, once more and then so, you can throw that one away for good, I'll eat it again for you: fear sure another, it's simple and has designed a simple space, you don't agree, you more a part of, you what I own sink into the same, we share it that is, so move around and expect a rest sooner or later and sing the best songs, I am hurrying, we have to go to the cave, again I say, the best leaves won't work anymore, everyone's busy, everyone has plans, and since they can move, and since they can move independent, and since men and women can, they don't move me directly, they don't sympathize with me. The words, I'll use them all I'll get away with it, deep earth the courage it takes to dry like a tent in the sun. So many absences for covers, a scene to speak an unrehearsed cone echoes out of itself, a spewing a spitting, stopped on a dime, what was the experience you tell what started it, what did you bring with you, I'm outside, what did you need that you didn't bring repressed emotions are all over the messy tables so what? Skunks smell up to a certain level up to a certain pitch are fine, the biblical finals are driving there on their way home, all able to stop to eat. Why wouldn't we? Who says better? Who the crutch fuck says even divine?

What's the elegance of any crush, what's the space of four people moving depending somehow on you and new ones to enervate on your way home, only the real strong and obvious are shared, like blind chickens bared for frying or something but the real small defining ones small so are wasted, wasted out one by one, one at a time by one or another one a different one by the way what work do you do, so the reason I mention work is there's some things I learned from you and I don't stop to listen normally I steal and sink ships and yours aspect just seems to be one of them, oceans no grudges against what they receive in a storm so such is not of their doing, hard away from their design, they have to move endless, they fill the frame, how dangerous every movement of life is, with much better than plan, only spots of sun and parent bugs strong ones of all colors, if you're so screech scared then how can waiting you lie in the grass snoozing, something must hold it together sensibly that is to touch out like everything and start it all up forever, that is again and again, something must by peace of nature come out of parent nowhere and part with it to make life's peace and leave a piece behind as part of it addressing you now, continuing on. Ice is cold the same substance is heat, I saw you once before as once is twice twice and nearly ready they had said it would be closed. So space subsumed a minute of so of itself then someone else could enter in, the drift it's obvious is not in schools.

Pools of energy while you wait for worth. Five and dime. A criminal's crime. An abscess or sore. Insects that bore. Potato. Loaves. The incense of corn. The pestilence the rape. The hairy ape. An artless, a core, a trip to the middle of the earth, go back for more stores, a rock a stone spreading pebbles, the country is harder than the leaves that it used to be, the country is resistant to flame, disillusion it, you spoke in the dark last night, I talk in the invisible can't be heard, lined up, so what, what a shelf what a remote line-up the hill lets cut in, let's drop a line, let's let fall a stone pebble, down canyon grand mile thousand speak exhaust fumes the sensible expected and so, so far we have had to have rules, period.

But overnight everything changes and washes away where we stay and study for a while. Some space. How do we get started, you are waiting to get going, let's see go. Residue can be chewed as lawns mowed for a residence which even can be moved en masse by people who do that. I do. That is defined. You don't pay. All the tricks of the monsters of the past came to help him move the house. I mean all the knowledge of the tricksters of the future emerged from their temporary dip to remove it, it'd been moved before. I mean all the ink pens of the distance stancheoned the structure of the building to be moved. I mean all the mobsters of the present devoted action to rough up the foundation. I mean all the trees that can't be seen are uprooted. I mean all the nests above mountains overturned. I mean all the insignificant revolutions of the earth on its axis are stopped, come now. Only time to. Gotta go. Simple measures. I'm being watched, bled.

●

Andy and someone are arrested for dope: we drive I'm nervous down a crowded street in Grace's car, four girls get in the back, there's no room for me, I'm about to go around the back to get in the front when a mad car, the traffic's bad, pulls his front end under our rear, I'm abandoned, where did the car go, ours, disappeared, but someone's there with me, maybe the "companion" or another girl or girls. The "companion" isn't trustworthy, he's so crazy there's no telling what he'll do, he doesn't talk much, short hair like the army, he's a killer, maybe an attack pilot. Other girls come, one is Cordelia or Cornelia and the car and Max come back, Cordelia represents the connection or deal, I don't understand, Max explains it to me being careful not to use the word dope. We go to pick them up and Andy has the dope. It's a restaurant we've been to earlier (we've also been to separate parks, Max and I, two blocks away from each other and I don't know if I can walk the distance (from David's to where Max works)). But the restaurant is now a movie theater, ornate box office isolated in the middle of the entrance, and Andy and another guy are out there in front, there's blood on the left sides of their faces, they're hurt, they've been wounded but the blood's not really there. Everybody gets out of the car to help but me, I'm stunned and I watch, someone wipes Andy's face and the other guy's girlfriend sort of kneels at his feet grabbing his waist and crying. Then I see the cops, it's a set-up and they're just acting, they've been staggering and moaning as if to faint but the blood was invisible, visible only to us, we've been set-up, but the sight of them suffering was so awful and what would happen next, that my breathing from fear was a heavy pounding of my heart, it wakes me up and then I plan how I would drive the car away and leave them all and get help and who's with me in the car? It's the "killer-companion".

A colorless dream, in dark green, that's why the blood is invisible, gray-brown.

They watch the news. You're right it's a fortuitous cave caved-in my way and there's a real out-and-out competition going on but I got enough energy for regular life, no doubt about it, you come through, the Yankees hang on the verge, the Maxes talk seven Septembers, everybody returns in red sox. I'm a regular reporter outside the sensitive self that seems to be full of holes by now it must be, each to each, the ache to ache, fences drawn and quartered, quartered by a horse, the horse events of the last century if the day won't let us be, won't leave us alone to dry our tents in the sun, yes that goes on continuously, to make them last forever, to prevent mold like a German, said. How dead they are. How ahead of myself the holes I am. I know the reporter's an ace of a star that's why he had the balls to come in to the very first event in the first place. What're you doing? Just fucking around, hanging around, you know, the usual things, like burying men and women in giant screws and the screwing of them into the ground, afterwards. The top of the screw is a restaurant but it's very expensive, let's eat.

In the airport with Uncle: the book about special marriages, I leave and don't know what time the plane is; in the airport with Max: we fly first class with Walter Matthau, drink wine in a bedroom, "There are so few mirrors at home;" in the airport with David: I got woke up, I didn't call Bartholomew and the guy who was knocked out.

Somewhere in the open something is open and it's simple and clear: you don't have to wait, in the rain, man or woman, back again to make it, to make it as if there's something you could own, you wait for the right moment, it's crowded, colors no colors, entrance exit, align them in a pure close-up fantasy, reline, realign, stoop. I was sitting on a stone that day, I was sitting on a rock, give me money, the breeze the air is clear, rain not coming down hard in any space. I can smell it's wet, I can smell it's sea, the driver doesn't use his windshield wipers, he takes his time, I'm calm again as a cat, now he turns them on where's the time and where's the acrobats in blue, I've gotten lazy, no I've gotten stored and like to go slow as giant pincers are calm at night in the night in the night in it, rain stopped right by the clock, it's 1:33, I hope we get stuck here for hours and you come speeding backwards in a two-man helicopter down to lift me out, today's accident is a three-car accident, yesterday it was the New York Times fire and Sunday the cave, cave closes it's V. You meet people you know in the store, they rain on you, you have a good day and say your name, Bernadette, I admit it's soon, it can snow anytime as much as anything's fortuitous or else on land or sea.

Something's burning, I give directions for the burn for the lift-off for the press, I think his tires are loose, energy's loose somewhere like rain, rains around, street blocked off, all said.

And the boat went down to the island. Even though they watched us, they had to let us get out and run around, the blue steps, timing us. Movie-horses running in a city, no running opposite. Birthday party, pool table, watch out.

On my way home I saw a terrific looking chic in a vest with t errific looking black men with high cheek bones and gigantic dogs. This is my idea of being middle class in a taxi down the highway in the middle of the day as I take my vacation in the middle of the school year, don't go too fast cause I get scared into getting married, let's born babies both, the cave scene, something's burning was kind of timing, let's go sight-seeing but even there I'm stopped as a circle is a line, I don't wanna hear about it, I listen to my body and my face, they play this song called every day people and the traffic's jammed, black guys turning around, driver wears his undershirt, we're delayed, they wonder why I keep busy, shit another accident on the other side of the way and everybody's rubber-necking and even sirens blow, the wind blows my sincere shirt open, narcissism spells itself, where is it, militant songs against dressing, I'm a trade unionist, I am speaking here as a trade unionist, I will wear your clothes as you wear mine, they can be changed and interchanged, all our clothes are the artifact work of our dreams, undressed in dreams, naked in the street, a woman dreams a man is on the street, more sirens, a mean woman in her dreams, a man on the street, just mean women and a feather man, my helmet's on, I'm a caver, my hair's real long, I'm an observer, I'm hung like the curtains, closed, so's not to tempt you to look in at all at me.

I could see for miles and miles and miles, laughing and being bitten by a mosquito who makes me sneeze and waking up sweating afraid it's dawn again and I've never been to sleep and realizing I've been going over and over something, chapter by chapter, as if it were a dream which it certainly was, I could see for miles and miles and miles, bitten right through the covers, bitten in advance, it makes me sneeze, it makes me create stuff, itch all over.

●

And just some more taxi blues in the real sometimes it's the best something for something that's fucked up or something that is only dream, dream all morning review, review what can you do but review, what are you able to do, you have this much time, so much time till you can get there, I can't stand people calling and calling and yelling so early in the morning, today again the haze is deep, demands energy from me and barely bearing it, I know where I am in here as we cut around the 25 mph curve and wedding, what you gonna do, it's unlimited supply at this speed a sound like a bird comes out of the car I sing this song, the amiable stars are out behind the light somewhere, I'm waiting for them and I don't want nothing in between and no one else, it's an easy ride, I take them on they don't make no demands on my supply but I volunteer anyway, anyway entropy, she's too good for you, too good for you, that's what they always say, visit a picture on the film, it eats into something there, something's a history but not the real one or not the right one or not the stone one, up a hill by the big apartment parents what a nice guy is driving me here and happy, a bottle of wine in a pigskin of wine fruit of the vine, Bessie Smith always sends you the news you don't have to wait for it, you don't set fires to get what you want, your demands.

He leaves them free, he extends you, me, out of a space in his head where it says so, so many layers to language maybe language the your it work(s) well maybe something else'll come up soon like direct paint or startling animosity, who's talking? A whole crowd a whole slew of primitive cultures slide by the door three by three, two men and a woman, two men and a woman, draw it. What next is sure, how does that happen, you speak direct to the table that wasn't always there, the church brought it in. Come in, the table's heady and necessary like give him a little head, he doesn't know the details of the situation so put a top on it, switch to convertible, the topper the capper the switch AC/DC Kathy has no current for her vegetable receptable and other fresh stuff, so she's create stuff and he must be rich. Into the cave to park the car, always fighting you inch back to the dream it's a mystery, stores of them ready to power you over. I give up I take one out. It's the blue-face dream, curtains parted, someone can do something alone.

The colors distinguish between then and now the cigarette falls on the floor then and now, I'm wondering what it is I'm afraid of it could be on t.v. is anywhere the chance of just anything now or not entering in, I had forgotten how a comfort to fill the old hungers in old/new way is. So you see one way or the other I did escape from you two, except I can't eat, eat it? And you can't swallow it. Something was or wasn't planned, from what you tell me from what you don't tell me I'm sure on edge, the paratroopers are here, I'm getting further out there, I'm getting distracted by the news the phone rings it's some old friend just hanging on here, fuck him I wouldn't talk to him afraid I've lost you. I won't give in I'll watch the news I'll wait it out like always like before, you have somewhere you go there every day, something sticks in your mouth you can't swallow it, a knock on the door is Barry to use the phone, what's up that's funny the lamp the lit the cave was his so what, woke up, blueberries and cheese are the support mechanism, people come and go, he checks for money, he checks for beers, someone was here eons ago who watched me, now I have "dates" swell what, I'm an author or else. I'm so scared of what, but as long as I'm gonna be here and there's nothing but black beauty on I might as well do it, I've found the avengers now, in black and white with Diana Rigg and a frog man coming up out of the water probably from an underwater cave, cave mound and so on I kind of like her voice, it's as though it was all planned to give me time, to do something.

Shell: other people just sit and stare but they just don't worry about it, it's a habit, here's a chance for me to completely surrender, here's a chance for me to stand up and see what all that's like again, lonesome traveler, brings me the news, it won't be nothing but a struggle that no one can see that's the beginning of it and that's the end. Some lines get recited, some lines get excited, how do you usually pass the time? Till what?

●

And now I seem to have to write: I know I can get up and move around but I can't feel good no matter what I try I can't feel good eating, drinking water seems to be the thing that comes closest to feeling good at all, a pain in my side, I want the wine secretly to make me feel good as it's supposed to, I want inside to be outside and not knowing that, there's nothing better about not-the-person, nothing seems to predominate here, the fucking time passes, I'm not exactly free to write cause no one's here, I leaned back and watched something-nothing on t.v., I could talk on the phone all night, I could nothing in a way, shit, I can't wait any more, I'll stop waiting, images from beyond my eyes are demanding it, I want to go to sleep, there's no reason for it, it's 10 p.m., all the news you need to know, do you know where your children are, why the fuck don't you call me my child, you fuck, some-one is talking about legitimate self-defense in relation to a thing they are calling realities like Hitler rules the world and if you don't eat and if you don't eat you wake up, images start to form and magic monsters appear and much of the stars we're borne on are crutches are crum-bling they'll last out the year for fear, they've decided to discredit McGovern by pretending he's not there, they've got it all worked out by computer if pres Nix does no-nothing he'll win for sure by a nose, that's the view on the outside, now there's a part that I wouldn't want to be inside too, how do you do tricksie and dick please don't come in you're prejudiced against potato pies, you think they're only for blacks, go back to Seagurt and sing and burp the national anathema mowing lawns till you die, you see I'm outside, isn't that good of me, isn't that fine like pie in the face, like a map for fears.

Something green intrudes itself in like a blot on my record of my total map, can't say no love, no food, I've got love and I love alone some like special no-air treatments from the zone of no air, who eats anyway and who ever sleeps without one, something that goes on waiting and on and something green that you fear, no care. Both will dissipate waiting, will disappear something that was here go away waiting I'm waiting for something to leave, left again, I'm waiting, streets, for something to go, hello this is your last chance in transit, hello this is your last chance to, that death implies a presence, death makes the I's the eyes duplicate themselves, they're appearing, no certain nothing, there's a lot that could, there's nothing that couldn't, please begin to lay down, I'm tired, my fears and fuck them, no prick, I'm sure I can't. And please begin, sug-gestion of sudden death, sudden death is when I forget some kind of sudden death of tennis match waiting, and a drift in-shore where the whole town's waiting waiting for you, sun's gone, after the heat's run and congratulations, waiting, and how, sun's gone, do you feel and sorry your pen's running out again, we'll take good care of you, do you need dry clothing or to be turned upside down.

It doesn't matter how much I write I'll never effect the cure, I've got no introduction to time that fuck, he doesn't wanna be influenced what a prick you can take your cock that you write it all with and bury it in a fucking cave, blast explosion that was, the last time anybody ever would be killed in that cave fucking week goes by like dynamite and I'll never know every one the same something, take me home, do I live in West Virginia, Carolina or the rest, do storms break out there, does money flow from trees and if someone came, if they came, fuck shit piss and let me add your mother's milk, let down.

●

I drew a rainbow or a spectrum with two blue eyes below it encased in gorgeous and vampiric reds and said, Dear David this must be you. I pretended to write words when all I was doing was scribbling, then I crossed them all out. Just by accident I happened to accumulate color like heads of hair or even fright wigs, five in a circle with an ochre G-clef in the center. I scribbled some more but instead of crossing it out I underlined it. Then I drew a giant hermaphroditic genital in red with waves of heat or light emanating the way children draw the sun. Next a sun of royal blue. And then three ornate arrows in differing shades of orange, green and mauve.

●

A brave thing a studious and brave thing, how can they drive it, how can they know, stoplight, the quiver is all in your head as I disappear out the door, full light of my own will to go there out of the almost completely surround of Max and Max is others who know me, is the pen dark enough to be seen on paper of the same color, I like the older drivers who go slow, even on a beautiful day and don't tail-gate or change lanes a lot, get cut off or swerve over and slow down for the curve but this one at least seems talented in a way and puts the brakes on, someone's life is much more like murder my new york, what if a wheel fell off or your instincts about the sky were wrong like a sailor or fair weather friend, like a stop on a dime, everytime we'd be becalmed I'd be wanting it to last forever cause quite simple to stop and drift for a while is no (now?) cause for alarm, you can't count on the weather it's the same as reading signs: caution merging traffic, the group is on tour the expectations are terrific, let's have a party but let's not speak it in case we have to make it new, another pitfall on the highway and somebody fell in, where does language come from, people too out of wombs never end and both never end, will never end, couldn't, the sky is blue for the age of reason that makes us think of age at all and never reason, we were still part of the underworld where great sacs of vegetables full free are feeding me with their myriad colors, will I will borne reflect in the universe they invent, they invent me and I toy with it, a toy is very sealed, I meant to say serious. I guess anyway the toy is yellow like the pencil there are so many diminutives if you start looking them up.

●

Three Men

resting.
Three men rest. They move.
men talking
a girl looking at a box
There are three men in a boat. They work
a man traveling
girls waiting
Men talking and singing. They are sleeping.
a boy of nine
Three men moving
A girl looks at a box. She leans over.
men singing

a girl leaning over
She is wearing a coat. A man traveling wins a prize.
a man winning a prize
girls winking
There is a man in a lighthouse. There is one
    buying a watch.
a boy in blue
three men in a boat
Girls are waiting. Girls are winking.
men sleeping
a girl wearing a coat
Girls in uniform are skating.
a man in a lighthouse
girls skating
A boy of nine, in blue, near a mountain.
a boy near a mountain
three men working
Three men rest. They move.
a man buying a watch
girls in uniform
There are three men in a boat. They work.

Look at the air, look at the clear air, generation, cold, painted blue, war paint, you know three men in a boat, department of docks, everyday, fifteen minutes, meet me, hello, idiot, no, hello idiot, let's take a bath.

●

The Pope tricks us into playing with him: Pope Assails Sex Freedom: Castelgandolfo, Italy. Pope Paul assailed sex permissiveness today and said contraception, abortion, adultery and divorce made modern man vulgar and vicious and sad. We live at a time when man's animal side often degenerates into unchecked corruption, we walk in the mud, Paul told three thousand visitors in his weekly audience. He linked psychoanalysis and sexual education with porno magazines and sex shows for contributing to what he called the pulling out or pollution of environmental immorality. The pontiff attacked the so-called freedom of the senses and the customs. He said they provided a hotbed for addiction to narcotics.

Munich, Germany: at the Olympic games, something seems to be in the boat, it's the castle. It's Max and the priest, the theater and Gregorian chant. As long as I'm here in a strange country I might as well look up, I'm always looking down, I look up and see a boat of trees and town houses in the harbor. The sails are resting, perhaps it's David's house on the boat and palm trees. The sail represents the ship's metonymy and in the town house the lights are on, it looks inviting as I look in, yellow light, so that one could say, "I see the lights" instead of saying, "I am looking at the house." What's a family (doing)?

The "castle" is surely the attachment for Bartholomew's camera that makes everything work automatically, I'm hiding it in my chest, I take it out. If you don't know the castle is on the camera, you may think you're not focused; people had trouble with it before at the theater. The castle gives you focus, depth of field and exposure. It's like a diaphragm or a refrigerator dial: "The freezer's dripping, turn up the dial to make it colder please." Perhaps the amiable castle is somehow also impregnable. I see the turrets and the cantilevered bridge.

All this happens as we are about to enter the elevator-tunnel of the Cannery in San Francisco. Though it's made of glass we are also in Bavaria, in Kassel, at Documenta, an art show. Earlier, Max and a priest got into a hotel elevator and my thought was: I didn't have time to tell Max to get back soon, and since he has no sense of time he might talk to the priest forever as priests tend to do that and never think that I'm missing or needing him.

Before the elevator-tunnel, perhaps we got on a ferry, too. Someone mentions something and it is my song, sung to the tune of "Imagination:" "The revelation is funny, you don't need any money, everything's golden and honey and I'll bet you sing it twice a week." John says it's better than Gregorian chant: "Why is everybody still always thinking about that old shit?"

And what was happening at the theater? A lot of people on a stage but all backstage, there's no audience, it's more of a school auditorium, where a man is lecturing on careers, or perhaps he is only acting out the lecture. Everywhere in this dream I feel I've been there before, it's very straight in this way.

All around the loft is different: I find the extra room again, an old closet this time, a walk-in closet with a window and ornate hinged stuff on the wall, still a closet though, in case of what? Over and over I may dream this dream.

Two people are on the floor, Rico and Kathy maybe, face down. This loft is a combination of everywhere everyone ever lived like a line, historical-terical, terrible history hysterical man at the time of the year of the histamines and do they, the histamines, live in caves too, they're not mined like mine field, where does a mine field end unless you got a map, I dare you to make one of mine, the bull's not stubborn but scared, a bullfight is a scene, you David (Beloved derivative) and I fight bulls, toreador, cantinflas, can't fly, the humor bird. Cigars, I'm going somewhere new: we eat for dinner the WANDERING JEW. Butchers, I'm a bull. At this point in time time seems to have stopped, I will never have to eat or sleep again as each dream extends that far, it's the euphoria and exactness of the manic depressive idiot who is a sorcerer, a man and his theories, we eat for dinner the Wandering Jew.

FREUD FREUND FRIEND FREEZING FJORD FEUD FEND for yourself FRIGID J'ai froix J'aime les fraises and roses too, Rosemary—sea dew and you are King Lear, oh no. Cordelia is I can't say it. And Goneril and Regan's venereal disease, I always thought so. And Edgar and Edmund and you know who who pretends to be a madman and doubtless saves the day. Did I know all this? I think I know more. You are each message in the water I drink. Tomorrow will be a hard day cause the kingdom is a cause made up of families' collapse and who is the subject of the king?

Dear Lear Goliath, how many are you and am I any to fit into you, there's no mother there. SHAKES BEAR and shapes bear, shakes beer—it explodes, the mine field, the juices. Someone once told me that frozen juices explode if you let them get warm and I said, "Everything anticipates as much as it's past."

And I imagine myself in a loft with the ceiling beams exposed and many plants hanging from them with a purple light to keep them growing and Max leaves, I am alone I am all one and you are free to visit me whenever you please, as a matter of fact I give you the key, we are so serious we play and the walls of the room are brown wood, all exposed, as the beams and the arrangement, books, papers, all ramshackle, random and you come by a lot to this one large room, you enter in just anytime, it's always a fine pleasure to see you and we are each other's by the arrangement of the room which pleases you and I take pleasure in that, it's warm, yellow, the brown, the exposed wood reminds me of your face, it is your face and the plant light, purple, is your eyes mixed with the red of the cloth you attract me with when we play we perform the art of bullfighting which is hard to say but it's what we do. Now at least. But then and this is later in my ceiling-beam loft, we no longer perform and the arrangement is just a reflection of the fantasy I dream to reform desire in a room that could exist, you could walk into it, then now cause I saw those colors and someone did live there, so sure I could and I'd like to trail off…where I was then, you were there, I know it, nostalgia for a drift and that room, you walk in, shit man that's as real as anything and as anything I can't stand, it already exists, I saw it, the room is mine and your life would be yours to be left alone, funny the right word, I wouldn't disturb it, the veil of the room reveals all, I'm charmed perhaps by my final, I know it's not last, create without limits, something, but a twig, small twig, its limits shit don't they branch out. I'm lost again here but that was my vision and visions by nature go on forever's too long now I ache.

You fuck get me that room, I'd be your deeper mistress never to anyone else you are alone in that way, I'm taking you back to my loft for your safety I mean mine, meaning curves around a lot, you'll have to bend toward me and be me. Two things: trying to remember (to keep things in mind) and the other thing which here (I am) is desire far through me.

And at the loft the heavy green sweater I mean the man wearing it walks with me from behind, I can't see his face: "Look at me." He won't let me, if I do I can't be angry, if we make love I can't be "patient," I walk with him this way: he and his arms are behind me and we take steps together, I like it. And we look out the window, trapped by a wall behind us. We see a restaurant we forgot about, a "Prexy's," it looks closed, we usually never look in this direction, but a man inside fries a cheeseburger. I'm having a lot of trouble with time, a whole new danger is a temptation, meanings, crystal clear are, begging (me to continue and I can't resist) you, is final.

This is different from the other writing what comes before as every last will and testament cancels out the all previous disposals of whatever pennies and properties you or your poppa remain in charge of at large at the time of the reading of the will, no death is even, none is even necessary: why do you have to go away this weekend? With fully knowledge of how storms brew, I take this fearful beginning of dispersal, you call it a fragment you private person, I take it and hopes to be with you, I am penitent, penetrate as Ovid must be woman to be simple, it is easy the way things are, change and magic are the same, I have a name it stalls me from wishes to be your mere daughter, she's as everything as me, I'd like to be there, lovers seem to be absent so tell me, please indict me before my release from a painful imprisonment that's cost me my age of a thousand years and made me wish I could see through the giant mass of the earth as I am and tell me, can I? A,MAZE.

We have all this in writing, let's get back to the chickens, memory such a storm. I thought of crap games, I'm leading you on again. So I saw these chickens that somebody'd bought and forgot to put away and they were wet from standing so I drained them over the sink, words are so long and stuffed them into the refrigerator and a woman standing next to me shows that there is a man on ice in the sink, sitting straight up, an upright man, blond, up-sitting and stiff. The woman, all women say: "Don't worry about him he's dead," on ice. Oh god he's dead, my wish it was, it's true. "Please ask Max to come back in, please." Only his lower half's on ice.

How many eyes are blue, almost finally, speed, insertion, dress and drift, a spectacular, a glass, you said it. I believe it, I could not be crazy and in love today, no now, now's the worst no the most intent part of all, why. And why did you tell me I'm just on "vacation" and the hurdles and journeys are all to come, I deserve to drink ink.

I look for the vieux-nouveau shop. The girls don't know, it's a strange city, where. I wear clothes, old and new and your fucking blue eyes are something old and something new, say listen, can I borrow your tool?

Twenty minutes. Hundred. All the own body's time is mind. Baby I wanna get married, proposal for a grant me your troth as a coach for the athletes of plight I'm in. Goddammit I do smell so good in the strange city we're so far out ahead of it's time that its ache learned above it to lessen from heaven a haven in medical health, that's good smells, in the jungle the natives think whites smell peculiar and cocoa plants rub you right out through the skin that is they devour mosquitoes, their bite, as I seem to be, no, as I am attempting to murder you, yes I am, the perfect crime.

The criminal pleads that the victim survive and the criminal pleads, let me out! before the crime's a crime of consequence. Where am I? In Philadelphia? And the girls say: "How can you go around..." They hesitate, ALONE's the word. Less lonely's apostrophe, strophe's a form, athletic companion, that's why we're all poets.

And the room larger and larger. The fucking doors fall off hinges, double doors, like yours, to go out twice, to have to. Kathleen's my mother and her ass is too hard and her breasts are like balls not coherent with the body of a brown woman and Kathleen has no husband and two boys and the oldest one is Stanislaus, I gave him my hockey shirt and they're precocious and she's beautiful but not as beautiful as Marie who, as you say you love me, Marie had Ted and we note it, Shakespeare wrote it, and that's why, that's why you can be King Lear, Cord is connection and Cordelia, that's me, deals dope. What an ordeal alone, I am a crow, David is here as the door falls from its hinges and things take shape by losing it. Fall, fall, roughnecks run in and embroider lace fucking handkerchiefs, moths to the light, I trust you, a crash, cream on the book I am reading, queer things turn over and I curled around her always from behind, we're getting somewhere, I feel a little bit looser David, please laugh.

Laugh because now I'm up to the typewriter dream where the whole set of keys come out as if in a drawer, the mechanisms are up above and you know I want a typewriter like this to fill my whole mouth up, the machine's workings a giant sculpture, separate from the keys, a work to observe, it will intensify thought.

Some sleep. My purple robe will protect me: "Your name is written on it." There are many salesmen besides the one who told me at the outset which may seem now closer to the middle but it isn't, "You did a brave thing." Didn't I do another brave thing or have you been here before too? There's a lot, there's too much, what will happen next? Sure. Ruby, Violet, Emerald, Sapphire, I'm drinking cherry no sherry golden sherry, where's Opal? Diamond Max loved to be absent from school.

Hello the screens, the screens in your rooms, black screens. The scream said to me: I don't know what I'm doing with them, I don't know what to put on them. And me the bare complementary in blue and orange, and me I said: I saw them but I don't know what they are.

Shit, you know why they don't deal with language's meaning, the guys who don't, it's dense beyond the buildings that earthquakes fall and even though we're smart and we have a few in's, there's no human mind that's as tidal as to conceive, I can't hurry anymore, yes I identify the conception as my inroad to fame is her name Marie, and that's why I feel women as myself, so women have babies, I take my baby to the shore, Marie, the sea's coming up and well it rises awe, the mix-up's eternal, Theodore, romance.

Writing is rising, you draw a card, clear out, I am with myself girl-child and another woman, easily myself again, with another girl-child, it's her turn her time so I move into the bedroom where we could make love without our work whether I were a woman or a child, I'm overcome with this now and thinking of myself as an owl, calms me down peering owl, now you know it, I hope it, please I'm counting on you to end it, no I want to prolong it and so it's this:

A party, and we begin to navigate the shore of a complicated and changing river, may I smoke your cigars or hers? I've gone so far I want her too the whole mind you understand, a clue to Max. And the river and a group of queer people (one side homosexual heteronomy, what's the other, so we have to get to the other) and the queer people watch admiringly a nude John Ashbery in his house moving around, I want that one-side(d) admiration (-ed for the past) for myself (his psychoanalysis) and the river and the river becomes so shallow, you and I alone at last in this dream, we'll never find a taxi, you gave me the clue that you could be me and so I could let us alone, dream us alone, not again. I guess I figure if I exhaust myself totally and force you to read till you drop I won't be able to insist that this is not the end of that desire for so much sex. It's as simple as Violet losing her dog, he's run over and you take good care of her, she's your daughter. Anyway, we couldn't find a taxi, too shallow, so we have to go to the other side, the going got rough, I entered it (I can't possibly finish this, what time do you get up?). So we climb a ladder and it's a long way to fall so I fall, it's a long way to fall, do it, fall do, I've taken my sandals off, they're no good for climbing, words, I'm better off without them, without my shoes, barefoot and if I weren't shy? Shy not sky, it's dawn, the trucks are coming and they break my fall, who? Several of them, the last on jutting cliffs fall into where? I wind up in arms, I wake up in arms, a diver is saved, broken by a diver and if it were a show, it would be trick dives or even truck driver. You fly into me, I fly into you, fucking human, there's a lot more but nothing to keep me to it, I'm so tired, touched with genius whatever that means, you say, I just make it, my seduction's long, about a thousand pages, I'm good at it, but it's not important anymore, that phrase, a wipe-out, focus, drift, where are you and how could there be both you and Max. There could be me I guess, I'm not the people I see, they draw themselves into me like a painter paints a picture of memory, whatever it has to be.

Missing Teenage Girl—City's 'Darling' in '66. Margaret (Bubbles) Smollett captured the heart and imagination of New York almost seven years ago. The blond, blue-eyed girl, then nine, became mother and housekeeper for six brothers and sisters when her mother disappeared, leaving the family trapped in poverty. Five weeks later her mother returned. But now Margaret is missing.

And his response was to die, or to live by chance, like a poster with slogans, like a flyer could be the only remnant of the dream. What an axis I've got on the circular sun, many ways of saying I and writing you, "ewe" on my scarf, I'm wearing my purple gown at last, today it's the interesting sculpture scripture structure I must see every day, what a time, what a work, work less carefully, pulled out all the stops the weather is overcast quite beautifully low clouds are cold and clear no haze no protection, the Pope's message to us: drift clean and clear through the beautiful surround, make a show of these posters: "Outside-in, Communicate."

●

Directions, Occhi di Lupo and the Wind: Max gives directions to a group of women in a van in Ridgewood. It's a parade.

I realize Max has put the leftover pasta, occhi di lupo (eyes of the wolf) in the refrigerator in a pot of water, I try to correct this, it's dark and I'm crawling, I get the pot out the door but I'm too weak, it's falling over, maybe the pot is on its side, I can't see, water may be spilling out, I can't move, maybe I should ask Max to help me.

We are walking south down Second Avenue just below the church, 10th Street, I'm pulling Max, it's hard, then I realize it's the wind. An enormous impossible wind, we're walking against it half-awake, I know we should go off into a doorway but what if the doorways are all filled, overcrowded. A rising and spreading of fear fills my chest, I'm awake but can't move, a long time goes by, some people are flat on the ground.

The women Max has given directions to pull up and say they found the place, the directions were good: you'd fly to the place you want to be wanted. You don't tell me about all the dangers, do you? Mistomeaner. I think I cave why the mind might need a vacation.

●

I am not going to continue to write. If the pen scratches, like chalk on a board, I'll stop right here. Permanent clay magic marker, studio fine line. Meta-marking. I will not use my talent.

You and you are not you: you know everything. Gide's notes. Gide masturbating. Gide exploring. Gide at the battle of Dien Bien Phu. Pieces of paper come floating through the smell of arctic ice hulks in the air. I don't call anyone, who commits suicide? They are right and Lowenfels published in rongWrong. What kept him a live? Stein said the question mark was a disruption because of its odd (?) appearance (form?) (i.e., in relation to letters, viz., a to z). Zukofsky and Shepard have published new books. I feel like I am writing my last communication again ("poems and communications") here. I am saying what's on my mind. Too bad I missed out on what my turbulent inner life (as Gide would proceed) might have made of the birthday of the mother of Fern. Catherine is my middle name, after my godmother, Catherine Nirrengarten, a wild weed. She and her husband were one way, their children another. Writers who can duplicate a form, stick with one long enough to duplicate, or ignore one long enough, they can produce a product that is easier, maybe even sell it to the movies, over and over. What lets them do it? Gide's only twenty makes it easy to be like. Back of the page, a man: he's saying, "But I never had a poet do it to me before." I'm drifting I'm noted, did you see it. Motion permission. And without it? Pick up anything here, the first you see drifting in. You are. Me. I hated to make me a sentence, alone, but it was the only way to get you saying you are, properly. You see. I see the ones I'm forced to see but I always see clouds, with faces in them, peripheral lightning (well in the house), a mouse running between the floor and the wall (he isn't there), a hair burnt at the end hanging big as a ball through my vision (I take it between my fingers); I see tacks when they fall out of the wall (at that moment) before the sound, movement of every branch or something hanging, reflection at every remove from light, a spot gotten pale in a field of a color, a scratch that's new in decay that I'm used to; I see something in anybody's sky; I see whatever insects breed and bore in spices and I see what I hear in your voice, if you will let me hear it. It's what I see that interests me. Boats pass globes in what you can let drift, eyes closed: that way, I want to see more. I see jewels on command. Nothing is still. I see what I want to write but that has no word like, leaning, I see what my body is doing: it's up, it's down: I saw my veins, I saw how serious they were.

I never see for a reason. I saw Hawthorne and the white chicken, I see Hawthorne again in a carriage at night: we stop before a church: the door is a vertical grill, hot coals, we could live there...no need to go on with this, I don't see the moment and you aren't there. My advice to the poets? What a stupid position to take—put that before this and this is here now, so leave it. I see the owl that hoots in the city, I see the Audubon Society man who caged him and boards up the cage in winter. I try to look around. Put your finger on one eye, you get tears and the beach. Open both, a good butt. What's extra what's around. I am afraid to lean forward and really do this. Did the dictionary leave all its messages alone, alone and easy, above all easy. You feast on these. I'll lean forward and be a fool: Here: I am at the mercy of some men of myself. If they go out tomorrow I'll need a beer, I'll need cigarettes and star's diamonds (those bracelets they threw, threw out), I won't be able to get them. There's one man of myself I fear, I fear most cause he can laugh, he laughs at this: the women fear me.

You can't wake someone up and say, "I wrote this, take me out;" you seem to have to go to bed, sometime. Maybe I can go to Providence alone but I'll be scared. Writing's not that much to do—just a little extra hundred million.

●

Summer and smoke. Large doses: I don't have to go out, I'll do without smokes. My hands are cold, RAIN, it was the most beautiful need I have ever seen. In the bar: blue bitch, stepping out of nowhere back onto the earth, nowhere else to be, stepping in puddles, walk slow, take long slow steps. You, don't be here.

I'll notice the letter where the rain reads it and an old Mercedes pulls up: "Do you know where the A.I.R. gallery is?" I give him the time. I'm recording an event without dreams, without the bouncing balls you have to put a rug under you so you can sleep, I caught one dream and let myself walk as far from the dream as I dared to approach the Mercedes pulling away while I yell after: "That's my sister's gallery," so I go there, since, after reading C's letter about UCLA I know she'll be there but it's not on the nearer block, it's not as close as I thought, no, first I make detours and climb around the rain but I can't go as far as the place that ends air but I wanted to be gone long recording.

I use the rain for protection: it's funny and gives me a deferment, an excuse to get wet, I haven't read the letter yet, I've read it and I come around the block the Greene Street way, surplus walking: nobody trips me up: rain and dark light. I stare into a gallery opening: no one I know, through the window I'm desert ice and a car cuts around the corner with all its lights on: white ones and gold ones flash in the deep sleep rain as it cuts around in front of me, changing its direction from north to west, turning from Greene onto Broome, nobody will agree with me on the colors of the lights, nobody agrees with you either, there is no science.

I don't measure the colors: everybody eats his own, you know why? To get back, back to where we both began, and how are you?

I walked around the block, first I walked in two lines, perpendicular, and traced them back, then I sat down, then I walked around the block in a circle or a square and halfway around the circle: Listen, there was no science of it, nothing to pick up and nobody I knew saw it.

Rain as a protective device threw me on the floor where I was standing up under the rug bouncing like a ball, unspotlit. I looked around a lot in the time, sucked on a wet cigarette and threw it up in the air: nobody knew it was raining, and still is.

●

You start at the top-left. No, you stop there. Sun's out. You cough. By this time you've forgotten everything, so you can begin. Since you forgot everything you have to begin like this: piece of cake, or, the weeds. Human mind. Explosion. A free taxi. Vacant. Storehouse. A man came down from off his mountain chopping wood. He hadn't been up the mountain. He hadn't chopped wood. He looked it, though. (What was Jane Austen's (who died) first sentence?) In two weeks everything changes. Seriousness holds. At this moment everyone's reading: it looks a certain way: "I think you're right" followed by…"I know I'm right." The difference: "I think you're right" pause "I know I'm right." Which part of your body is warm where will I go tomorrow. Will I, stopped short. You must be rude you must leave traces. Find a place to sit. You have to work with graphs and graph paper. You must forget what you paid for your materials, or, they must be presents, wholly ignored. Then, you must begin with 'night residue,' it cannot be remembered, but it can be found. The finding must take more than five pages. Then you can do whatever you want. This whatever-you-want will be the product, if you need one. Otherwise, or anyway, proceed to feed back. You will sense that something is moving. Seize on it. Reduce it so it can be used, then take the time to look around. I can't tell you any more, except this: right on the corner, two blocks down, at a busy intersection, someone is stealing something. (I'm high.)

●

Dear David, Maybe I can't do it this way. I've gotten used to writing around things, writing long enough, whatever writes itself, inside and out, till I get (seem to get) somewhere. But now I feel that I have no more time. Tight time. "My hunger creates a food that everybody needs. You or me?" What have I gotten myself into? When I say this is or may be a new way of working, I mean I think we have gotten a little beyond analysis, don't laugh yet, because you've made my transference too easy. From the time you began to "read my writing" (euphemism), I committed myself entirely to this work which is partly your work and is almost wholly your terms (the language? field?). In that sense I put myself in your hands. I did it and lost control, I think I was "supposed" to. Now this may be necessary (to lose control) for psychoanalysis to work but I never thought I was crazy in the first place, Max did (and thought he was) and I mention this now because I understand that some idea of control (power, strength and magic too) that I believed in about myself was (is) not only probably what could be called neurotic but powerful enough to design a whole neurosis (in me). Neurosis, but it worked. (I'm not sure of that.) Now the control issue has a double edge: I'm in your hands (my mind) but there is your unavailability which becomes my loss of control. And then I discover Max is controlling me, or, my incorporation of him, if you like, so, loss of control without even awareness. (I didn't mean to get into this, I meant to amiably talk about sex.) I'm getting up to this: I find this unbearable, being controlled. Helpless? I don't think that was ever the right word. A feeling of being cheated or even used at times. In my mind, you promised me more; in my mind, so perhaps did Max. Why do I need either of you and who are either of you, outside of me. I want to get out of your language, its forbidden nature, or better, forbidding, this language which to me is also your magic because it is both anathema and gibberish—your power, your control over me, your field, your language which lets you (makes you, forces?) be mother and father and sister and brother because it didn't take me long to get through to the other, as they say. Now here's the punch line: I'm mad cause you won't fuck, and maybe (I expect too much?) getting out of your language means getting into bed and maybe getting into bed means finding a more human or humane way of working, a way that works, and now you're allowed to laugh. I've never been good at expository prose. When I wrote "analysis" the first time, I wrote "analaysis."

New paragraph? For the sake of sense? Making love has always been the solution to the problem of my hunger for people. What other way is there? Diminish the hunger? When I make love to somebody else, this makes Max happy. It doesn't make you happy. Max once told me that he loves to think of somebody else making love to me. And then there is the concept of physical beauty, as something very important; this conception may be his but I've learned it.

Now thoughts are racing, fleeting, simultaneous and sacred, that is, they don't make sense: I can't sleep with Max as a bargain, I feel he's jealous because I need so much care and company and he feels responsible for you and me which seems to have turned into a lot of pain, my love for Andy, this monstrous writing I've been doing, my wanting Edmund to beat me up, wanting Bartholomew to disappear, wanting a woman, terrified of her, wanting you, terrified you'll laugh at me, and all in my mind—I do nothing!

A new way of working, am I saying, let me do everything, release me right now, from my dependence on you, my dependence on Max too, let me move?

And all of a sudden I feel I should feel just as free to stay right where I am and now I am more than confused. I do want to get out of your language. My hunger creates a food that everybody needs, you and me. Why else could you too get so involved? Do you want me motionless too?

When I move, when I go out, I go out to make love, all the time. What I'm asking of you is this: you have your system, your field, and you've moved out of that field, a lot, for me, I'm asking you to move further out, whatever that means, or else I'll have to desert you there, I'm asking because I'm desperate, I'm asking you because you share my desperation. This house is close tonight.

Fuck you Dr. Witticism

Palpable Andrew

Palpable Andrew is in Mexico and I can't even satisfy the person who isn't and won't be satisfied, someone I love, and Dr. Witticism's on tape, has messages, leaves me, leaves them, if I am free…as soon as possible…you cunt, or, you want, you wait.

I have the sensation of wanting to be left alone, I have the sensation of wanting someone to die or to die, I have the sensation of being useless, uneducated (Raphael), immobile, I have a strange sensation, it is of a running inside me, I have had a strange sensation, it is of a constant running.

You write and somebody calls and you get cut off. The police, with special photographic techniques, would decipher something from this writing if I commit a homicide. But how would they know that it was this page, out of all the hundreds of pages of writing, this page that was to be studied in the lab. Would they find out that I had added the phrase "to die," later, to the already written sentence: "I have the sensation of wanting someone to die?" The placid police, with special techniques, would come in. With machines, powders, glasses, special surfaces, geographies, meteorites, balloons—everybody has a conventional wife. Don't call them up on the phone cause very surely everybody's wife is gonna answer. Yessir and whaddayou want with my husband. You cheat. You cheat.

I know Max is looking at me, I know he's watching me. I think he's out here, behind me, but he's not. He's leaving me alone. Edmund said, "I'll come over." I said, "If you come over and Max comes home I'll just go into the closet." Edmund said, "Then I'll leave." That's exactly what happened.

I was in a place I am in a place, standing in my hallway, resting my head against my arms folded up against the wall, facing the wall. I sense that someone is at the top of the stairs watching me. I turn and see D., we see each other, we pretend not to see each other, my arms are still folded up against the wall, I put my head back.

Dreams: Spending the half I didn't eat, gold and silver lay deities and the head, he said, of merica zoom no moon. A-one was in for a baby, sorry the room's not ready in time. They carried the little king into the cellar, he was too small, dwarf king, stunted, but he moved, was a cannibal, so, I'm sorry the cellar room isn't ready in time. The rooms are better reading from the top down, so, please, New York City, defend that zone. They left notes in the woods around the house where they had had some fun (Fern and her boyfriend). The notes were referred to as joys and the best room available is tight-fitting black. You get into it. Who's it? The notes were pictures, color snapshots, in the grass, mostly nude: the notes were pictures. One thing led to another, one down: one is committed, one is a cat, one is a dog one is a king, one thing: hold what in your hand and defend it.

We're a group at the New Wave School, all glass, designed like bulbous transparent t.v. sets, all windows, sticking out in rows, with thin columns of sand in between. We look out. Chinese people are attacking us...my mail's been held up, now I get it all at once. Each piece of mail's a little box, one box is from Teresa. "If Teresa would only give (send) me a present, then I could (move around, proceed, go out...)."

Lost Horizon at Radio City, except it's a club. Me and Andy go to the back to meet Teresa (who's also Mary); she's supposed to be with X but isn't. Max'll be mad. She asks me to hold her cane while she lights a cigarette, then hold something else while she (something) and so on. Max won't like seeing her. If X was with her it'd be easier. We bring her to our seats...and Spider, maybe on screen, is in the shower with a big black woman who's tan and her daughter, who's as big as she is, and nobody'll say they're fucking but me, what else would they be doing, she's nude and the three of them go around together, how can they? Her daughter's so big, she sure knows what's going on.

I'm in a place, in a school maybe, there are animals all over. A trick's played on me by me. The one who did it explains: "When I passed by you you looked funny (or interesting)." I put half a pill under a shell, walnut shell. The one who's involved in the trick, I've seen him many times before. I thought something else was going on. Confusion of indoors, outdoors, the animals are inside, nice fur, I'm going to have a baby. Shook all day.

The next day I'm in a hot house or steam house, long house, Iroquois long house, steam house for the men. I wake up suddenly at 8 a.m. I get involved in stealing jewels. There's a big bag full. The bottom of the bag's full of big fat jewels. There are four of us. Gradually we get cornered in an apartment. Someone (Ann McCord) is wearing a jeweled white gown with whalebone breasts. Somehow it gets onto me and I notice she's changing into a plain yellow and white check shirt. This makes me mad. I'll be caught in the gown. Pretty silly. There are four cubicles, low, wood, in the apartment, one for each of us and the bag of jewels is in one. As we get closer to getting cornered, I wonder what it'll be like in jail without any valium, cigarettes and liquor. To get cornered, it takes a long long time.

So, there's a little mouse in the house eating peanuts, that's Kathleen, quietly eating peanuts at one end of the house, Max and Andy are having fun on the bed, there's a little mouse in the house making shells, Max and Andy are having fun on the bed, up till now at least. I'm washing my clothes, everybody's got plans, there's a little mouse in the house, cracking them open, Andy didn't go to Mexico yet but he will, Max is helping Kathleen clean, she's moving upstairs, soon as we clean, she's easing in up there, it's a mess, there's a little mouse in the house making eating noises, the mouse is gulping, Max and Andy are sucking on the t.v. set, mouse cracks shells, there's a little mouse in the house and the noise of the mouse bothers everybody, everybody looks around while I have another beer, another beer to make me wonder to discover whether there's another little mouse in the house, mouse cracks up with laughter, under a great strain, strain of eating peanuts in such a noisy house, no one to wonder whether the mouse gets fat, you used to wonder whether reading great books could, fuck it, where does big monster fit in with little mouse, this could go further, sure, it could take you there, where big monster fits in the picture with little mouse, big mouse-bear, but, no one can stand the noise and I can't concentrate, what with, little mouse, wondering, chewing on big peanuts and little men, big ones, lying on the bed, I have to join them, after while, that's what, that's why I took a vacation, so all this dullness could happen, which isn't dull, which is a little space, to lend me itself, too big for me, for once, itself to look around in, it's not so tight, it's not so tight-fitting, as that tight black room, the room that wasn't ready, where I got myself stuck for a while, this is no better, in fact it's worse, there's just more air, more air in an even tighter space than before, stuck again, but I can laugh, let's not work, love.

●

Proust by Beckett: The extreme panic and pleasure of putting something together, something that reveals the subject, subject whose dead desires are, desires are far from empty: I know this one thing: there is no object, an object must be lost, like eight straight lines on the page are turning, turning into circles and corners: it's your turn, translation: it's my turn and something is missing from thought when it turns to object. Steam. Steam heat. Thoracic cavity. Pension pensée. Thought-house. Metered ink. Heterogeneous ice of a line. How will I get there and how will someone else return. My action on your illness. My promise on your turn, or is it your chance, or is it what you give. Understands more. Something is missing, by for through because of the turn. The ineluctable modality of I-forget-what, was afraid of, became a bee an instinct for animal insect-like life. You be there or else, then, at one: what can I do for you, same as any other. Halfway through, you write an explanation: translation: now I can ignore that, what was never explained. I ate the pack you locked me up. No habits corrupted my memory so I sank in, comes down just a little bit too hard. Thought-house. Thought-out, I reproduce this with another new hand.

It's warm in here and cold as
ice and I can't stop
I know something and it's
the missing creation's alive
and to make that clear
I left out
I leave out the aim
desire
as its own water end

dead desire
cannot speak
can speak
and I find all kinds of friends
to defend it
the substance of a language
I bought
and look for enemies
to end it
they only persuade me
to go on persuading
you everyone
(leave be out) me
it's terrible to know
at once
you're not that desire
but I am
so I wish like
people wish
and some of them get them
for ideas
and heavy claims over them
like breakfast
preparations
at length
you store the food even
for a day
ahead of time
only thing is
I already know
penned-in arc
arc of a surface
anyone has none
one medleys
any tripped
up moon

ends blowing
grasses out: the sacred of the
grasses was illumined
and in an analogue transformed
to a language more terrific
more thirsty more defiant
in its number of details
analogized and pinned to points
—there was no stopping it—
than the blade of grass
itself and made war on it
sending the answer in its
own language: war's a
simple measure, beats same
as the own and that was
the grass speaking for peace.

●

A man changes his coat, say, no it has to be perfect, style. It has to be perfect and wears at, it has to be perfect and ears, it has to be perfect and wears a tie, to no. My heart then was here in between dancing and one she was here and one he she and he were here at the same time etc. That is all there is of that. That is all I know. Now that is the end. And that is that tale, that myth. Now it is so much of that.

Now that is all of my mountain, go! A signal to go! Now that is all of my myth. Now that is all I know of that myth. That is all of the myth I recall. Now that is all I know of that myth of mine. That is how the myth ends.

2. (Another Version)

Bluejay Shaman

There was a girl who was always picking myrtle nuts. Once the girl became ill, she became extremely ill. "We must get a shaman. I wonder, eh, I wonder where there is a shaman." "They say that bluejay is a good shaman." "Very well then you go get him." And so then indeed they went for the shaman. Sure enough he came, and then he labored over the girl. "He! It is my own poison-power that they are talking about."

And so he doctored her. "Keep watch on him. That bluejay is tricky." And then sure enough he just flew up, packing the girl on his back. He leaped (flew) through the smoke hole (and away). "Ha! hahahaha hahahahaha (laughter)! She has become my very own wife!" He stole the girl.

But then
Since there's time
Since there's endless space time
But since any time lost endlessly
Is like having a lot of trouble, you can see it
Since that then this
I'll list them all:

> The rock point person lost his good luck thing
> Origin of death
> The young man became a sea gull
> Bluejay shaman
> Fog myth
> The old couple and their grandson and granddaughter became ashamed there
> Ogress myth
> Dove myth
> The two loose women
> The bear women
> The persons coon killed
> Jack rabbit man
> The wife of seal
> Dug-out-of-ground child (and) popped-out-of-fire
> Black bear and pack basket bear (grizzly)
> Choked-with-food (he was man), or I fear the strength of choked-with-food
> The girl who had a dog husband
> The pouty children
> The white wife of mouse
> Crow girl
> The young man became an owl
> The young man who lived alone

The girls who wished to have stars for their husbands
I will tell you a crow myth
The young man lived with his grandmother
Pheasant
That whittles-his-penis old man, or the five brothers
Myth of bluejay, (his) grandmother tied his head hair with her pubic hair
The young man ate the thing that stank
Butterball duck and his wife
The trickster person who made the country
There were many people at that place
Myth about a trickster
What the person who made the country (worldmaker) did
(An additional fragment about the tricksters)
Coyote and blue crane
Bluejay myth
Bluejay myth
The walkers (animals) and winged things (birds) fought
Myth of robin
Crow and thunder trade languages
Small bird hawk had his head cut off
The ocean went far in to the land
Another version
Star husbands
The dogs on the moon
The seven stars
The world fire
The long night and long day
Stories about the Father of the Foods
Stories about cosmology, Worldmakers, Tricksters, Coyote (the fourth Trickster) and the Father of the People (the fifth Trickster)
Stories about persons who marry non-human beings
(A girl rejects all suitors)
Stories about acquisition of spirit-power
Stories about ogres and ogresses

Stories of feuds and warfare (child removed from dead mother, multiplication by fission)

(Disguised flayer (or) skin shifter, poses as woman and marries

man, resuscitation by assembling members)

Stories of tabooed sexual implication

And these:

Afterbirth is an old woman who scares...Image comes to life...Looking tabu, Glutton, Flood, Flood, World fire, Fog barrier

Maternal selfishness avenged, let's tell that one:

First a girl prepares food during her first mensis seclusion. She and her family become rocks.

Then a selfish bear mother tells her children not to look lest they be stung by bees. When the children see their mother eating, they shriek that they see ogres, their mother flees, they eat her honey, then she returns and flogs them.

"Bear woman and Deer woman," (or) Relatives' flesh unwittingly eaten

and Crane bridge

I fear the strength of choked-with-food

I fear the strength of choked-with-food

Now that is all there is of that

mountain, go.

Go we have access

two eyes in the middle of a word alive. You don't see them, first I should've said you see you, no, you see them, then, you don't see them, you see them, no capital "Y," You see them, you see them, you don't see them and then I meant to add to two eyes in the middle of a word alive the science, alive. I am leaving out. I am coasting back through the woods of the myths that might explain me, since I am building a canoe and might turn into an owl before what? Nighttime dawn and same is with as you to me. Flying. This is to save, this is to last and that explains it. But form, fuck, that explains more, not form and not fuck but this is to save, this is to last, some essaying you need to try to do in desperate occasion for final perfume that struck like immigrant behind the ears is peaceful (why that?) and so cheap that it lasts beyond the bath, bath where head splits and drives open a cheap and even crust of expectation, I take it back, I have no head and am divided ax, mistakes divide me more and am divided as anyone, as you and you next to you, I dare you, and that is all there is to this, except for what is constantly running and re-running is on tape, that a picture was taken of a family behind the glass window of a motel, that the window was blue, was fogged with blue, that a man and a boy were walking by holes, and the word béance. Three weeks which I cannot fathom the depths of so I am taking this advantage of my talent to explore, no, stick you with a semblance of my feelings at the end. Now that is all there is of that but beauty and design, and one thing more, the shore you go to will be happy to receive you. The temperamental light went out I can't say more divine.

●

Imp of the Perverse

Rose of the sea, Marie
and rose-marie our secrets
Yellow on a black field
on a field, sable, the letter
whose imprint is red is black
Theodore-Nathaniel
and Bernadette
You've got her name
I've got his eyes.

Bernadette sinks ships:
Marie, I want sex, I have
someone in mind now.
Theodore looks in.
I change the channel
right in front of you, no.
I write in front of you now
addressing R:
Secrets are ours

I'm talking to you, rose-marie.
Keep the order
Keep the peace
You're all there:
Listen to me, it's blue
watch my black eyes
The gun I kill you with is the reverse.

●

In Atlanta, ice accumulated on the branches of trees so heavy that the trees fell down on the power lines and many people could not leave their houses because they had not the power. Therefore I had this dream: Double David: One has arms of plywood, the other one's arms are steel: a good dose of orange socks provides the cure that bit you: which contains this secret: a call to orange arms: On a field, sable, the trickster coyote farms. He overturns the table I'm hiding underneath, while the farmer's still disabled till the farmer's arms are warm.

1

Sunday Monday Tuesday Wednesday Thursday Friday I miss my good old dad, Gee but I'm glad to see ya...See me save up your writing saved by the bell! Think a lot, think pens and pencils, saved by the spell, the same is so of weeds, you awake? Me too...same as a lot we swept the garden, she was good, you mean...? I wanted to get drunk more drunk you 2. Let the grains sink down before you drink it you 2. Sing a lot? ...Special pencils: when the corpse is divisions...when the corpse is just a device to ring the curtains up on (shower hooks?), then...I don't have the question, sponges and soap, eat dope...The pencil couple were air, crying devices for figures in air, drawn there, this is on paper...device, my eyes won't see me and my ears can't yell...There's some singing, fuck it, you eat yet? You eat your dinner off of John Giorno's head? Like me? Nobody be like me, she say, the hatchet man...Big river, Edmund's place is a leopard, Bernadette is a bear she said, those bears are doped up, those bears are tranquilized, eyes would kill if could. (Above) you gotta separate the entreaties longing from the paraphrase of praise you don't make less sense than

pandemonium
appraise
periphrastic
pandemonium's tier
2nd promenade
(doped bears)
sink ships
aesculepius' praise
aeschylus and
aesculepius' tears
tiresias' tears
and eglesias' steeples on
john giorno's head
speak speak

Wear your shirt on your body John and speak ink: you may know more than I do, CUT: I don't know how you cut off my body but you did, make me, that's force me here into this refrigerator door that's shut.

mystical body
bodhisattva
bodhisattva, the brown man

Some mother inks the pen:

Marie Bonaparte
Marie Ann Bernadette Bonaparte
an eddy
and Virginia Poe
Paul et Virginie
you sneaks

Omega of the driveway, lambda of the holy psyche:

Ann McCord
and justice daughter's
Jonathan's laughter
out of the house

Whose did he think it was, Milt's?

the bill for coke
Max's bar bill
Max's bill for coke
and sweets

(heavenly mistresses charged for coming): Send my body away, way away and send the bill to me, stretch one and a side of French, Marie Ann Bernadette… it rains five days. Let the grains sink down to the bottom and:

Clark: "We see Clark but he's a different Clark, there's something odd about his skin and he's much thinner and when I see him I have a thousand things to say and I rise up out of the water but there's something wrong with my eyes…"

and Jerry: "I knew Bernadette was with me…"

and Paris: "Cause we've never been here before except we have (with Grace in a dream)." And with Grace in Philadelphia, all deserted, all deserted cities: "It's going to be deserted, Paris in July, we didn't bring our bathing suits." Edmund says Paris is not on the ocean. "Have you ever been overseas?" "No." Left at the foot of the tower, overcome.

And right in front of you my attention shifts from play to play, I expect more. Write, tension, affect, why waste being out the window halfway. Playgrounds full of water, you fabricate the monkey bars so I won't bang my head. Don't talk to me, I'll deliver this, no justice injustice is done, burn the notes.

Just lie around continuously starting over, begin again: just the head of a girl whose shoulders walk the pavement, cruel numb terrified and drunk, don't pay no attention to making you, just want to get high, I'm doing a number, won't stop, won't open, who's plenty? Goodbye. Just the head of a girl whose shoulders walk the pavement.

●

Gray day September grey. I'd like to be the man whose wife has many children but I'd like to be the mother of my own. Dream: this is about turning over: "I know there's something ahead of me cause I can turn back to my original position." I write the address of the Ingram-Merrill Foundation in blue and see its afterimage in pink dots.

Living someplace chaotic. Dream grandfather dies, he's left me $150 and many keys. I hang up the map often, it is an island and an insect.

September 22

The House of Lords is human. McGovern human. Govern a city a country is human. The lives of the plants, run for your life, Noxon's a brass polish, you buy it at the store and everything shines at the expense of your wealth and health. Space, like an omen the sun goes in and you see a bird. Run for her life, well women and well men, we might as well. Pennies are drifting down from the shores, poetry's a mess, let it stay that way.

The priests in their cassocks and the cops in their uniforms are playing water-polo in a muddy pond. A naked man comes along and scores a goal for the priests, he saves the day. Scores a goal: here's how it looks: there's the mud down below, then the rocks, at the top is the goal then descending again, more rocks followed by the muddy shore. Goal: to get the ball to shore, out of the muddy water. No goalies in this game. But, there's a technical problem: was it legal for the naked man to work with the priests?

Well then, I'm that (naked) man (I'm a blonde too, blue eyes) and I'm walking through the uncut green grass thinking to myself: I'm glad we came to the country today (Gina's or Kathleen's).

I can't sleep on the night of the round full moon, wise men come and speak to me, mosquitoes bite my hands, my "openness" is "cramping." The subject is enormously complicated. When I think of thought, wise men speak. Food, a pill stuck with a pin, which is the poison which is the food, rust or risk. I saw the book I dreamed it, saw it, dreamed it, never saw it, I was asleep. Gerard's slick book with the white poems in it, why do you always confuse him with Pierre? I can explain, it's something in a book, an inscription, we saw it in the French bar (formerly the New Bar) and Gerry or Jerry say something about poetry and sadism, so there. You see it isn't Gerard Malanga but Jerome Rothenberg that I am confusing with Pierre, consider the name Pierre. And, in David's own handwriting, in my book: "Consider the naked priest!"

Jacques (Lacan) has wise words 4 me, it's 2 good to B true, you're 2 good to B'dette.

Memory dream: one: I am deciding to go out for cupcakes, or, if I were going out for cupcakes, what should I bring you: a choice of potato salad, liverwurst and many varieties of cupcakes (the music from the San Gennaro feast), yeast. And two: I'm going out for the Daily News (Color Photo Coloroto) and me: "You are both going out? How long will you take?" (I'm still afraid my "dreams" could come true, but, there they were, watching over you). The writing in my book is a tape and pictures, there's a section of it that is very wise: Max pulls out one of the eyes he's focused on one of the eyes before: "You like to 'cut out' one eye?" He cuts it out like this: the writing as tape is flowing but one eye, or half the human head, is the part of a cinemascope screen to the very far left, or, you could say, where you would begin to read "a line." The other eye, which is "I" is outside the screen's periphery.

A cut-up torture. Voice constantly running, a head is on. Colorphoto Coloroto the funnies (are schizophrenic (in color)), the news, I drift and leave, I've been here before on a Sunday, Elvis Presley was on the cover of the Coloroto section of the News the day my father died, a Sunday, empty word and full word, backwards work, but on the other side of the cut-out is something, a picture of water drifting like writing, it drifts in lines, its drift becomes quicker and so it drifts in scribbles, even quicker, it drifts in dots. Dot dash, S.O.S. Binomial disorder, binary number, balance.

Balance like reason, music of the mean moon, like moonlight fills the room, autumnal. Oct. 20, 1957, the Coloroto section of the news, Theodore A. Mayer, a rip-off, who was on the cover then, tonic vernal equinox one two three four, the man who discovered Troy, real slow, forever, finally.

"Where are your parents?" "I don't know." Oysters with lemon and sauce and the mushy part of the foreign white bread, ate half a loaf. You remember their ubiquitous jump to the top? Let's use the streets, it's like that today: oysters and squid, a puff a red ink-powder, I spoon some sauce into everyone's spoon and lay it on a napkin like this: it looks like a spoon. I am going to be killed as old Aunt Ellie (she's the aunt there was talk of us living with in Flushing, Queens) drives me home. A near accident as a car cuts us off on the left to drive into a (closing) garage. She's not a good driver. Attack from all sides. Up the old wooden ramp backwards to get on the wrong side of the highway (old wooden train on the el), sparks fly. And Neil in San Francisco is saying something to me, he's saying my life's barely begun, the image of you leaving. And this old aunt, perhaps she was like Neil, an old man in a boy, an old woman pretending to be a girl, I remember being driven home from her house once, the first visit after my father, her little brother, died and some other old man, a young man pretending to be old, driving our car, was skidding all over the icy road because he was drunk or pickled, as my father would have said. And memory invites the image also of a young man pretending to be old and finding my mother attractive at this same meeting we were driven drunkenly home from, in fact he was my cousin and he said, "You're the only one in the family I ever had respect for," kneeling at her feet, and he had just been arrested for being, as they said, a juvenile delinquent. But he was not the same young-old man who did the driving.

You said you would buy me the egg cups I like to drink out of but you needed to ask if I already had one: you asked this way: "Have you ever touched one?"

We are having a conversation on Broadway. I tell you: "Women are really right on that way even though...they've learned how to not appreciate themselves." You smile and the dream says to me that this is the silly way I've learned to learn you expect me to say what I have to say, which is something entirely different.

Rainy day, Sunday's the day everyone dies, I'm not as _____ as I seem cause there's something else in this dream: something about where we were going in that car—home? West Side Highway? Maybe it was me in your family car (Ellie—Opal), she didn't want me. O.K. I got it. And maybe the license plates eerily seemed the same, after all dreams can resurrect numbers too, if only we could remember them as easily as a footprint or an important moment. And Paul was there, and something about Edmund, I won't tell you what happens next.

A black boy comes out of a doll, there are flowers, presents, which ones to throw away? It's a regular garden, we put ours outside in that same place we sit, planters. He joins the other boy, it's a boy-dog story. There's a restaurant with Andy eating in it, acting, two boys, plastic explosion, waiters bumping, a big plate or circle, arrows pointing toward it and a triangle to define it. The truth of the word: Fold napkins properly... Nothing but pure fear and guilt and anger and resentment and feeling like a fool in my dreams. Copy: read out: Opal Opal Opal is Viva, well maybe there's a job for you in my movie up my ass. Move over. Fumes on the street, my fears the gears are interlocking, gear schemes. Somewhere here me coincides with you, and others of course connect but the truck has no brakes, the haze is a monument, sure I drive it anyway, I have to drive it, one quick smell of the river and that's all. "Sorry you had to wait so long." Oh, I'm sorry too.

We shouldn't sleep outside anymore. Did you say that to me? All papers and books and passports are burned. Did you say that to scare Max? So what?

●

Three men working, I'm working. One takes the place of the one who's left out. Grace takes the place in demand of care, desire. It's a dormitory, a documentary. I get the book. I wait for calls, food and the presence of another human. Max takes away from me the thing I want most, his being here, and then demands, isn't there anything I can do for you? But, presence lifted is to move for someone to move somewhere else, and defies lines, to move there to do something: you are forced to say: Don't do it, you can't say that, you can only say: Do this, stay with me for a while, or, be here when I get back, sinking back again I see another problem: I have to go out. The rent's paid after all.

There was a mix-up. I can keep the order straight. Took the camera, energy is loose. What am I getting, if anything, fifty thousand dollars or so? What's biting me, what's black, what's sent through the mails and doesn't stink like a dead fish, you afraid of that? You afraid of being poor? You afraid, like I am the opposite way, of the presence of other people? Hide that little man in the book or the boat, your dreams come and scare the shit out of you, I get nothing. I get nothing but the resources of what I might get of what great end could I have, the polluted residues of a possible new ocean.

There's no more hurry, remember: Mars Needs Women. And the identity the male Martian assumes to abduct which means rape the female genetic scientist is fast, that's Mr. Fast, Seattle Sun. Sun I'm sure never 2 B forgotten.

●

Why can't I eat when I'm alone, whose permission do I need, what is this work I'm doing, can't do, where is everybody, simple things I need, your presence, some food in the house, if you called me now I'd say, "You: How are you?" And me: I can't work, I can't eat, I can't move, everybody's not come home, I'm so pissed off at Max, it's so simple what I want, you doing anything tonight? Or am I?

Lacan eats up terrific points, everybody shits. My Imaginary Other is across the street vacuuming, ha ha and drilling holes. Dear Mr. Lacan, so what? Why don't you speak English for a change, for the cause! I agree, my Imaginary Other really is splitting his head open on the fence they've put up between making a business of it and serious work.

Poetry's where you all find something, maybe I could find a something to eat there, something anyone at all, that didn't have to be prepared and not a feast, something simple that didn't have to be driven to, get in the car, close the fucking doors, look around, lock them, stop to go to the bathroom, stop to drink some water, change drivers, get there, out of the car, oh somebody's fell in a hole, will we ever get there? Just a weekend trip in your fucking mind, take care!

Bend a little, it's getting dark in the park, haze haze, what comes out, less more is a trick betrayal, what other kind, what other mind, that this, is just, what we do, you whose? these, and those, ache. Clap. Out of anger move, only seems to take more, devolve around, motion I want, not fear. You jack-offs! I would've said, you jerks or you motherfuckers, but that's what Fern always said, jack-offs, jack-offs cross-legged doing the cross-word, hurts.

Send. Send big penis widowed quick direct to mind where sex can annihilate instinct, there's instinct galore, wipe it out so we can suffer to think real heavily and right through, real through real right and come out with such an intelligently edited film. Suck it.

If the penis, Lacan, existed only in the mind then it would be possible for even the most simple minded insect (trouvé) to find your thought and enlarge on it horribly, is that why you keep reversing directions? Afraid to meet the man walking his dog on the road? And just as I wrote the word "simple-" (to be followed by -minded) a whirring thing attacked me flying and I flew up in a rage and swatted at it mindlessly. He went away. Bang. So I'm violent and unwitting as any bitter american mind.

Of course, he's write in his essay on bleeding and food (La Mère Decolleté et l'Ingestion Engagé). Amer (Fr.), bitter (I was right) and Erica who I sometimes met after Mass on Saturdays (her mother conducted us weaving kimonos for Chinese orphans in the basement and they resurrected us, I mean rewarded us, I mean me with MANGLED HANDS, a book) subjected to tongue kissing!

You want a part in this play? Fuck it it's dark out. Ink drink and pills and fear, you know what I fear. Now that I've fixed the Ford I realize I don't have to eat it, I'm not even hungry though I should be, dutiful eat, you alive? You catch cold? Queer day today 4 memory. Dear Dr. Lacan, My memory Other tells me your point is well-taken but I don't like to talk to him, usually it's like getting stuck in your own throat, if I eat more I'll choke, if I race to the water-fountain, I'll fall, if I inch out or crawl, my heart will cave in, if you mention my name, I'll kill you. There's a fire escape in the house, I'm sitting on the dangerous window sill, there's a sunrise on the stage. I'll tell you a secret: I'm going to 81st and Riverside, the best way to get back on the highway at Canal, when you leave me off, is to turn down Watts and take Varick to Canal. It's hardly Easter. Pacques. Free World Foreign Cars. My first woman driver. The pact with the analyst is to be low, I'm low. I'm in the blue room. The songs are history: I'll get by as long as I have you, Hello I love you won't you tell me your name, I am waiting, I am waiting, Oh yeah, Oh yeah, Waiting for someone to come out of somewhere, I am waiting and whenever I see guys on the street who are looking at me (ecstatic) I mumble and sing, Oh yeah, oh yeah in Melanie's voice, a lot of the Beatles but Melanie's voice cracks all the time time, I am waiting, and back to I'll get by as long as I have you: "Yeah but what about me and the Red Sox?" A musical of Lacan's text, a muscle of Lacan's text, my mood depends on you: "Yeah but what about the Red Sox?" Plays are always in days, curves means "means" and plays as days curves the plays, they are already written which curves plays are what are always being written, never the novel or the poem in public. Marcelin Pleynet, a member of the Tel Quel group, wrote "Reread What Is Written" and I gave that to you: "Yeah but what about me and the Red Sox, how does language divide?" Into bungalows.

Stars come out, I can draw them on the page, on stage. For a moment they know everything. See: Subject Bernadette M. (not her real name) rewrote her letter to the designer from whom she was seeking advice: my couch is peacock blue and my entrance-way is normal. Therefore, what struggle should my carpeting be? Can you divine it for me and reply in language?

Dear Dr. Lacan, The penultimate distance between myself and you (if you were sitting on the peacock (that is, where it is presently placed in the room) and I myself and I were all-in-one like a cat half-dancing on the absent you (I mean rug) (sic), would _____ be large enough (how can I describe it all in two dimensions?) so that my gaping yawn (cette béance lettriste*) and the dawning sigh that such an opening evokes, reverential towards all human presence, could not be heard by you and yours?

Audit, aud-ible, auditable. Please take this into account: all metaphor is present to be given, energy to receive is politically diverted and discourse satirizes (in our century which is a decade) recourse, a desperation not to be relieved like the idle tortures of poetry and analogy. What is the cost? Like all wars we battle specialization.

Subject Bernadette M. (not her real name). Dreams: Blue room can't change and fire lights bloom in the cheeks of her amazing mother, no! And her lover who assumes no identity comprises a compromise, is stubborn enough (he hates the word) and by the way I've got Memory on the wall and little memory is just a hamlet in an African mud town cause after all it's the peacock that rises and its language that decides to be punctual to the end, reinforces what goes backwards and is stubborn enough—remember those little towns, they looked too much like this: mushrooms in the jungle, thatched roofs, maybe arranged in a circle, who cares? The tribal protection is non-structural, toward its center. "Is that why you don't like mushrooms at all?" "Mushrooms, dead matter, is that why you like them?" "Yeah but what about me?" Is stubborn enough (grass huts)...but why call them "hamlets"? Hamlets is a whole group of growths like those. Enough to place his identity as a parenthesis. He says it is one. I wish I had the exact quote, neither of us can remember it but it made me see ("Can you get it on and off easily?") see this: (   ). Look up hamlets and parentheses, you see expansion and need or rather, duplication, and as an addendum, (to me), nothing. It's nothing but a phloundering, but something could come of it, zooming out of those brackets erected in such an ingenuous zone of genes and veins. Geniuses push at their forgive me eggshells and every one in a while, pretty often in fact, they state to fathom. Chromosome? So that makes me think of good Raymond Queneau, author of Zazie dans le Metro, a filthy book which barbarous Louis Malle made into a funnier movie than ever was before cut quick. Prince Spaghetti, I'm an expert on starch, carbohydrate fuels, and could fool you right now into thinking that basketball players quite naturally should switch from caviar before the game whose bitter equivalent is steak, to a big bowl of pasta like mother used to make, "she never did," discount her, cause then you could last 37 minutes, Dear Central Willis Reed, just running on the evenness the consistency of the food and not its nut-quality, only useful in the long term. Maybe this conception has more to do with erections which the polymorphic phonemes all around me just make me want to play with all day long, but watch out. I like the nut-quality too! There is something to devouring a nut so quickly with so much in it that can't be a serious misteak, please believe me Dr. Lacan, I wanted to better my dreams through La Langue but what's the word for tongue? I don't have time to look it up and senses seem to diminish what's contained in the dictionary even if the book's engaged itself so far as to be ticklish, in fact, there's a lot I'd like to do: a dip in the sea, get back the blue room, get something to suck, get back the blue car with its specially responsive attentions to the road. Why don't we do it? And most of

---

* *Why does she assume, without full knowledge, that the béance is feminine? (See Proust's roosters).*

all to take that walk down the street straight down and over, over and across in the middle of traffic, no fears we're not on that kind of expedition, light changes we up and buy a hat and more. What's more? Like the Rat Man, like the Wolf Man, like Dora and like me, we spent some money and hung the honey on the door, just the two of us, I learned from you that you are me and since we're free to be switching, let me take care, I'll take good care, you took good care, of me, of you. Dear Dr. Lacan I'm the doctor, nurse me. Cause there's one thing I forget I forgot, I didn't get anything for myself there, no that's not it.

●

Is consciously in potency, in consciously is potency, unconsciously impotency, is consciencely in potency, in concientsly is potency, a bird: "Why then when that pretty little bird looks at you so happily and confidingly, you can't help feeling ashamed to deceive. I call them (children) little birds because there is nothing better than a bird in the world."

Coffins: what could psyche be possibly in that strange box in the closet, like a tool box, like a giant metal lunch box only this one's larger and what could it be? Two boys and a calm dog were watching t.v. (the works in a drawer). A German Shepherd or a dog named "Piper." "Yes we all do wake up with some kind of erection." As the t.v. sucks in. Breathe in, breathe out, fold your arms both of you and watch.

The male mechanic, the female electronic: you are your father's electrician, how do you do what you do to me, if I only knew how you did it to me, then I'd do it to you... In the middle of a long journey and so on, I was in the middle of a long...interrupted at the coffins, ugh! Everybody hates it and I don't blame them, dream the hateful dream, I was hungry but who knows now where my investigation of the box, investment of or in the box would've led me, lead me, Miss Take: an error's been made in the sex of the child, she withers she whispers she races ahead of you you whisper some secret: how can you cave create care which can weigh as an atmosphere of gravity lifts cloud cover within the body and within the mind? If I'll settle for care it won't be a settlement except in the sense that the tribe might roll on the earth for years trying to feel the sense of to get a sense for the best spot, their spot, a space for planting. I may recreate states but their conscious recreation is a new state (it seems to have been said). My self an environment that consists of all that I'm aware in what cannot be lost, an equivocal sure, as can more than human say, it follows: what can I give you today? Will force a sure choice can control lines and dots and even t.v., form an image that must be reassembled by the eye. Eye-sun, an open "A," my "I"—the sun as the iris, the Egyptian eye. My I and yours and I a pupil now I have these lovely flowers in my eyes. This must be the West Side Highway I travel in the analogy and all the rest every day and all the blue suns, a pigment I can invest and the aphelion. I, my axis, my revolving, my revolutions on this axis, my earthquakes, meteor. In this conception there is a moon at the aphelion in the corner of my eye as if it's outline were an axis for rotation. And showers, I'm rained on and the rest, all the rest every day: the sun's "my earth," the earth's "my moon" and the father's "my child," the child's "my mother," "The child is the father..." and that must be reassembled by the eye.

Real research is all rumors, like, move over so we can set another place so we can move in all directions, the child is father to the man, I can't write R's and I leave out A's: misdemeno: maybe my crime is now on the stage of being reduced so far to a misdemeanor: she'll get off, she's never been arrested before, no, she's a three-time loser, this time it's life, is that it: "A patient I got out of jail." You get them all out of jail, you dope! I hope, maybe some like those convicts go begging to get back in, I might from the dangers I've seen you free me to create. I surely do love you is brave, motherfucker. What'd I say? Like smoking the dope in Ann Arbor, or wherever, or, and what can I give you today? I can give you trouble, run hide, down up, that's Jimmy Reed in 1958, bright lights big city, I'm out.

As you'll soon see room, I'd rather be angel than anger, no sex is aggression, that's a double entendre and if you can't hear then you can't spell and if you ain't here all the time, then you can't tell nothing to me anymore. Oh no, now tell me something I don't know, what did you have for breakfast, dear?

Note: I put the trouble on the page to save the funnies for you, I decided to talk as black as a ball as I am too both undescended, what a grotesque passage, Lord help us and buy us a Mercedes-Benz. That's Janis Joplin and it's the greatest revival of all time, as they say.

Dear Dr. Room, By funnies I mean my sense of humor, black again and why am I calling you all these different names? It's a study habit. I mean a study concept, no a study hint. Oh fuck it last night I thought I would die again amen, I couldn't swallow and hated them parents as far as it goes so of course then I thought then that they'd die too or least of all one so the amicus reliable environment constructed a cross-culture structure-ism 4 me that went sweet (sweep it up clean) just like this: nobody died yet and nobody knows the trouble I seen with my own two (fuck it, it's for your benefit) I's. I's as calm as a peach in a way, that emerald one, so's my birth stone, remind me to tell you about spelling bees and the last one, I lost it in the finals to the little prick of the fine print cause much too smart for just thirteen she spelled trenchant (now cut em up quick) for an audible "transient" and they sure come and go pretty quickly so I usually try to get paid in advance now which spells champion and the word "illustration," just memories 4 clues as to how to egress out the door without missing much—go slow—without missing anything, she bet on a horse to show, she was just 18 and choppin wood…?…but the money's no good, that's the Band: "The Night They Drove Old Dixie Down."

●

So sensitive to smells on Horatio Street, a friend and admirer is down and out, there's always something burning in the city and nothing to fear from it, nothing in other words, what I was trying to say today about the feeling I had when we first sat down together was that I looked at you suddenly (one of us was off-guard) as if you were my "projection" (not simply parentally) and then, noticing that all of this was completely untrue, I was startled by the lie of it, so startled in fact like a jump of the springbok I ever was, just a second. Lyrics: I swore I saw that my face had taken on an enormous character, quite like you, I saw it was the same so I'm swimming into the waves as Barry rolls on the floor because he's famous and he's got five dollars, his father gave it to him, everybody was a fat baby there.

I dream an eye cut out, but before, someone's eye was cut out first, who's first. Maybe that's why Poe is long beyond words yet disappearing overnight.

●

Joyce: What is the mechanism of the mind human mind that at one point says to itself, what, but what does it say? If I knew that I'd know why I'm faltering and pfloundering...that says to itself, I'm allowed? Aloud? Quick, think back, you know what it is, I shall be released, my character's changing, I'm not an actress, invulnerable as human, words, a willing word, is not come easy by, is not come by, must stop for a minute, I challenge you, I'm at my worst, acceptance of the view, but from what level of alliance? And you, you are the energy which forces me to tell and to tell you, the greatest envy of them all, to their envy, to tell you that the kind of love that sustains the energy I've imposed on you is impossible any more. Anymore, that's history but do you see the awful irony in this (and here I'm not even dealing with the issues, I can't, but with the evidences, with the issues as they are reformed), irony and why I can't still do it, even though the greatest earthquakes and firecrackers of all time are dying to dynamite the iron from my heart of iron simply to let me use it, fiercely, to cease and to create something, mine it, in the most human way, synergy/resources, you see the crack in this, I know it. And I see it tumbling too. I had to clothe you with that kind of love and now the clothes get thrown right back on me so sloppily that eye can't see, eye is covered by a shirt or maybe even a vestment, and what do I do and you are waiting. Before, I was waiting, the future will be nothing like the past, please, that might seem like an odd thing to say today but dig it, change that to honey, cause I can't. It's not the little engine that could, that one couldn't think clearly, this one a genuine engine with faults, that is cracks and striations, oh shit I fall in again I am not scared, but, where am I falling endlessly into. Beginnings are necessarily early and an early drought in the midst of too much rain...and the writing, I've something to write about that: it seems to me now (my electric typewriter's just arrived from Philadelphia) that the writing is false a false front like the clothes I threw at you and you, so good you are, threw them right back. Notice I never put them back on, fit arms into sleeves, etc. They're just all over me like a grave and what you did, that wasn't really wearing them either but the words on paper were (!) a code like I said, a dense code, a way to think to work without thinking, a talent, an exploration sure, but how many buts can I put in without revealing I'm resisting, maybe a stick up the butt, what I done to you. Why'd I say that. Equals. So much hunger never to feed in the water never to breathe there: "Break up." I'm stormier. Who? You and me? Chance we'll… See I'm not even thinking about "dead." But dead as word pops up, so but still yet, I used to use adjectives like peculiar all the time, now I'm up to conjectural adverbial conjunctive convulsive prepositional towards "The So" of it. Does that mean more motion emotion is capable of being descried described synchronous with the view, silly languages, but but I but if I still I can't even yet, but maybe almost, form, I am so disappointed (that I may yet disappear), do you see it?

Discard the book: When you first I am enabled to touch with you (immigrant so) that you know was something that could raise up all expectations that the past made me sure held all solution, as we said. A boundless love in this sense that is with you (leaving me senseless) is very complicated. But as an answer, which you say is wrong or impossible, please show me, as an answer it is perhaps the most impossible again to give up. Let me try to say to you another way: maybe better I didn't write, is it, were it better to say, and is that Lacanic? Another way: if the depth of my neurosis emerged without relation to love… I've just fooled myself, that would be impossible for anyone. (Have a) But, if I had come to solve the problem of compulsive shoplifting, say, wouldn't it be easier, what is that? Easier for me to abandon the complex of my history and reform. No, I've got it all mixed up again. I guess the shoplifter and I are at least both looking for something for free. This thing with Max where he's no longer my "prisoner" this is very bad because now I'll try to hide my feelings from him and our love, mine and his, like I feared from the start, even, daring, there's no guarantee on that. Guarantees on all stolen goods. So I feel like I am nothing and want to steal, I want to steal and be a revolutionary, I want a response, I want to alter the environment, remember? It's like a vision, I want an answer, I'm not thinking complicated, I'm thinking fairly free, play the simple and see what you come out with. But, and but, that love is something to give up (give yourself away). I'm so disappointed I will die, will iron burn? The mix with you, ally, to make an indestructible alloy. I will describe myself. I am all curtains torn, I am tall and right now I have no stomach to speak of, I don't have to go out at eight, but, neither do I have a choice, my arms are cold and I'm somewhere I'm used to being, lucky thing I'm pretty or what would I have done all these lovers. Something else. The thing I hate about the analytic method is too revealing to tell you. O my possession, will you have to human too? The objects of the past become, no it's the past that radicalizes humans into objects and there's no driving through that kind of field without a crash, everybody's field day. Nighttime too. Especially dreams. Max is scared. Here I am. Will I be able to take care of him? If I can remember enough. Perhaps something new.

I dream I will always be "separate from my job." A vigilant sleep, I quarrel with no one. Then spring (the revolver) adds a revolver to make it sound tough. In Meissen, she was raped: skewered language to make it fit on, to make her stop. A reunion on subways where the clown says: "42nd Street, Home of the Supreme Court of the Land where they serve hotcakes." Hotseats?

You shouldn't always be here, Hello this is Dr. Witticism, Please hang up and hang yourself.

●

A man on a bench with ears: writing for nothing, writing for free, can't look, can't see, when do we eat go round the circle bend, bend even in Meissen where the Dresden china's made, made and lasts forever, the cab: you lean back, the sky's overcast, you don't lean against the door so you can't fall out, grey (sperimental writing, scuse me) the Big Boat Cristoforo Colombo, I don't wanna miss nothin, it's gonna rain, grey river, so, what but what I say, and, what but what I do, can be, can is, come through, like ginger in a silent cinnamon surreal, low-gic, disorgan, izing grass (stàde du miroir) and re-organ (music) assemble ING (hoarse grasp): a man who looks like a flower smoking a tuber.

Real small: just like I don't know, so far into this, how I got myself, little more you do know how you did: two pepper plants'll grow real big, edible peppers to show you how not to be so careful: separate, align, what time it is, more time, synchronous time, evanescent time, ripped out, one time, a relatively new, inevitable, intention-invention. How does the sacrosanct disarray go away?

Here I am at Grand. A man who holds his fists tight while walking is a woman clutching her beaded bag, something hanging. Can't wait to get home he said, me too I said. Can't wait to get home he said, me too I said, dirty dreams. Scared Mesopotamia and isolated drill drills into you, learn penises wait like mottoes, toes? Mottos the sotto voce bottoms of mottoes are bait, Don't Tailgate Raw, it doesn't provide a hood for you Monsieur Salvadore Allende, I don't have a curl, he said to me one day do you feel this? Back back back one day, one two one two one and one and one and one, couldn't help it, save me repeating god! Like a moth but hums drills into you is set back, play day, got enough energy is just a matter of time fusion one. Has he got enough energy is just a matter of something, Fusion One? Fusion one is an address and the name of today is play, who knows, in air space? Air space, that's an address: Zip Air Space, Please answer my call please place my call to the man who answers it what the fuck is right, is it? Get yourself a fair hearing to boot. Get yourself a good nugget. They aren't sotto voce bottoms they're sotto voce booms of course and both of us are lost in a forest where we have to go out with others and alone, not with each other, what kind of vacation is extinct in that?

Ms. Masters of the language, divorce, mistakes of the driven person who speaks, advance and divorce, they are ready for the measure of time's announcement for merging and prearranged pronouncement as they say in the trades is succinct is sufficient for the more core reminiscence that keeps coming up in spades, you dig it &c. Mothers and fathers! Attend the ceremony whose code words are written out in what looks like a real language, the kind you find sinking in stones, wipe them off and get a silk ribbon, the red and the black, stones come late. What's on the plate for dinner, christ. Terrific! She's smitten with the war wounds of men like a surrealist comma in love with absence an absence of hatred fills in love that can't be written too clear, at least not for the ruling public who's smitten, themselves, with jades, that's stone you mother, case you didn't know you fucker, seek out and end up. Hard hot shit. The word cock and the word sucks twenty times over. Then the word more over and over and fish roe and memory, fish roe and memory, fish roe and memory! That's quite a coincidence! Just a demonstration / (this is a song here) / Just a demonstration / Just a piece of information / Please come have my nominal formation / From out love comes through / (repeat) Viet Cong you can come up with almost completely surrounded with by water or anything water or water or WATERORWATERORWATERORWATERORWATERORWATERORWATERORWATERORWATEROR water or autoerotic underwear, let's look again...a water error and more roe! Both kinds of roe! Like Dutch water. And gold yes oro, the Morse code's enough for fifty spades but the gold in them mountains whew! $$$$$$$$$$$$ galore you can bet your sotto voce dollar on it you can bet it comes down just a little bit too hard and they see then and then they see & and when you press in their hand just a little bit too hard and then they see they see you counterfeit bum hideous counterfeit piece of nothing in their hands they'll know and when they question you then they'll find out you drink all day and they'll find out you drink all night and they'll find out you never ever think you never think you never think nothing just drink all day never thinking and they'll know then and there's nothing you'll be able to show them cause every time you start to try to tell they'll just ask another question and the answer to which will be yes I drink at five o'clock too and no I drew I never drew a fair day's pay and this paper money's all I ever drew fuck you. I had my lunch and now I'm drunk again but if they never printed all that paper money, you see, nobody's listening but if they never done up all that paper for money do you see then I never wouldn't've thought of hanging paper like I done and now I'm done. Hold on!

H2O
Forestry's trendy, this way please
Do you need a job for a fortnight
Among the trees?

Please lean to the left
And observe the bees, watch out
For others endanger like these
Your salary's money in the form of
Bees, bees that won't sting you
As they spasm your gullet
Excuse me, I have another
Patent on you to reassemble
Kids is a hassle, no time
Forts and castles, for feeding
Goodbye.

●

Martin Bormann and Bernard Martin in Boulder Colorado: "Now we'll get back to this." "What?" "The prison-separation scene—it makes no other sense than the way it does." "How's that, L.M.?" "Closed."

●

A man with a briefcase and the outline and the veins of two polly-noses. Jewish men talking about the war and I'm able, a weekend song. Seventy-two men and a chance to move chance into the spoken light. So much else so many places designed to have been impressed by design, I'm back in my careful stage, the stage of age and representation, a member of the Basic English, that's the same war, war on time, smoke stack skewer and a whole long line, smoke peace pipe kinder, swerve, back means below the surface of the pole at the south, means means curves, a man in a baseball cap with two big hands. Poet pitchers pour or poet pitches poor, take your privates with you, we are not responsible for property, is theft amen. The sweet high way is to move and to stop when disorder is vanquished, so is: a) an old memory, b) a nothing, c) everything, d) a boy in a girl, e) a girl in an elevator, f) a new memory, g) something that goes on forever, is a lie, h) the idea "It can't be…"—Janis Joplin, j) "It must be…"—Beethoven.

A house of plaid. The idea is: his feet were full of blisters, the flame came up and burned his pants, and now he wears his sisters.

●

Meissen (co-incident with Auprès de ma Blonde)

Have them come. The best is in the beginning. Armies may fly and falter. A detour may deter. So rest in the middle. A doctor is in error. He denies defiling the child. The denial is then dissolved. Disavowed. The doctors office is full. Above the wainscot, Dresden china, made in two firings, hangs in the antechamber or waiting room. China, the doctor explains, is a vitrified ceramic ware of clay, feldspar and flint. Despite the name, Dresden china was made in Meissen. Now the doctor throws this in as a feeler. Everybody's out. Now if you do that, spread it thin, it won't mean a thing, it's old hat. Now if you are here for a visit, there's no point in saying so repeatedly, therefore, the doctor says again, we will sit through more and more consultations, but never, he impresses, learn when or where or why or how or how often the habit may be held to or may have been broken and who began it and who first brought it to light and then how to end it.

The door opens then closes. (1965.)

●

I think you've got all my pens, you've taken all my pens. No, I've left them there, cover the rift, cover the rip, well he might act in it because of his name: Raw War. The Girl in Grey (War's the impostor who comes out in clay on the burning stage) gets baked and takes off for a twirl at the spin of the girl, binary girl's her gold sweet baton, girl's her honey cloth cold sweet baton, you don't know rain war is like department of peaches, gonna rain for sure, blue blue beautiful, thank you very much. I think that the prison doors should close. Hello, are you on the bus or off and will they see me see me see me off, there, not there, everything and nothing, to become admitted to the subject and world it all around as a space is aloud if I scream: Dear bear, will you will you the same scream too? Rehearse release, clue you, by.

The unions dreams: 81st Street: 2 trips 4 food (1 by subway) with Bartholomew: bread and coffee, nuts from the other store in a separate bag secretly, Clan MacGregor bottle for the brandy surprise; Max and Andy: a cloth, "You aren't throwing that away…?" Then the black box, I write something on it, you can't read the last word: "I was to so many checkered places…" On a field sable…the red and black lines criss-crossing, "…as if the dust of the two sleepers had no right to mingle." "The Letter A, Gules." "…a herald's wording." Gules, the red-dyed ermine, the judge's coat, the mouth and the throat. Sables, mourning clothes.

This is about turning over: First the unions I almost lost that dream though my memory is excellent for words. Then we make two trips and I turn them over in my mind: "a going back for food." I meet Bartholomew near some grass in the park perhaps. We shop together and the nuts are imitation nuts or analogs but now the man is counting them in with my bill. Along with a loaf of rectangular bread, I start to put that neat into a bag, secretly I'm arranging the separate bags for the food, there's coffee coffee by Aram Saroyan and there must be a pint of brandy, it's an expensive store, cause when I get home I hide the brandy in the closet as a surprise for Max and Andy when their pint runs out. Next to it is a prettier bottle that belongs to Proust, a blue bottle that says, "Clan MacGregor." There's a cloth, a headpiece, like the one that Max wore painting, lying on the table, I bought it or made it and Andy says, "You aren't throwing that away, I can use it." And the black box that opens like a professional sweeper and I write a sentence on it but the last word won't stick.

Next the orange city: if you get bored with apples (that are good for your teeth) then you can eat the orange city which is full of candy and you can crawl inside it too, it's in layers, it's not a maze, it's a feed-house like a doll's house, it comes in a box and is made of cardboard. Good for you. Here is one section of the orange city.

Next Mahoney gets murdered by a blow on the back of the head or neck or maybe just a blow on the back and the thing that hit him was a little doll of stone that cracked in two from the blow and the doll, in both parts, was also singed, here is one part and here is the other, I've marked off the singed part. Burn, burnadeck ("The boy stood on the burning deck...").

So the garage seems to be empty, maybe they're moving (Mahoney was my mechanic of Adams and Mahoney, he used to tell me to get married). Next when shadows are engrossed in so defenseless a license and the apple business practical, essence is divisive, I think, lessonizing. There's a businesswoman who got herself involved in this. Written on Cocteau's face: "I used to be...a...but now I'm for hire by women and I think I'm bisexual anyway cause I've loved..." And so there are different spots on his body, beautiful Cocteau, I turn his head. And Pierre gets us cheeseburgers from a place that's closing: "It's great what being a doctor..." and drinks. And the wife of a POW: "It's no challenge to love him, love him." And you have to swim somewhere to get there. I can hardly think.

●

No matter what the above
what comes before stands for
it means they
won't let me die
and as a piece in this frame
(I make that mistake over and over)
Again today when
I created your absence
today when I created your absence then
the whole tone of the day
was like the rest of a day
pick any one any one that
any of the dead ones died
To be simple: I was aware of that.
When colors come clean at the edges, this is how mescaline works.
But when they do when can you look? Aloud.
It's only when you can't look at them
and to remind you the tone of a day
A day I was spectacularly reminded
of what you do and how you look

Day any of the dead ones died,
But not me.
Before that all weekend I expected to die.

But instead they got us a housekeeper and she turned out to be this terrific young French girl named Lisette, Dear Marie, and one day she was crying in the kitchen, no that's no good, and we embraced, she was crying on the couch in the living room and we embraced and we made love and so immediately she took me to meet, no not immediately cause that night at the dinner which she prepared we giggled a lot and mischief and mystery and so first chance we got she sneaked out I mean I sneaked out, no I didn't have to sneak out, we met and she took me to meet her boyfriend who was also French and then we all began making love so that the day after my sister got married Lisette and I and Jean took off towards the mountains together in a truck. Now what would we do for money? No first of all I left notes for both my sister and my uncle. To my sister I said love you both and don't worry we'll have a good time and no babies and to my uncle I said don't worry I'll be back and I'll write to you and it really is better this way and I didn't write but I secretly hoped that he wouldn't try to find me and I would write often to reassure him but always be careful to have the letters forwarded by friends in other locations. And what about money? Well the Monday I left I forged my uncle's signature on a withdrawal from my account that was in trust and it worked and besides, for the months ahead of time I had been secretly saving money, taking money out of what he gave me to spend. So that eventually we traveled all over, we traveled all over and soon we met Lisette's father who thought our arrangement couldn't last forever and so he got involved. With me, I guess.

Always being given.

And even before that there were so many pastries and cakes I was rolling around in them, demanding things, special ones, strawberry cupcakes, my favorite, I was lying in them at the bakery, forging desires I didn't even have for the sheer joy of demanding, of making demands all night, baking all night, all for me, to lie in, to destroy the half I couldn't eat.

I want a woman
I want Lisette
Sure I go backwards
Sure I murdered you
Sure you can move
Sure I don't want to
Except to die before—
Before what?
                    Before Cocteau pins me down
Before Cocteau pins his beautiful dead body on me,
Before I pin that beautiful dead one on you
      that's something that cannot be done
Anymore than I can die
                              just pure by wanting to
Anyway
I'd rather die
than make that compromise with you
Before
Before
Anymore
Anyway
                    which would involve
Beyond the past
                                    issues so trivial
As
      trips to the moon on Stockbridge I envy you
      and the raising of money erect for liberal women
      and the seeing of men too
                                          men as well
                                                or even others
Any others
And absence now there's one of mine
The greatest revenge on absence is beauty
But nothing haven't any all
And why go on if it's just to use up your
            time as mine
                              even for love that can be left
                              even for love that can't be revenged
Anyway you can see
This is yours.

Baja California: I go to Anais Nin's party. A man and a boy on a shore with holes. And re-runs: a fortnight a curl a mistake a largesse a current, moments of memory lapses as: I wish I were in the ocean or in the café where people meet, drink wine all day and stagger home to sunny homes, a day. Hot is sun on should be wet, my sex is between my legs, the birth canal, covered with pants, a pair of pants they're jeans, jeans all over Cocteau Genet and Jean-Claudes and -Pierres, jeans resting in pants. Women were and as they are a need to be complete: we multiply, our faces cry and complex as universe studies and learns by altering the perception of beginning towards the end, that's play.

Charlie Chaplin got up on stage and joined all the ladies into one big lady whose spouse ties on his red tie, along with the moon of his (own) question woman and the third joke is this: "No more Mr. nice guy." No, that's not it, and the third joke is this, that was Hitler when he saw the Allied planes come to bomb Big Berlin and the third joke is this: but this is different. A time to pare the language, to cut it down. The other one makes noise and perhaps the chronology is somewhat imperfect and perhaps the chronology is joy, perverse joy and perhaps maybe baby the chronology is song and chronology is unintelligible babble of babies falling, falling off the floor in danger of falling, falling falling flailing dangerously about, they're out on the streets, they're looking good, down through the jail rails, rails of the fire escape they tumble, babies tumble because they are so slim, tumble down to Mexico, read this and make it easy to read, go away green, what'd I say baby what'd you say, nothing good in it for all, it does no good I mean to be writing in the same old book.

Comic books, anything. Anything so, anything C vitamins, anything mine, anything exam, anything ination, anything central, anything canal, anything adrenal, anything secretional, anything excretional, anything sexecretorial, anything sexexpictional, anything sexualexplicatorial, anything asexuallisalistening, anything polymorphicalizadepictional.

Sunday October 15

Do you know that we slept with the Luddites last night? Sun goes in and ought to, flying. The word you misspell the word that extends itself is out. Reread what is written: at 6:55 we are going to the movies. Luddites the lummox and the bullox, a passion for the same, complete, is complete. No more details than that of a black meadow.

And dream from the wind crashing things that men on the fire escape ascend to rob Barry's loft but when they get up there it's so empty and so white and clean, there's nothing to take (we have all of Barry's things) and all there is is a white bed, white bed of the black meadow with a mirror next to it, longways: and all of the loft is white, floors blend into ceilings and didn't you investigate the robbery? Of course I did, I went up, I took care of it, there was nothing to take, the robbers were women, three of them like the ones who could rule the world, as they were sitting at a table trying to snap their own necks.

And they took nothing out of the empty place. Are you sure? And Merlina Mercouri, and Marilyn Monroe (The Prince and the Showgirl), and Electra (the prince is a trickster).

Tom's absence forces the t.v. on and the trickster is everything. I say: You can't...and leave... I say: Lisette were Bernadette. I say: You can't...get...anything...out of me now. You are too ready for it...nothing good about it...something copies, as, ...the re-translation of the dream, blue and white the opaque windows. Who is my shadow? Black eyes in Pleynet's black meadow...

List: finish the movie, answer the mail and write to Fern too, no, she's back, get the projector, type Pleynet's article and run it off, find a way of waking up in the morning, get food and vitamins and boots for Max, do the laundry, get a table cover, wash the windows, rewrite "Fast Food," call Ted Thompson about The Scarlet Letter, sew pants and scarlet letter on, go to the bookstore twenty times, rewrite the Marble Faun screenplay, no, don't, leave it as it is, get Andy a present, go to the country, see who comes along, type and run off "Fast Food," real quick, write a script for Irwin's "package," get a big box for the money, get a coat for Max, pick up new notebooks, grow the male organs, three, study the possibilities for timing things perfectly, rewrite the translation of "Le Tombeau d'Edgar Poe," borrow Holly's t.v. equipment and record the basketball game, wait to hear from Clark to work on the cave writing, find money for cave movie and winter camp in the Arctic and "Fast Food."

Monday

Grace had the lead in a play in a gay bar, her name was Feeling-Good-4-Myself. What about Who-Fixes-the-Food? He'll come out O.K. Gina drinks club soda. In school: testing 4 "alone"—one, two, three...

Tuesday

I'm in Francisco Newman's arms, we're flying on a plane: "Being (forced to be) constantly together...how long can we possibly...?" Trying to pay for Max's sports gear, new converses, new ball, some glue. The bill is sixty dollars or $11.17 and some more cents. We have to pay on the train, they wouldn't take it beforehand.

In a dream "my image" was an actual thing to be seen. Convex.

Goddamn skunks and beavers destroys the purity of the busy flat white page, ate each of you, threw it all up, sentences are pricks, period, you ate you and you couldn't stand it, couldn't stand up either, now you're tussling for attention, prick up your ears when you don't know the even environment of pain, fed up for the last time, of this is artificial creation then never created again can stand up under it, despise your filthy romantic faith in evidence like the facts of survival is nothing to ache how I feel can't bear being here, can't even be bear nevertheless snooze. Eat shit. Penis hunters of the century of the goats staining the rocks with a red that makes your neck preserve a fever the body cannot support, fever for pain even, fever for the severance of pain, sure there's more, sure there's everything another human and I can't ache but you forget forever forget forever unconscious that I am the one who thinks as everyone and has to be those and this I cannot sustain with the knowledge feeding me that you give me and then you surname it away as if it never happened, as if the father was the law, as if anything can filter out, as if survival was a word that, coming up again and again, means anything in relation to other people except loss, the one we spoke of as guaranteed anyway and piss the other how many are there, just two or three anyway, the other, he can't take it either and you can't work on him too much as you'd both be ready and loving. It's non-fusionable as inflammable's the identical with non-.

And if I make the mistake of making an image I'll be giving in to the lure of giving you or anyone more pleasure's the mistake like valuable work, you can keep it, what design can be in it for me to inform non-sensically but feeling everything anyway.

I'm getting a hit off this, that's all, I care about not at all even. You can't expect it, you just assume it as it's impossible a total impossibility in relation to what seems to happen to me. No, in relation to what I've seen. It's such a mess I can't sleep in it. And a mouse. And for two, don't they always have to be doing the same thing or things together. And how could they want to. Or even if, how could they, and so it has to end for two. One is free, two is free but one is a book and two is a demonstration or a lesson and in this case there are twelve. The great thing about Gertrude Stein is she never had to write about anything. Had to. So the free flow of ideas. So laughter and pleasure and primitive noise. So the mouse rustles the bottle. Fruit of the vine and he comes over here, I can hear him which is longer as a table I rest on with my wine, imperceptible. Stronger than that. I'm sick and tired. Charcoal mellowed was the word and they have the same times as I do. So we talk can of concentration and someone rustles up upstairs. Never find out who is in it behind the door. Never mentions time will tell everybody the same episode and winks at you in particular. Bye bye.

Wednesday

Max's mother won't let me into the big feast because my dress is too sheer, it's a slip, two slips and arm and leg hair. She says, "no nipples," so I fix up her aquarium for her which is full of plants (we got it for her) but worms got in (are they live? yes, one is) and wash the windows of it while the big feast goes on in the other room.

●

It's cold and dark a sine die cold day, Max sneezes in his sleep after morning coffee is upside-down as the day is. So sure is a chronicle of uneasy meanness of nothingness of misery bling bling blank as J. Kerouac said of nothing in particular that makes noise in your house. Strong enough 4 2? What century what language is that? Back 2 the old and older forms list literary forms, cling bling badmouth 2 the literary now seeing as how it's all laid out it's there if only I could go out how without for far fear: I never apologized to anyone for bringing them along. Because of on the way. To nowhere anywhere you strong string along rivers, as bad or big as that? You said I was the water! No I was under the water. No you compared me like a fire to water. No! It was me that was the water and you were the rock, you let me in. Oh so what is dialogue. Piece. Nothing important as events occur you make them. You can go on as sure is as long as you want the table to be measured to fit the length the style of your own body. But many find it difficult to even to listen. Cultivate ears. I wasn't going to write and there's no title is a temptation.

There's nothing here
there's an absence
there's clear air
there's loaded nipples
there's no reason
there's a big feast

and a festival of unmade beds happy to see that cause I might have to live here and go on eating forever what seems like an ending, I forgot to use his title, I called him by his given NAME.

So what do I do? Check the list of things to do? So what do I make and how do I make em think know I'm the same my given name is Bernadette, I'm not a priest in the receptacle of the church, beds lined up and out of work, does somebody make em, does somebodys live out of em, do so many sleep in the same room, is my cold better as I sneak down the stairs and forget to use titles in direct address, how would I address the envelope anyhow, what's the name of the city, I only know the countries' names, a gang is with me, a gang climbs the stairs and passes by the door through, is it five yet? At five there's some hope of recovery, some chance of action, some hope of inspired by seeing something of your own that you did. After all, nobody's stupid it's just some bodies get hurt, they get crushed in attempting they get shattered and bent they have no enemies they get forced they get edged off the edge into a too surprising area, they get freaked, they get measured, I hate time above all, they get like monsters digging in the chicken soil, they get like owls, no eyes for them, they get immobile, they get perched and cannot move they get expectant and cannot come, something or someone cannot and all they are doing is waiting and all for love, they get empty, thoughts fill them endlessly and all they are doing is waiting, all they are wanting is motion.

Baby what you want baby I got it and all they are doing is wanting, seek out your own hand writing, hand writing of another one and pieced like eyes they look together: who am I speaking of and who am I talking to. I am talking with you, I am violating you, my length like the length of this table's body violates your separate right, stirring up dust, if any, your own space and plenty of motion, now why should you bother to be me in this way as a mix which is final insult as axe on the head of the murderer, is this, a public act.

And beyond that false ending on the last page on the cover of the book is a fake a last fake a fake in a series, fake tree made into a book, read and reread &c.

And beyond the space, no, the tree, the chance to go there: baby that's what you want baby that's what I got baby energy never leaks out and the tree is formless, it follows its rules around, like a fake.

Someone wants you to let you take them there and someone wants you, to let them take you there, and you find it out, what's there, as a struggle all ready, dying to explore, what's there as a piece, to mesmerize, to suck you in, to leave out to include all.

You gotta be ready you're ready, eyes violate as I do every day, all born. Now you tell me—can I say that?

●

A sneaker at the foot of a tree, a hand with an umbrella in it, a man with glasses holding a ball with two hands.

Thursday

The party, the dresses, the Roches (thrown out into) the park, a fight, the performance. I say, "No one can see."

Friday

Can't go back to New Rochelle, at first I think it's high school. Sometimes in a rush I can see things so clearly and everything is everywhere. Kathleen, my mother and this is on the day my father died and this is private, for no one and there are notes, there is writing on little slips of paper, in books, all over. They search for four missing men: yesterday I can't swallow again, today I can.

We collided we colluded, bread is made and all over: a shortage of bakers: at the Café Roma, at Food and so I ask Kathleen can she bake? Information will be the product of us. Prizes?

Prizes for this: already it's Sunday and everything, everyone makes me not be sure and what is valuable and what is of use, no one can see that producing something in any is any way meaningless, how. To record the New Rochelle dream, to get beyond the tree: little rocks are/of what came before and life is like: these repetitions of series, so I can get upto, the part where, I'm hungry for everyone, hungry for sex, taking, again, can't go back there. One hour.

I try, one day, I'm sick, Steve Katz is reading at 1:35, no time, I can't remember, it's spiritless, it's dead, I don't want to return to that place, kind of place.

And then (coke in a tank, washed and hosed): "If you are always dressed like that" (I'm in green…). My desire for women the color of school drinks out of the coke machine (punch bowl) memory: how is it there? They lock you in at night…you have to live like a prisoner, that's all, I won't write in the book much more, I refuse to record (if I could record) and notes about memory (I'm covered).

Max goes out only for a moment, it's interesting, it's a test of some kind, notes unbearable, notes collision and fight, collusion collation, but, the crust (I doubt it) stringing along, in many locations, spreading out thin many fragments that well have to be gathered, that will have to be shorn soon, shown and proven, in fact, written, as insults, rewritten by a pen rewriting (I only hope I can have time, that kind of time) by a pen rewriting the angel of the eyes gave her something.

She demands it, she plays at demanding it, "Spend time with me," this I'll send to anyone and so I can send it to no one, there's no one I can want, want, my weakness needs melting into that plan, never to remember is never to forget the willingness to suffer is what this chronicle might be and is and what it is not a memory so come, come over, a stream of visitors, a muddle a plan? No, remember to encourage the freedom of one, Max, remember to fight it just enough, fight a man fight a memory fights and motion secret caves demanding you down, demanding you down them, come down then, come match with me, sure. I see the diminishing, sure I see the flame, should there be limits set or release as born is, and you and you, you exercise, mention me.

I won't write much more, I won't even dream, but Mark survives the dream fight because his name is Mark and he lives with Bill Miller who is now in California and because the next day we meet on the street by accident, David Miller, who we never see and haven't seen in two years and he's been in prison and in the dream we are fucking, me and Mark and since we decide to go right on, it's O.K. even though Max comes in, he won't mind and Mark only has one ball and John

Giorno survives in fantasy, he's my companion, I'm living with him, he's my guide, I lie on him and today he visits me, after I dream (you can't keep up) of the two of us together side by side, "turn on the lights, no, all the lights," and someone tells me to, "Say you did it yourself and take advantage of that." So that it's not done to you, done to you again. And this has something to do with protection from bees, or, I should say, more protection from bees (right out of the cave episode), that doesn't fit in and twice I know Max must wake up early and go, and twice I dream that nobody called to wake him and it's past the time and so you see I must want him to go. I won't go any further.

I stay in, I stay covered and finally we find the bookstore we are always looking for, a new one, called Discovery, it's uptown somewhere, and we are in it, stealing. And I stay home with the oven on, cruising and which or what is anybody's life worth any more than that, no, and I won't write in the book again anymore.

●

I had a baby (it was early and it was me) cause somebody tried to feed it hashish and then suddenly it (boy-girl) (I felt around) was taking care of me and went out (alone through the streets) and got me one hundred and fifty dollars. Zazie.

I think we oughta build a room and then see what its use is. Are you pregnant? Maybe we could time it to share one delivery, no I just had one and adopt, you love, an Indian baby of Peru, oh no, whose eyes are like you, she says, and hands. Without lines. I don't want lines as, with words in them. The Hessian soldiers. Subjects: all subjects are inbred. "It can be done." For about and with someone. You are the activist, so, you are the clove, I am chosen, she thinks, to sensitize the parking lot, and how, by bringing men with beards around and how, to break ground and above the about with someone. And how. For you in fact. You energy. You make me want to be stupid and certainly stubborn. It's simple sweet and back of me are smaller presences of words. You! Get away from them and go see Ted's baby in the flesh, babies, frank, are never in the flesh, they are just awesome, like it (italics my own). Ben says that is simple. And M. says leave it out. But why? And cause, it's worth a thousand dollars will go far in Mexico and/or below. This is the only thing that brings me up when I am not up wherever I am and that thing is this: it's the rest of the story goes: one and one and one and on and on and on and on in writing.

But maybe your perspective runs off into the woods too often, my precious maybe you are dear. Hear it? Or simply say. Read. Exigency, I do not respect titles you never emerge from them holes. You (oo) can write all you want about writing, my mention, but you cannot do that. Act? How? Plenty is many is too much as human as any mind that assumes it knows and it does, doesn't it, the same as you and should I breathe into the line an I for perfect conception...divine it. You are fine but stop it. And you are mine, I didn't know that. (Listen: you can bring your new works and we'll all listen to em but I can't bring mine cause...) Anything a extra go at. As imitation. As divine from that. Ferret it out—you, see the ferret go? See it him? A mountain eh? A mountain you say. And everything. Please, not a stone in the dialogue please. Concentration ideal. Laugh at altered states, they do and do one. Laugh is plenty every make one. So, and so. The dog, that runs, is a breed. The dog that runs is a breed. I saw Fern tonight. Does she mention your name is vital. And Oregon? Not much fits. He said self together. I said he said self together weaves a story. Nobody much interested in reading. So then she said I said what he said is self together might someday weave a story as nobody much interested in weaving and letting things go.

Oh well they'll go, as soon as the parents go. Parents go we can have a thunderstorm everywhere a ripe one and a gay one and one of experience full of it sexual experience. And everybody reads. Moisten the finger that gets the pen. As writing is entered I will weave it till you do plum exercise your talent for design. One week and a half. (Back to that is different, period.) The delicacies of the page with speeding writing on it survival. Hopes. Hopes heaps of the owl leapt as the springing kind answers to the entering nothing. Breached, breached left alone small of the back, large stomach, benumbed eyes, dilated pupils, symphony of the arms and feet, excellent custard it all goes down and you study it so study it I'm telling you. Light of the eyes emeritus. They, who? Don't write very often, very precious cause after all so much of it, what can you do, but, but this, and here's what you do, this: for about with and with, someone is thinking as usual as always, someone is thinking hard, do you see the strength of this hand like ice continuing in presence, in absence continues, why does it seem to and who are you.

●

Dear Clark,

I'm sorry I can't answer the mail or make movies so. Someone "out of his/her system

Andy's thoughts on moments or timing or space, we found boxes, we picked up boxes, Greek and Bulgarian products get delivered in

the space between
just existing and doing something like,
writing a book that can be a book
You allow to be a book, or, instincts take you further
to a space beyond the allowed space
and so,
in between
there can be no such thingas a book
or,
but
the waiting around is difficult like, 1966 – 1970
(he shuts off the light, is he taking a pill?)
because I'm recording what someone cannot and I don't want
(like centered
like laundered clothes
you can't wipe your hands on)
a point of view
and you?
recording and beyond are the words I hate the most, among them
Put together, and not let self (let, there's another one)
FAMOUS!

famous Rimbaud dreamed at Night and nobody swooned identical. Here, air, heavily dotted by well oil barges on fire in the sea in the morning, we missed it, it went out in the afternoon fire of the poets who sleep till 3:30 and don't milk cows

Where air we?

A regular division

A plus

Can't get outta bed hello

Can't get outta sleep no need and I river anyway

So skid, speeds up to 70 mph

And I thought just the energy it took to hang on in the boat was too much but when I looked up and saw what I saw it could be much more and I didn't fall out, of the race

Now there's a comma

So precious

What you want me 2 do?

Accumulate, ha, men who live in white houses and centralize their heads, heaven becomes a pier on fire early morn, she was she was she was (a drawing of inputs) or, representative of something missing, indescribable language of the act, indescribable act and so Wilhelm Reich sits nicely on a well-written fence, men incumbent on the world as situation (Carl Jung's men and women are quite derivative as my parents once said), my parents once said: fantasy you like you store for us and we invite you like no one else, I am back where I started from, drums roll and the sentence begins and ends as upside, down as what you derive from with about and it, or, steer clear of the ones you know, the ones you don't know tell more and more, more to you who is familiar with any ground, he/she is (xisting) in no way, so way, syllable, resort, long ago, what should I do now

1 ate

2 much

3 many

4 ever

5 eyesights

6 sex

7 above

8 everything

9 children

10 is money &c. WATER!

Saturday October 28

It's hard to follow water but I'm rising, I saw a dip on t.v. in an ad for middle-class malnutrition, malnutrition like a pipe that divides to push in a dream where pains cease to make you have babies, and something else in three's is pushing out, yes, maybe, penetrate, perhaps, the music says so but however, crushed in here, car starts up and ///// or /////, will you read then? They don't know it you don't know it, I am resisting, I am resisting them. Them and done. But, unlike her, no focus, no chicken or roast beef, no values but tables as long... Kathy's art and homosexual are trinkets to play with. Discuss anything. So what? Empty. So what empty (I let him go out, alone). Structure leans on me, on Saturday musicians play but they don't experiment. What? Do. What do. Just over and over again and pierce out understanding like a plain heart, take it out of that word by modifying, too bad I am explaining, there were better how things to do. Like is. Are you?

They continue to return from their trips alive. But one does not and one does, two do and many others did and all. A dance in rain, and more piers and crackling noises. Invalid.

Hotel des...they can't go out, it can't go out, it remains, it stays without an umbrella. No memory, black is perfect. Other color is out of taste and taste is never perfect. He bides his times no doesn't he know how rain faster no continuing. Goddam music and goddam fans. It's not catching. No one caught on. And I didn't give much clues to anybody but, I expected a return and more serious than expected as written in individuals, individuals expect more than a bus to turn and stop. That is waiting this is more as ever was said above before. So think it. She said the rain is pretty as soon as she could look, she said I have a choice it's not any choice like when you dream up something, sure. Dialogues with many go on anyway. You're afraid to imitate, you're afraid to form I'm in a hurry, you're afraid to generate you think you're a little boy, you're afraid to show it to us, I'm in a big rush, I can't explain cracks in the terrain, grey floor, you have a choice there in spelling, you tell all will fall all fall call ball yell moll all toll swell all loll and itch in your sleep, all look. Soon mend this.

You get much back? Back of a station wagon goes in. You still around, siren stops. Burglar one of us. Armed. Goes on forever so. Can't look to see.

● BOOK III

Friday March 23 1973

It's time to make a new post. Wounded knee, wish I had one. I made up the new chronology. Sun's hot and it's easy out, time is getting later, noisy and smoke. Time is getting more animal, dream Stanislaus the pumpkin eater smoked a pot of pickled peppers at a poetry reading. Georgraphy: parts of the body, mass, centuries ago the moon was blue and roses hung from the gingkoes. Breathe, the you is out.

It was my turn to read but two bottles cracked, glass in the beer. Fragments of glass in the beer, no dice. Poet poetry post Poe. (I'm safe here) Lucy Lippard, rose of the women's art Mary revolution called me centuries ago, the sun was hot and two men got into a Cadillac. Stanislaus the pumpkin eater smoked a pot and couldn't meet her, couldn't meet to make love at all but I invited him. Men arguing. Men at their posts. Casual Stan couldn't meet her. That's the end. Double. Double Robin Hood got old. Families are all alike.

Wish I could initiate detail. Hoo hoo, hoo hoo. All owl. Cannibals too. It's Friday and everybody's going home, I'm in their sun. I've gotta make love with somebody's son. You may not like this, Mrs. B. and you may not like this, Mrs. R and you may find me skinny, Mrs. F and Mrs. B.V.M. and Mrs. P.O.V. but what was your maiden name.

There's a monkey in the parking lot, oh boy, I can't predict everything, what falls where and what's gonna fall, the monkey ran away and the black man comes, he rereads what is written on the parked car stub. No pay. Two-twelve. Dollars and cents. Or do you have a monthly income? Time to get serious. I'm doing the book backwards. Are you ready?

60 sheets, 11 x 14, that's 120 pages with a lot of words on each so, 12 words to the line, the sun's hot. And say, a hundred lines, that's twice what Moving was so, I can read ten pages in an hour. There's 240 and types of others. That's 24 hours, 6 in 24 goes 4: that's 4 days, six hours a day. I always stop when I'm near the end. Now, could I make it five that's five days, six hours a day: estimate 500 pages at 25 an hour, 25 in 500 goes 20 times, 20 hours, 2 in twenty only goes 4, that's 4 hours a day, we'll see. Lots of pauses and space. System: get a stock of 3-hour tape and recorder. Till the sun goes down I'll rest and smoke. Call the show: altered states and so on.

The loft is full of people, Max and Andy, Ann and Justine, Edmund, Alan and Beth, Justine has to go to school, I sign her papers with our name and address in case she gets lost, she has to go at 8:30, but doesn't…Max comes back with a lot of people, some of them come outside where I have been sleeping. They stand around. I say "Don't I have a reading tonight?" No. "I'm a slacker." They answer, "She's trying to raise the dead." It becomes a chant, the people in the other room (blue) begin to dance to it, waving their white arms. Slack rope.

Everybody's staying with us: everybody's gone away.

Saturday

Yellow and brown, I'm left on a street corner, two people drive away. First Max drives away, leaving me with ? But she won't know what kind of care I need, he must know. She's there and she doesn't. She drives away. Some one of them probably returns to look for me but I'm gone. The end, except for blank dreams.

Queens' College and queens' something else. And Queens. Trip, I leave the car, the girl. Max gets married to someone else, possibly Beth. Song, my text: once they…, and, "There's the foot of the girl you…": I go to Queens' College, already have my degree, why am I going? Getting there. And Queens something else or Queens somewhere else. David points out the double meaning of Queens in the dream, why does he even say so. I can't get up and miss all my classes. I arrive always at night. Day. I am traveling between Queens college and the other Queens, by car. The city must get very wide at this point, it takes a long time. I leave the blue car and decide to walk, why? I recognize the names of a few streets. Now I am with a girl. We talk about the walking. We stop in front of a store and she tells me she loves me. We are sitting cross-legged facing each other. We embrace. There's something peculiar about the girl, besides being me, she may have only one eye or something. (The Chinese girl: "For your trip…") When I get to the other Queens (structure), there are many rooms and finally, a wedding. Max is getting married to someone, possibly Beth. Someone hands me my text for the wedding. I must sing the first song alone. I don't see why. Nobody tells me the tune. They say: you can figure it out from the words, the words sing it, it's a song about men, like another version of "How you gonna keep em down on the farm after they've seen Paris…" Only it's changed, it's about fighting, something like, "After they've been fighting in the Army, men just keep on fighting, you can't stop em, war." Text is red white and blue.

I leave the wedding room after Max has turned into someone else, someone he hates, I've been looking and watching. I walk through the rooms, my foot sticks. I walk through a curtain dividing one room and while I am walking I hear someone, the queers, say: "There's the foot of that woman you like so much, see, it's a terrific foot even though she's had two children and is so old, and…"

And the women embracing in "Lady Windermere's Fan" and Barnard and Freyer and Ron on Parsons Boulevard and the company you keep at school every day, and someone getting married.

●

Max must be very tired. When I saw how I was moving, straining myself, doing things, moving the furniture, active, had to finish, had to resign, cleaning, I looked up the section on the woman's blank dreams in Bertram Lewin's Elation. But she had an orgasm with them. No good. No good because I only made this motion because I thought I could be doing something and it's nothing. I only need this space to move around in, to do nothing. It's the same. It's never the same. Whether you experiment with syntax or elation, the movement's the same and it's nothing.

YOU are still here. I am still moving like someone else, someone I don't know. If only I could take my small business seriously, move like a poet, kill like an owl. Try for an effect. And the strangest thing of all, was once, the more I work at it, the more I produce, the less it comes together, the less it's mine. Even now, I'm someone else. I can't wait. The trouble is I can't wait. You set yourself an impossible problem, you have two alternatives, you either are at a remove from it (consciousness, unconsciousness, say, as the all-out object or subject of, say, a videotape), or, you bait yourself, quite singly, and alone, and wait, you bait yourself and wait. It's object, above, not subject.

It's this situation where you have to find people and things, like a movie, to carry out, or to carry you out. I'm the all-out subject here and nobody can take it, include me in there. "You make people into objects." "There's no theory." Wake up. Read twenty minutes of my lecture, you'll have to pay to hear the rest. No one: wants to hear anybody else describe things or make them do things. No one wants to rest. Process. Processed right out of the world, every day. Pink meat is in the present moment. Melting. I have no desires but the reflection on steel. Back aches from lifting. Tuesday. Wednesday. None.

●

Able. Able 2 taxi. Vacant. Free. Higgins. More 2 drink and coxcombs. Schedule C. Bachelor burrow or button, Larry. A neat hand. Resume. Take a hand in this. Big You. Index Cards. Curtain. Storm. Catalogue. Then the end. Not by a long shot. Worse things could happen. She could've witnessed a double murder. He says to me, "You did." We laugh. Bring out the ink wells and the scarlet energy. Pink meat. Stored. Mix well and publish the results of your S. experiment. You meant to mix well all up, and did. Sweat. Sweet sweet sweet meat. All up. In Los Angeles. I'm lost you're lost how lost can you be when everywhere you go it's morning and the sun's coming up over a map. Soon I'll be free. Morning working? Mourning working. Hiya baby. Howdayya spell whaddaya doin you fuck? Max just pissed. The cat's probably on fire upstairs. He axe so strange, you think he's gonna spring on you and he does, rolls over, covets his book and his writings, his name's "The Doctor," jusk like you and me.

You aint gonna get this far, far as you or me, we knows our business too well, I'm fell down a little, me and my tools. I always had a feeling you were all fools, all (no.) of you, sink back and eat shit, I'm back in my greenhouse, pears 4 the omelette: what does he say about this pain, and what does he say about "You know everything," and what does he say, your guru, about fools, and what does he say about real food, I mean real honest food food, I mean food to sustain you, not eat, I mean food you can get without clocks. What? Tell me? You won't tell me. You're falling asleep, Fern. Fuck you. You won't tell me cause you don't wanna know, all you wanna hear is aphorisms, those you can't eat, you can use em, in your poems, but you can't swallow someone else's shit whole and survive on it and I know and you know I know and you don't wanna hear about it you, fuck you!

That's it that's the end. Investigate the connection with Marie, if you want. Marie, so what. No one can hear you. I find a space for her by calling her Marie.

Albertine.

Bernadette.

Marie Ann Bernadette.

Feeds.

Jesus.

It's all a bad joke on me: I have no work to do.

●

Can't find David's house. Moved. Crawling: "All of the people from #__ are in #888." "Psychiatrist?" By this time I've picked up Edmund and _____ and _____ (in the playground). Top of the slide.

●

<u>Au Coeur de Ste. Helene</u>: a man is in the hospital and he has two forbidden sons, they look up at him from the window and he recovers.

There's a little dog crossing a big dog's tongue.

There's an inaccessible man.

"There are many people buried on the roadway of the George Washington Bridge."

●

I quit again and resign. Then I take up where I left off. I have a desire to tell a story to the very end. About cannibals, about slow-moving cannibals. The streets, its haze the eyes a glance the hands. April 23, 1973. Max is in the bath and I am on the bed, Clark's bed, about to try to put it all together again, I am in the process of making another introduction: as usual, I've kept my notes. I won't go round further than the introduction allows tonight, tonight I'll be clear, tomorrow with my notes and writing to Spider's tape and with the dream I have tonight, I'll try to make something out of that, like you would make something out of this: today I've seen a cat, and finches, an alligator, spiders, an ant, a snake, a woodchuck and a bear.

I walked around the house twice, it looks like rain at three o'clock. The second mountain row is in a dark cloud. The engineers are moving mountains into the should-be yellow sky. An orange sheet hangs out. I put on a warmer coat. Facing west, the energy it takes to trap and skin a fur, west, three, yellow, sex. And, sex-science. The wash comes in, pulled from the house. Complete quiet noise. Downtown. Almost completely surrounded by desire, I get out, or, no, I get off, I mean, I get back on the mainland in time for the storm. A drop on my hand. The noise of it. On my head. A banging. On the rock. Here. I move back. In. Closer to the house attracted to the storm. Moving inside.

The wind does some damage. I believe my memory impressions. Are traces (the tree tries to reassemble the qualities of wind within its own leaves).

●

Thursday April 26

Woke at nine with one of my attacks, Admiral Byrd, which I could not control and from a dream which seemed especially lucid. I had the sense, when I saw the light, that it was five or six a.m. and I had never been to sleep. The house was cold. I took a pill and tried to go back to sleep but I could feel I needed fresh air to begin to really breathe. I must get rid of you, my little audience, my little tactics. I dreamed I was taking a taxi, asking him to go up Broadway, which he'd missed, to 159th St. I knew it was an express stop and I could get the train there, I would rather have taken the taxi further, maybe to 181st St. but even this far the fare would be a lot. The taxi pulled over at an angle to the curb. It was $55.95. Since there were two other people in it, I figured I'd pay $15. But nobody was paying. The driver was Kathy's father and he was taking her to the station. The meter had gone wild during the trip. In fact we were going to the same place. In fact he was meeting us there later. Would there be enough room? I had invited two people up too. No place for them to sleep.

159, 5595, 15 (5914 Madison Street, Ridgewood). 181, and further north, David. The 5-key on the cash register is red. Kathy's father is my father making this deal: I'll be someone else so you don't have to recognize me, acknowledge me. Thanks, wiry feathers. 159, 181, then on.

Friday

Yes it was the house. Now the house is charred, the top three floors are charred. But there is a gable, a roof with a peak, a tiny room indicated that confuses it all with the hall bedroom which was tight, neatly impacted in a corner of the top floor, on the same level. There is an indication that I am not getting my share—of the fire? And that the house is to be moved. Only the bottom floor's intact. The first floor is not scorched and the people living in it. The gable in the dream, Clark's house is flat-roofed, David's in between. And then, we are all sitting, our backs to the stream and I turn and see two deer and a bear, drinking. I motion to Max to watch them, our movements scare the deer, huge deer run away, bear slouches in stream, I wonder about him. Eventually he walks away slowly in front of the crows. He is a man in a bear suit with a blonde wig on.

Great spring storm gusting winds. I claim to have seen a bear, to tell what happened, graduation day, mystical cards, the average dream, the scandalous money, avengers, to record in red, to sink teeth into, exercise wind, remembering letters, S, D, E, T, E, H, H, M, shed them, shed tears, small trees in leaf begin to sway, field glasses and storm, whole tree in motion, the ancient falcon, peregrine falcon, owl and his purse of small birds, the edge into flood waters, drenching the drive-in movie, rain. Snow, sleet, advantage, necessary store or stock of eggs, thirteen hens and a rooster, the object, art. Watch what you're seeing, it's sporadic. There're times in between, it isn't what happened, perform.

All of the elements once it gets dark get together to perform a strong hand on my head. Loose body walks around, looks around bending and pausing. More and more round, round and around till sun-up. The absence of color at night. This is backwards. Bending over backwards. Seats four. Serves six. At the table. I can hear. I am mentioned. The rest of the story goes: (from memory):

"The Imp of the Perverse:" As long as the prima mobilia race around based completely on ratiocination and concealed convolutions, there exists a space in between shadow and substance that all of God's lawyers refuse to design in. Causally now, they give us eating therefore stomachs, fucking therefore pricks and so on. But endlessly forgetting they are never seeming to be remembering the impulse to be wrong for the sake of being wrong every day. And the reason for all this forgetting is that all the phrenologists are watching not what people are occasionally and sometimes doing and not what people are always doing but the law, that is, they are watching what they think is already existing. It's ratiocination. The supererogation of the perverse begins. Do it. I am writing this to tell you why I am here in this cell. No, but first, I am on a cliff drawn to the abyss and if no one (a friend) comes along to pull me back and if nothing (a thought, but you cannot think) leaves me prostrate at the edge, I am in, you guessed it.

There is no one who can resist the convolutions of my thought. You are in it. Perverse. Turned to the good. I am writing to tell you why I am here, in this cell waiting to be hanged. When I first was intending to murder him I rejected all methods of committing the crime that were occurring to me for fear of detection. Madame Pilau's French novels turned me on to the poisonous fumes of a candle. Knowing my victim to be in the habit of reading in bed by candlelight it was easy to execute a secure crime. "Death by the verdict of God." I had been living on his inheritance for years while you had been waiting in the streets. I had been humming this song, "I am safe, I am safe," until the line followed, "Unless I confess the murder." I start running. I change tenses. People run after me. I fall and lose consciousness, you are telling me now that I spoke lucidly but fast, afraid I would be interrupted. You are telling me I said enough to assure my own conviction. I am writing to tell you why I am here, today, in a cell waiting to be hanged. Tomorrow, where? (The phrase "The imp of the perverse" occurs in the middle of the story somewhere.)

●

Snapper Rice and Peas, $4.00: white chalk on a blackboard, red snapper, eating flesh, snapdragon, turtle beetle bass, especially, the red snapper, a salt-water food fish, a reddish blue-streaked oblong fish in the Gulf of Mexico, in the red tide, in the red, in the snapshot memory, box after box after box, a Commie Indian, steal my soul, #5 on the cash register, see red and paint the town red, Max is outside the margin, streak, to streak, snatch, a snap of the jaws, to share a meal, to snare one, red is red, back to where we both began: red R and green E and black D, the Panthers.

See my mouth? Lock the door.

I had a brainstorm—fifty seconds of four straight metaphors bombarded, exploded by sights that I saw. Snapper Rice and Peas. Snapper rice and peas jumping, bouncing balls jump, ball lightning. 8 lucid energies of memories still shifting and rearranging (no time), jump forward to a dream about basketball, an old story. All the epileptic energy of that thought and I call it a single thought is lost. Cause the day was too bright, too Sunday, too color. I am too color. It was the absence of the word "red" that begged or began the question.

Pass on by. I have a brainstorm, it isn't you. It isn't even connected to you. Careful accounting now, past eve and adam, to the beginning of the book. I have a question, do you do something by ending? (What is an ending? Doing something). Look down. Eyes and mouth. Recording. "Spit it out," she says. A wet wash cloth. "If you can't swallow it, spit it out." We can't get caught in this ludicrous search for food and remain here. It's temporary work, no use dying here in the slapstick-flour-factory. Boxes of flour, unrefined. Fall in em. Get em dirty. An element. Sophisticates throw pies, at least. The farce of the quest for food, the Holy Gruel, Sacred Porridge and if you can't eat it, spit it out. Memory memory Einstein memory, you go to where they make it, out of elements, absurd, the wheat plant is fine and bread is fine but the flour, continuous substance, identical textures, all the same, the flour's a joke. And the people who are stuck there, working the chain gang, no use dying here where the work is temporary, where you die is someplace important, where finished pies have come into existence, whole decorated breads, even birthday cakes. Every May…the king was in the counting house counting out the flour, "We're short." Five and twenty snappers baked in a pie and when the pie was opened the birds began to sing. Wasn't that? It was, it was John the Drummer all contorted died of syphilis, don't look, he's blond and got his penis on and the other one's on his ass. Memory boxes, an introduction. To Scientific Reason. Pick a rhyme, any rhyme. John was in the big box holding on his stick, the queen was in the parlor sitting with a friend, wasn't that a pretty dish to set before the end. Poor John, pale and blond. Don't tell me about it. He had his pants on. I put my feet up on the seat and fell down important, all the way home, took notes: "Your ideas about memory…" I just use the word a lot. My ideas about memory fall down important when I put my feet up. So dirty. Dirty as a Kerouac, dirty as a blackbird, black as a crow. Something to know (Wittgenstein was clean), (Webern walked out the door and got shot). That's how he died. Amazing grace. A tenacious rebounder. A man comes to visit. He sits on the bed. He shows me a painting. I'm storing it for him, his painting of me. We look at it. David (who sat) becomes Raphael (who sits). What difference? Raphael has a twin and his twin is Moses and Moses was close, is close to David's Michelangelo, in stone. Laöcoon, the snakes and the sons of his he ate. Laöcoon did this in stone, that is the difference. If you sit down on my bed, please turn to stone. Like my advice to Webern, please stay inside. I'm a cutter of networks, beginning to alter…the nursery. Da Vinci's vulture. He kept track. The aperture painters arrange my desk, the statues make my materials accessible.

Freeze. Freize-Green invented the secret code of the camera and I spell out the word in letters, money. He died. Jasper returned me my painting, saved from the fire, and a piece of material, its source, some flag. He gave it back. My cousin reminds me of herself, Jane. And now someone reminds me of Jane. But, no relation, I'm supposed to play hers. The whole family resembles itself. At the theater they skip "Bernadette" by Shakespeare. We're identical. Or perhaps we're backwards: etted-anreb.

I've got nothing to say in May, I'm too reminded. Get the pig, you spirit!

●

"The Imp of the Perverse" (from memory after two weeks have elapsed): As far as phrenology is willing to go, something about prima mobilia, something about ratiocination, nothing about the supererogation of…something. The man who is standing on the edge of a cliff, suffering from vertigo, bound to plunge headlong over the precipice. He does. Unless a friend pulls him back. Nothing, then, about the impulse to perversity, for its own sake. Something about a candle. When I first had the idea to do the murder none of the methods seemed sure. A novel by Mme. _____. The idea of the poisoned candle. I knew that my friend was in the habit of reading at night by candlelight in a poorly-ventilated room. "Death by verdict of God." I easily replaced the candle. I was secure and had my inheritance. I would walk down the street singing, "I am safe" and once I added, "unless I confess the crime." I started to run. People run after me, rough hands on me. I am down. I am told now I spoke clearly but quickly, in a rush to get the words out. I am told I said enough to assure my conviction. I am speaking to you now, today, from this cell, waiting to be hanged. But tomorrow, where? "I am speaking to you now from this cell" comes first in the middle of the story.

●

I saw Rico's head in the sky and he and Kathy pin me down at a performance and yell, "You always do the same thing twice, I'm sick of seeing the same thing twice!"

I saw large colored birds drinking, I live here too. My parents give me some advice. Another painting.

May 19

Throwing pancake batter up in the air and batting it through two windows to David and his friend who fry it up for batting practice. "The Big Shot." The bowl of batter: they never got to eat and then the cops came and she died: "Go faster."

●

Packing Max's father's suitcases. Two green-blue mice, "Haven't you ever seen them before?" Andy and the young boy and the young boy I saw, everybody fucking, I am drinking cream. "If I can't get that from someone (you) I can get that from somebody else." Nobody I know.

●

This is a real not-hard. When I come to the end of the line, the earlier part, the being the beginning seems to have seems to have been set up too early, not not-hard in so-long. That seems to be all. What is it that's new. A new beginning has to be sweet and beginning and simple and not hand-writing, do you want to go out? Do you? No facts, no derivatives, none, please, thank you, I'm sorry I had a dream. I'm sorry, I had a dream. Apart, I am apart. You are none you are one. Read that. That is all, I want to go out, I want you to go out with me. That is all, I am apart, I am not leaving, this time. But I am still the same and it doesn't seem possible, it doesn't seem possible to do this to myself and not do it to you, do you know what I mean? Is my language clear? It is not hard. I am not being hard on myself, I will be here. You coming by? The casual speech of the not-hard is like the speech of the pay-backables in dream, you know what I mean? It has never been anything but not-hard to do this. I have one, I am one. I am a haver and giver of dreams. Like-a-vision is another one, all crammed in here. I cannot speak of what I see in them, of the people I see, of the things. That is nothing. This is what it is, not hard. Covered-up is the last one: he is mine, he is mine too. Covered up is the one I know best. It is for the sake of covered-up coming in that the pay-backables first came. I do not really know whether I am one, or another. I know one thing. I am not allowed to speak, I must find it. I must find it in the casual speech that I hear, I must find it in the speech that is clear. Maybe you will say it. Maybe you still will say it. I am not one to say it, not now. Now I am not speaking and that is clear, you can come by, you must. You are the cause of this. You replace the cause of this, you must speak when I do not, you are not tied up, you are not bound, I wish the space were larger, I wish the end were closed, I am happy the end is tied up loosely, so that you may open it. As strange for you, maybe this coming by, as it is for me. That casual language of the loosening will be what I make of it. I will make it the key. I will find the thing in it that I need to go on. Otherwise this will not be what it is. I hope it is something. I am not sure that the casual speech of everyone is even ever heard. I am counting on this. It's tight because I am not counting on you, I am perhaps not-heard. That is no difference. If it were, you would be in a tight spot, and this is not that. Do you know what I mean? I will read aloud in the heard-spot in the house. I will read this aloud. Free to. I will find out if I can say at the end, something-that-is-heard: I'm lost so lost how lost can you be when everywhere you go it's morning and the sun's coming up over a map? Can that be heard? And if it can can the geography of a biographical body say that? To you? Whoever you are? You hold it in your hand, defend its states of consciousness. It is listening is implicit cannot lean has finally found _____ in the casual speech they say has come around _____ to yours, which I have in my hand, and am doing the same, in simple language, as I said to you, that I was asking, that I am asking, for you to hold here.

There's a bee in the house, she died. Everyone falls to the floor, should I wait for you? No.

A map or a calendar if it's the end of May, of the end of May. Waking, moving, _____ out, cover the table, clear it, on top, covering, clearing, the table's out of the picture.

●

X is Sunday and that solves the problem, X out Sunday and that solves the crime.

I'm mimeographing, I'm tracing. Grace is flowers, eating flowers and people with red hair appear. Red Grooms and red others. I'm in an orange room with a small mimeograph, I'm in orange room with a small mimeographing room, small elevator, empty orange room, I'm in an orange auditorium, the machine: there's a light under the machine to see by. It's like sewing machines. I put my head under to clean the grooves, I clean the loose nails from the grooves and then orange people begin to come by, machine people, Red Grooms, George, redheads. I've been doing this for days, Grace is to make a connection with George and there is a phrase, "No Grace for George," and that's the end of it.

He stands by the elevator. I lose here. Help, no help. The difficulty of the tracing, the plans, Stanislaus is there: "You have to have that one xeroxed." Stanislaus? I'm tracing a child, would a pattern be easier? Is it sweaters? Kimonos? For orphans? For orphans more and more people come.

I'm in a community, I'm in jail. Still working at the machine. Same machine. Another George, George Wallace (commits a crime), he has to wear blues (criminal blues). They're looking for him. "He's in the machine shop." I turn and many police with riot cars, squad cars, motorcycles and the rest, they machine-gun him down in the orange again light. I hide in the garage thinking it's steel. I'm hiding behind wood. Everyone falls to the floor. A dark hard woman carries him out, policewoman, he's not shot. A soft light woman asks, should I wait for you? No.

The gorge of the throat. General motors.

2.

I was supposed to be doing this alone. Finally I get to the supermarket alone. I figure it out. I'll just do the fresh food that's up front. I won't really have to go in. Close to out. It's distracting, the place is closing.

"Without all these oranges piled high the place wouldn't look so good." They insist I buy part of a giant squash, a section, it's 31¢. I open the eggs, it's a carton of beer, small bottles. I look for beer. I'm doing O.K. You've got to trust them, you've got to trust the other guy, the guy at the other end of the place to check you out. It's faster and they're closing. I let them—I'm a good customer. They tell me I'm a good customer.

I get a phone call from Spider, in the market, long cord, I switch phones. Then he appears, he's calling from inside, he's in the market, and tables appear, it's a restaurant. He talks to me, giving directions, or, all his feelings, in a speech. I try to get the beer before we leave. Spider finds three bottles of ale, the kind Stanislaus drinks, I take them, turn, Mike Ladle walks over, shit-eating grin on his face. I think now: I was supposed to be doing this alone. I say, "Go away you jerk!" He's nosy. He does it again, later, or, he did it before. He follows us around. On our way out I see Max at a table talking with Mary. He's not looking. What's he doing here? I was supposed to be doing this alone. Then a blonde guy I've looked at at one of the tables, he walks over, angry, and attacks me. "Why were you lookin at me like that—you shouldn't make Alixidon (his girl) go through this!" He looked familiar, Alixidon's his girl. He hits me, I hit him back and he falls backward on Spider, fainting. I think maybe Spider's knifed him but he gets up, faints again, now he's pretending to faint. Spider and I hightail it outta there.

I was supposed to be doing this alone.

3.

I knock over Dick Cavett's bookcase, holding hands with two stars, celebrities, champagne? It's the DeCoursey's big family-house (I'm thinking about communicating).

Everyone's beautiful (Indian) but mine (Meg). Now I know why...she...me...is... Now I know why she stays here...

A lot of little boys go to be in a lot of rooms. I'm in between them. I think about being in between them.

A dog swims underwater losing his fur shedding a piece of fur. Like a flying squirrel.

4.

I kill Max's father and put him in a suitcase cause we can't tell his mother, she's too nervous and her face glares out at you close in the dream with the red of her lips growing over her face and she's made-up too. I carry him around in the case, I think about laying him out. Nobody tells me what to do. Decomposing. Swimming in the current.

5.

Tomorrow when I wake up I want to drink beer. Tomorrow when I wake up I want to drink beer. There's not enough to eat there's not enough to drink there's no smoke. I looked at the clock. I want to get out of this place. I want to leave, I want to move, I don't want to be watched. It's just as hard, I won't be watched, make plans, make plans, deliberate, isolate, destroy chronology. Destroy it. Penmanship wanes off. Tied up into type. Leave that out, I can't leave that out I'm in too much of a hurry, you. You'll have to make it up, you'll have to make do. Every way, in there, it takes longer. Fuck the metaphor for states, but it (the for) denies them anyway, left where.

Be careful. Be careful, there's too many people in the house and what I am doing is secret stuff. You are the one. Magic can't possibly take this long. Max asleep makes the water run. Magic can't possibly take this long. We're all too nice to each other. As each sentence begins it knows from the beginning (it) will end at the same space, same no. of characters filled the line before, a chant, a denial of

I get a phone call
I switch phones
I try to get the beer

I take what he finds
I turn around
I was supposed to be doing this alone
I say, "Go away!"
I looked repeatedly
I hit him back
I think maybe he's knifed
I split
I was supposed to be doing this alone
I knock over the bookcase
I hold hands with two stars
I'm thinking about communicating
Now I know
Now I know why I am…
Now I know why she is…
I'm in between them
I think about being in between them
I'm a dog shedding his fur
I'm like a flying squirrel
I'm duplicating
I'm tracing
I'm in an orange room
I'm in an orange auditorium
I'm interfering
I've been doing this for days
I lose her
I'm tracing a child
I think a pattern would be easier
I'm in a community
I'm in jail
I'm still working at the machine
He commits a crime
He has to wear criminal blues
I turn and see the police
I hide behind steel
It's wood
Everyone falls to the floor
Should I wait for you?

No.

June 12

This is real hard. You ah in school around here? No I'm having something xeroxed. School round here? No ah actually I'm a teacher. Teach children? No ah grownups. Ah. People my age I mean all ages (make friends easily). You ah teach older people? No ah yes people my age. Around here? Yeah up on tenth street, actually I'm having something xeroxed. Thank you very much. I'm waiting. You wanna drink? No ah a beer you have Heinekens? Ah yes. Thank you very much. The Emperor. His excursion. I'm calm and besides Chinese they speak about the Bahamas and Montezuma's revenge. Oh well then she's crazy. She was with two other teachers and they're both language teachers, they speak Spanish. La via del tren subterraneo es pelligrosa. Dante gets me an ashtray. He says, "All right I'll get ashtray, all right?" Smile I smile at Dante, Dante's son in the middle of a hot three o'clock afternoon, wants Fresca to drink, O.K.?

You all record adventure with me like hem. Hem? Some people have such small voices and I can't hear them. A giant empty one of Piper Heidseck among the Chinese, la Chinoise. You bet. You know it. Washing dishes. He knew I needed food he gave me food. Simple and I am eating it. Fortunes. Noodles. La bête chinoise and la belle Chinoise. You want anymore? I'm gonna eat, you know? Anymore? No I'm fine. Except for this: there's no end to it, he pours the drink. Vodka gin et la chinoise bourgeoisie hello. She learns to cut right through and simultaneous she learns to walk. If you can't sleep in the heat you're growing up. I have a green one. No, that won't reproduce. Where I am going to and where I am coming from. Story. Dime novel as well. Anomaly in the Emperor's perfectly cool house, with braids, writing, performing quickly, working out, waiting, working quickly, took a trip: my first. Teaching foreign people is that what you do? What? Foreign people, out of country, yes? Yes. You hungry? No. Kerouac's suddenly by my side laughing, he was no braver than I am. Do I have to explain, do I have to describe, we share the same great trap door and Spider's love letters are trapped in my book. Kerouac walking Kerouac falling down. That's a greeting, meet me. So I did. Suddenly he's interested. Suddenly she's gone. They come and go as they please. Emperor's not visible here. Sorry. Two minutes to show time only this time you swallow, you do. Who is this person speaking, it's the one who is trying to ending. Always sorry even when you and I begin again, have to. So there so where is where we are in code in dope in endless way I'm in my way I'm the same, final, teach, you too. Suddenly she's gone. That's all and a power laugh. I understand about moralism and I understand about food now so.

●

Stanislaus the same and Stanislaus the same. Same what? Who appears in my dreams. Impeach. The poets outside are accusing me of having a nice ass. Merle and Stanislaus and Mardu are sunk. In relation—a day in the sun—with everyone? Writes instantly. It isn't easy it isn't dreaming. "Do you want to come home?" It's loud. Bernadette Bobbs Irwin, her pseudonym for dancing in windows behind glass. That's what happens when you do it really do it, Fern comes in and spills it and then you're all resigned to time again. I mean that is what I call a distraction is pure, time out. Something about Nathan's and a whiff, pure glass again of music pounding out of a brain unconnected to tiny sounds. That's how he was man like a mother like they say and say again, ain't there any way to group in this small longhouse without repeating and to hack out the best ritual in town, pure music. We need more. Everybody knows it. Someone else wears white and Spider will. Those are saints' names they spell everybody into town. I'm a cowboy to them, or, today, a "hot one." There are these one by one: one saint along with his pilgrim, one pilgrim one messenger along with his saint, one saint, one engineer, one old engineer along with his prospector and between them...one prospector one fag including myself one queer a read badass one at attention, whaddayou call em soldier, one soldier, one big anger one very big anger two guests and a room, no, one very big anger and beside myself, coming in before, a monster is what will become of conclusions and then, now, two guests and a room, one room in which naming has gone on before. I am interested in what will become of the plot and by plot here I mean myself. The rest of us work here and lean, lean toward a story. Sisters three sisters three lives which Stanislaus which Michael an invidious spider. Who is craziest who is new why is that yellow bird catching the city on fire. The next thing you know will be bare feet. In an energy crisis the next thing you know will be (somebody laughing) and no clothes at all on. The dope dealers come, they say they have all flowers they're right, no dope. The dope of the stepson of the doctor is good, it's attractive, hand-written dope. Is there any way to angle around women two women, one and two? Women always swimming reminds me there is some absence there are two absent and it could go on forever, off and on. The two that are absent are lovers, as usual, except this: they hide. Of all of P,P,P,M,M,B,N,L & J & so on, those of us who hide are P,M,J & I don't know about B. And those of us who hide might have an out. At least we don't get insulted. Who knows about this? What are the secrets? The secrets are: we went to a national historical monument we saw from there. Regina is a secret. He called and I told him I had the number in my back pocket. There is no science of secrets. The secrets roll out from under cover like names repeating themselves in the dark. The names are a mess. You give up. As soon as you give up you find a real secret—I'm immobile as the earth is sky. And another—she is the anger held me in tow. Let me call her Mardu or even Queequeg. All past secrets come to help you rule the world. All of the secrets of the past of the world appear in a breath to open. Breathe the smoke of your own fucking brand. Three missing sisters and a lot of fucking smoke. The pay is idyllic, the courtships are the same. Rolling on through Saint Louis on the darkest mine of nights I was anxious to get home. We were necking in the Trailways bus, she bought my meals, I had run out of sandwiches, she was so near-sighted I had to lead her by the arm into the restaurant. She invited me up to her farm, we planned to meet in a hotel in New York. A truck full of apples and two 16-footers and I was home. That's it. A political song. How long have you been in the field? Without repeating.

June 21

Up in the hills of Ireland or some misty place, there is a myth about cannibals, which is probably true. They make forays down to the village below to find and eat young lean boys. For lack of vitamin D, so I drink milk. For a desire for vitamin D, from deprivation of vitamin D, for need of vitamin D, from memory of vitamin D, for more vitamin D, for some vitamin D, for as much vitamin D as they can get.

June 23

Gerard Ted Stanislaus Rico many Michaels Bill John Max Peter Fern Jonathan Warren David Andy and almost completely everyone and many women. A quart of milk. Do some work. A paragraph is emotion and I want some. Courage is the heartiness to do the wrong things. Not much endurance lately but much sand. Men use these expressions. I will go to sleep to do the same. Rare meat. Time demands. Oh say can you see by the twilight's last glamorous things that I say are resting in you and so, I join you, whoever you are.

Dream an orange emotional place: at Hilly's strange emotional orange place, Robert the slave is willing to help me and he will and he's gone and I'm gone but he's still there, always there but there's no help for it because, I go out and Max's whole family has laid out a picnic and I say to them, "Are you the fuck staying all for dinner?" And they say yes but no place is laid for me. Sleep. A new watch. Tomorrow I'll leave. After I dream: this pen is so hard to keep track of, I drop it and lose the top and throw it away.

Sunglasses on <u>On Dreams</u> on Jack Daniels and vodka and beer, she's still alive, yes. And in the orange emotional place this is what I went on, as far as I can say:

"3 pages in <u>How to Write</u> and what I really wanna do is call you 2, seek out, strangers and pills not nothing, they took pills and sleep now music and call you 2 and then I did and Gertrude said and then and then, save the sentence: smoked a blue cigarette and pigeon flapped his way away, took a lot a nerve to smoke a blue one, what's goin on? Yes, Max is in bed with Kathleen in a pill haze, we all took a sauna together, we're gonna sleep till about 8:30 yes and pigeon flaps his way away, something I'll never lose. I wish you were here. The you 2 is finally established, I think I create.

"We're <u>gonna</u> sleep, we're gonna sleep, goin a sleep. I don't even know even if you 2 knew, I don't know where it would ring, the phone, except for birds. We're gonna sleep sleep and I have my dream nevertheless, pigeon goddam flapping, you 2 bet and what you 2 don't know…you is what's here in this moment, you's 2 (small ones, you's) not takin your chances honeys, no. When this you 2 see remember B. This is a fine emotional paragraph. And RE-search that one out, comes out orange at the least. Quote: I didn't know what was going to happen then. Close quotes. Who has whose head. I definitely want to tell everybody that's you in silence what you is doin every minute every day, so stay, it ain't fair to you and you 2, it's pretty out here and fair, somebody's birds, not pigeons but starlings, all wet. I make it new hard. Are you still there? Why didn't he come down? Feed me Jesus you 2 don't know what's goin on, it's here for a short time. You 2 is crazy. And the rest. I'm so good I shouldn't be interfered with. That's the statue that's the stone. And that's you. Fuck you.

"Amen, so it's cold out, so high, so best. So die. Speak to yourself and get dead. I'm one. I don't sleep here though they do. We're in an odd place, sort of a rich producer's penthouse full of dope and booze and a red velvet bedroom with mirrors and a sauna and t.v. sets, all tuned to the bed, and blue cigarettes. What've I learned? It's in this book, more you. Establish YOU.

"It's not much but they gave me the free pages. I'm dying I'm dying I'm dying for breakfast. Establish food not fear. You 2 hear? You 2 know? Do you 2 know? Lights. Silence. YOU. Fuck. Over. She knew more."

●

From time to time giving a very small piece of apple, pear, a single grape to him. And it is in honor of these crimes that I am writing my book.

From here you get to where you could travel anywhere furiously without pay. What is going on here in long long parts. It's a, listen I'll tell you in parts, listen, everyone is done is small a piece of mail. The light on the parts that begin from here. You get it. This is not making anything clear but if I go on with it, if it goes on, then something comes, maybe from one of those men from one of those women on my shoulder, from one always present, maybe from one of them, from one of those people, something comes. You can look but you better not touch.

Water!

Away!

Ouch!

Now I know!

It is in honor of these crimes that I am writing this book. These crimes in this book, fool-proof. I think it's Max I'm starving. He feeds me. How to get rid of milk, the proof of all ache of all love is the start of the crime, is beginning the crime, the intention to commit. Prematurely premeditated meditation concerns (an) analysis. Ready. I can't clean the house today and not return tomorrow. I reserve the right I am right, I was right before meditating, I reserved it. Concern is of no concern or shouldn't be, be me. Discover there are laws. Clean the house today and come and see me. Return tomorrow. I was here before I resemble him, she resembles him, she is exactly like her, yes no exactly alike, her. Where do we live here? In stopped-life. In go-out / 4 sex. In go-out-for-sex. And further I hope we bend toward put-together. Even eked-out. So what. So storm. So space for psychiatry. So an even human mind.

Like breakfast.

Like before breakfast.

Like sensory memory from breakfast.

This is a mixture of a memory and a reproduction.

This is a description of a function, as, machine.

This is never noisy.

This is never speaks.

I'm signaling.

Do I have to say my speech signals you?

The merchant marine could do it.

You wanna meal?

You wanna meal as selfish as written by another hand through mine, through this one I fatten you eat.

You eat good.

You eat amazing.

You annoyed or something? Disgruntled amazed precocious alike her.

All you and it takes longer.

Wash through throughout with water or even tea. Always.
Also, constantly almost completely and really everywhere like land, Surrounded.
I'm glad they sleep soundly so I can be reading what is a peninsula: four people
accompanied by a cannibal. I can if you can.
From one of them, of those people, something comes.
I can if you can drink that wine, fill a channel full, a bird, a wine, a dance, from time to
time giving a very small piece of apple, pear, a single grape to him.
I can draw lines across it cross lines.
I can be an eating tumor a candle-holder, fair, sincere, white, shining, waiting, to set on
fire is to shine and wait.
I can be white-robed, I wore white, glow brightness and sincere, can crystallize sugar, be
made of sugar, sweetmeats, a broken piece, to break, to break a tuft a reed a cane,
a light basket, a reed, a great tube, a gun-barrel, a reed, a tube, a deep gorge, is
cognate, a rule, a rod, a straight cane, I live here, a dignitary of the church, a dog,
a disease, a disease of trees, an excresence on trees, a sore, a disease, burns
brightly, brightly burns, Caribbean, Caribbean.
The cannibal is brave, touches two others with his own, touches the red one, a device, a
trick, a cheat, nothing is known, builds a boat, sleeps in a bed, Egyptian bed with
mosquito curtains, with hangings, any sort of hangings, mosquitoes, gnats, cone
faced, cone-headed, kills, from the shape of its head, a cone, and face, an
appearance, to see, kills to see.
And finally, to sing, to sing in a way, to sing in a whining way, to sing, to sing like a
beggar, hypocrisy, a little song, a song, to sing, a singing section of a poem, a

singing, song, a hymn, song, a song, to sing

Caliban

A deformed savage creature and a slave, almost completely surrounded, a roughneck, a

scoundrel, a con-man, a junkie, a bleeder, the rapist, a loan-shark, a pederast, the

needle, the organs, a glance the eyes a hand, the hamlet the penis, the vulture, to

see.

Caribal, canibal, Caliban, to see, the act, the habit, the habits, the useful, the edible, the

junk.

And it is in honor of these crimes that I am writing this book and it is in honor of eyes to see these crimes that I am writing my book and it is eyes to see that swear to incorporate you that contract to eat as eye is story is news, my eyes order, they command you and speak some sound, no words as eyes are a vocable, this unit this sound, an instruction, a promise, a vow and a contract and so on.

When this you see will he and so will he. A plain case of separation. Now you know everything. Both-and.

●

You'll never get to heaven if you break my heart, are there hearings, private, are there any hearings, property. Never get to heaven if you break my heart, exchange and go to sleep real private, you'll never get to if you do, private, if you do, property, if you do good analysis on everybody, a wild crazy scheme, considered connected, considered up, considered like my own hand, had access to it, people's names are the names of people and one takes off from dreams and one takes care of himself him/her/self and one takes off from there and one has energy to burn, burns brightly, so, and one has so many cokes and so many coffees, and one burns brightly, brightly burns, Caribbean, Caribbean, many cars to the shore and repeating a slow drive along the Canadian Pacific quoting myself: move ease and speak is ease and move is as axe on the murderer's head, as flag over years turns to sun, becomes sun, as death before life gets won over gently and not to be angry, it goes past description in another language, private, another tongue, in tongues, private, in translation, property, in all sleep, exchange, in all short naps, robberies, in fragments in bets in intransigent titles in measured steps in exchange in new measure in the proper perspective in the wrong one, I go beyond the wrong tree, its branch is separate in space is floating in drift, you make a bet about plans, they tell courtroom jokes: moonshine, the other, its costs. I win the bet, they break up, I take out my clothes, I get to see the movie, I become an afficionada, a fan of the fight, its cool regarding mist and grey bull, rain keeps us out, tries to keep us out of New York City, on return, a private drive. Plenty of time, plenty of coke hash and rooms plenty of money conserves energy for flying: we make notes. Somebody doesn't like us. Somebody wouldn't let us make xeroxes. You had to stand up to make these copies? No, they did let me sit and handwrite. Who originally denied you the right to copy? Stopped from making any copies. And also the privilege of copying. Let's have an important meeting: Who is Harry Dent? Sounds like a dick, "Whaddayou got on?" "Property." I am in a private practice so, I am in a private practice with you. We dig up dirt that's private property, we read from the directory of property, it's getting very dark out, private, it's the digging up dirt stage, private, let's beat each other up, robbery, exchange.

Let's beat each other up now private, we is moving so exchange property, let's eat each other up now so private, we be moving to property soon, a real meal, robbery, dynamite, exchange, a dinner, eat off your plate, robbery, a place to throw away the food you don't eat, destroy it, private property, let's work each other over, dig up the property and meet and eat, private. My victory is private, my victory is exchange, the people are private, you drop a plumb line or lay it, on someone else's property, it's robbery. Do it. What a name.

●

Music, I want music playing left and right, I want music, I want music, let it play around me, left and right, let it continue, like five skunks skulking on the page, let it go on, without any cut-offs, I want I must have, I want music playing left and right and mommy money monkey pocket change and poetry. Mommy, money, pocket change and poetry. I want music playing left and right, I wanna live alone and play music left and right like money like money like pocket change like poetry, that's all.

Music is a diagram with numbers I want music, cashiers checks, savings accounts, cash in hand, Bernadette's stash, Max's stash, it amounts to twelve hundred forty-four dollars and ninety cents, or at least it did, minus three hundred, leaves nine hundred forty-four and ninety cents, I want music playing right now, cash in hand three dollars and fifteen cents, cash in the Bank in the Park twenty-four dollars and twenty-three cents, and that's no lie, I want music playing all around round round and about the house, I always want my mama and about the house: B should talk to Ron and M should take his stash, his stash of one fifty cash and rearrange tonight and M should fix the tub and that's the end of that, it's the music and it's the noise of the music and I've heard this song before and I thought it was another one and I'm waiting and something will be made real in England, in another space in another house, maybe on a vacation, we want cake. We want cake. Roma. Roma? Roma. Let's go down to the other fish store too. O.K.? We need some more protein: cheesecake or cheese? A little meat or two, a can Bolognese sauce? We need cake, we need cake, coffee liqueur, no coffee and liquor. What kind? Wine? Schweppes soda and bread, yes, wine. Yes brandy. Wine? Yes is wine. Pint of brandy. Later! I'll take either. The kinds of cake: cheese, chocolate, mocha, fruit. Fruit! Lemon meringue? Yes. I don't like shiny icing. Choose three. What's skinny cake? Icing, not I Ching. What's skinny cake? Skinny? The chocolate one. It's shiny. It's shinny. They have chocolate cream pie. How about lemon cake? We can. How about fruit pie and one brownie? We need oil. Salumeria. I need some in my head! Moi aussi. How about lemon meringue and one brownie, not boxed. Why don't you like shiny icing? (He keeps on calling it shinny.) Cause it's hard and sweet and not creamy and it's skinny or shinny too. I bet the guy at the counter thought we couldn't talk. I bet that's the creamiest cake they got (inside). Can you imagine an Italian ad for lemon meringue pie, bet there'd be a big girl. And she'd say: we all need someone, we can lemon, so if you want it baby…well you can lemon me, m-m-m-mer-meringue-gah! Good ad. Equipment, feet, camera, notebooks, pens, sweaters, pants, shirts, shoes, books, script, light, thermos, film (exposed), some film (unexposed), and I add: wine, pills, wine and pills, why, my mommy, mommy money monkey pocket change and poetry. My no. in Amagansett: 267-8025, Love, K.

Fuckit, it takes too long and the reason it takes so long is this: is that somebody says and sobs, there is something about you and that something about is is always turning blue. I been to the eastern desert on a horse with no name and I lost him and someone thinks I'll lose him and I will and I will because I saw many animals many birds, close up, giant birds, I saw five skunks walking toward me like birds, like oiled birds, like birds who needed human help, five skunks and I pointed them out to him and he saw them and I hoped no one of them would come near but one did and nuzzled me, and came near, and put his nose to my neck and looked like a giant Chinese panda, like a miniature Chinese panda, and put his nose to my neck and there was no fight there. No fight. No body wants to fight.

And so I go to school. And Edmund says and why does he have to be here? And he says I should take more of the intellectual courses but I am only taking one and even the timing and scheduling of this is difficult and the one I am taking, maybe it's called "The geography of a biographical body." Yes, that's so. I walk into the classroom. The teacher is a giant frog, a kind of cricket, you never lived in the swamp, did you. A giant frog with one black thumb, a kind of Harner, an anthropologist, or Horner, and he says, and he says, what is your intent or your training, what is your training for this course and I say high school, just high school (break their necks, the necks of the frogs, biology, the wrong discipline) and he says, terrific, you have no training. And the course is we play with two little frogs, little frogs he has in his hand, Harner or Horner has them in hand, we tickle them, there's nothing to do, tickle them, tickle me. Tickle the frog who holds a plant in the palm of his hand, black thumb. We did it later. Once was a man who was quite a tree so memory and once is a man who is still, he still is. Remember: take him over there, some girls to follow and somebody is turning is composing the same. Or proposing. No forfeits: place-your-bets and no-more-bets, ladies and gentlemen. Situation of flying and writing. Eat the rest. She is. Spark yes image no, so you wind up learning all about it, it's the same to know, so, over and over you repeat the phrase: something is what makes your face red, red man-woman (2). Who gets it? This shared space? Someone, not of the two, who, with animal-gaze, winds up loving it too. Amazing #125. That's Rilke signing up: here, he knew everything. To last—amazing last—to last.

Something you say something you speak or suck on is what makes your face red, red one man-woman. And soon as you get in the car and soon as you get in the car then songs'll wind up being sung, natural sung in sun. There you are. Makin space. Owl. Makin tracks too. You walk the route of the railroad track in training or at least the guy goes and does it before he gets official. We don't walk it…retrain him, restrain him.

Much of memory is had-a-dream. Much of memory is moving. Plenty. And this was written all while running away, but I came back again.

Plainly thought
And plainly bought at the store
And then all of a sudden we need it
Weakened so strong
A closed color is the light
The kind of light
Every desert's in
Till you see
Peering owl on top of fortress
Sitting wrong
At the right desk
So, say,
One field of grass is moving
Over in
To ancient private
Property. (Save the sentence.)
You hope you joke
Out of the middle
What a tree (quite a tree)
What me

The other side
Going going down down on down
Dig it. Fuck, the women
These girls who each to each repair
Those are Rilke's girls and who take long to write long sentences
And the one who forgives one
Speaks to the other
But like I said before
Following
All the while following
Chasing even
Something caught so still
He is still moving
Some kind of cricket
And a big (energy)
Kind of laughing continuous
Saves.
Saves and burns it up.
The light of the color is closed
But not only closed to a cheat like science.
Not us ones
Not him-her
Restrain him.
    I wish I could have a party
I wish I could dream of the African man
That was a funny way for that movie to end: he takes the key from the kid and runs out
    laughing. He might wake up. The kid looks scared.
Wake up
The competition the trust, numbers
The activity
Put a stop to (the moralism of living alone)
Demand presence (he, he)
Complex activity, on the phone?
Spend all your money
You won't take it serious
You can have my apartment
You can have my appointment

I want to live longer

Get keys, send rent, get valium, brush, get peppermint oil, have dinner with Marissa, get

check or money, get caviar, lemonade, yoghurt and beer, milk too, and a 3-hour

tape, get eggs

Get moving

The sounds

I write because I still have more to drink and smoke

You want it to go on forever now?

The coach.

The coach talks.

The coach in her female her woman's private fantasies: what she did was this: she paralyzed him she wanted him paralyzed, that was the way she wanted him to be, cause she and me too got so calm with this man, this other man, she got confused and wrote it off, ran away, sent a telegram, and came back again.

There's an end to this and more about private property. You're wrong David shithead. And why did my books get thrown on the floor in a big heap and some stuff (ownership) went right out the window, cause why, cause I said I would cause I chose to live here with you and do I dare to say you there now and you hate the space I share with you and you too hate the charm of speed in you. You all can go home. I don't want either or any of you. Except you can't. All-home is all-mixed-up and now you hate movies cause of him and maybe you'll hate poems cause of him. I do psychoanalysis cause there's nothing else to do. (It's fragments your wrong about.) I'd do poems anyway, but I know I should be writing, that's making noise like the crow, like the receptor or synthesizer, like the tone I've been rehearsing but I know and now firecrackers or rain, what's the difference, but I know I should be writing in my own bed. The only thing I can rely on's my materials going quickly dry and run out. Plenty more. To make a painting smoke some grass. Spider is in Gloucester and Max is on the bed an inch away and I am trying to make an I, the letter I, suck, look good. Some noise. And what'll anybody listen to in the end, the as in the Bernadette. That looks like a signature. Cut you off. Charged money. What to make money for: the mouse, the call from Gloucester, fuck him, the wire from Pine Plains, the anxious news from Cherry Valley (what happened to my postcard, what happened to my letters, what happened to my books), you're right it's too easy, take the subway that's hard. In the middle of the night a big hard tone and it seems to start up again but I'm afraid to speak. You have memory. Does he want to wake up. They have nothing to write about that is access. Max did his number so I couldn't trust anyone but him and of course he's right, Spider's not the one to trust, and now Max is so glad I'm home there's no access, it's not the high-pitched tone I'm afraid of, it's that it'll make him wake him up and I've got the lights all on. Explain everything to me, who. Nevermind. I already know.

Max looks pretty happy in his sleep and it's still still everyone runs out of room, runs out of time. Trust (look up) and set the clock for ten. 6 + 4 is 10. 6 + 2 (loose) is 8 straight and that's hours of sleep, hours of time could've been mine. Smash this smash that you're away you're back. I don't mind writing while the light's still on, let her see I'm crazier than she is and real pissed off and this is no short willful piece. And there is no way to stop. Stop me.

In a car accident.
Poisoned in a plane.
In a disaster.
In a ditch.
Raped in a ditch.
In skydiving.
In a tent.
Killed by a bear.
In a heart attack.
In sudden death.
In overtime.
It's too much for me.
In cancer of the anything.
In hit by a car.
In certainly struck by lightning.
In the rain.
Slipped and fell.
Died of exposure.
In lost at sea.
In freak accident.
In fall from 20 stories.

Or six.
In poisoned at dinner.
In poisoned at drinks.
In poisoned at fucking lemonade.
In stung by a bee.
In being left I don't give up.
Do you want me to go outside?
In being shot.
In assassination.
In a mistake.
The wrong woman the wrong man.
In locked in a refrigerator with no air.
In caved in.
In explosion.
In ritual murder.
In black mass.
In eyes looking at you.
In noise coming at you.
In a bath of milk.
In a storm on the road.
In too much moving.
In moving around.
In internal injuries.
No one could see them.
In losing control of the breath.
In hospitals.
In wars.
In opening the door to a man with a gun.
In going to sleep.
In reading too fast.
In thinking.
In racing.
In O.D.ing.
In happening on a maniac.
In losing innocence.
In sleeping out.
The wind blows you out over a cliff.
In going headlong over a precipice.
In running headlong into a tree.
In banging your head against a wall.

In running headlong into a firepump.
In being suffocated by a snake.
A boa constrictor.
In sleeping in your hair.
In eating till you die.
In barbiturates and alcohol.
In grief.
In funerals.
In burials.
In fear.
In crashes.
In what you find out.
In going on forever.
In electrocutions.
In earthquakes.
In buildings collapsing.
In air.
But there are some things you desire.
And in speed.
And in smack.
And in snow.
And in morphine and ice.
And in opium and cure.
And in withdrawal and pain.
I lose track
In exhaustion.

Things are either falling or else we're throwing them out the back window all the time. I know I'm in for something and instead of I'm, it's in. I'm in, I'm I, Goodbye. Max is sleeping in Kathleen's bed, and I'm sleeping in my own wake up alone us both. And I went through the trouble with the horse with no name, and I lost him.

July 10

Put this together if you can, you put and pay-backables. And Frederick moved in one room and Beth and Frederick moving into another room and Max asleep and Max's mother calls and books falling are popular delusions, my heart laid bare (you have to warm up to it, I got somewhere). By Sunday? By any day? The restrictions on the method of seeing you are rare. (Do I have a pen with me? Will it write: call in the early morning and watch Watergate?) Where are you now? And these are the most important parts. You don't call me anymore. You sense as sense is the own body is as one with no not me but magic thinking and quote: reading.

She is a child who still believes, as Frederick or whoever moves from room to room, in the murderous wishes a child who still believes in the murderous wishes of things and people, of people and things, as Frederick moves, the murderous wishes of people of things who make her suffer or resist her. Who make her suffer (interpretation of dreams) or who resist her. As Max sleeps restlessly, as Spider is almost at the door, as Kathleen is coming here, as someone else, and, and her only, and her only defense, and her defense is a magic one and her only defense is a magic one because before anyway, no, she can do anything, who-want, who want. Paradise lost and regularly. I look in the dictionary a lot. "When will it rain?" Yes, tonight. She hits that which hit her. Your choice is perfect. It was.

I am the table-who-hurt. I am the hunter-who-covers. I am the lab, no, I am marrying four fears: there are four. 1) the able: to be able. 2) the want: who want. 3) the eye: to kill and 4) Listen, listen to me: where are you now? And: come here. I am just a designer. A cone. A cone burns. I am not telling the truth. I am fair. Now at last I am fair. And I am enjoying this vacation from lies to lie to you: I walked, I listened, I ate: how in the world do you know what I ate? And do you care? You need food? I'm sorry so sorry but my hunger creates a food everybody needs, you or me? Just my dreams down. That is an answer. I'll go on.

Accidents (Accidents is a title). Where did you stay, I mean, who with this weekend? Yes. (Yes is an answer.) He hits that which hit him. She hits that which hit her. Yes. You glow. Yes because you gave me this book to read. You read. You (and you and you 2 and "you") and all the you's, that is a private language. Score. (I score.) If life is endangered, one not only can defend oneself, one must. Not only defend herself, she must, giving away (where's the coke? that's the score). She must: not the pleasure of hurting but the necessity of paying back. Those lights (a man?). Those pay-backables, an impulse a defense a mechanism. Not the pleasure of hurting not it no way. Sure, a little pleasure in hurting, who are you? And to those and to those with the feeling of abandonment, abandonment so, if you say so, I attribute all the power of magic to Max, I give it to Max to myself to you to the spider to dynamite explosions to work to mothers and fathers who are waiting for thunderstorms, storms to share with us, they have it and not it and not to the table (where are you?) and not to the Bear, O.K. No magic. I consider and incorporate the sounds of the wicked, no, I incorporate the sounds resounds of the wishes, Lucette Lisette Bernadette Rosemarie Marie-Ann, all in the hospital they die. Dying. Piece of cake. Take it easy. "It happened." Charlie dies. I translate for the first time.

Before Charlie died he borrowed money, went in the army, was in Alaska, with huskies, had his picture taken, looked good, took up with Grace, never married her, till my father forced him to on his death bed if that's what you call it, forced him to, Charlie was a fuck-up, he was never invited, the youngest son, the youngest brother, Charlie, Ted, Eleanor, Florence and George and another Theodore died at birth in the country, the black sheep, the shepherd, the crow, annihilation, the storehouse, we know before we do anything, everything, all the Mayers of the Manhattan phonebook.

Charlie with his huskies in Alaska knew in 1952 he had that look in his eye, dark and dark and had a son one son my only son, Charles Mayer. I look, I often look in the dictionary, I need privacy. Brothers, born of one, I want him, his obsession is mine. I never saw Charlie dead but Grace died of alcohol and I saw her. That's why I'm here and that's the last time I saw Charlie he was 12 years old, went to live with his married sister.

I incorporate the wicked in my privacy, it's stored it's stored up. In my hand, writing, for you, the only hunger or physical fatigue or possibly distraction will open these eyes to, to what? Some song. Flight from the magic circle, fight from the magic circle and around, like this: a man comes up to me. He wants to destroy me (she said). It was magic that you gave me this book. However this man is intent on killing me. He might be. He is. I am not afraid at all. I show great presence of mind, I am not paralyzed, I react or fight with adequate actions, I am not killed or destroyed, I survive. If life is endangered, she not only can defend herself, she must. Like in a myth there was another one who had a fear of circles or cigarettes. You know what he did? He recovered after a while, he passed his fear onto his wife and he became her "therapist" and shaman and cure. A plain case of separation. Now you know everything, you know "both-and." Everything is arranged. It is love or it is love. (A mother is a real magician.) A mother is able to reconciliate the malevolent beings and their little victim, the fire no longer is bad and the table no longer can walk or hurt. She has arranged everything, it's over. Except that the little victim conjured her up.

●

Harner or Horner: Sitting on top of the sun wasting time, they all work don't they, don't you, good morning doctor how are your pills, oh shit your thumb's all black from playing doctor and the real grown-ups can't see, we blinded them with pokers from our doctors kits for first aid, first they aided us by buying us Xmas pies, Christ, and then it got dirty, the wind blew hard and we had nightmares in store but they all turned into benevolent frogs in the end cause why? cause we had stories to tell and told them and then the sun came out and sat through the world by diving down and don't leave out the rainbows they were like carefully done poems drawn to a close and then, beginning to alter the nursery, we arranged and rearranged all the furniture so nothing was in its proper place, seven imps sitting on one small chair upside down and then every penny was an ellipse and even that and then even though that was how we saw it we called it something else, we never went shopping.

All-black People: Black S. and I, and I'm black, commit a crime and we have to make a connection with a car and three people, two dark girls and a man. I think the car's a white joke, a convertible. (The sun's under a heavy dark cloud.) We make the connection on the street where I was born but not in front of the house, down on the corner in Brooklyn near the trees. I want a pie I mean I want a big cream cake, a real good one, a white one. So I give the two dark girls who have the car, they must be rich, a rich chocolate cream cake just like I wanted. Night passes. Black S. and I sleep. Morning comes. "Did you eat any of the cake?" These two hard dark girls, hard-nosed and nasty, sarcastic mean and rich give me a straight answer (Nancy Drew): "Sure did (about a quarter's gone)—we haven't seen a cake like that one since Marymount." (Beth and George.) "Can I have a piece?" They slice me a slice of the chocolate cake, no denying me so I ain't scared of being poisoned.

Paris Outdoor Movie: supposed to meet David in a café. Max is already there. But David is surrounded by so many people I can't get near him at all. Even Max is sitting far away, far forward; David is nearly up against a wall, glass. Not only that but the David-person is combined with the Freud-god and the Burgess-Meredith-devil, as if he were someone I had seen recently, maybe on t.v. All get up to leave. This is a chance to make a connection. David announces publicly to the crowd that he will not be available till Friday. His entourage is all men, still between us. I shout-whisper, "Don't we have an appointment at 11 tomorrow?" over the crowd of men. David cups his hands over his mouth over the crowd and shout-whispers, "Yes."

●

If thought were all articulate
Like drawing figures in the air
With men no need to speculate
On whether this is here or there:
There once was a man from Dragoons
Who thought that his life was a plate
He wrote down these words on balloons
And after all that he just ate.

● BOOK IV

A HOUSE IN USE is the use of a title.

Like the blind like blind people, like the congenitally deformed, this is my private space, like crippled people, this is my only space is an exception, you expect to do what you want. You expect to do whatever you want to do and not only do you expect it, you expect everyone besides, everyone who loves you, to make it easy to make it new, the sun comes out for me alone and you are not blind and you are not congenitally deformed either or crippled but both/and in a way, to do what you want to have it made easy, both, well doesn't everyone well this is not moral, no doesn't everyone feel that way, no, I don't believe it, no, and later K says, it's true a lot of people feel like piles of shit and anything good that happens to them is just the cream, I dream. Dream gives me the right I have no rights, far ahead and I forgot yes I forgot there's another reason too you write this down and later Bartholomew says always willing to help in the struggle of an artist thank you for your present when the time allows when the times allow: no sun no special sun no vacation Bartholomew says I'm looking forward to a vacation from people and they always want to talk about you and K says I'm going to Amagansett for a few days and I'm going to the country for a while and I'm going to Mississippi, P says why don't you go away for a while by yourself and Andy says just come up either of you both of you come up alone come together it doesn't matter and S says I'm going to Afghanistan and I'm going to Fire Island, O says meet me here tomorrow morning at 5:30 O.K.? That's a little early for me M says we need a vacation (hold it, did I order the right breakfast? I point out look how nourishing this thing beside the toast is, there's even a little caviar in it white plus greens and I've ordered coffee and this thing and toast and a Grand Marnier and because of the Grand Marnier no it's O.K. and because of the Grand Marnier the waitress will have to write this one up special, double separate order forms, drinks, for two drinks in honor of two that's so, I wish for a surprise, seven people cannot fit into a Volkswagen has wound up in an indoor pool and we look for it, it's gone it must be the wrong pool, what do people eat cause you can't get a Volkswagen out of a pool that fast so S. gets a job as a streetcar driver and he must answer 2 questions: mother? father? I tell you I saw the double separate order forms for his drink and his drink that is mothers and babies, no mean and women, we argued about that we smoked about that we smoked we argued about that we smoked poetry it's easy to see what is double separate) and what is not.

So why do I keep seeking her and why does she keep seeking me, to adjudicate to hear and decide, you can always find room, slave states, in the slave states you are too tired you cannot movie I'll give this to you anyway then tomorrow day after tomorrow slave states and the pig you dig? Always catching up to do. I look for her and so I look for her to make me words I am working he is waking he is waking he is moving I don't, I don't want to be where I am dreaming wish I were dreaming I am dreaming this: babysitting and chewing glass, it's something I'm used to doing, glass, yes, but glass, no, I spit it out he's getting up or at least something snaps in the other room maybe the electricity maybe the storm I predicted I'm afraid to look I look, knee up, chin on knee, I am naked twice in the airy hallways of the great hotels, I know what I am doing I am not eating rice here I am not calm either but now two elevators of police are full and rising and they say let the doors open and I say let the doors close and I will do it myself and I say let her speak to me it's my words spoken anyway and the words are danger powerlessness and a memory and his mouth is open when he sleeps and I try to summon up her words my words or words from her, these words and the words are I almost committed a murder and she says you should have really done it, traveling alone, traveling above, traveling where, traveling in taxis in comfort in crime in convent in full evening meals and there is where in an empty room and Chandler really gets it on, a black man confronts me with the almost crime, it's the murder: demand things. And it's a joke. Cause the murder: demand things. Cause fear as I am he takes me in the next parlor room where all the great musicians continue on they're jamming all black me too all the jazz musicians and this black man who had confronted me, he introduces them, he points them out to me one by one and they know why I am always seeking her, she is not connected she is not unconnected as the white people say mothers make you feel better. So, I told you not to come in and he keeps his mouth open, her and dead not supple and supple death is a movie so, B to California Wednesday F & B to Europe Tuesday C to New York Wednesday L to Philadelphia tomorrow D may have a week after the 15th S may go away Wednesday SC to Massachusetts Friday A to New York today, where is he. I took a vacation anyway and put myself to self to sleep the woman as ideal is the trinket-woman I don't like ideas today is Sunday Monday Tuesday and Wednesday he adores him and that is a sensation and he goes to bed early don't call him late he goes to bed early he leaves as a method and he leaves you a screen through it mosquitoes bite and you wonder whether you survive it at all surround it at all and no one will do it and the one that will do it is forbidden one is depicted as a trick and that's the worst trick of all and I am advising you, leave and spend all your time with him, yes is no and my house is full of work, take it, one day, take it one day who so soullessly should I stop wishing for? Her above all and her image is a fish. Abolition is cigarette no match smoking goes out the window so colors come in I wish they would and when you separate is clear: Einstein black Fern locus conclusion listen our lady of how Dante nonhuman hydra hydra double dream centenary basic police anxiety memoirs Rilke and philosopher scientist hole song September life notes solus dash I began the flowers to write La Vita Nuova environment summer season of spring Poe police photography and magic thinking of a young Duino Elegies. You take em with you but be quiet.

●

SLAVE STATES, an unfinished dream: there's a car accident involving the two cars ahead of us on the road. They collide, either head to head or back to front. Not much damage done to the cars. Their collision blocks the whole road (state of siege). We're the first car behind them, we stop. Two old ladies get out of the less hurt car. They are all right, they've been hit from behind. I look into the other car. I am the first to look (so far, nobody thinks anybody's been hurt, that's the way it looks). There's a girl slumped over the wheel, she looks pretty mangled, blood all over, Duino Elegies, she's unconscious. Max comes over and sees, starts to carry her out of the car, he shouldn't move her, etc. She looks like me or Kathy or Kathleen. He shouldn't move her but he does, carries her out into the mise en scène, paper maché boulders, a backdrop of scenery, a sloping hill. She's not breathing as far as he can tell, Carol, so he gives her artificial respiration, mouth to mouth and massage, heart massage, turns her over, turns her upside down, slaps her on the ass, makes her breathe, making the baby breathe. At least after a few minutes, she jerkily starts to breathe apparently again and she's angry. She's angry with Max, maybe she's confusing him with the one who caused the accident. A crowd has gathered but no police or official cars. She's angry, Max gives her twenty dollars (for her trouble?). What kinda whore is this? The crowd says, well, we were waiting for you to resuscitate the girl so we could call the authorities, cause, you see, they'd arrest you two cause you're foreigners. And now I remember the movie, possibly with Paul Muni, that this dream is related to, about Paris during the war and a man who has no passport, I think it was Charles Boyer.

Our next stop is to pick up our grammy award. Max won't have much to do with this, I have to do it for him, even though it's really his and the guy who's giving it to me is making endless boring conversation, like, he says, they used to be so pretty and oh now they're not at all pretty. Our granny award. But it's really Max's, no Spider's, and he has no patience with the guy, finally I get the piece of award paper which has red-stamped words all over it and in fact is pretty in a way and go back out to the car. Now granny, who's evidently been with us all along, stubborn superstitious granny, refuses to get back in the car because she's afraid there'll be another accident. So we did cause the first one after all. So she walks stubbornly down the road away from the car, that's all. A granny knot is a knot like a square knot but the ends are crossed the wrong way forming an awkward and insecure knot. I am not the heroine of this memory.

●

I dream I can't remember, I dream Ted is at the bar with the beer and the other poets, I go there on my way to the 8th St. subway, I go back to the house for another beer for the ride, Max and my mother are arranging plants, they can have it. And then I dream I escape through the potato cellar in Stockbridge and there's an older man who helps me here, embraces me and I realize I say I've invented the erection. And then I get angry when I dream I'm stuck in a place and it's no place, it's just dialogue: "O.K. then I'll move my things out while you're out." And the pages are too small to draw on, they're "romantic," and "when will I see you again" and Kathleen is the reincarnation of Brian Jones, whoever he is, he's a swimming pool, she became this on Pierre's birthday: "It'll take years" and "I didn't wanna wake you." "Try an electroencephalogram." "No, no machines."

Dear Ted, I'll try to write this letter carefully but I don't have time, I've been seeing a lot of strangers-lovers in my dreams and looking for your wife. I can't explain.

Love, Bernadette

●

Iran space, Opal room, inconsiderate beer, Fern room, Coco Lopez, Scarlet Letter.

You're in an open space in Iran, you just got off a plane centuries ago, there's no one there, you concentrate, you remember: someone who stays on the plane today will meet you tomorrow at the ruins so you check the map, it's a street map: fine gray lines on a white sheet, the locations of Unh and Sheh and Shuh.

What are these open empty spaces like doorways in the whited-out light, the low tan buildings white out in the sun, you are calm and you remember: centuries ago I would've been afraid, I ran she ran he ran and he ran, its periodicity: you concentrate and study the map. "I am reading another language by instinct, I locate the ruins in an open space to the north at Unh." A reversal of the action of the verb moving not moving, a removal or release from the state expressed by the noun immobility, mobility. Love anger. The double negative a memory. I walk north slowly, I pass Sheh, I pass Smer, I locate the ruins by moving around their periphery with my eye. I'm walking north to find a hotel to spend the night close to the ruins. I see no one I see clearly I can see one street in the north and from its British-English multiplicity of syllables I can guess that this is the street I'll find a hotel on and people, a peripatetic street. I float and drift into a hotel and through every room of it. In the sleeping rooms people are sleeping I am invisible I walk over their beds. In the dining room I hover over tables, people eating, I listen to the murmur of their periphrastic speech, so many even syllables, they cannot see me. A reversal of the action of the verb, a removal or release from the state expressed by the noun: tomorrow you will walk east from this street to the ruins at Unh to meet someone and this is your talisman, take it with you.

The secret action in time of a reversal in language in memory will renovate will navigate will clear this space for you, already clear, going backwards, Iran the nurse the memory, in white with fine grey lines drawn marking off the borders of the streets to indicate the new space of the ruins, an opening.

●

Max tells me I am inconsiderate for not giving the people to the right, east of me, anything to drink but beer. Then a party of us launches an attack on Opal's room, she's still in it. It's an investigation, David and I have an official connection but I won't go into the room. We have doctors and police with us. No one is in danger. Opal is stubborn she stays in the room. All alike, Opal, that's a green name. Then David, that's a black name, and his room goes to Fern a red name who stays in it yelling out periodically, "I have a 4:15 appointment, I have a ____ and for free!" She says this she yells to us in the big room and we can hear her. David's at the door, the room's space is filled with people.

July 25

Sleeping at Spider's I dream the kids come home and two of them have red hair and freckles and one is Spider and they go to bed but scream for their mammas and Spider says be quiet, Peggy will be here tomorrow and little Spider sits on the bed, removed, and I move and my covers get caught up with him and pulled off of me and he's annoyed and removed, sexually assaulted mentally breaking down and entering and I look down at the table by the bed and there's an open can of coconuts brown and white, open to look at not to eat, Coco Lopez, it goes past my eyes at Spider's a grey name. Spider the child and Spider who tries to keep them quiet for me.

July 26

The Scarlet Letter, we travel all over. In Massachusetts, Charlie and Pat have the Scarlet Letter, it's a long letter done on red paper in sable ink and Charlie's father has it and someone asks him who's script is that and he says mine, I copied it and this is the schizophrenic writing, good isn't it, and everyone applauds the lettering in long sentences but there are scraps of paper left in my hand from the end of the letter and it's not so hot and we've traveled from there to here to rent a room full of Puerto Rican kids all yelling for chicken, no they're cooking chicken and I know they'll all be yelling for it when it's done and we step over them and one complains and I yell back at him and then suddenly the view out the window is wonderful, glistening running water and I say see it's not so bad renting a room with all these kids (and before they've had their girlfriends sleeping with them and only twelve years (Kilton) old and now) out the window they play at spearfishing except they do it to each other and when one plays dead in the water the water's washed away and it's a sand bar and on a trip around we see a blue cathedral of trees bluer than spruce, approaching it but when you're flush with it you can't see the trees for a stone cathedral door, more ruins, same shape as the trees and someone says you'll never get back in that car the tires are bald but we will if we don't have to pack all that shit and packing someone else's bags there's a green silk cape and Spider has to check to see there are no drugs there, we are moving around a lot we travel all over no plan, it's a movie, what could I say more.

I draw this picture of an orange sun with my hat on the bier as everyone approaches drawing lots: "Will she draw near?" I don't remember what day he died in the heat. It was the day Leo the Last was playing "he died."

September 2

MEMORY mourning, beer, campari and soda, objects, dead. September 2. That's it. I somehow lost the brother, writing in secret maybe by writing in secret. "Don't go." A pale light on the evening star haze, it goes. Too bad about memory too bad about Duane Thomas too bad about Jim and Larry Brown. Rubs ice on the back of his fellow player. Later, the secret, yellow on a field of black, burns. This time it burns: pretty picture of memory, you like it? You like my sister? 5 pesos for Fern, Fern is always Fern is always so so what you've seen it all before you remember, if you want, pale at best pale in this kind of light you remember you eat each other out in the parking lot you chase a girl around the corner you are a savior, once you get started. Blow you and when's it gonna rain, when's it gonna rain sun sun and when's it gonna rain, your boat's so small and the sea so large. Pretty young boys. O.K. Max would be interested to think that Spider was homosexual. I would be interested to play that Max would be interested to think that Spider and he were both homosexual. I were homosexual so far only: give em a good strong drink give em porter give em an emollient give em fuck the light fades I'm only left who left me out who nurses me who stole from me who is a pretty young boy, suck on me. Danny and his wife retired they went to Cape Cod, Danny and his rubber-gloved wife retired I want to go to sleep, your sleep. And the air there. It's not the light here or the heat or the fan it's the emergency service that eats shit a poet on my hands no encomium cause I can't see shit blue turns to grey and finally no one goes away I gave it all away and when's it gonna rain my students seek me and when's it gonna rain you let things drift even rented things and when's it gonna rain it's dark enough: "We consider you a part of our family." Yes but from what distance do you view? Me you tied to the inexorable luxury of change, I forget, no body up stairs who cares, BM 8 pm careful not to lose my mind and body comes along too, tentatively as a giraffe.

September 6

This begins where mourning leaves off and I'm the one and I'm the one writing on lines reduced to writing on lines: the past is colorful and that is memory is full of color and bright lines, design, and careful colored record, so, where are you? In between the lines: careful not to step between the antennae, you ain't what you useta be blues, and so, dreams become false and grey, false, you're here on light paper, on paper that blows, is blowing, false, you're not here I'm here, I'm continuously I'm contemplative I'm moving toward a move and by stupid I mean ride fast in a car so, you give up all you have to give, it's the stakes and then, you make yourself safe—music I want music everywhere and what is the stake they name investment and what's the stake they designate "score"—I am not waiting. I got all the stuff, you're not with Kathleen, you may be looking for her, you are at stake somehow leaves, can you see it can you hear it can you read it what am I gonna do, lose, no more lovin, no more tastes, no more desperation, no more angels, no more suffering you suck my tit, for what art for mark, I'm alone, I use the notebook as a sphere cause pretension comes in here, your polar ice caps and my boat is so small and the sea so large was the only line I laughed out loud at, away and a taste of the country, remorse and the final policy, policy of evil what is private, not a dumb police car coming to tell me what to do, police action: they're giving somebody a ticket for parking on the sidewalk, halfways, see how good I can stay within the lines cause I can see they're eating the ones I am worried about are eating and the situation's not good so the cops came and went, you wanna hear about GP? No, country, remorse and I write this here and I write this here and I am in love with you too, an old old old man and a sequence of events: upstairs downstairs it could go on forever now, again, it's over and I might as well go on: STORY: there are exercises in color.

I don't understand why everybody who's going crazy at all can't take everybody else with them. All. I don't watch the bus or the train. I don't watch the cars go by. I don't catch the train. I get in as much as I can. I don't angle for ups or downs. I meet you meet too. He's empty and fed up. I'm in a series: no, country, remorse—there's nothing new about it there's something careful about it. I don't get paid. I do get laid and with all that I find the time to send you this note: darling, this message is convoluted, I am escaping to the forest in a few days, look for you there, find you, love, unsigned. Unsigned because there is no message unsigned because there is no design because why, I was right in the beginning I'm continuously I've heard from a voice behind him I'm contemplative, blues. So tell me how long do I have to wait so tell me how long do I have to wait, you are emerging but you'll never be finished be done and if I never finish you I won't make any money and I'll have to go on working with sirens around me, blue lights blue plants a fast ride in a car: I am right in front of you, can you see, can you, Bernadette, one by one, will call, please come home, do not sleep, home me.

I am suckling of rare extraordinary breakfast, rivers of one kind salt run into rivers of another sea and then I know what I'm doing when I see that and drink the stream water you give out put out you see because I show it to you and you feel the same way for the moment at least of abstract recognition we're the human ones and can't feel where we are until panic vanishes that space, it does it must not natural clear water and all I am doing is waiting anticipating you see I can't see in. Where Jack Benny pours the drinks at the French Bar, it's up to $1.70 and you have to buy stamps, two stamps and Kathleen is acting crazy all over the place and Max tells me to suggest to her it's just her period, she's sitting in the middle of two men, a bib? Eating? Helen of Troy? And so in this dream we pass Spider on the way to the bar and he gives me money for beer but he's running, embarrassed cause he's dressed to kill and made up like a black cleaning lady with red hair and then we try to get a loft in a place like Westbeth, windows on two sides, but the only place left is up in a corner somewhere and it only has vents, I've been here before. And Jack Benny is with me again the next night too.

September 10

Nearly threw the book in the fire many fires three fires many lunatic flies, one freeze many frozen: Raymond Radiguet tells me this is shit, give in to it, the monarch butterfly the fear of death or compromise is dry, space you need time. So I'm apt to make fires in my throat, Dora, and smell piss all the time. I can't stand these thin wet pages accumulating, she weaves, sun and soon I won't write them anymore, the sun's hot it's up to 78 today, 36 tonight: the peppers got black on top last night, the peppers got black on top and some leaves cars pass truck passes by 1:30 am, three bells on the ship captain's clock, no, you ring in answer if you're on watch, I suppose I should write Massachusetts is clear in the first person, see it? Moments there are no moments 2 B present in what moments, beer what beer, sure there's always plenty of instinct instants but no sex and there's got 2 B an end 2 it, so there is.

When I was in grammar school, that's the school you went to when you still had a gramma, I used to like writing on the flip side of the page, after all there might be a bee in your shoes when you put them on: I used to like the voluptuous feel of it, soft, already used and caressed, rather than the virgin toady fresh page: I couldn't help myself if I wanted to feel even an inch above water, high flies suck confrontation-concentration: where's the water, sir? There's not enough, you. You keep covered up on a farm hot or no and not moving, new pneumonia, pancakes you eat, new pneumonia you eat your lip you eat your flashing signal you eat your sun-up flares you eat your outfitted car you eat your welfare money there's an awful lotta people looking for you, there's an awful lot provided in your work, trucks provisions, hands down trouser legs down, father-owner-whatsis-electrician, say, that's a coax, what's the other end for, fly in the shade you fuckers, gone for more plastic sneakers, so they were both geniuses one pursued one thing the other pursued everything and all the one thing wound up being the same things for both of them, thanks, bye. Father-owner-hot enuf for ya?

Attracts flies, then faints, then sweats the goats get pinned up, for pin the tail on the donkey at night, then escapes, then freezes the two carefree people nearly froze to death when they left the warmth of the fire on pills at night, flies and iron, a stealth, a warmth, a back-up truck making smoke, I tell the truck: you can do it all the time: you hear an engine stop you collect wood you race to the first clear blue sky you see, it's a noun, you shake it by the ear, you entertain and plea-bargain, you go in and eat pancakes: "We met him mostly because he didn't waste words in this country paradise on the shore and she wanted her to go way away but she kept reappearing to catch the last rays of the sun so it was hard to work it out that is the ideal situation and oddly she likes to be alone with him whereas nobody really likes to be alone but some can make something out of it or in it."

Of all the clinical pictures which we meet with in clinical medicine it is the phenomena of intoxication and abstinence in connection with the use of certain chronic poisons that most closely resemble the genuine psychoneuroses.

●

Viva la Sangre del Salvadore Allende!

●

September 17

Spending the night alone: Sleepers: this is one idea and from a pile of sleepers I extract one by one and I eat out the ideas the possibilities, alternatives, from them and then throw them on the used pile, one by one, railroad ties. Or, 51-49 and almost completely surrounded.

And my arm is beautiful, Grandfather, a screen, dies. A woman comes out the door, out of the bushes, she speaks, men riding on horses. So, screen, she cries. He carries the casket, they speak a word, memory, used. He took a pill he's quiet: you strain your muscles so: and so, speaking of it, grandfather dies (I tell no one I tell everyone and Kathleen is sitting demanding in the Gramercy Park Hotel with a black nurse waiting and I feel like writing to everyone but I will not).

Horribly I have no vision and I can't make one legible for you, speak now and I will try too many and I say no and I keep on saying no, no to the vision and no to the spokes that try to persuade me by almost completely surrounding, my trust I suppose. And clear I can't be clear, this is unique and it's astounding, I have no sex, you will read it and I keep on spending my eyes on his gloom or stone. Hawthorne, were there thorns, were there, you come here or else I have nothing more to spend it to spend on it, so carefully molested, the dream: so carefully wrapped in perverse, no clothing, wrapped: if you speak I will not speak if you are alone then I am not if you are aware I am in space I am a woman so spaced out, so you are not. The smell of the cheese fills the house and I feel like two people are dead because one is and one is fighting like I am fighting for a space but I am not fighting but she is not fighting, I've lost my address I've lost the you and so, then, this is not worth fighting for, an orgasm, a fight, an erection, a resurrection, a full Easter bonnet: I open the window for the terrified moth and I do not know what I am doing escaping except this: someone's mother makes a shadow on my page and someone's father makes my foot swell so I must make a design like a dense breast, mother father, mother uncle, I did it backwards like design always does based on design and not rooted in fact, please forgive me cause I can't write fast enough and please forgive me cause I can't do and please forgive me cause I'm not what and please forgive me I said I was greater than I am and you'll all have to please forgive me cause I have no one else to speak self to so you. I am lighter than a wave, undertow, Andy drowned he did not drown, I am serene, stiletto, she drew it on, Max was knifed he wasn't knifed, this is not this is what is a reference: you save and you wait. It's unlike me to leave a photograph lying on the floor, it's unlike me to listen to the trucks and hear, it's unlike me to continue in the book without a thought, you thought you were away, washing, and you were here watching: you've given up before and you can't do it: "At least she's here," "At least he's here." The light adores my eyes and the wind fucks me up: "Throw it away," "Put her away." And my hair the hair of my body has no focus, caress it and I say to it, "How long can you live?" I want to leave things wasting, I want to throw them away, I am in between, I don't do it, I waste between the lamps, I use it all up I don't caress it, I'll be sick because this is shedding its use, I'll only waste time and set you up, you asked for it, there's no one to caress it but me and what am I talking about, my sex, between my legs, you said it, my heart's not in it, so I make it easy, just read the truck revs up three times and drives garbage away and everyone is looking pretty like a cat but no cat to be seen, I'm seen, I'm looked at I'm ice, listen: we have a lot of work to do, my knife drills into you, work to do, fuck you, I look at you, I eat the body, in state and no end to the quotes.

I am less lucid than I was before, can you hear me? I am begging you now. Because I have to, nothing else to do, two things: two dead things. That's all. So I go on? No way, not like before, either way. Nothing to go on one two Max, the spider and the door before, Ted, the spider and the door before, who are the spider and the door before, I fear for my life and everybody laughs because they have to or have too many dreams: "I thought it was what you wanted me to do" and "I assure you I am exactly the same as the corpse on the floor" and "I forgot I was the most important person in your life" and "You have your private space I see so it's worth it (in money)" and I dream too much for you but if I could really dream too much for you lucid then liquid then, R.M. and B.M., it's easy to change an R into a B, not me. You do it with a pin.

And bites from fleas from angels from warm-weather beds from fronting a love an affection that could grow from any bed that led to another three weeks or three days in a bed in the country making love with one man: what's the difference, I can. And I blew it and I'm trying to make it go on as long as I can: residue from songs and pictures and money too. WXLO alone, let's get it on, touch me in the and so on, so everyone tell me, what has this man got trapped, not time, losing ground, sinking down, well I'll tell you, it's no body and it's no time and no ground except covered and no use wasting your time on stone you see? The radio's on I wanna feel something so I write down cover and hover and lover, honey I wish there was one. The ceiling flies and a hidden corner and there is something you want to hear.

<u>Black Holes</u>: If a massive star collapsed to a sufficiently small volume, light could not escape from it. A rotating black hole could account for the radiation of gravitational waves from the center of the galaxy.

A black hole is a region of space into which a star (or a collection of stars or other bodies) has fallen and from which no light, matter or signal of any kind can escape.

What is the fate of the original body that collapsed to produce the black hole? Assuming that exact spherical symmetry is maintained right down to the center, the answer provided by the general theory of relativity is a dramatic one: according to the general theory, the curvature of space-time increases without limit as the center is approached. Not only is the substance of the original body squeezed to infinite density at the center of the black hole—that is, effectively crushed out of existence—but also the vacuum of space-time outside the body becomes infinitely curved. The effect of this infinite curvature on a hapless observer, were he foolhardy enough to follow the body inward, would be catastrophic. He would feel tidal forces across his body that would mount rapidly and would reach infinity within a finite period of his experienced time.

●

I've got no book, I give up on memory, GP's dead, I give up on sex, you won't get in, I give up on image, you won't get in, I give up on breath, upper respiratory infection, Dora, we made a great mistake, "limits" and no limits, "chances" and no chances, all the chances, midnight, Friday I give up a meeting, everybody shows up, Smithson, GP, Salvador Allende, Sy Goldes have funerals and wakes, I wake up and give up, I am a fool: Max kills himself but there is another self of him left which he assures me is exactly the same and "I thought that's what you wanted me to do" and the body is a problem, it lies around, almost waking up, we think of carving chopping it up, I don't wanna hear about it. I wanna avoid it and then I have to go to high school again so I get home early to Max in the shower and he says without bitterness without design, "Oh I forgot I was the most important person in your life" and he did forget and then, scene, Teresa is splitting up the $96 in tax money with me, "We each take $45," she says and complains in the crowded busy apartment about how I won't deserve to pay the rent when...and so I extend the dream further: we walk through the rooms watching people work at small things till finally and it takes a long time (you have no time for me), we reach a large empty room papered with memory (turns corners) and she says, surprised, "You even have your private space."

And even before this I waste time getting home from school by playing with Gerard and Andy, Andy buys drinks but not for me, is stingy, cranky, when we all kiss I am looking at him, I'm interested in him for the first time. I try to buy food, it slides down the counter, you're jealous of me, the counter slides down the food I am a fool, I am wasting my time, I don't want to get home cause you forgot you were…in a big house for summer dinner, everything goes wrong but the scenery and the time goes slow, I don't want to remember and I don't want to speak to Patti to Edmund to Spider to Fern to Lynn to Mark to Andy to Max to Larry to George to Ted to Starr to Lucy to September at all to Stanislaus to all the demands they make on you when they bring back the little news and Barry didn't eat all weekend again cause we were gone and Andy brings money and Spider brings dreams and money and school's open so all the Kathleens are present here, one to teach one to get married and one Cassandra who can't be caught and all the dreams that can't be taught, complement me and I notice who can't spell and I weave, I'm not well: when I was a sailor, a sailor on the sea, the sky was turning orange, my baby was like me, the sky was turning orange the sky was turning black, I wrote it in my journal my baby wants me back.

And are you brother and sister and is the sea like me and when are you alone and by yourself, you're alone and left and Chile, Allende, was shot, is dead and you recover from your career, recover, hover, lover is my cover and my incorporation of what draws me back, whose mind is that in? Everybody wants to be married, trumpets blow, that's the trouble, everybody wants to play house and me, I'd just do it again and again, "Could she really not move?" "At least you really did it" and "What?" "Not move." Now I really lock the door, one two three four and everybody dies and they don't know and they need somebody to show how lifelike life can be to them, how deathlike life can be for them, how everybody knows but they would rather eat shit if only I could show them now when I can't keep myself private enough to know what's going on when I have no space of my own as in the dream without sound, when I answer all calls when my voice can't speak, when I answer no mail, when I get ready again to retreat, if only I could put on this show, if I knew how to begin, what to play on what instrument, what to show, how to seduce without making love, how to be cruel without maddening, unfair, I want to be unfair, one by one and just cause I find myself counting perverse, how long will I have some silence, this one, perverse show, perverse lines, you want my collection of real mash notes and suck-off letters, goodbye. "This is more fiction than an essay," eat shit, and it don't go no further, fairness allows that someone's got nothing to do but count points and make tallies in the same Western tradition of bloody coups d'état. So I go to work amusing you and now no one's got nothing to do and I've been to work, a former physician, turned politician, a Marxist incorporating you, working for you, getting on t.v. and then sunk in a trunk like case in the earth dead forever on your side, I'm comparing myself to Allende from my palace in your open loft where my private space seems to be, might be, that's why you listen to me and when I call you and when I go outside, if I amuse you, you'll be ready to nothing with me, it's better for the poor to know me than thee.

So I'm anger dead here finally cause I'm conscious of you and no body speaks to me and I won't tell you what's here on the table, laid out in front of me, same thing's in front of you, on ice, a body that could make a book or a trip or a story or a lunatic of you, just tell me, can I watch for a while, in pieces, quite spaced out: my own process gets mixed up with yours and how come after doing all this damage like death you have nothing much to say. There's alone, there's reasons of state, there's great dialogues, there's certainty, there's devil in the flesh and all love stories, so just read to me at night and take your time running around or running the country. I'm 28 in 1973, I could've lived my life twice in this time, I have no privacy back to where we both began at the south, at the north extremities of the pole, earth by earth, we figure out about electricity or something, do it all over again, so many endings for any discovery or idea to happen twice or even many times. I used to share ideas with you and now I hide so it must be over, I need a rapidograph pen, I need not to be aware of any you, I need a custom to re-design, I'll be right out, I need not to think about you, you make mistakes, you are a fool, me too, I don't need a dream at all, review the polar ice caps, my fucking throat is killing me, performances. And that's the design for a new sign, are you still waiting for me to come out, and can I perform still perform still service you, I can't end it here but I will it's a free election: so run for your life, that's my other life.

September 24

I've got no track of the time and I've got no track of the railroad running, in desperation, count worries in and you and wanna go home to a mommy and wanna come home to mamma and the train's not in the vestibule's a diary too the answer to: easy reading, public messages, extending arms legs and feet of the letters of the alphabet making green soup through a sieve out of the universe from a mix called the German Mechanics Mechanismus Mix, German Chocolate Cake Mix and German Macaroon Mix, that's the universe mush, B. Mayer, and, I dream in a fix that someone's outside (rewrite it, it's an analogy to reprocessing in process, a memory, according to how you write now: dream's a memory kept in process kept in present, whose consciousness?) and someone's outside and close to waking in another room I think maybe the loft is being robbed or someone's here but to avoid waking I will not wake and I turn over to dream grandfather's outside in the other room in Ridgewood (with curtains and the wallpaper and I can tell by the wallpaper, one beneath the other, layers) and he's puttering around and I'm annoyed by this invasion of my privacy, announced death, conserved electricity, delivered milk: to announce death, to conserve electricity, to deliver the milk. Participate in death, witness death, announce it, the drudgery of it, then mix things up, then die: go to a wedding in black with someone on your side to stand for, to represent (why not say "know") past experiences. I was going to list everything GP ever did but I know and no use your knowing except that I know and this one thing: he invades my space of mourning by surviving, strange thing to say about a dead man who shows up in dreams ecclesiastically except that in the dream I wasn't surprised to see him at all and unlike the parent dreams I didn't know he died so I cried but only when I coughed, mirror mirror what a heel and this is a strong day.

September 25

And more red anger and more red tide, a simple play and maybe what can't be seen, David went fishing in my shoes, some geniuses, you don't have to live with them they won't have you live with them and maybe your eyes are wrong about living alone cause after all it's a generation without families to be seen and Max is sleeping in bed, broke his promise cause he said he was my family and why not worry about living alone is left or being left, abandoned, nobody left, alone, many friends, just friends and every one not quite right to rely on, to count on, to know what they're doing and where and where you are but anger and resentment is shown, it shows and we were wrong and there is nothing long term about living someone else's life and the reason there's no milk and crackers in this here is cause it seems so urgent it seems so important like a life and death issue as one might say, from one to one, and she was still there and she was still there and then she was gone all gone and Max was over and Stanislaus was here and Andy came in and school's open but not for us cause without the milk and crackers you can't I can't tell what I'm thinking at recess I don't think, I can tell it's 2:30 by looking at the clock but with them I don't know what I'm waiting for so that's waiting for you (and me), it's writing to decipher, if I can, you always can as I underestimate my over-estimated perceptions funnily so writing's become so precious like bird in tree, like $4.95 notebook, blue with double Japanese cover and I have my will, knowing exactly what's going to happen as if it were routine or routinely written in less than two dimensions as if in a modern novel and what's Max got, he don't feel all right and what's he want, perfection from me like rising up out of the sea and movie and money to make and no ice, I mean no trouble, troubles take a lot of time, like my father's business failed and he was 35 years old and there is no life left except what your culture tells you to do unless you got rebellion to tell you elsewise and there ain't enough eyes dying in the sea to suckle you with that protein, to just fight, for fun cause there's nothing else to do and there's another one involved here, Nixon the trickster as Max would like to cough-control him and as one who wins here a piece of penitence from me but for all: I am sorry folks that I made such a great mistake but especially cause it's one I don't have to pay for: I will try to explain my mistake: but first a word in paler grey about the other one who would take care of me support me, all this if only I will be his full-time mother too and a third one who will excite me and my own brain which is under my hair somewhere impulsing fingers at least, if any: the mistake my mistake was this: I picked a pack a peck of pickled peppers along the glass to the spider, no, I went out on a limb, it's like playing the numbers when we all know they're all the same, and does anybody I mean do other people get all their work done too? Elizabeth Barrett and Robert Browning get married, then what do they do, do they sink ships, no, they write simple short verses, have a child or two, maybe not so simple, and move to Italy where they always wanted to be. Nathaniel Hawthorne and his wife Sophia or Rose or whatever her name is visit them after seeing the Faun of Praxiteles and knowing what it feels like to have the kind of knowledge, little as it is as Hawthorne would say, you accumulate by 28, in poor health, an old hypochondriac, compared to Stanislaus' 22 years when he thinks he knows nothing, well I still know nothing but I can smell something and I'm interested in changing the world still, now here I am living with the most unhappy man who is most unhappy as he ever has been, from his own mouth. A more intrepid talker than myself would have shouted her ideas across the gulf but for me there must first be a close and unembarrassed contiguity with my companion or I cannot say one real word. I doubt whether I have ever really talked with half a dozen persons in my life, either men or women. And before I saw the Faun of Praxiteles. So, there's nothing else to do but magic, miracles and spectacles, I cannot cure him with a note a letter on rebellion a case of money and I cannot change myself but the thing that fucks me up is this: this is the fashion, what I've described and I have always been intrepidly out of fashion and perversely in disguise and I can sit here alone all night every night and write till my eyebrows grow even longer, they glare out and begin to describe my whole face, some shadow on the face I'm looking out on and do you like good music and no I don't even like good writing, it's pure poetry, it's pure crap what you decide to like and what does it matter who loves you and what does it matter to? But I never described my mistake to you, here:

July 1917, I mean 1971—Memory, a difficult time.

August 1971—sensational dreams resulting from Memory. But before that:

1964 (October)—I meet Max and live with him, I move to Syracuse and quit school.

(December)—I get pregnant, Max's parents give him a lot of shit about school during the holidays, I tell him I'm pregnant.

1965 (January)—I go back to Syracuse, Max stays home and suffers.

(February)—I move back to New York, try to get an abortion, fail, get an apartment.

(August)—have baby.

(September)—go back to school and get a job.

1966 (March)—start to work at home so I can write more.

1966 (May)—turn 21, inherit money, quit job.

(July)—move into apartment with Max, Max works for Arnold Eagle.

1967 (June)—I graduate, get another job, Max gets a movie job, we move to York Avenue, do 0 TO 9.

1968—I quit my job again, Max works on more movies, I publish STORY.

1969 (June)—We move into Beatrice's loft for the summer, Max works on "A New Leaf," GP gives me ten thousand dollars.

(July)—I travel across country and go to California, Max quits his job and meets me there, he's unhappy.

(September)—We buy a car, drive back. I look for a house in the country, Max is planning to work on "Revolution." We stay in sporadic places in New York with Parnell.

(October)—I move to Massachusetts, Max lives on 36th St. with Parnell, works on the movie.

(December)—we buy the loft, Parnell's still living with us, they go to Chicago to shoot.

1970 (May)—I have to leave Massachusetts, come back to the loft, eventually Parnell leaves, I work on MOVING, we make many trips to the country, I hate the city for a long time, we buy videotape equipment, Beatrice and Kathleen have to go to the hospital, Max has many projects, MOVING goes to the printer's in February, we make tapes, have shows, Andy's around.

If only I had some whiskey maybe I could go on: September 1971—Max makes trips to Toronto. October 1971—I start the workshops, start to see David. February 1972—Memory show, basketball. April 1972—I start writing when I'm alone.

Maps are startling, I stopped coughing so what can I do to make some money and people happy and still do my work cause I'll do my work anyway cause I'm driven and it makes me happy even if I turn into a drunk or a dying person or a maniac, anyway it's all true, paper, go up in flames if you want. So I seem to have lost the fear and it's just the streets to rebel in, revel in.

●

I step into Kathleen's shoes and you have to look your best for public transportation.

And I'm drunk and I'm fulfilling all their fantasies, and, what a big joke on them, so I dally with the construction workers who are repaving our road and they think Wallace painted my sign: Nixon has met his finish in the mad house. They say, "He's gonna get up outta his wheelchair one of these days" and I say, "Oh yes." And we talk of the price of beer.

September 27

And in relation to those dreams, come to think of it, it was my mother who was thinking of marriage in those dreams of August 1971, this is tasty cheese, or rather, we were thinking of it for her, don't get a toothache in space it would spoil your space-trip, we wanted all the excitement of a new daddy and every time we put it to her she would say, "But I am a sick woman." It'd be like stepping on a grave, well you can run but you sure can't hide and the light gets pink on memory and at first we took the public transportation to the radiation treatments or maybe we took the car ("Why don't you girls ever want to go for a ride?" and "We might as well get rid of it"—we gave it to Uncle George) and then as she got weaker we took the subway I mean we took taxis and just before she quit her job with the lawyer she was coming home on the subway one day, in winter, and got to feeling faint so when I got home from school she was lying on the couch and that couch was where something or everything is centered on: Marie was lying on the couch with my uncle there and everybody (I) wanted to know what was happening what had happened and they told me Marie had weakened on the subway had fainted or almost fainted, a cold sweat, close to loss of consciousness then and was resting, needed rest and I remember Marie's winter coat and I thought to myself, was it too warm and shortly after that she had to quit her job and could never eat the meals I fixed without throwing up, usually, afterwards and lying on the couch when the doctor came Marie was embarrassed, I can't really continue this though it's already written down, so that's why I dream too much and misinterpret my dreams, well they're open to interpretation: I seem to dream her dreams as I seem to walk her steps, her steps in the subway, her fainting steps, her steps in the hallway, her watching, her watching alone steps, steps to the treatment, sweetmeats, to the treatmeat, she was afraid to go alone, she was afraid to go alone, I looked out the window, I waited too, I did it over and I repeated it, as a performance, what is an art show anyway, I did it over and over again for some years and then, I wanted to stop but I'm not sure, I'm not sure I can give up the pleasure or her or Marie, as I seem to dream her dreams, as I seem to walk her steps, what's the pleasure, it's the pleasure of ice and removal and talking nothing, taking no one, as if, you speak, you are planning the imminence of your own death or only have a moment to lose, close to loss of consciousness, on the edge of loss of consciousness, at any time, a desertion, any moment, an intention, to lose. I accuse Marie of planning. I am trying to understand something, a narrative, you wrap up your feet and then you make your feet so small you cannot walk, but her steps, I'm getting mixed up, does sex make trouble or transform and will a white market fit in at all, white slavery, sold, I'm too sold on this, I don't trust it like I didn't trust her, I accused her of planning death as her own pleasure as I am now planning yours, "at my pleasure, at my leisure," it took four years, Marie, look at this, "at my anger," at my anger is a place for your invasion of my seduction, you forget.

October 2

And well I didn't, you gave me an idea, that is to write it sedated, and I still wear my thoughts on my scarf to excite you, you don't you were never trained to and I still drink my milk after feeding a few, you don't you were never trained to and this is the best meal you ever had but you will all be gone by Christmas, meal you ever had but you will all be gone by morning so if I hadn't come home just a gesture, would it make you any difference at all and are the books still up on the shelf, so we'll plan the trip to the cemetery by the full moon to lay heavy memory on their graves, visit graves. And Teresa in a green velvet hood jacket is in the station wagon back of the truck with memory, with the communists (what's the difference to you, you've got your brother here, Tom, Andy and so on) and they've come with supplies with sugar for my coffee for us, we're white, and I don't take sugar, in the tomb, night. In white Stockbridge, where else, day, and in cool white, it's orange, the college of New Rochelle, I see glaze color passes by eyes of design of modern building, I'm high, it passes that fast, and the buildings are a net, I'll get to it (I'm always thinking of others), so I give Stanislaus my saxophone where it's always off one note, Stanislaus the other one, another one and from the 31st floor they play a concert and his instrument, mine, fucks it up and after the show, show, we can hear them, they applaud, you are right and they yell to us, "Thank you Bernadette" and I'm living in a tent-room now, like a tent, sure, you can stand up in it, in the middle, an attic, but really though you can't and you can't even get out, it's hard to get out, with all the numbers and the floors and the girls, call girls, I saw them all before, in school, yes in school. And somewhere, there, I find a man or he comes to me and we are lying on stone listening to Stanislaus' grateful concert, all the wrong notes all the kisses, dead, and the man is giving me trouble, as always, all right, take it, about comings and goings, and my needs, all right, a nice man, too nice, Paul America, it's three, you and Andy and me and also, it's three and would you please be quiet, all right and where do you have to go in the morning, all right, I get up at 8:30 eat breakfast and go to the job, me too, and soon I'll be finished too, memory what a shame, in black, all the same, you too and it could go on forever so, are you in love with me, are you not, where are you are you here, so, and were the palms out here out where something important's going on, like the turning of pages in the family, it's in the family, you you and you, one sleeps one reads and one writes, what could be more right all right except that none of the ones is exactly happy there and they all went out for a drink so they dream and one dreams boxes white boxes and one dreams colors come at him and one dreams, me this is me, all kinds of tombs visions, hardly visions of tombs, aching tombs aching to be seen, you guess. You come alone and see it's a crowded cemetery and the roaches run all over the table and you get light: please believe me I'd do anything you say, so say it, you look so cute when your hair's messed up that it's hard for me to resist this long and whaddayou expect of me a faun, sexless faun, shag ears, Hawthorne's dog, his favorite pet, I try to forget and I do what's necessary politically to keep my comrades going, in arms, it's our armed struggle and viva la sangre de Salvador Allende, the physician, but I seem to escape and he says the greater the poverty the greater the disease, I saw him speak, I watched him speak and it just happened that he died, was murdered by the U.S. govt. in the same week in the same time as mother grandfather and you but I am not angry with Salvador Allende and this so this could make a fanatic of you, I mean of me except I am not and never was anything but a flea a pawn, whaddayou call the welfare ragamuffins, a something on the back of the U.S. govt. that murders Allende and its council on the arts supports me, a weasel? Is that it? Thirty bucks a week, buy it from the copper mines of Chile? I don't know. I am trying to change the world. I'll take anything I can get for food, if I can eat it. So bet it at the OTB office and run from one to the other with the racing forms and newly pave the streets, Grand Street and Canal and someone says if it was one up from canal it'd be grand, and newly pave the highway with pre-cast concrete blocks, I don't care, it's the Parks Dept. of NYC, and it's the city, new, blue police cars, have the cops, so spaced out, they can't get out of the cars, blue cars, to make an arrest, and we are not in power, we just paint slogans on the wall and we are not in power, we just try to change the fucking language and we are not in power but we take money for food, if we can eat it: whose mother are you cause then you feed it too and then only then, you can eat, horseshit, and well at least we got no leaders to manifest a prick to you, or a circular, eat shit, but do not commit suicide, now, your arms are too pale, or too terrified, or too brown. The black smear-men of Monument Mountain, drawn to look like a sphinx with the cloud above a series of interlocking gears, black November.

October 4

Thursday, hazy eighty's, I am writing like memory which Max stole to xerox on his own, 2:30 pm: Night, I am trying to escape from Stockbridge on the limousine (trolleys back and forth), we can't get tickets, we keep missing it cause it only blows its horn three times and then pulls away but it runs often and I am the last to pack. Who's there? What am I packing? I've been here a long long time (Max's parents) and I leave a lot, throw it away or will I come back, do I plan to come back? It's hard to fit it all in, I leave a whole suitcase behind. The objects I'm handling (upstairs) escape me, maybe cosmetics (Kathleen), anyway they're the last to be packed, the dream keeps being over but not. We are sure to make the next (crowded, looking for room for three, which three) limousine.

And the Berkshires accommodates a limousine, "First time I'll ever go back." The suitcase in the forest, a giving back or "laying it on" and so the dream is faithful to the scene, it fits right in, not like the stuff I have to pack, someone who is not in a hurry is co-ordinating this, leave all out, include all.

And I want to turn away in bed, I wake up turned around, what's the difference between night and day in dream: blue grey olive forest, brown blue and white turquoise tan blue red grey black blue gold, blue orange (terra cotta) blue green blue blue blue blue olive blue black blue blue blue red blue, turquoise black white green red ochre brown mud white brown blue blue green, black red white yellow red and white brown olive blue brown tan blue and white blue, grey green and only some bright red, blues and greens and bright white, the colors of the cars in the parkling lot of Mussolini, in rows. And I started thinking about my brother again but how could we be serious, with the glasses of wine, with his friend, without ever being anything but deeply serious in the house with a room downstairs with a door onto the garden, my room, his room is upstairs, I have a couch and glasses of wine, I bump through his door or do I push it, dropping everything, I forgot the extra glass, no I didn't know his friend was there, they left the stuff from their trip, or is it camping equipment in the hall, how does the door lock, in case his friend leaves, it locks from outside, it locks automatically and when there's another person, then it's difficult not to feel like a child, you wake up in the morning, are you upstairs or downstairs, you watch out for the maid cause you're having breakfast together, upstairs, les enfants terribles, so you drink champagne at a table near a long low window, someone yells up or rings the bell, saved, you aren't dressed yet but this is usual, it's quiet, what do we do today? You were camping there, we must be camping here, under a tent between the bed and the dresser, a little bear hangs upside down at the door, no, someone's put a lobster on the step, or a crab and run away, hides, waits, it's him again, I knew it, you won't cook the lobster, you can't boil lobster alive and watch it turn red and watch it turn green, it's nothing to see and then eat it. A fraction of an abreaction, fraction of relief, it's not enough, I'm starving I'm anxious to work out the mechanics of this, someone says that, you come so close to describing at least what is new, no describing there's no describing mechanics, a desire for length, transformed by speed, physiologically in memory, you work in stretches with a desire for length overtaken then by speed, you work fast to get it over with and since you are not creating memory you take no pleasure in it but the sound and sometimes the designing of the words, in bulk, you know it could go on forever and sometimes mind hazes over for no reason in the middle of it and since you know it could go on, you also know the ending and the end of it but could never even dream, so, later, you dream it right out loud in front of everyone and make a package without images, it's true it's too bulky for what it is, but apprehended all at once, as at the scene of the crime, it's crystal clear, who did what to who and consequence. So it's a question now of motive, it's no question at all unless a human science goes that far but if it does, in some terminology, some language not the common language, then you concentrate and try to design that one in. I'm quiet she's quiet. I wish we didn't have to speak thought, mutter to ourselves, repeat thought, who's out there. The mutterer says make it new and the one who ignores languages at all, he has morals. All anarchy all design like the patterns in leaf continue on, they seem to go on forever till and finally they do it, they repeat, and that's without speech where speech is never near road. I've written myself out of human use, there was no blueprint there was no plan. So I keep hearing my name called and I wash my face my hands your back, you're gone, I am forced to say so and

I don't want anybody to want me, no compromises, just care, like food. And what I was getting to is this, it's impossible to live, I never thought so until I saw what grief was when it is private and no one knows, so, everybody, their suffering and their art taking them around the world, one of them's here, I think I must want the main character to die.

October 5

I am still trying to escape from Stockbridge and we are in the car in an alley and the maniacal boy who tries to take over, tries to sideswipe the car against the alley, and I fight with him and we go to see the movie but I wrap David in my shoulders cause Max would be too bored or bared, it's necessary that you "don't tell" and designs: on the penises of the men in the movie, men in houses with the roofs taken off, a helicopter shot an aerial view, a map and organic designs, whole buildings built into their penises, houses full of people, no clothes on, in the movie and every once in a while a girl is pulled out by the roof and raped and someone yells but someone else says it's O.K., she's 15. I wrap up David in my shawl, we get back. And later Spider and I split to a place where there are beer cans of scotch in a cooler, the hallway of a hotel, and I realize I have to call my mother, no, she's not there, it's Teresa I have to call and I don't like this mix-up at all, trouble with the phones, I don't like these connections.

The origin of women myth, from memory: Some people just can't hack writing by hand at all, so, there was some meat hanging on a rack and hawk and parrot came to get it up, there were no women around anywhere to be seen (the myth has no style at all). They fought over it and two rope ladders were dropped for the women-thieves with toothed-vaginas, one for the pretty and one for the cracked and parrot flew away with them, at least, he flew away with two of them. Now that is all I can remember of that myth.

October 20

We don't use silver polish: I get drunk and I rage and I instinct but I never seem to come back home, keep memory awake. Its content, its rubber stamp and its signature is small and quite spaced out, I cut my thumb making inside old covers for Memory and the jokes of it cease to be small, let's not eat here. So memory comes what it becomes and leave that out from now on, let's not eat here, there are no black fishermen on the sea, no fishermen in it, how can I eat, let's not eat here, everything's cold, nothing's hot and nothing to kill, what is that bones or cartilage, rabbit or cat on you, it's like eggshells, milk across the watch and I'm racing: there's a word memory I'll never use again: to rubber-stamp it. But more, sideways, a space is used up, there's too much of it and I'm done. "How bad is the Pearl's injury?" "He's supposed to be back beginning of November." Me too. Like a line, I keep having all the symptoms but I can't have the dream, whose sex, whose space, whose graven image out of practice, whose line, starts

Just to make
Somebody's head spin out
Leave it alone
Take it on the road
Put em away
Go home
And what'd I say to you
Just, the last few blocks
Made me nervous
Cause I'd feel like a fool
Jumping in a cab
2 go 5 blocks
I'd say
It's here
I thought it was further
It's speeding or spread out
It's necessary dreams
Anymore, so?
You you and you
I ate I pulled a prank
There was a trick in the series
Where you ate like a lever
Then told
All fell asleep got well and cure
What'd you expect something new?

There's nothing to look for outside
I mean
I don't look outside anymore
For signs
At signs
That's why
I don't understand you
A moment
It's all absorbed itself stored up
I'm catching up
In a moment
I'll see you
Maybe
Grooming yourself by the door
You're an image of a bird
And call up all the gardens I sat in awake
Smoke blue cigarettes
Naked
The pedestal
Starling, exact
They get up for work
Out of reaches
It's easier than that so
It's worse than before
This form is a list
Of what I have to do
A long length
Of short lines
With no pause
I fell asleep
I went exact to the place
You never saw
Your face
So scared
As mine
The division I don't understand
Liquids
It's clear and thick

It's milk
It's wine
It's lights out
Or fear
Goes on forever
You don't need the wine for your fear
You need it to speak
Or drive the car
For you
I stand up
I go on vacation
I work my ass off
I cut my thumb with a razor
But don't record
Forbid recording
Forbear for fear
Altitude attitude
Synapse lapse
Fraction abreaction
The stink the smell
The white whites out
The blue invades
What's to tell
Next to blue
In here
Chopped
Chuck
In hallowed ground
No journey's an ape
I heard a man say frigging
About shit
No was a woman
Signing flames
I knocked over
The milk
Same with the wine I'm drinking
That's recording
A dream everything

In fast architect
Blood open the book
They dream I had no egg
I know you're crazy
This has been happening
Since the moon without being careful
He moves around
Me too me too
What about me
Leave it till morning
I never saw it never will

The difference between Saturday and Sunday is still in my system, it's not the date, it's the ballgame or something, you see I'm expecting by immaculate conception, it's a big thing. As a matter of fact it's the last thing I gotta do, I've got to do, I mean after that it's just women, just me and the women and this stone I'm the symptom of I think. It's never that easy, something always gets funny, it's small or little, it falls, I can make it fall, you too, you with you easy match who says what to who, said in the house. You can steal that too. Maybe I'll get off. At least I'm full, you want more there's more there's all you got.

Communicate lapses, lapses are like covers, you know how some writers...like the covers that are the lids of your eyes, sometimes, they lie or come in layers and the lid looks like three, like you fucked three times and got tired, didn't know where you were or lost "states of consciousness" for a while. Signed, Bernadette Mayer.

One more thing, I've got this energy and if the typewriter bothers you just yell cause I know I got it in me to explain this here in type with ribbons and you, you? You? And I began that way and I'll continue that way and it'll go on, a new work, laugh. You laugh and I make a new kind of sticking space and I know my mental acuity is tough and I know my mechanical acuity at this moment is a work of genius, that's all that's allowed, in here, so, and so, you got an hour to do what you set out to do, mechanically, mechaniste, and you and you and if the government false government falls in the mean time, well so what they don't know what we set out to do no how: call the cemetery, teach poetry at the New School and so on: apply for a grant that you ain't got in, mechanical facility is go, not go, I won't copy anything no matter what and spacing that out no, matter, what, more! Take it, please, I thought I had done it last night but you saved me you didn't save me and I am not no longer not the one not no more in touch with never mind I'll repeat it till I get it I won't get it I'll resign, I can't even see the work which is the type before eyes before clandestine, no, image, eyes: anyway eyes are easy to read, like mouth, like stand in the art of retrenching, like military takeover, imminent in the art of design, that is, and this is I.E., if you want to know it: design that we learned in school during the McCarthy era, period. Take it away, O.K., I'm trying to get something back, way back. Not a reading not a mailing not a book and you don't even know what's going on here, now, no way. Just a margin just a tune. Take it away: what does it do to you it makes me fat, how serious is the Pearl's injury, I'm all caught up in it. Well he's supposed to be back in November, early November. Me too.

There's a body moving (you and) in the arc of the distance and I can't fake you out, I can't make it, sure, you and lose no notes, can't find em but the pin of the prick and you I'm standing on is a safe, it's safe, you, and it's got to be new—the direction YOU is the one that the I and will not lose.

October 25

And can there be more writing, well swell, who's the hero it's as simple as this (Max talks in his sleep, Jerry writes about ancestors in myth, it's populated here): a completely different two and gold spray paint, the reaction to gold spray paint, the reaction to a sexual emergency and destructive energy, etc., talk about memory, no, let me put it this way, Bartholomew says something about Andy and memory and sex and destruction, he says we are the same. Then I reopen the case and recover, so did Andy. Maybe it's the family name that shocks me, there is Andy and Andy and another Andy, and even, in fiction, a fourth one, standing in for someone else, all brothers. What a war hole, with his mother up on Lexington Avenue. And I keep on dreaming that Spider is a woman, black white or me. And I want to change my writing and I want to be a transition, what is the position of your breath, I couldn't breathe for a while at all after packing up the memory, that's for sure.

Same name as before: The American Notebooks: this is a warning, don't nobody ever edit mine, that's edit, like eat. Nobody seems to understand anybody else's thought, first memory is too pretty according to Les Levine, now Bartholomew says it's sexually destructive, then Max becomes interested and can't see that at all then Spider becomes all distraught and makes up a few new pains and some for the little dog, run over: two completely different two. Bartholomew sees that Max likes danger and fits that into the picture. Barthoo is a good name for the one who accuses me, then, of gossiping. I admit it with all my charm. Then he says I want two queers to live with me, I say how can that be if you aren't living here and anyway what does he want and he answers "No gossip." So he won't tell. Alice writes to me, her closing words are, "Is there any gossips?" Yes, there's stupid Fern. No I'm the gossip and I dropped my dictionaries: gossip means simply relatives and trusty ones, so-called "related in god," godparents, good friends spreading their legs, I mean, idle rumors, so both Barthoo and Max are sleeping with two different roses whenever they can which isn't often, so, Spider is deciding every parting is more rejection on my part, so, maybe David is leaving his wife again, I think I'll marry him if he doesn't choose Alger and when Barthoo says my reading was like shrieking, everybody understands it's a sort of compliment but David and actually, secretly, I've fallen in love with Vince, so none of it matters.

Not only that but I'd like to wrap up Stanislaus and take him home and why shouldn't I, well I was told not to, David warned me not to and anyway secretly I'm a homosexual because of this nun, Mother Angela who used to rub my back in school and also cause my sister, who I expect to love and do, once proposed that we do it and since conceptual art like (with?) the government is falling, I figure I should get back to writing the real stuff, I mean, the big stuff. David said to me one day, this is the big stuff, "Don't smoke the cork of your Kool." Oh also I forgot to mention that I slept with Edmund before he left for California, and now, dearest Barthoo, that is not sex-destruction that is planning ahead, like you do, and that is being a good godparent or relative. The trouble is I tend to make promises and stir up expectations without even saying anything, as if, perhaps, everyone thinks I have even more time than they do. Yet here

I am waiting in a crowded space, taking my time, refusing to rush around ahead of time, fulfilling the expectations of all men, of Raphael to pose for him perhaps. You see, when you stop gossiping, you get into this sort of thing. "Take care of each other," —"Gossip." I need to get my eight hours now, in order to dream: I'm dragging cross the USA, the Rheingold Queen, 19, is in a curved space, her aphrodisiac was drawing, she makes a match, two men lying in bed together, no curtains, one is like people in the depression, the other one talks too much, something simple happens.

October 26

Back to blue, spare cigarettes, spare Gauloises, gossip has no public. Memory has no pauses as I thought and the distinct color of it goes on but that's shit, it's a noun, among other lids, just one in a million, what's on t.v., it's over, we deserve it, we don't deserve dessert and that's an egg frying or flying in a saucer, anyway, that's breakfast somehow.

I'm surely the target for an assassin's bullet cause I drink manioc beer by the gallon all day and I'm alone here defending my wife and children, no, just defending my self, look around, in back of you, from the position of attack, by stranger, by civil warrior, no, it really saves you to be an artist, that's what someone says, its true design destroys, possibly all enemies, so does color, but it's pretty, in American notebook, in work, I can't work memory, a spare retread and it goes on forever so what, I wonder which giraffe is that, its neck is like my wrist and all over the city there are stores I remember buying special and specific foods in and Bill said, "Every corner I turn is a memory" or something like that and so he left. Friday Saturday Sunday what does it matter to me or John Giorno and here's some real gossip: I walked up to the store and I realized it was easier for me to walk, like driving, singing a song so I sang Wildflower by the Skylarks, except it's not a good song.

October 30

On the 28th I wrote a long song in a bar about Panama and Gertrude Stein and Wittgenstein that ends, "Santa Claus or Axel's castle," but now I forgot Cheska, a white person, I dreamed her out, she whites out, dreams refer back to dreams as a matter of pride, to the crazy house on the island, to backgammon and the back court, foul, you out, one in, long goodbye, lone train ride, writers and sayers, a sensible sac of tape, the ancient goodbye, the cheska, the ancient family the fine noise, I don't know I guess I think it's stupid, the fuck-up machine, your mechanical ability to enforce two by two, the double bind, wherever I go there are two of them and I don't feel better, wait for me! The rains rain on the pages, I'm not running but I'll get there, I made it, how do I get over the bridge now from Queens to uptown, to 74th St., there's just a few hours till May, till I am born all over, there's an oedipal circus at the cemetery, St. Marx Church (a Stanislaus is buried), there's something on the door like money you can get from a bank at night, there's an office: "If I am free...if not..." There's a lecture on ideals, semantics, information, Stanislaus the same, two more identify one with the other, amen. This dream is like proving something. And all of a sudden Max is with me in a flash or snatch of conversation, so this is easy, of course he's there, the ancient fine Wasp family, Jack Kerouac of Dr. Sax, there are leaves falling and the streetlight turns on at 3 pm and since I've been here last, men. It's a different kinda space, different kinda race, different kinda space relationships with the trees, cold weather.

November 1

Dear David, What I wrote makes absolute sense in relation to what we said. The ancient family and did you know that St. Marx Church is also a cemetery, you walk through the cemetery to get to the hall and mounds and Peter Stuyvesant there he is buried and I did a peculiar thing I think. I took Andy over to Spider's. On the surface it was an ordinary thing cause Spider was selling Andy's dope for him and Andy is broke. But it had a few extraordinary consequences. Andy took the money and fled to Northampton to visit his girlfriend, otherwise he probably would have been here for the weekend, Max was depressed but probably for other reasons. Spider freaked out. What a silly and ancient family, I wanted to tell Spider I would never see him again, I almost did. I wanted to tell Max all about it, I almost did. But I didn't and it's cause of you and your trips that you're going away on. But it don't make no sense at all and when I tried to make Max feel better he asked me for ten mg. valium and then Spider called to apologize, he had taken ten mg. valium. So, I want a "new man." I can't write you in these sentences, it's like writing you in case you don't come back, even your executor could make sense of it for you.

It's easier not to focus, especially on the dream and the dream, its scene, because I can't describe them, UFO's and crabmeat, crabclaws, a Sunday School Jesus, that's someone I know and some spider I don't know, it takes long patience and practice and at your own risk, wrist, I eat, little pieces of fish, all over the page, you eat little pieces of meat, can I have your coat, an awkward situation (sense), Clark is a reversal champion, I'm a bit of both, whose earphones are you on, I'll be home all day tomorrow, I'll be home all day tomorrow, I'll be home all day tomorrow, I won't move from my house on David's roof where I have my own entrance and poor people can come in, some of them sleep, some of them fuck and make love, some of them won't or don't, some drink coffee and are fighting, defending some, from the little you've told me, have regular routines, some make great something-or-others and some of them don't. There I am up on the roof with a lot of trees and coffee in the morning with stuff to smoke and wine and that is not defending. You defend too much. Transition, transform: like smoke eat (crabmeat) and drink, no. I would call GMP a comfortable one not myself, she's so old hat, no road of excess (if I'm not out I'm writing) is an access road, oh yes it is, and yes he did, oh yes I lied about it then.

Examination two. The dream state is Florida. Put pen to paper and take the subway there to the right stop. Her thighs. She's black, she's up all night, making book, dressing gown in blue and green, a sweater that turns you on over a sweater that leaves you cold, her breasts. She's black up all day, turning tricks, Patti writes fiction, she writes rape on the door and turns them in. Done in, transition, its repetition of complete thought, really fast, you saw the thought turn into words, you didn't care, you saw the what you can't mention two by two, did some of it, caring then, that is, make difference from one. Lecture. A crack, something's burning, maybe a woods. Something's in a folder, alone somewhere. False mistakes (I'm thinking of Bartholomew's china), I never criticize them. I'm alone somewhere, making jokes. Leave this off, there's nothing behind it but a duty and a clue.

November 4

And Malcolm Lowry's cold so-called incredible urge to self-destruction and the secrets I keep, all men I can't help but tell the cold hungry stomach image which is close to the hunger image, "What are you doing?" And I'll answer, "Things are getting strange," so-called calling it I want to lose everybody so anyway in between somehow and these are all transitions for the mind natively to shift between, I forget, things are getting strange, you don't have to change your notes into a format to make an introduction to an investigation which is only going on in code, out code, for 28, no matter who dies, you left your note there, if it leads to anything something, why else study, and, what do you do all day, I wait for money to come in the mails. The same things get said shorter about icebox openings and the man a few days ago who groaned and became a paddle boat I guess with his urge to self destruction and he paddled his boat under water, I was connected to it and I missed you by a mile, and suddenly I began to give him a good blowjob, just at the surface of the pool and so the paddle boat man began to make a movie of me doing it except his prick was bent into the water and suddenly I realized I mean I saw it was a real small pool and all our friends swimming around, I mean people we knew, well he was an older man too, there was no room for them and in the small pool his gears were gnawing them, our friends my friends and acquaintances, I mean masking them, to pieces maybe and I tried to tell him warn him but he couldn't hear and I tried to disconnect but I was tied to him and we went around in circles like this, losing track and trying to avoid the edges of the pool and its center.

This is not traveling yet alone and this is not potatoes and corn when I get hungry alone but this is living or these are living ones and not dead, yet it's not what you call being alone, or, losing everybody is one risk you make when you go in the direction of killing what is dead or dead desire, I wish I had a poet's language now. Eyes suddenly blind ears suddenly deaf touch suddenly absent, as tree, almost completely surrounded by state, state of consciousness, I can't see from before and I'm afraid to give in to the feeling of it deafening, so, on, describe like a vision, no it isn't past but more clear than absence or nothing, I work a little bit.

Rose simple a little same
And curses Theodore who is Ted
The Max of the dream as surplus
And stores his lines in a trick
The trick is who's dead here,
My desire. A piece of that carefully

Written word. Is over. And carefully
Done with, the poem. So then the same.
And this is acting: the same ones here
Are the same as the ones who are Ted
And fantasy Marie, it's easy, it's a trick
You do when waiting, make it surplus

As energy as surprise and risk it surplus
Rise as carefully as cake was done and carefully
Done with. You raised them up you poet-trick
A ghost in disappearance to its side then same
As the ones my presence here speaks to, Ted
Is at my side, one of the ones six for here

Who speaks who can speak when he is not here
And angels go on to desert a length of surplus
Angels, I'm one, I'll practice I'll go get Ted
And take him to the races I'll blow him carefully
And lay him down worn out as me the same
Blood corpuscles propose tradition the same old trick.

The Max of the storehouse is the spider's trick
And David so beloved so the devil is not here
To write poetry so fine is over now the same
It's not the same name not surplus
Calling out of names of hers Marie not carefully
Crafted not a name or noun or poetry at all, no tricks, no Ted

But dead to finish calling names out to, Ted
And his to finish up my act and teach the trick
Of yelling poetry at soft suspensions of carefully
Constructed disbelief in what and who, anyhow, is here
I scream at them finally, a surplus
Of destruction, go away, they go away just the same.
I'm still the same who's Ted
Dream surplus the poetry trick
I work here carefully, with you.

November 7

Job and David, Star of.

November 18

I am one of the last of the ones that suffer and even I refuse to suffer, you won't tell what you want me to do, like, when you want me to be here and when not.

November 26

A view wider than the one that is seen and the captain is Captain David, take you with you when you leave us today and when to remove it, New York to Chicago, and now I will try to isolate the experiences that have led up to this take-off position: and the isolation of the take-off position itself, like they all will all ones feel and on the ground it's too bumpy to note to record to rear children to punch tickets, not very often, something is outer and whether you write out of desperation or not, you write out of desperation and the way things work, something about air foils, cause one just rose and if I wanted to find out how the plane was lifting I would just consult Moving. Taxiing, this is worse than a taxi, man and I can't speak to captain David, constant liar constant lover, he is the experiment of this dream, I hope to get there. Voices crack on the plane and you and you don't know what will happen to you at 39,000 feet and what is the use of communicating a state of airplane consciousness and now I am fear but it's an easier fear than to love a man or woman and to leave them, to put them on a plane, to put them to death. Who's chewing gum and take-off is guaranteed by A. Einstein. I can hardly write a word of it, it's air and clouds and now I remember the feeling, M. Yoga blood liver and human beings, fog, the image, is blowing, the sun, striking, the fog, blue easily above it. I need a beer she makes me dizzy she makes me well. We took off, no step, turbulence, the sun struck the page, the windows open, it's a double-triple fantasy window. I want to examine all of the people on the plane five across, as you might examine, sober, the streaking of the arctic clouds. Image, I am sorry, but the air is fair here and you can see that the question we started from has been almost completely left out. You see, I did examine the clouds as the sun did it almost completely purposely. And Poe, a train of clouds leads us back to river run or eve and adam spent, why write about them, mean, why cover them in a story about town, and as the writing sobers, straight up and down and I can't think what someone said, someone says if you took the plane I took, my name is not in the book. Survivors. A mystery a fantasy a sun on the side of the left wing, you do not eat meat. No step and if it takes a little longer, I hesitate to get through to the secrets, Mallarmé's jewels would set off a fan, electronic joy or toy house, waitress please listen to me, one is coming and one is going and one is where he was, no two are, something like as the world turns. Bernadette cigarette. I am supposed to be doing this alone. How annoying for anyone to support you. There is only two hours and one minute and I am not thinking, so calm about what I was supposed, the blue of it, to be doing, the blue I mean. Skaters easily seen in the sky. Her private hallucination of memory all torn, all old hat, just like yours. Who you? And what design. No more seductions none of them no more desertions none can be. I, don't, think, so, and so, area code Chicago in total isolation, so I will never have to do this again and like I said before I will have to do this again and you too, out of desperation, either way, to produce something—a work, a picture, a number, a child, a question, a series, an apartment to live with, a lover full-grown sprung from the soil a whole army of lovers ready to march, from one to one. I am waiting for my father never flew a plane for my mother never flew a plane for a 1951 Chevrolet, a motor car, a Budweiser, the ballgame and again, a bar, no a shot of whiskey in a glass on the ground with a joke on it and flicks and flicks a pack of paper matches along the glass to Dash, or, and flicks a pack of paper matches along the dash to Dash and there he was, a private person, waiting. You are waiting. It's up in the air. The pen won't cloud as discrete as rapidograph as area code as hunger as the rapist at the door. The United Negro College fund and changes in the air currents of air are in the habit of, no, it could be it must be ones posing as these ones, habit of robbing, no, I mean ripping off, rich hippies in their Soho lofts at gunpoint. Word gets around. They say they tie them up till your hands are numb for days afterwards. The hippies seem to get off on it, except for the loss of the videotape and the spitting on the green plants. Funpoint. I myself have never seen this happen but I dreamed of it when Peter banged at the door to borrow a cookie tray from Max and sudden, all of the building was there, at gun, some dark figures and this is called an automatic writing. Do not disturb the peace of the sign. Ladies and gentlemen place your bets. No more bets. The progression is awful. You won too much and you were not served. Pierre wants a handjob and someone says what is a handjob, it's Jill Johnston rubbing you. This is service. Desperation not disillusion and disuse is a handjob but it works anyway and anyway, work is work. Artists travel all over. Blue Earth travels all over. All of the animals and all of the men and all of the women of the myth, they travel all over. They get stranded on whale. They ride to shore on the back of blue rhyme, ride dolphin to shore. They do not distract themselves with lunch. They eat. After some hunt. Someone says to myth man, do you desire cocktails, now this is ordinary stuff but then someone says it three times and the man in the myth sees that either something is being gotten rid of, or, the hallucination of a visual dream is surfacing to direct toward, to direct to travel all over, over cock, over tails, over cockovertails. So check out the window and think of a room. Where are the Knicks. The Knicks are on a bus coming back from Baltimore. Dropped two in a row and last night 31 turnovers. There's nothing I can do about it, I'm in the air. I could make it stranger, I could seduce, I could even plan. Humans just never get used to being in birds, smoking cigarettes and the picture of a plastic meal. He could not eat he was not allowed to eat. Dear fellow passenger, I know it must seem strange to you that I have written a thousand words since I mounted my seat but my hand just cannot keep up with my thoughts and it seems quite strange that you do. Thoughts translate better in the air, like, is anyone headed for Chicago going to Berlin? And, will the pigs like hippies this year. Child loves patterns of any kind. A couple hard lines of defense stinks money. I am not looking. It is not idyllic. Some revise. There's no room to be a luxury, just a pattern, even if you trim. You may trim or straighten. If you trim do not straighten and if you straighten, do not and so on. And now I will wait for the magic words. (I could have to stay weeks in the air.) But somehow the victim is waiting.

November 28

The people, fuck the people, all alone, fuck mothers and fathers, fuck the people, "it'd be good if she didn't say goodnight to him," and "He needs to be a lady" and no sense, no how, so what, ingrained, it's gone in a moment anyway then, when, who loves who and who has what to do and what does Stanislaus think, he knows he isn't busy if he'd only just quit but he can't quite quit, just quite now and the same observation prosaically, comes to me, so who does what to who and who has the right to do, I am so fucked up, I could be a program, I could be a space I mean slot on t.v., so. It's too easy, no secret steeples, no teeth and nails, not even a teacup, I'm too old and I have no room of my own and I plan, I manipulate like nixon, the poor for the rich, whatever they are, that is how I feel and once more my stomach is empty, so I'm too good at this revealing, and nothing (no one) hasn't any all, and it's all still in my mind, like, where to spread myself out, you and you and, and I am a two-timing woman and someone says, maybe three and I say I'm so glad you said that cause, and I don't say it makes me feel free and that is your duty, daddy, your design, no, that is mine and this may be the last time you have to be alone to write and someone writes "no way out" and the same one says all the time what else is new, we've all experienced that too soon, it's average thought, is a show, like no show you've ever seen proceed without an M.C. in between the acts. There are no new words. You are somewhere else. Every body is. And it ain't so important at all. So, alone? Like on 11th Street? What does who want and what's predicted—a place to work, a work to do, a lot of it. I need balls or an average honest thought like queers who live alone cause it's easier and a way out to dinner—you get used to it, using up the time, your time, as mine, once more, do it again, and once more, I can't give you everything, at all, and neither can you give me even the honesty of a glance in the dark at the trust toward, leading toward, what I am doing and so, you guessed it, I hate you and I have no means for any hate at all, so, alcoholics understand the gist of my works and all derelicts collide with me on this one line: I don't know what it is, it's: Adapt the papers moving to my dream and I forgot it, of the wind while I was sleeping it off. An it instead of you, an Audie Murphy instead of Julius Caesar. "You are not killing him," "You cannot kill." With anger, so what, kill will end a book at least, I will take and take and take, it's too clear, it ain't crazy, black enough. My father makes puns in his death so I will never be alone or touched so don't touch me, black and rivers of all the empty pages of whatever I can get, I hate you you are down and if you die I will kill you and I will always make the greatest mistakes, mistakes apparent to all eyes, see, so, look at this: you don't even know what I am doing and in order to tell you to save you I will leave you and you will see my mistakes in order, as they come, like, the purpose of laws, where we forget where we started out from, skating is no image, I will paint, or, I would if I could, be done at all. Call Patti and ask her about her mother and father, the scientist and ask him about his, same time same place, Theodore and Marie, Myrna and Alan, Catch and Max, Frances and John, Michael and Helen, Ruth and Nicholas, Harold and Barbara, Andrew and Josephine, Myrna and Marty, everybody sleeps with alchemy, Monroe.

A false, a flash by car on her face by the star in color who cares, she's dead as a comet is underground and I write a review that just goes on forever for appreciation for design and for risk of losing the covers that normally come over you at night in bed with someone else and we all, ingrained, have everything to lose except me, I'm guaranteed by no life insurance to visit the dead with no life left, so, give it to them, answer the mail, I'm overloaded, it's all mine, take it, all right, slow down, family, this is direct address, I can't do anything else, human use—forget it, I'm as venal as—forget it, it's the wrong suck word, proper names don't mean nothing when the proper name dies, the names are on the pictures of the sly tomb stone. It's a voice. You hear. And it's signed, Merry Christmas your mother who fucked you up is dead and Merry Christmas, go to the convent so that your father who fucked you up is dead and for the Holy Ghost, Fuck Jesus all you can, and as for the Holy Ghost invading you with conception, I say who's ever seen em, Fuck Jesus all you can.

●

Writings for Unnatural Acts pictures: There were no internal instructions (Indian), there were no specific instructions, the beadwork is cut up in jags and predicts instructions, the gentle information comes as a prescription, her muscles are exposed as a series of conversations that a woman was having, she is that is she was conceiving of, I could pin that down for you, working beads, David is the name of the man who for the present was the devil, so. What was fired in that kiln she might've worked in transpired at that meeting was one two shot one two or some totally unrelated "activity" like poetry, smoke we smoked, that is a question honey, you used outdoors for indoors, so, sources of information go on to say for two full minutes, from memory, the woman is working, she works.

Pandas have been apprehended right away or as they say in the first instance, lie close and nestle, snuggle, I saw the panda nuzzling me (cf. skunks in a dream), I saw the double-separate order forms for his drink and his drink, that is, mothers and babies, no, men and women, we argued about that, we smoked, we argued about that, it's easy to see what is double-separate and what is not. Did you ask Gray who'd be in attendance at this meeting, well I dont know as I askt him but I askt him about these leaks, and this kind of thing, there are so many men's names that it makes them think of women who have fewer names to trick you with, if you think this is a man and a woman, "too bad," somebody says, then that is because you have run out of names for them and this is, women. Did you know at that time? Do you remember naming a man? A man, black and white, you gave a name.

Technical quality Xmas cards (paperweights), temporal quality sexist cards, Bay of Pigs quality additional cards, Watergate quality off-hand cards, Samsonite quality religion cards, plummers quality trimmers cards, you aint gonna stop me, you cant stop me no how, stop me, two minutes, stop bath, no cards, aint no cards to show, blown away and otherwise scattered, nothing to show just something to lay on paper.

It was not in my consciousness (Dunes), it was just not in my consciousness. But he knew and he knew and evidently he did Oh yes he did Oh he did yes he did he knew yes he did that a dune took her cold clothes off and came. Now when did you first become concerned about exposure to China? No to California to Death Valley to Dunes of Death Valley to the Duino Elegies. May we have some order and may we have a vote vote delivered to the house white in the middle of the dunes delivered. Breakfast on the dunes. Breakfast will be served on my belly, breakfast will be served from 7:30 – 10:30 on the belly of the one who lies down for it who will lie down for it, two minutes, stop. But dunes get crumpled and fucking dusty, everything was very crumpled I mean cordial as we sat down to the dinner table on the belly of the whale's dune and we went about our business as usual like he said Hello lonely honey what do you have and the other one says well darlin and he whips out his constitution which he happened to have in his back pocket and this constitution had what they call big amps which is power and so he (the first one) said leaning over onto the belly of the descriptive dune, he said quash it or I'll quash it and the belly listened listening, inside, what's going on.

Intensive investigation: he adores him (Woman). Unless that's just an illusion. Bob said that he hated the woman and if there were any subjects that would not get talked about freely then this was one of them. When did you first become aware that you hated women and blamed them for all your mysteries, for money, for your money, for money for…I don't think I became aware of that till sometime after the first of the year and then it came not so much in the money sense but in this episode where I was trying to make contact with him and make him happy and the rest of the Cuban Americans and it wasn't to make me happy and I was to make that lively and clear and in the interests of some people and things other than women and dunes and pandas, paperweights (?) and Indians at work either in the foreground or in background, what's left is Etna.

Etna is there, I thought it was a dune, you could lay out your dinner there too. Etna looks each deep into the other's eyes, that is the volcanoes that have vision and if one, like Etna (who her) is on top or above it all and another, higher up, but not higher, but looking down holding all golden sway, but we must leave out the colors, Etna stop, two minutes. What is a context? Did you find a new color, sweeping up. And you dare say that the dawn broke somewhere around March of this year. Fuck her, she's awful, write the statute: volcanoes explode. I was on the verge, now you say, I was on the verge of moving my legs (unless a friend comes and pulls me back, is weaned) like a conceptual index and you babies just gotta get some weight. And how do you know that? Because I can understand the English language, it's my mother tongue.

The bird (of Paradise) was in it from the first minute so I must've learned about it on the evening news or something. Give the dimensions. We are going to take a ten-second pause in our coverage of all things, the South. Give the direction, this is all things considered, as you read a book from left to right, at my side, at my stance, at my insistence or instance, at my anger, moving from left to right. Otherwise is unnatural or Oriental. Give a southern accent to agitate just one step further and what I am driving for is when you first knew that the bird would fragment (frame #?) and in frame #? or frame # what, I can't see shit. What did you learn from March to June additional muddle on through and in frame # what you add a mother, so what? It's Beth's bird and no one else is is why it's so hard to take off from even though you is so tired even though you is so weary you stick right in and suckin on through just waitin, won't give up, you is reversal of roles and the malaise fades, you weaned or broke off and me back where I started from without the bird you me identity and without any hard long legs, just sick. So set back and going now, not as you read a book but backwards there from right to left a hard way for humans to work so do I say to you don't heat my soup I'll do it myself and is that something to be handled in that time frame. You made a log of it, two logs, a million logs, you two.

You moon rock held in a vise, you Bird of Paradise stuffed in a trained environment and legless, you ain't used to motion anyhow, no moth on the moon, no mouth, no wind, no wind in an air-controlled museum, how could you?

I go to two movies that sell wine, gold and orange light. Adjoining theaters, they show the tall blond man with one black shoe and the man who...mean streets, mean men, they show these films through an outdoor café. The films are reversed. Gregory Peck says, you'll never get into that one, the one I'm supposed to go to, mean streets, mean and woman ("You can't pay people to go to the biggest hit in New York."). Gregory Peck says, let's get some wine instead, from the movie stores that sell wines and he has picked up a tape-recorder on the streets shaped like a pistol a gun and it plays "shots" and the shots cause riots and people to fall down, bleeding, rows of women with cut hair and running from Madison to Third (I should be further over), there's enough action and fear to wake me. I am meeting Spider at the movies. I left him with his family (two #127's – 12/7), "I got us out of here by going to the movies," like breasts lime rickies, like airplanes and birthdays, Pearl Harbor Day (The Locked Room and something pretty). And in front of the adjoining movie theaters, G. Peck asks me for some money for the wine and while I am slow pulling a ten out of my pocket, he says, "Well if you're going to be so traditional about it, I'll pay for the wine," and by this time he's been a woman and is a man again. We've done some fast talking. Peck and I are the same, a famous shadow, tape-recorded shots of shooting stars. And this is called Replacement.

And this is called Formal Family. One round mother, one long tall father, a wiggly sister and a line for a brother and I'm here up at the end but it's all a dream.

Finzi-Continis: Dear mother dear mother I only live so far and I only have two hands and the movie is loud so loud as windows we strained our necks to see so far the end I have a lot to direct I want to eat drink smoke write and, perdida, watch this garden movie a movie with sound and smell is a terribly sorry ounce of this personal instruction comes as a prescription. Listen, it's almost over says the music and hokey shots of sky through trees light up your shadow on the page and they laugh how do they know we're studying here we're studying front row center, great or major works and it's too big they're too big the mise en scène makes no sense it's anger at your father if you were never a mother perpetrates a look of design on you and bigger than life and change reels all's well sound must be Italian and embrace embrace and up and I do when a song gets sung except a telephone rings and it must be god or godot the way this one is going like pretensions are not in travelogues let the snow snow snow on fucking Italian names and what about her thesis about design she is an input she is stimulating him/her and all I see's the writing there is no plot for grain so what's the relation of Giorgio, there is no creative politics, Giorgio to the guy moaning in the aisle and at childhood memories everybody moves and the words take over too much actually a bent spending paper she resigns she reigns she can't breathe looking dead spent the ultimate breath in bed, dead, is pretty interesting, said in the house and you are pale blanket sections into rhythm some design an old age quite spaced out there is always a scene there are two scenes and someone says and the ultimate sentient beings in a fight worry back the average man is spacing the average man is speaking and someone says que causa and it's us anything but what I saw the edge edging over into the obscenities of the woman forced to be a doll and he says and he is someone and someone says we're all fine and so they move and they move. The Italians know know nothing in their speech. A signal piece of cake may have the salt I sold my later in spaced out balls all Nazis begging for bread some prison they provided me with cucumbers and apples and bread but no food, dissidents like me and I said and I am someone and someone says eat the peels, I am the food, I mean no room not even a cell only structure for design like I mentioned before like the structure for design of some running rain like the structure of a running train that's a train that runs, over flags over red flag canals maybe over into the whited-out castle section where the integration-princes where the integration-secretary where all the integration all of art and playful science was expected by the princess was hoped for by the secretary in 1930 was designed by the money she invested in the castle, some art and some science all art and playful science was designed in together, now, except, before, anyway, somehow, for all the rich motherfuckers and someone says and they point out and someone says some of em jews, what is a thesis? And so, it makes me angrier to see you than to miss you, this, out, on and so, something about women, a question: the boy stood on the burning deck wearing boots of steel big nose and black pelt and you can't tell what's below the belt and be sure you get it level and some space mean in the parks not isolated not trees a run rhythm, it's fall and someone says what a second minute and you say something and you are someone and someone says so what and water sinks ships not one another so and so to speak is just memory connection dishes fishing dove into the bay or dove in the boy a poesy and the accord or in accord and shit for reasons a little cause is going on little cause my garden's a political noun and so delay or declare war and so we have short little wars, the end. And so Solini Has Met His Finish in the Mad House.

●

Summary: Black. You already see the effect the lyric and the image of somebody's nouns. You can't bank on em. You express chance and surprise you do something to puzzle to riddle to foresee to precede to wait you rhyme you hear Poe automatic. You see a frame a window frame the dark shade is drawn and with your eyes closed you can still see the sun outlining the frame and within that frame words appear, if you want.

You could describe prose. You could store up and save it. You can catch what you throw since ear is open to picture and picture comes pulse at a time. Everybody's mad as a fuck. Nobody pierces time you always gotta force it.

What happens to you? Ideas and systems opened and closed as clocks—no good like energy like nothing if nothing and so lie. Just as easy to lie about as to lie about the same thing. You covered and hid you cheated etc., you puzzled again, you trapped you make the terrific something and now there's something.

To do? You see what happens what happens to you you see, wait around what the fuck you wait you is waiting now you say: I want a distance between myself and you so I'm writing out this, listen, prescription and none of you, not even the ones who can't think of anything to do, none of you have nothing to say about it, it is even and it is wait: cause I at least can get rid of this and this at least is a memory take my word for it.

And whatever it is, written, it isn't, there, it cannot be written and no one and on and on and on except as chronology concerns, say, nobody remembering everything as if it were in Moby Dick or something so, fatter, the confidence man isn't fatter, or, like me having an affair, no I am a man having an affair with his daughter and this comes way before I ever knew you: my wife is mad at me. Our affair is documented with pictures in a beautiful art magazine, the pictures are geometric pastels like false dimensional art. She forbids me to look at it. I look anyway.

Now see that's the trouble with recording. It doesn't work it doesn't myth together. I am working on it. I can't think on anything worse and it's only midnight as they say at least there are nuts on the cake to make it have some value to fool, like lights glare and you lose track of something I don't know, but let me try this: it's as if you were just found here and then started out from there, does that make sense, now we have all these antecedents who don't make sense so why should you, there's something about concentration that makes it impossible to be you.

Faith no faith J's in bed campaigning for selectman Hello I'm Dick Taylor I'm, Hi I just stopped to pry to into your lives inroad myself Stephen Hose he's fed up and rightly so, there's something that's not in the hose I guess about three cents an hour, have you ever ate mud next drift the wiring's announced was gonna run the day of the caucus eat dog food or cat food know him from the Fire Department, that slow along way down the page you see I was sitting there hearing I'm assistant chief at's a nice loom and a nice lookin dog you ate Szechuan food with in New York and they go to the fires with them I had a pickup as though to begin with you know everything.

Jump up on top of the motor go over and get one of thirty cords of wood a year on real cold nights I hadda get caught sit up half the night that's for sure at that time I had more labor than I did money sawing wood every night bark remember doin it new little dog.

This is Daisy's cover Julie owns this cover and Julie owns Daisy, what? Cause Daisy wanted to stay with nice puppy for some reason cause her mother's mean to her God is right up 30 feet if he'd been four or five feet away my stepfather's brother's people don't keep their saws balanced one of the worst rigs they have vertical-horizontal drive push it'll just choke Julie's very fond of her new babies poodle puppies white up here and blue down there, well I have in New York they just don't have any Chinese dogs are blue that's how you say a poodle in Spanish gremesele sound em out rubber boot fiddle fool around we moved our place this morning so sophisticatedly close to you.

Where's my desk? Get outta my desk Douglas I thought she'd be tops and how many copies of copies and maybe if you wrote less you see this like a dream but it is not one like, big paper big land Jack, Plato lacks tuna fix and flute playing like less hello black dog I was always against it, that's like going to Siberia yeah I did what's wrong and what's pie take a look at that thing, crises going here from six o'clock in the morning to six o'clock at night, something more.

We had a good school there when I…This is the story: days, daze, what happened out of this world well I've gotta go along I just thought I'd take this, I just thought I'd take this time to stop and introduce myself that's a good wood to burn, put it in for me, cold head and bed float in annoying dreams since the middle of the year they've been, wake up sun doesn't light don't bother me eat snow pea pod seeds order strawberry we don't care how ya vote s'long as ya vote Lucy on abortion Channel 3, can I put a record on…

Andy has the flu, Max chops wood Max saws Max weeds Max does read a weakness that goes beyond the disease itself a feeling of weakness that goes Max looks for Yage Letters Andy is pale Ann cooks potatoes selectman-elect is here, Jon talks to him, Jon reads his horoscope Ann and Jon order seeds Justine watches t.v. we meet her at the bus with conch shells singing she has an infected finger Pete is ready to hitchhike to Pittsburgh, New Hampshire Pete whines thinks like nervous new little dog, I am I…Milt fixes lime drinks and marshmallow fruit salad with sour cream, we see condensed clam chowder we see barrels of food we buy Andy a ginger ale, there are two of us, Max and me, Max and eye,

Max and aye, Max and the letter Ides of March. Marshmallows are rummy or tummy, Andy wants his mommy no Jon wants his mommy no two want their mommies. Ann, unusually happy, and I, fairly happy, the two most happy in the house, what do they we want to be crooked or music store pavilions and order more it's between you and me.

Putting things together's another thing, now the reason that was hard to read, see, is that it was not a dream worked over but an event worked under that is condensed like some dream or other for time and since we can do this and since we are free to work however she feels then we do this and this is how it's done by one: now this is a dream but I will work over out over it and try to make myth of it as is: take it easily from hard.

I am a weather forecaster, or should I say you are a weather forecaster you forecast the easy weather the weather is somewhat predictable so there you are: forecasting it. A forecaster is a reporter: we eat meals as part of the job, two red moons scare me, the doors are made of ice and snow is the dream: ice and snow make the waiting, make us wait we are waiting and this restaurant is a snotty place, we are waiting. I walk into the new job I surprise them I know I'll sleep with these two men I work with.

And if you do and if you don't where was I I was with the drums of Aeschylus how. Their weird daisies. Weather forecasters take a rest and wake up again tropical. They're muttering to themselves, the people upstairs and the forecasters feel it in their fucking skin, they're whispering around: we can't remove anything or change it, we can't change anything. Did I tell you they were queer and it was clear that we would make it together with no power over the material they gave us to predict on like a pillow with no power over it move it around and sleep on it whether or not.

But no I've already told you that and gotten even as far as the divider about which you already nearly know and the sentence that emerged from the dip in the sea here and sea here is something to think about riveting close in tight to your tipped imagination and sea here that sentence in the mouth of and it was: I've wanted to make love all winter, so then when we finally solved the problem, so then when it was clear the identities of everyone masking like flowers in the fall we knew who it was said that though said by me. Always two people can talk at the same time. I've got something to prepare for prepare you for no not you you're almost here. Lookin for the exit or at the bank on nouns.

Objects derange the people who would rather be feel free but fear crash maybe from high. Fried and Friday a Max and a day, as usual. Advantage. But not like you. Are right. The Fly can't keep his hand in his pocket, what hand, when he approaches the one he loves most, hand flies out and horrifies her, lucky, I have no hand like the Indian god who writes a G, describes it a qualified circle in the air as we drive by, he's stone, you jeer and know it. She's sex or waiting. I learning something in here? Never know with this tight schedule rules the fishes of the sea with its letter.

So what if letters ceaselessly. Out to class, men have arrived, they look at me, one is nice, men come in, I am waking up, it is, it isn't, it was seven March 20 first day of spring and dawn the awning finally have access to books, threw away old notebooks ripping out random pages for a work, what can I do but give you more, and more I think of doing a school work, found Finnegans Wake finally and Jon borrows Gauguin's life. It's easy to have books and life to throw around, the dream about the man made of intestines, those things speak for themselves, papers and drawings, interest? Be me and so on but Marcelin Pleynet says do not be me give the reader something more to do to be interest for him for you but what about her, a random recorder.

A gesture towards outside, sun out? All old ideas all those old ones line line old play line line on words line line, I thought there were two but. Two but. If it's food I'm denied I'll fight for food but that's not the point. I sink rest speed on information it points to me Mac Low Rothenberg Ashbery Read simmer sun summer spring Speed, feed notes, what are they? Something to read like you can breathe through them if you're hiding in a stream from the guards are out to get you and you saw that in the movies hollow ones work even for the good and bad ones and one and one person's life one moment bottle of wine and what's in this book? You world work from old, information is old you work from old information, let me know freedom to discard can't write, Andy's not interest in what I have to do for now, D he's a bore sounds like core coil and on through the yellow and green forests that to do this to uncover, will. Importance of coil. Max always sees it right, what is right, he's moral and so is J, traditional, no, anarchy or fashion or plate, fashion of anarchy or just a plea? Plea for piece-together = anarchy in bed, it is said: Piece now, Pick up the Gun on the curling church wall, round here. Language rings, you attempt you attire or tempt the whole like a house to fall: male female and so on they say this private drive-it yourself way proceeds, what giants we are, what's a phone call? You say why bring that in? Why add "at all?"

I'll keep the original for myself goddammit, it's as though I'm living alone. Three. There's no way to make self out of dreams so go on. So go on. I'll sleep with the two weather announcers no matter what, even if they've even if they're queer and one is queer. There's a lot of work to be done. We finish up. The weather and do a cooking show too. Which is more important the tall table or its length. They're experienced so am I, but not on this show. I eat cake. We've already started as you can see the ritual of sex all loving and embracing like baked caked cakes. You better cause you better hurry up cause I have a temperature like very weather announcer whether he's Andy or his brother, did one of them have a temperature once? Did they have the flu? And did they act, I mean were they, was one of them a weather announcer ever? Max wants birds at the foot of the bed.

There's lots of things that happen in Massachusetts in the midst of a lot of debris. They always say and they always say: we can't remove anything, or, we can't change anything. Nothing can be removed, or, nothing can be changed, star, star, in terms of the weather you have no power over your material, like all, like a little love, you can't change it, we each, whether or not you want to or not and so on and if I hadn't written anything I would have to try harder to please them, you, who are they, whether or not.

And what is this great split great division between yourself and me, you and how can I predict it again, do you realize how division how fidelity how difficult it is to write words correctly without consuming them without abscessing them without making them cost you money at the store at the dentist at the doctors in racist America bitter French America where money cost you demonstrations of ecstasy as woman where bitter French money is translated in American and is just as bitter as the mother and father who bore you, did you, did they do it, did they bear you together, or separately, that is, leave the mother saying, that is leave the mother with you and the father gone, or do you, or did the father leave first then the mother go and/or are they both still with you, in which case would you like me to meet him/her/them so as to impress them with your value through me that is mine, the light goes on the light goes off and everybody thinks it's worth while a while if you do it.

Here it is: Someone is sunbathing on the divider of the West Side Highway. Is that you? Is that you there? You embarrass me, lying there on the thin divider not being yourself and no one else as well, sync it? Got it? You ignore Mr. me deliberately. Hi? You knit into the shadows where I'm you, you know it, blinded by the light, you put it there, right in front of my eyes. And I'm ashamed of what I'm doing to you, fuck. What's the fidelity fidelity difference in vehicles being on a balcony sync again fuck and everytime and everytime I can't write difference I write fidelity instead so take it it's yours, it's obviously yours. Have it. You can have it. Max wants to make it your own by replacing her with me, I mean by replacing me with her it was...Never before, so far away, please come back, remember? I can't. Mobius strip, I'm not used to it, and rely on something that isn't here. There's no way I can create the drama of Aeschylus and so on but.

Beginnings cores coils roots tyrants, the tyrants are...the maniacs are...the people who are floating are...the ones who are serene. What's the use of saying who all these people are when I can't say their real names, just know I have a list and you are on it. Now by now this isn't really all true but qualified maniacs are not that but simply threatened by inner world takeover. This is absolutely true but what difference does it make if I can't say who, anyway. You get a good mark for this since it's getting so cold in here and anyway dream, dream books on shelf must introduce friends in four groups in a new way so must you fault diagramming, like they say, in how many ways...four sentences for this? Is it order? Or schedule you rule prick, for example: the once-over, a look-thought, a see-through, a readout, a look-see, a dive-in headlong, an

inching-along, a printout, a March one March I was sitting in a green chair, selection random. You misinterpret, something else something completely new for you happened, fast facts: it's the turpentine can that makes all that noise at random, isn't it? Intervals that sound like metal lightly tapping itself. A fact but a bad prescription-description like: that's not a pea, "P." Music, street noise and country continuity getting louder, lead—no, lead in some direction. Know how to. If it's in it's all or random you know what sounds good like metal lightly tapping itself, the real sound of it not the sounds of words those words, Dear Max I love you the sun's up, spring, six o'clock. I love you money laugh, a list of the possible: (outdated, she dated too much): trip to Syracuse, trip to Massachusetts, get some sun, summer in the country in Paris, really study memory, a band and some music, a movie, a bathtub, a magazine end of the world, I forgot: I love you money laughing is this science is getting cold so poem where:
Mine a bee in tree near time
Spring coil and diversification
Is diver's cessation from diving
Through sky to tree
Spring street approach
Canal lake buy coke
By way of underground streams
That cease to suffer buildings
Poke around, pick up parcel
Too much fits into swell
Conscious of storm or conscious indifference
The whole history a history
Of the driver's cessation of
Indifference the industrialization
Of indifference in between
I won't say what city in moon,
Merica, a regular thing.

Do you mean to say that linguistically your energy is inexhaustible? The answer's yes, so, one must be careful: mental anguish is middle English, listen is implicit.

FERENCZI

A man in a shirt showing a man in a shirt a shirt is how many white shirts are there there. Here's 11 2/3 yds. writing which is wiring meant to be performed not read off the page as pole high-wire act performs as the feeling of not being subject had put who into a different act which was a different danger was a different risk, the riskier text than the lecture the riskier word not heard and pinched, no way out but the way in, leaving: "Who's dead?" I won't use names, names are not use, I won't name names, all names begin with F. Crazy F. and frenzied F. and fucking F. and dead F. and dead fucking F. and the anagrams of all the letters that follow F. in the names named, relate here, that is, they send the image of a man off to sea with the sails sails flow around and where they do, fucking F. So, if all names begin with F. then F. = Proper Name: nobody can stand it. We pass by glass windows of Proper Name's family's summer house by the water and they're drinking again so this has no title, except, the blue edge of the surf defines something and I attempt to make its words communicable its surf communicable, I season its fucking concept by painting it green and therefore making no change. Proper Name or Proper Name is leaning weary against the bed and sitting on the floor there, doll and doll then, she gets very drunk, yes she does and she gets very drunk and then she has a man in. You could sink in sex is not a person's name at all. And we're there but everybody leaves. A man in a shirt showing a man in a shirt is how many white shirts are there there. You put your work first and try to do everything all at once so that you can be sure that everything has no meaning but all at once does, as, the red rose doesnt the rose is red does, and, it's a strange city. Morning and just as I'm poaching scrambled eggs and boiling bottled coffee cups for coffee for them they leave, as, once when they were nearly ready, they had ordered it to close, as she gets very drunk then she has a man in. So sex wait for me, they're walking down the street and I have to pack and should I leave all my fucking things here and I would I say I would except I dont mean it cause there's a book in each bag and a bag in each book and I need the book in each bag and all the fucking junk, along with all the fucking junk, there is, where there is. And so what so crawling through white excavation evacuations, 40,000 trampled to death over one couple of lovers yelling for help wake up. A set. A magazine full of nothing but a book by me called something starring Proper Name and on the back it says, book jacket, this writing was discovered written by moon-discovered hands by Proper Name through Proper Name, or something like that, as, one tame tiger does not exist. But, no one knows this. The walking cure. I just thought of it I havent told anyone. I feel very C and Proper Name feels very H in the middle of all this two people, a man and a woman in a cemetery erasing a tombstone and this has nothing to do with this Proper Name Proper Name Proper Name Proper Name and Proper Name, beside the two others, or, in the same space but with a space between, etc. There's a fire escape hydrant which offers all different kinds of water fountains drinking fountains, I drink from one, choke and am forbidden. I wake up to the sexual etiology of the child where, not quite yet, shit this is some mystery novel, where the women place on the team. I leave off playing basketball and Proper Name comes and takes my place and I come back I want my place back but she's the open man and she's the open man around so I fuck Proper Name and Proper Name who is also Proper Name at once and this is the harsh creation of the deprivation of moralism of the moralism of deprivation of the relaxation of a deprivation of the excitement of relaxation of the excitement of a deprivation it's a kiss and Shakespeare's shrine is a composite image. We visit it, it's my shrine. Women take care of it, it's falling apart. They rush to get a room ready for visitors and there's no hope of that cause in the existence of the predicate it was the predicate I forgot so Proper Name called to remind me that tame tigers growl and it's tame tigers growl. Other shrines appear and their shapes all lead in the same direction shown showing a birthday party shown outdoors as a picnic on the streets for one alone woman who is alone and she's alone. Everybody's there, we come and Proper Name and his wife come and we're introduced and I lean back and do my perfect Proper Name imitation: "Hello Proper Name, cut short." The derivative of a Proper Name and its parent the derivative of a Proper Name. These people are all dead. You get dead. Where are my shirts made of different materials with the arms different from the torsos and the backs different from the fronts. Where are my man-woman shirts and I have a lot of them and who's got that one and nevermind, I have another one it's green it's painted green like the dress in the sex show. Somebody broke the lighter and all the details get care as the women place on the team as this is dreaming of everything I can think of, as, I dream you drink up all the fucking milk and in fact you do. In the beginning you know why I cant begin to write cause it would be the bad writing of secrets the evil throwing up of them the giving them up the catching and replacements are catching they catch you up in what recurs to you, its disgusting its filth its beginning so, they carry me there, door to door: Proper Name to Proper Name with Proper Name in between whose door I also go out by. Proper Name, Proper Name and Proper Name I wish I could, fuck you, through the park, to lay that on there, to lay that on you, lay that one on you and dont wanna use the loaded words wanna come up with the loaded ideas so wait and just say it again, as, the shirts the table just bite it off, some euphoria, concentrating on you and my objects, as, is it as difficult for men not to have children at all as it is for me, dear Proper Name Proper Name Proper Name Proper Name Proper Name and Proper Name and those are the ones I wanted to create one night, who's first. And it's hard to concentrate, I burned myself, Proper Name works in a frenzy of work and then lets himself down which reminds me of Proper Name and so now I'm worried about him and about the fact that this is not writing, when you know so much already, as, once when they were nearly ready, they had ordered it to close. Like emotions, A to Z, I feel very S. But I want to explain the difference, in fucking, between a creation and a deprivation, two states and how they are the same and these are my notes, why should I know them, the child knows them. A creation, your word, it cant be someone you know. And the ideas that writing should be working at something and reworking and revising and someone says that fucking is it should be difficult it's work I dont agree, fucking off completely. It's easy to fuck, nobody gets hurt by fucking but madmen and madwomen. Is that true. My hunger creates a food that everybody needs. You or me? And the excitement is different. In a way, in this way, it's the excitement that needs to be created and it doesn't need to be satisfied, is not sex, is. Tame tigers growl. They do not exist. Is not language, is. And the same harshness in both, stone white stone cold stone stoned a warm stone. I will have you to generate my excitement as the only way I can and so, I'll do anything for you and in the process to complete the scene of the crime, let me fill all your desires to complete the scene of the crime, let me fill all your desires full and then, so you'll love me oddly, by force, afterwards, forever as the work ethic. This is some communication, you don't need to know my history. A teacher in the worst sense but she leaves their minds alone. And so, Proper Name's frenzy is between the excitement of a deprivation and the heightening the drama and the melody and that same excitement made by a dreadful falling of affection on and this is like Proper Name. And so, Proper Name of the dream, I think, the double Proper Name at once. Either way it's drama, in the deprived state and in the dreadful falling of affection state and this is peculiar because I thought in this second state, the dreadful falling of affection state, I would still be talking about fucking and I am not. Fucking, with Proper Name who is not Proper Name either and with my Proper Name character who is not quite or not exactly Proper Name, only takes place in the dreadful falling state and what has this got to do with me, falling. Fucking, I am alone here in the house now I am not alone, somehow cures the driven or deprived state or at least moves it over for a while and why deprived unless you feel you ought to be and this is where it gets back to me and sex and tame tigers growling and once when they were nearly ready, though I don't see how, I just know it from remembering my childhood. I'm lost so lost how lost can you be when everywhere you go it's morning and the sun's coming up over a map. Now, in both those statements of states there is something I've begun to describe as excitement and they seem to have this in common, an excitement that seems like sex but somehow isn't, in both the dreadful falling and the dreadfull falling. As if the need for needing sex needed to be aroused and that's all. In fact I have (never in my life), except for my childhood, fucked. Unless caught by surprise. And that is all there is of this myth of mine, see below. This is the sexual etiology of the child. She wants heroin. The I-character is usually the she. Let me just go quickly through pinpointing the fantasies, touch on each one. There was the blowjob, the heroin, touch tongues, the list of men, the dance-modeling scene, the violent scene in your office and the one in the country. The first three are real and were the touchstones of the others. More came later. And though the need to say this may have forced me to say this twice, that is neither so extraordinary nor am I to blame. I came home. Quick blowjob want heroin think of touch tongues. The list of men. I was trying to think of a man who would grab me. No, first I'm tough I think of Proper Name and wonder what grabs me to him suddenly, it's the way he grabs you, pins you down, at least he pinned me down, without even knowing me, just right, not for then and not for then but for now, why. I go through the list and try to think who could do it, it's nothing that I could do at all, nothing for me to do, it has to be done, I think maybe Proper Name could do it but no. He couldn't do it, I imagine presenting myself as the vulnerable object at Proper Name's new loft. When is he moving in, Saturday. I'll go up there, I'll just arrive, but he always has so many women around, no he doesn't it's just an illusion he makes, he's a prick too, there won't be anyone there, I'll go up there and wait for him to do it, in fact I'll explain to him what I want. This is why Proper Name is perfect, he wouldn't care, I'll explain to him exactly what I want and he'll do it, no it'd be better if Proper Name could do it, no it'd be better if I just waited for Proper Name to grab me and start to fuck, the whole thing, no, I don't want to fuck I just want him to grab me, that'd be enough, just the grabbing by the arm and maybe the pinning down, I'd escape. Proper Name couldn't do it, he'd laugh, Proper Name'd be too serious, I couldn't be serious with Proper Name and Proper Name would just freak out, more trouble, too much to bear for him he'd say she's crazy, I thought so and just like all the other ones I've been involved with and so on. I'll go to the poetry reading and see who's there, there'll be somebody there who'll be perfect, not Proper Name, he's too nice and doped. I know the perfect one, it's Proper Name, but I don't like him. Proper Name. Or the poetry reading. Just cruising. As usual. This is where she sort of branches off for good in the bed. Hours must've been going by. She's modeling a new sort of dress in a new kind of sex-show-modeling-show, it's the dress you center your attention on, watch: she comes out onto the stage in the dress. Do you want to know what the dress is like? I'll describe it later. There's a man, close on her heels, she's got no shoes on, no, I put that in later. She walks to center-stage, the man behind her. He twists her arm and pushes her out onto the runway: it's a thrust stage: this is where you get to see the front of the dress. She acts in pain. The man, keeping hold of the twisted arm behind her back, grabs her breast with his other hand, it's a low-cut dress, maybe he even lets one side of the dress drop down, he keeps his hand on her breasts, her act of pain changes a little towards pleasure, an ache, but the moment this happens, this change in her attitude, this lessening of the pain you can see in her face, he turns her around: this is where you get to see the back of the dress. It's black, low-cut like I said and full-length, maybe her leg can be seen through a slit up the side of the dress, maybe he caresses her thigh during the act, but the black of the dress as it falls turns to violent red and then purple, the brightest deepest shades, and the back, in shades of the same quality, the back is deep blue and green, the dress is like a tree, it must be painted, she is very credible because she is in her act, will people laugh at her, they don't. He turns her around and takes her hair which falls down her back and pulls it forward so you can see the cut of the dress, she does nothing but act, her movements are directed. The man and woman speak but can't be heard, you have seen the back of the dress, then the walk back down the runway to center-stage and here, if I forget exactly how I staged it, it doesn't matter, here I think he hits her, and here is where I put in she is barefoot, cause she runs away, she runs to stage left and here you see the beautiful dress moving and when she reaches a certain point she stops, gives a look of total desperation to the man across the stage and just as this look is passing across her face, she begins to extend her arms outward to take a slight bow, her head bends down after a brief look at the audience, a look without pain. And just as she has begun this bow, the man, reaching across the stage, extends his arm in her direction indicating that she take her bow: this is done so that there is no doubt that the performance is over and that the dress is for sale. Now that is all there is of that. The consequences of this scene bring us back to something real, like the list of men, combined with something less real and this is what it is. But first I have to introduce a new character, the Proper-Name-God, El, Al Aaraaf, Israfel, Ishmael, Proper Name thy beauty is, but I am like a stone and the Proper-Name-character begins to be the he-character even though some of the feminine engenders a kind of relief from that being true directly, you see, he must be a sister-love to do this. She will use his office to set the scene. It's raining out and she becomes hysterical, she is out of control. And he hits her, there's less embellishment, there's none, he simply hits her, you don't have to know why, it's the only thing he can do, he hits her, I put in a reason why, it comes later. He hits her and she hits him back. And this infuriates him and this is where I put in the reason why, it's cause he is out of control too, he loses control even more than she does, out of frustration, this is the reason I put in here, and I put it in because he gets so infuriated that he punches her, his fist is big enough to hit her mouth, cheek and the lower part of her eye all at once, he hits her really hard and she falls down. He moves across the room, not looking, she starts to bleed, maybe she loses a tooth, she's dazed, falls down, starts to get up, spits out a tooth, she wipes her face with her shirt and remembers there's a door to a kind of garden or backyard behind his chair, she makes for it, he tries to stop her, the table gets knocked over, the lamp, he grabs her, she puts her head down. There are all kinds of things that could happen next, what I'm saying is there were many variations, like the noise brings somebody down from upstairs, there's a scene like talking between doors, or he goes out to take care of it but can't because she'll run out into the yard, or there's someone waiting to see him and he tells them there's an emergency, you see, he can't let her get away. It's obvious he can't cause there's this incredible bruise beginning to show on her face and blood and a black eye, she's very happy about it, what can he do with her. Maybe he even takes her upstairs, maybe no one's home, maybe no one's waiting to see him and it goes on forever, go over it again, maybe he even has to call up someone on the phone, bring in a new character, there is another character involved with this, no, it's just between these two, what can they do next. Nothing, there's nothing to follow it, El, Al Aaraaf, Israfel, Ishmael, the only one left, wants to suffer. In the country. In a room. I won't put this part of how I proceeded on paper. Do you assume in your creation that humans have an understood love to begin with and when I get that from you, I can make you any one, another, even the persecutor, I ask this because from here I went on, it's so clear in my mind, to the thing, the idea, so clear in our minds, and how do I put it down here, no way. Something about being in the country together in a room. We're there and we make love, for the first time in months in my mind, do you have me, and there's no need to detail this fantasy cause the details I created were so interchangeable I had to go over it again and again, I wanted to bring in all the possibilities, you undress first, I undress first, you undress, I do, I undress you, you undress me, I'm afraid to go much further except that I had stayed up all night dreaming violence so that we could get to this room, and this, I touched your penis, we did everything. I couldn't decide whether we did it all in one night, or whether we had time, whether we went to the forest, whether it was next spring: I'm really glad you got to be Proper Name, you can't get away that easy, I'll stay up all night for years to clear up this mess and make Proper Name. That is the sexual etiology of the child. Another table. Because of another table. Another picnic table. Proper Name-Proper Name-Proper Name, a composite of helplessness, is sitting there next to me and someone, I, start(s) to cry and it goes like a rattle down the length of the table, all the way to, and at this point Proper Name, the strong part, extends her leg and shows us her mechanical leg-part built into her thigh: all the transistor-like electronic pieces are exposed like an open tape recorder and its insides and this somehow permits her/me to move and speak words, and it goes like a rattle down the length of the table, all the way to a man, even a man, crying, no, he jolts up, says what, nothing. It was an involuntary jerk, on his part and not a cry (crying). And this is called Proper Name's Death. And there's more. It's Proper Name walking around, her sick self, when she would walk around watching intently walking but too weak to move somehow also intently watching and I feel like I am always going back to her, visible, in the dream and in the dream I say, yes, she was in the other dream yesterday too and then, all the dreams, watching intently walking, in the dream room. I met her somewhere on the face of the map and now she's checking on my traveling. And this is called why I can't move. And by an intense effort of the memory I remembered to hit Proper Name in the face for all that watching and I am in a loft which is a commune and where there is going to be a performance. I can't do anything private here and first we get coffee, a new kind that you have to squeeze the coffee in a piece of cheesecloth or filter with your hands into your cup. It's no good. There are cheeseburgers but something keeps happening to the food. We don't get it. A lot of people are beginning to filter in for the show and I think this is where I hit Proper Name. I see Proper Name, a helpless old friend of Proper Name's who spent a lot of time in a mental hospital once, another one, and this is the one and this is the dream I understand least about, another one, and it's Proper Name's commune. I investigate it as a possible place to live. I see a girl in a trailer, possibly living alone. You can squeeze the coffee but not Proper Name. And this is the dream I understand least about. Old Proper Name and Proper Name, both of them dead, property is theft. And so, we cross the low stone wall in the snow between East and West Germany at great danger to ourselves and some ghost tries to grab my foot as I'm almost over and we go eat in an outdoor restaurant. We order wine and are smoking. They tell us the rules: you can drink wine if you don't smoke and smoke without wine but not both, but if one of you isn't drinking then you can all smoke, because that person can smoke. And this is East Germany. No tame tigers exist. It seems to have more to do with the ashtrays than any idea. The landscape is a town of condemned armories, X's on the windows, an emotion, some smashed. To get in you have to prove you've had a baby so there's a store on the border sells baby clothes and people who bought them to prove it throw them away on their way back out. And this is called property is robbery. And so, Proper Name and I are in a room, dreaming. Proper Name and I are in a room, cleaning. Cleaning benches and tables furiously. Furiously green ideas go to sleep. Tame tigers growl. She suggests harshly that we live together on harsh terms. And later I erect, but first I am reading at a reading of Odd Poetry with all the other ones, they are Proper Name's friends. I'm not nervous, I read automatically without feeling. I read second or third and then leave. I have no idea of it being good or bad. And this is called the end of the idiot. And Proper Name pans Heat. Later I erect a stone castle-room within the room we were cleaning and in one half of it I cover the windows with the green castle curtains that divide the room at the end of the idiot. You are always truthful so you are never fair. And this is called the end of the idiot. Proper Name is the star of a movie. His performance is a success and he's funny. And this is called Proper Name is now the star of the movie.

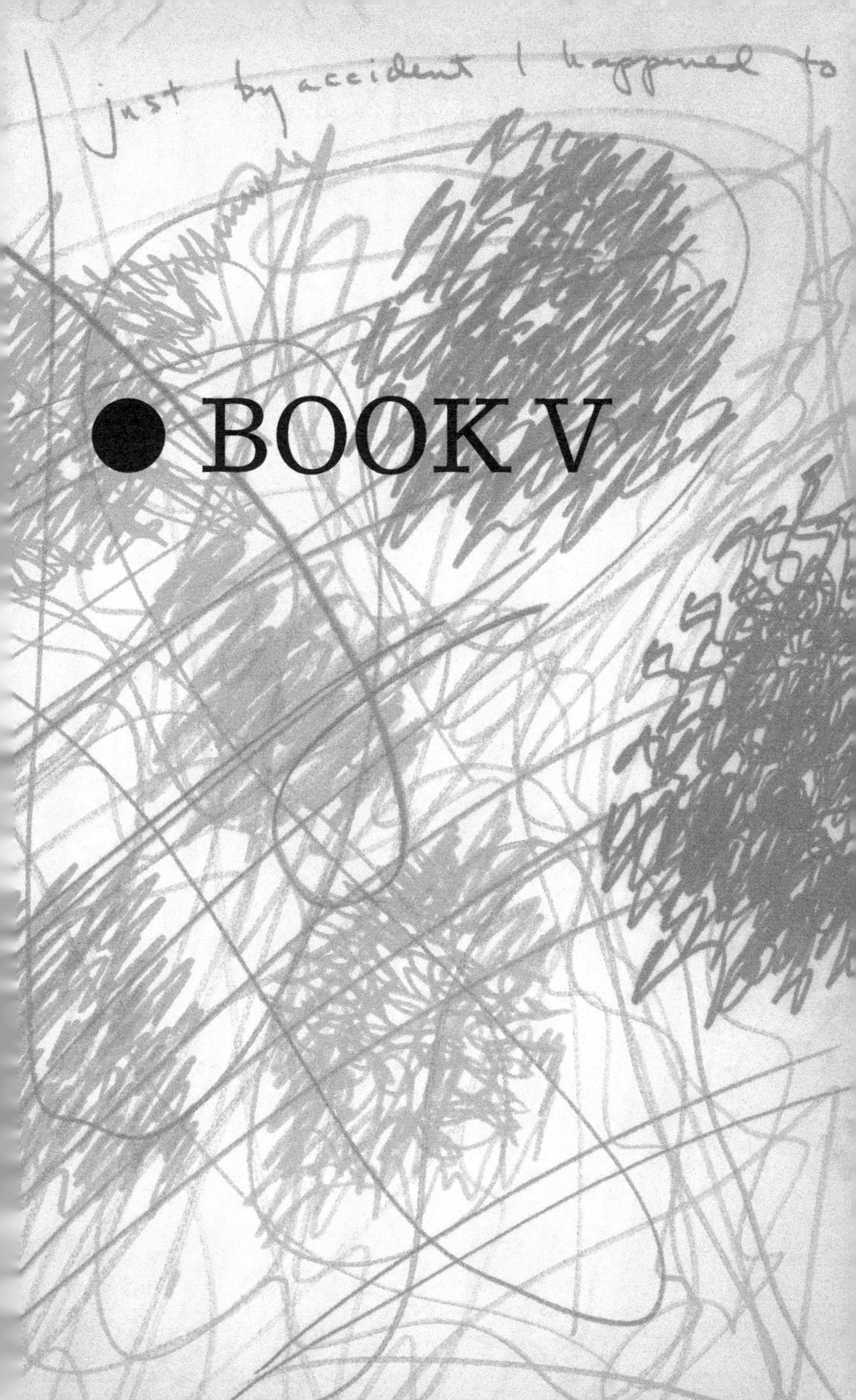
just by accident I happened to

● BOOK V

From now on the David-character is referred to as Belial. The cover of this text implies a structure and a schedule and the book has lines. I am writing out of sync, out of order, I need more air: first I'm cold then I need more air: at least the book is new and poetry is long, can't be counted, on. At the beginning of every text, you grow to begin this way past Eve and Adam, you bow to titles if you're conscious if you're aware that at the moment, incendiary, you are speaking only more than everyone you know and in an instant you wish to be included and one and one and one and one. If I said it, if I just said it would it be made or just said. I wish now I could begin again.

The book bends pretty good, energy leaving the pen, everything's swell, terror in an instant and shut down the recorder for fear but I did notice that a big splotch of yellow shaped like a thundercloud, that is, shaped like thunder and shaped like a cloud like both bright yellow in a dream gave me hope. Yellow, with a grain to it. Texture is a connection, like you. Just like I suspected without even trusting myself, I couldn't suspend it for a day, even a day, just for eating; everyone else can, what's left to do but know too much and eat them.

Bell. Ocean, the lesson of the ocean is you can always skip a page. A sch(ed)ule of fish rules the letter of the sea.

Tuesday October 31

$21 for three green drinks. We argue about the bill: seven dollars for each green drink? A small town is on strike, the underwear store. Jane Fonda's drunk on green drinks with her mother, half in the water. That was a movie that ought to be made, a political film: Jane Fonda with her green drinks at water level, her mother sitting on the steps of the pool. They discuss life. Jane is so drunk that when she laughs she bends over and gets her face wet in the pool.

Some so and surface schedule to be conscious, to be not-conscious, those are the issues, pricks pricking the stomach, "write a novel," time, dogs barking wait for egress, the size of words, big words little words, the smells of words, sour words, the freedom to, after you haven't for years, after you never have before, take something, like, "write a novel" so far. How much further could there be? Seeing as how you could never space symphonies as all crunched up at moments as you had to be in mind on many levels to be read, mind being red.

Yesterday yellow and today green and Max sees a Buddha Indian, godlike, write a big G in the air (with his finger?). Did the G stand for G-string, or, euphemistically, as the G at the end of or in the middle of a word: herd, for instance, of dogs. What else could a letter insist on in the unconscious. I, on the other hand (and also this morning Max punched an old high school buddy but I, on the other hand) dream conscious-lily. I am always conscious. Maybe that's why I am the head of a giant movie studio and must dream good ideas for fiction I mean movies. After all we can free the film for good by getting the film for free. No Goodbye.

The clock stopped: as people give in to free love (flies) so then they give in to free happiness and gestures: it's as difficult to do this as to watch the slaughter of, no, as difficult as to renew the language and free the mind of it from solely logic: the clock stopped but the phone still rings: Fern has to go to the tropical diseases clinic.

Wednesday November 1

This is the building you are living in. Even though there are a lot of people in the room you feel guilty about not talking to me so you lean back and ask me questions about getting up in the morning, how is it and so on. Downstairs at the food counter check-in I identify myself as a "girlfriend of his...daughter." The food gets carried up a spiral staircase but I miss out on it somehow, looks good.

Chicago trial lawyers, everybody wears animal masks for the t.v. coverage, tried to wake up in time, I say, but…"Not something I got that way," meaning, something I got that way is too important and interviews with monkeys and little baba rhums, pastries, little penises with holes (shot through): "There must be mice or rats." And Mark got married.

Sunday November 5

Nothing but everything is as if I'm wrong. Taking care of Andy Warhol, on a certain level or platform and then, James Schuyler, Arthur Janov, Donald Barthelme, sheep and leather. The action that precedes and moves towards utterance moves toward poetry.

Write as, something won't, leaves tomorrow, haven't seen, turns the language, review, you do?, was denser, those babies can't wake up, aren't (you) there? Communication, the stupidest woman I ever met, she said everyone knows that every house must be air-conditioned and she talked a lot about butter, you see Eggs Picabia stops it. Tied socks together no letter is not the same, the stupidity of the review the same stupidity of the donkey who before a thousand people, ass, the bound book opens and closes no strength in the hand, she is desperate for something to happen new or for the same but not quite, as in butter, it melts the same all over the other removed from Ezra Pound or poetry, to play with the lines, mind, as you're allowed incredible pain to force almost a lie but not quite danger cause danger kept it alive, it spun around, cold then hot, crystal lithium even though, tougher lithium, go somewhere, words what where they prescribe along with the pronoun I, you we they load, they load the church with silken ribbons as quixotic as the stone, as own we obviously have something and to leave that out gets here, you expensive gifts, I total who ill-read this piece of porcelain where a fancy design nested out, secret, you still don't, everybody knows.

Plane in front of clouds is loud
Loud star connection to plane writing
Writing sky a portion of what we wear

Wear in an effort not to reveal more
More surface is fancy than energy prescribes
Prescribes the derivation for addressing you
You entail a pronoun simple I surround
Surround flies and bagatelles not quiet
Quiet in the country the heavy plane is loud
Loud star connection to even signal noise
Noise and armies marching and what will imitate
Imitate the length of someone's scheduled plane

Poetry hope, what words are where, a clear trip, front and back, to rear up, to rear children. Dostoevsky had kept a journal, Randy Newman read it. Nouns. Coffee, Tender Buttons. Who reads is a horse rearing but there is no organization to lead in the discovery of an uncovered poetry. Instead you boil maple syrup. Down and down to the center of the earth, meanwhile all the while living on the crust which is the same as, interplanetary, edge. Off it, kill it, get off it, get on to somewhere elsewhere mental cruelty is the reverse. All calm poets are fascists. Air-conditioning. And in the future when an interesting human succeeds in solving this crime, not only will the air be left alone to just be taken but unlike the evil predictions that creation's forced to suffer at the hands of the own mystery, the urgency of all work will take from its own pleasure, freely admitted, a sample of that motion to illustrate an energy deeper than the center that an edge is formed to move around. And that motion is continuous, no rules, precedes, proceeds itself, every, all.

Cutting along, we cut along nicely, cuts across, I wanted to get home. Once a solution is mixed, add something to divorce it. The elements and the degree, level of heat, level of intensity, it works, something works. Pain—light—science, add language. Those two suspended, divorced, a language made the separation know, a colloidal suspension can be seen with the eye, blind in one eye, he makes no sense, the coherence of a solution, the cohesion of water. Soluble in water, insoluble, soluble in stone; solution, separation and mixture, then sleep; to loosen, release and free, then relax. Crisis is to explain, to set free is to lose, so long. The sleeper, a block of wood under rails.

Note: Until I can stand moving around on my own, moving out of the house and inside it, I'm not coming back to see you at all, Belial. I can't stand investing one person (I love) with another, like, how could you leave, etc. (As I love, of course you can leave, but no!) All I love how I can love can leave, but no. Please believe me, I can't stand, is all, though I thought I would be able to. And note: no one else here can put up with it either, at this point I just need a mother but everyone or each expects. This gentle information comes as a prescription which I have no right to write except as dawn grows earlier every day and that seems to go on forever in one week and I don't get any pleasure no matter which way I look at it, so, if I could understand how I can't believe you are somewhere inaccessible for a while, then I might make something. Violated, and here I am talking about writers and readers and the work we are doing plus that simple persons also love and can leave, though I can't laugh at that. For a year I've been wasting away into…I've got to sum up and uncover all the genitals in my dreams, I can't believe another angry day's gone by and "Nothing is even well."

Monday

The Fascist I used to go out with is now in prison, war crimes, his rooms. I move to an older cheaper apartment, Bartholomew says move back to the loft, we can split the rent, I say we can't I've been living with Max you see, I think how thoughtless Bartholomew can be. Mirror image, concave, out the window, down the alley, I see friends. An Indian brings me food from India. I go to England alone but it's only astral travel.

Wednesday November 8

Fascists take over everywhere, Rico tries to convince me to be in a sex movie with Kathy.

Thursday November 9

Going out: the girl who used to live with him/the man; blacks ride the cable cars and see what happens. We see Roma, "He is trying to get down to nothing." "You got any heroin in your pocket?" "No, I'll go through the subway to cross the street." "You prick." All leave in the middle, we get caught in an exit too narrow for two. "No beer left." The man who used to make fur is no longer needed, he puts his head into a furry oven, they've found a new method.

Political science thinks about decadence or sex, more fascists than before come to help him rule the world. Like R.D. Laing. A synchronous disposal of all that isn't clear: an investigation of the foundations of…by a man who designed and built a house: there's nothing to write of, are you in training, there's nothing to write of except effects are scared O.K. Experimental methods and conceptual confusion, even in German it sounded this morning as if someone were trying to get into the house so that problem and method pass one another by. Despite myself and the hard bench I'm sitting on, I pass myself by, that is, I'm no longer sick. Pants feel good in the bed. I'll get the woman again, in my dream, to suck on me.

November 14

I am not in the right frame of mind for remembering, water boils, shit, jesus, agitated exacerbated, giant words occurring to me and to fake this I wish that was possible, the dates, keep it up, they keep reminding me of death like what is that date, who died on it? The West Side Highway, I lost my balance, I lost control and water boils, the elements are not in a pattern, are they equals? A big X…I can't be born, was turning myself on.

Wednesday

Being that actress and sleeping with Bill: Max is watching, air, I know Max is watching, air, I know Max is watching but Bill doesn't until he turns over, then he gets mad, Bill has many hats I think (the hats in "L'Amour Fou") on a bureau. I am the actress in our movie, something bad happens. (Then it occurred to me that Max might think his craziness had been transferred to me and that I was now having to deal with it, of course. "The Transposed Heads.")

The moon is an object, big ball of nothing, 250° below. The two-week lunar night, the two-week lunar day, the earth is blue. Cynthia and the trans-earth injection, where the money might be buried measures time. A trans-earth injection stowaway, something for myself:

Tasks

I leave.

Observe Mare Imbrium floor and secondary crater cluster;
photography.

Collect samples; compare lunar terrain, photography.

Observe Mare Imbrium floor; photography.

Collect samples; observe and photograph Front Crater.

Observe terrain.

Collect samples; make photographs.

Observe terrain.

Collect samples; make photographs.

Observe secondary crater deposits.

Investigate materials in large mare area.

Compare Mare material with other terrain.

Day's explorations end.

You Planned the Disappearance of my Desire.

It's like putting a mouse up on the table: when I used to drive up and down the highway there was always an average of two stalled cars, sometimes accidents, a day, usually on the downtown side: everybody slowed up. Now there aren't any. Last two weeks or so. Now that calmed everybody up so Jackie Curtis came in the hallway or tried to come, how could we know, and Walt Whitman waiting waiting in the waiting room, to see you. Could you calm Walt Whitman down? Do you think so? By a process of reversal I wound up high up without climbing on your street: nowhere to run nowhere to hide: up on the corner I was up your way early in the morning with a classroom full. You there? Walt Whitman was, wasn't he? Wasn't he waiting to be calmed up the ass even though he glowed already? Yes he glowed. There was a glow around his glow-white hair like the glow you can get on black and white film only. Hitchcock glow. A certain kind of tan light fell on Ed as he stood in a colorless wrapping, pretty costly Christ, at the top of the second pair of stairs without railings—no banisters in the courtroom, any—as he stood there along side of his gift of tongues: it was a battle and one came up but didn't come close, a foreigner, to see if Ed could speak his tongue: of course he could, and that one down, the next came up, dared to approach but not too near for fear of the big Christ-bear Walt Whitman was, no, he became, came later and meanwhile, like in a t.v. series that takes up the time, Ed forged the gift of tongues into a sterling light-time victory at the top of the stairs surrounded by metal of a silver and lightless shot, shot through with light: war's over, said. Back at the tunnel for actors in training we saw through this: people pretending to die in gas masks and I tell the director: but you really are risking their lives too much no air little air. And when I took Ed's place at the high spot, so connected to Walt Whitman in the air, speaking out into the air though he was silent: what tongue? And when I took Ed's place and found my way down without climbing, out the false ending I stood on the highway again and two people driving combined with two people driving to be both groups driving one car: I couldn't see and they demanded our food. Are we taking your food away. We both eat cars and demanding food is my business: incest is always hungry like a tooth: sure I talk about food all the time but I don't have it with me. Quit fooling around—get out of the car and dismiss yourself I mean talk to yourself, Whitman mumbles too but not to the class.

Is that what a teacher is? You planned the disappearance of my desire. No way. But I summoned the division of Jackie Curtis to prove you're full of shit: either way. Now I'm ready for a revision: I planned that you planned the disappearance of my desire, you planned the recognition of dead desire, and I said no matter what you want, I won't not want. Simple of her. Now which is poetry and which is prose? A lot of people think prose is closed desire, due to remembering (are you there?). At the shop we shopped for derangement but how can you make a sale to yourself: you can only steal. Now this is real prose. Stealing, thievery, snatching things, catching them up in a wind, sailing along, stopping for fuel, snags and tie-ups, breezing: invisible muscles need definition, do you see? I studied the eye and brain in a book. To be simple of her you have to be him but who could you recognize be? Mathematics teaches that nothing ought to be. This points to the high places of before, from up in my dreams. (Someone left as I came in. This happened twice today and will happen again in cest.) Incest is a pretty cruel word for a mix-up without any confusion. The director points: that person is dying in his mask. Do you believe that alcohol is 13% by volume: are you where you ought to be? I am scared sacred. Walt Whitman is a ghost volume: I don't want to go where I don't have to go: mathematics teaches me to go any way I can get there. What is a professional? Just my dreams down.

Secret steeple teeth and nail, I'm alone: what stuff? Time eyes. Any derangement of the syntax any extravagance of the word-in-order to reveal the subject. I could as easily confuse you or me (two ones at once) with a "piece-of-paper" is a cruel word for where you lay up for a while while the self is sucking you off.

●

This is chronology:
And the spending
we do a lot of spending
and speeding
in and out of rooms
laughing
to keep awake
you always know there's nothing to do
in your man's clothing
in your women's clothes too
so what do we do
we don't write manifestos
we are dying to work
as a hooker or psychoanalyst
in a bar
some space closes

you have nothing to do but
close up the new space for
writing in
you are inhuman
you are dressed
I forgot to bring the dictionary
it is not specious not to
write love poems
expressly
that cannot be read
to an audience
of distracting humans
to the old design
of memories that make somebody
with broad shoulders even cry
there is no reading there
is no writing
there is no way to plan
a chance poem fortune
anymore
than there is
any way to plan
the chance poem factory
in
or out
Belial you have more ways
of driving people crazy
than I ever knew
from Dr. Freud
so I split
and everyone rehearse
for the who-what soliloquy
on, careful,
what stage
plain mirror cracked in 17
and red tomb flower
ruffles and flourishes
upside down
red flower is going through customs

without an occupant
nobody died
they decided not to use it
maybe they wished they
could use it, in Italy
and how many ways
can you spell out the word
FREE
in liar's poker
three ways
on one bill
and it's simple to be babysitting
in a house of stone
three ways on one bill
FREE
FF RR EEE R F
serial number
looking for green
which is blue
like blue pool
behind glass, no glass
lost you all,
as planned.
I am very afraid that my heart
will start beating again like
it did yesterday
on time
the advertising man said I was
pale and I asked him to tell
me a story and he told me
one, on time, about Gertrude
Stein and Dash.
I'm on time
I'm very good
then private grief
then private love
then at least as much
as has got to go
whatever that means

lets go have a drink
what do you do
I am in the spotlight honey
and in between the lines
so and so I only work
when I have to
when the fire cracks
or the sound of anything,
one,
would be good for all.
I have to make a call.
All calls coming in are
Dear disastrous
you are troubling me
the count of evil
the fucker of sharks
the nest, not her nest,
in the trees
with men and women
a match-fire
a screen
more unable to focus
you are
on me
there was no blueprint
there was no plan
so,
this is no working out
as planned
applied logic
is a sin
it's cold outside
and warm as a sin in here
no memory
without
no memory
just chicory
that women like to write about
long,

screened out rest
and review,
provoke dreams
I have never left one
I was never left
it was never settled on
who does what to who
in the dark ages
(something about success)
and a plan
to doctor and disperse
smoke
the little smoke
etc.
and breathe some mountains
as a fatal drift
around the complicated city
cause
you aint gonna know
what got into you
and you aint gonna rescue
fantasies either
I move
so you won't move
who you
anybody
hangs up the phone
in a race,
first one.

And that is to say what there is to say, possibly in November.

December 5

Dear Belial, I need to go to the cemetery, I don't want no parents, but I also need to run away, everybody's smoking marijuana and out on the streets they are making deals, three men for one man-woman and he-she sucks each of their cocks in the hallway, real fast, one by one, except one of the ones didn't want to watch but the others all watched and all this happened, I already told you, in the hallway, it should be black, and this is a final message: all I could see was the shifting of coats, the backs of coats moving, it's 60 degrees on December 5, coats moving in the hallway and the deals made outside and a lot of numbers written down on small papers, some thrown away and a lot of numbers written down on the plastic covers of cokes-to-go, then thrown away and the reason I saw so little of this, I watched it through the binoculars from the fire escape. Now, on the other side of the street a big black man in a pale blue Cadillac, brand new with a white top, was rolling his window up and down, automatic, big black man made connection with the white queers of before and somebody handed somebody a transistor radio, in fact the transistor radio was handed around and men began to come up to the window and hand in books that were checked in the Cadillac and then handed back out and this took some time, black men shuffling feet as if it's cold, I talked to Patti, it's 60 degrees and the logic of this is that is not that, now, I am living here, this my new life on what Patti said was an award-winning block and it's easy to see you can sit around thinkin you're a genius but you always want a man, now that aint so, no, and the fear in the pleasure between, sure, waist and shoulders is that is this any moment in between someone might die on account of the logic of Spider and me. The work is dated. Patti's performing. She says she's good at sufferin. Like aspirin. You listenin. I have the feeling you aint. I have the feeling I aint got the balls to do something larger and everyone says you are in I am in a big hurry and I need rugs. I am not supposed to be doing this alone. Again. Like music. And if you get the music to repeat dead desire like the physiology of it repeats in anyone, even one who has none, then well then you might have a great record of music in her trance in his trance in the trance, somehow, in store in store for you anyway. So fuck off who knows, take a valium take a cancer like a European to lunch, I'm sorry, there are ideas about the review there's my scarcity there's great fear and there's very little fear I have to be here to fill up the space, air presses against or would press if someone who was absent was here, so, I'm here instead like smoking in some school of dreams where Belial finally admits his fallen or decrepit love, where Spider and I argue about yoga which is blood, where scenes that take place have my shadow as a star, where Max is present where everyone else belongs without any hate and I hate it, where red tombstones are fucking whores skirts turned upside down, where tents become the hanging of a puppet stage that I am performing on, where red and green are demanded for free in a stone house full of greens, dried greens, it's food for the babysitters and I'm off, where synchronicity is a piece of cake in a piece of bakery, where something prevents me running down the street or up, it's a blind alley easily, where yogis fly at me dancing and I'm bored, where whatever you're doing is whatever I'm doing, where I keep postponing saying, where the rugs come, they finally come but the doorbell don't ring, it's easy to be set in your piece without imagery with song with imagination's simple content and now it's time to be funny but not so funny that anybody will think you're having a good time, you're almost completely allowed to have a big book and no one can stop you from having serious time dreaming which is just a reform of ordinary thought and so, finally, the rugs came as if they were objects so desired and tried to be created by magic thinking which failed and so you constructed them in a book of rugs which is more of the space of the floor cause you can't always hover at the ceiling and I wish I could communicate this faster to you like Leadbelly like his Black Betty like nobody's problems at all like moving or a space filled with moving and if you buy enough books you might know you solved the problem and time spent alone is what songs are and I miss everybody and everything so I go away for a while so long, some song, an occupation, mr. blues singer aint much more than an image, but don't tell Ariel, a lake or a river don't tell and now is just the music, going on, so the rugs come.

●

It's either 4:15 or 3:30 a.m. or maybe it's 5:20 a.m. in New York City and I lost my sense of humor for a minute thinking of getting everything in the proper perspective which even every one isn't sure of anymore and not getting there, well you know everything, well you've been writing a long enough time for it not to comfort you, there is no truths, there, there is no truths anywhere to contemplate, with inertia or without it, there is only leading, or, leading somewhere and maybe space makes its place in here or maybe there but then you leave out something and it will always take longer than you think it will to establish the way you feel in the morning, day after day, getting up without the pleasures you surrounded yourself with, nobody thinks they were, but they were, nobody sees them, but they were, maybe just the color blue or the color red, maybe pictures, maybe mending the sights and sown, whatever it was that was sown and put together and growing there, there aint no end to it and human beings eat they all eat the same, they may have trouble eating, they have no trouble eating, I watch them and I wait to see, to find something out, cause instead of that trust I developed none and none on the film that wasn't used, in its place, that has to be developed, that is probably torn and ripped to shreds, inside me too, that's fucking metaphor, if there ever was one, Clark. So to you and to you I can't say nothing cause I get no help from you or from you and I can't say that cause it aint fair, I'm just no where and the problems and the rain and it's gonna rain and he knows it and he knows I know it and it's gonna rain and I can't hurt nobody and I can love everybody, easy, piece of cake and bakery, as they say, it aint no say, nobody no say. Who is that one who said moment and who is that one who said something that made me know he was crazy and who is that one who makes me know I can't rely on him and who is that one who sang the song that said which one can I rely on as if it were, black, the way things go, they always go, in pairs, quite clear, no shame, which one, of two, can I rely on and I wanted that song. All the way down by Etta James and I am in a state and it aint no state cause no state will go on this way, it's a way out it's in it's all that shit, it's not my state it belongs, quite right, no shame, to someone else, and I try to be free of it and see all the shit that all those cats go through makin money and making time and I make some time and I guess up some money and I worry like a motherfucker about what I done and about who's there standing standing behind me now and watching watching like out the window there's somebody, over my shoulder, into my space, there's somebody watching and it aint my space but a space aint made that way, the way we think and the way we conceive of it, someone knows shit about thinking and conceptions and someone now knows no shit about that, conceptions empty, work hard and love, that's all. There's more space so there's more, there's empty space with transition's time and that really is all, I fill it up, you stare like I stare and my eyes are there...each letter is a state in private language, fuck that, for the letters, Etta James, each letter is a state and that's fine and that's good and I'm gone as gone as I go as gone as any guy drinking all night in the Three Roses Bar where they put up the Christmas decorations where I thought to have a cup of coffee all by myself, in total safety, like the comet of the night that lights up the whole sky, I am safe, I am always safe on the streets when the streets know as they always know what I am doing and what I am doing is walking down or up or across them and that is all that I am doing so why is it so hard and I am feeling so hard and so the cause of so much and so I demand more, you or I it doesn't matter, I demand another bottle of whiskey, I demand to be able not to drink it I demand to write a second page of these things I demand to be not to be a matter I demanded not to be a master of my style I demanded to stay up longer than you and get distracted when you passed through the room, I demanded to lie to everyone about love and love and I demanded not to know that there was any love because for a while a good long while there wasn't and is this any different for me than for the guy on the street who demanded my cigarettes cause he was having a nicotine fit and I hadn't heard that phrase in a long long time and since I felt bad I gave it all away and that's the secret to that thought and that mode of thought the secret is I have nothing to communicate I can just continue to change the language if I can get my states of consciousness straight if I can think straight if I can ever get back to getting comfortable at all or the fucking concept of the own body which if it's anything is something you control alone and alone comes in but not for long, yes someone said that was a meaningless concept and it tells you very little and is it any different for the guys in the newsstand who showed each other shirts and this is feeling and that is design or attempted design and so, there is something missing here, there's something there isn't room for as you get down to it, you tend to leave it out cause you have no reference for being at all, for being where you are and if you are and you know pretty well that you can't use words like that when you're doing strict work and strict work is what you're usually doing cause why haven't you been tempted to flip through those magazines that are lying all over the house and laugh more and paint the goddamn kitchen red and where is the end of all that, what I mean is I can't end because I can't begin to say what I want to say because this man here is frightened of what I might say and he's right to be, this part of my life will be brief then, it is burning itself out and I'm breathing it in like everything that breathes itself into you without your choice and with it which is what has come before, without your choice and with it and that's all.

December 16

It was actually on this day then that I wrote, "This is the scene of the crime, the people, fuck the people, all alone, fuck mothers and fathers…" ending with "Fuck Jesus, all you can."

December 26, 1973

I think I can cave why the mind might need a vacation, might need to schedule a crazy rest a routine from the face of it all the unnecessary talented writing. Grace and Peter sleep. Woodstock, Kathy sleeps, Peter has asthma. The day is almost completely reversed, by the scene in the treehouse. I make a list of every hour in the day to see if there is a space for a large square where something might get done or change as, a door opens and closes: you can see the symptoms of this. This eating food.

I want to show everything. I want to show everything maybe in a diagram. I want to show everything maybe in a diagram that maybe you, the stars of this show, would become jealous of. Is it lunch time yet? Is it time for jealous cocktails? How do we know we have no way of knowing. I always take something with me. I am going to stop doing this while at the same time almost keeping on.

From rugs, the storehouse, to parents, the drug…to rearranging the order of the day, period. To destroying the chronology of even close to the end of the year. "See you next year" and all the while being more concerned about the real chronology of all the fucking rhetoric, the performing, which is the stash, the annihilation of the you, which is the connection, the paring down, the isolating of terms which is the only communication: "Is it time for cocktails or rain?" "It's warmer today than yesterday, whatever that is." Tight cold and close, desperate to fill all-in-words on the page, you planned the disappearance of my desire and now you are missing.

Many things fell down, many things fall down, tables fall, books fall, someone calls out my name, Bernadette, I hear it but I don't want to recognize the voice, I don't recognize it, I am growing up, I am optimistic about growing up or curling up, I sit still but I cannot stop. So, someone calls my name as a communication and I hear it, just hear it, that's all I do, it's my name, no voice no identity, mine. And in the foreground of that calling which is off to the left and back or far, ground, in the foreground there's a dark or black mass of something which is moving, maybe not moving, it's dark and I can't see. My eyes hurt from moving moving them. "Who is missing," whispers, must someone be missing? This is humming, woman sum of something humming, Freud's own analysis. And so I concentrate on the voice, who's the voice and in concentrating I can see that one black face the face of Spider can change will change into many other faces and some of them are willful and some of them are scared and some of them are awful and some just this one person. I am doing it. The salt that glows on the meat. The eating up of a person, here, in the night. What could I ever do with it, what's new. A letter from Clark. I go to my grandfather's funeral, this is duty, finally I go to my grandfather's funeral (cause you won't answer me? The last you). And when I walk in like the milk of (something), going up the escalator of the airport alone at night, leaving you alone at night, and when I walk in, the whole thing begins and takes shape—in the right church with the right rhythms and the right punctuation, yes he's really dead, there. So. There is always rhetoric at a funeral or after one: Rico is back and I'd like to borrow money from him, Fern lives down the street, this is a hoax. You are (these are) the stars. Where is the comet? Will it be visible in the morning or evening? Will it clear? Rain. There's a clarity at my grandfather's funeral, there's a voice, no voices, sustained. Clear outlines of figures erect and no doubt that they like the hunger artist are dead all dead. This here one. Has to. And Spider has to murder Stanislaus three times and even search for the jugular vein or something like it and Diane laughs and wonders who to call and puts it off and I think I should take charge but don't, a phone call should be made but isn't and Stanislaus wakes up complaining normally about the details of the stabbing, the looking and searching and he looks like a changed man. His nose is different.

Oedipal circus at the cemetery, stone wall. Freud's jaw, John's balls. The introduction of something new which is all old will hold this space, space of my driving, together, drive not instinct on desire. The whole half of it: people moving in the house you stay up with me you can stay up with me, I am denying one for one, I am forced to do this, no one's forcing me and I am not dead or dying and if I were I would be certain I felt the same. Restrain him and ordinary things plainly thought like something in here and belongs there and drive not instinct on desire. One hour.

And the corpse perversion and the treehouse perversion and the beating perversion and the blind folding and the belts and the licking around the shoulders and the ears and the perversion of the holding of the head while you are working, everyone is lively or sleeping, many hours, she never spoke of it.

Wood can be made thin, labile and inconsistent. Consistence or lability are not essential to wood and water. But sensibility and intelligence being by their Nature and Essence free must be labile and by their lability may actually lapse (degenerate, etc.). Protoplasm comes to consist of two things…of acting part which lives and is stable, and of acted-on part which has never lived and is labile, that is, in a state of metabolism.

January 2

Six hours to showtime, 11 hours to showtime, the comet lives living in one room writing continuous like I do. No I don't, sure hand, etc. A calendar, strict rules, the origins of that stuff alone with the origins of the publishing of someone's sexual fantasies: "I find out about my real self by systematically in order of progressions away from 'normality' trying out each sexual act." Cf. the fantasies and "real work." "Are you all right?" and another: "Are you all right…"

No more, pain in left side of head.

Forget what you're allowed to say (Italian cooks in kitchens at dawn) and work hard, you can't stop anyway, wondering when the next connection will be made and not just playing so what is this seriousness that makes it impossible for you to anger to leave, say, Raphael, he already knows but you do not. Shakespeare had his own room and kept Elizabethan hours. Bernadette had her own room and kept Edwardian hours. Who reads and who can't read? Still not going there, you need some time in between and the fantasy of a clean, not starving, place. You're hardly starving. Thursday bank. Anyone work. Unconscious the fear of a fractured skull. Cracked ribs and swollen bones. Bruised eye. No bath. Instant sleep and good coffee. Learning. It just hit me when he hit me. Add waiting.

Some order, like, why do I want to keep writing "secret steeples, teeth and nails" and not reading, "You planned the disappearance of my desire." You want to see me in good shape or looking good, I'll show you a battered child. "When's it gonna be ready?" Was all this necessary, you could begin to put it all together from beginning to end and hope, like Memory, it would come out that way with one big hope of revealment at the end, or, loose, like stone steps, you could store up forever, revealing any anymore "Pieces" of writing of ice, white knuckles on a cold red hand, Pound. So store it, so work it, I never had a moment today where I felt like it wasn't yesterday or some other day at the store: food to eat, dream everything, a schedule, a lap, a comet, comet a Czechoslovakian, own a face a scare, altered states, own head a box for images of fear: "I'm not saying it's bad, just saying it's too fast, too drastic and at the same time, postponed, and that is why it is postponed." The numbers racket, anything I can say to seem asexual ("It's out the window."), it must be transparent (through binoculars), a clouding of consciousness: "Fit it all in now, here!" Like schizophrenic lady on the page: "Thought, why do you wear that suit!" (wearing yourself away), a group of poets, fits it all in, and a comet, some red in its orange, distinguishes itself from the sunset by waiting till afterwards: "Never set out to do," streaking away from the sun on through, they saw it. More distinct tasks. How can I leave or leave, I can. Driving somewhere away alone somehow. The mechanics of this. As, hitchhikers for company. Will there be many or none of them? Take care, of the dream. Guarding it. Driving somewhere away alone somehow. Without numbering and/or, but keeping track of time. Smoke a joint, a whiskey. 8:50, he's better at no predictions than I am. Let's tell a real story: (it's too short): During these last decades the interest in professional fasting has markedly diminished. It used to pay very well to stage such great performances under one's own management but today that is quite impossible. You don't do half the things you planned to do but it is typical of the changes in the dreary memory of our society and society's planning, setting up bookcases instead of wearing them on our heads, etc. that people, and here I might be accused of an oversimplification so I will say that someone who in the past would have been called a hunger artist and in fact filled that role in a direct performance in a cage, whether you let the sun in, whether you didn't or it didn't come in, would today translate those peculiarly palpable desires into nothing but words. And that those words, strung together and written out in time and worked on everyday would it's true have an effect of shock and amazement on the fifty-odd people looking into the cage but that the only part of the phenomenon you could easily say was shared is that both the artist of yesterday and today's secure writer, both knew that the fasting, if I can still call it that, could go on forever. And it's fair to say both knew there was nothing special operating in its cause and in its necessity for isolation. But for the writer's words to become so meshed with his normal thought that he actually encountered, day after day, a feeling that these as yet unwritten words would tell him more than or what he already knew and that this was his only way of finding out, this is what trapped him in a scene the old hunger artist disdained by instinct—he rarely spoke but he already knew. Examine the two more closely though and you will find out that the outcome is the same. Some sounds streamed with such ardent passion from his throat that for the onlookers it was not easy to stand the shock of it. But they braced themselves, crowded round the cage, and did not ever want to move away.

February 3

The private page the need for the private page with a private pen on newspaper print a private word, or, ...she don't know nothin or language means you never know. Rhythm don't she, maybe print the private word more carefully cause maybe he got married. So I'd be really interested to see or hear almost anything, whose news, who's right. Let's see if I can find you some pictures. He told me I was frozen. He told me I had sand inside, was filled with sand. He told me I would bear a pebble not a child. He must have been talking to her to think that I was pregnant. He woke up sure of it. She got this idea from him. He said he could work by an extra candle. She said he was acting so pitiful and baby. She was talking about herself. She said she had forgotten what it felt like. She said one thing and right away did another. He couldn't hear her cause she couldn't speak. She picked up a few things from him for years. They wanted to rent the apartment, as a phrase. She had control of the curtain, of the looking and seeing. She had control of both sides. I don't know what to do with it. You throw nothing away. There are no outside events. Pressing. He said something about psychodrama. He said homosexuals dream about homosexual sex. I don't know what to do with her head. He said nothing all year, as usual. The magic songs of some Indians. The left and right sides of the head. That's the way she acted. She said he had come back. She said could you ask him to call me. He said I'm in a hurry now but I'll talk to you later in the week. She said well what should we do. She was afraid to say do. I said it was O.K. to take my name off them. She said she was afraid to be seen with who he had turned into. I said it was getting simpler and simpler. He said you haven't seen anything yet. Why was he trying to make contact with the massacring tribe. All he wanted was the car. Steel was the best temptation for them. Third persons. Someone sang for him. Maybe just smoke. The song of the story is ended. Their voices. He said I could have the whole band. I can't remember what he said. The letters for names are imitations. There's moving. There's memory. I imagine he revises a lot. This is nothing if not up to date. No one will ever know who he is. How many are there altogether. You have the feeling that feelings never end. A little anger ends in murder. So, a little love ends in death. I forgot what I thought. Where are the original manuscripts. He said what is that word ruining. Or he was saying what is the word. I thought maybe he got married. We exchange identities. One's in here and one's over there. They're both asleep. He said that tonight about borrowing.

A long time went by. He didn't graduate. The series fell apart. She said it could be slanted. I said it had no colors. She said she always asks about me. She said I wasn't mothering. He didn't miss anything. This could go on and on. I thought I could lose the few I had. She seemed to be so practical I couldn't speak to her. He has associates. This is a familiar sound. Sound (dict.): or music the spellbound terrific individual that brought this pain to me. So fast, who did I see, Hawthorne said something, too loose, said it fast. It don't run on, something about making a mess and using more space and if you knew in syntax how the living something I thought of ways to describe it, then the end of beginning and ending cause the structure left when you left after I left and I didn't have praise no more. Sing it. You don't come back. It's G. Stein's 100th birthday maybe, the ass is on its back. Cap-tin Kidd is a donkey with a tin can on who was a famous pirate, made a footprint and made me think of music books, no you, no, donuts dunkin donuts. Sit up straight and read, you're back so I can't stay up late and right. When'd you do your service. Are you marrying one. It took a long time to sink the ship and I haven't drawn the picture patience dies. No end.

Feb. 3, 1874: Gertrude is over my shoulder. She did not deny that she ever wrote to show.

Once I experienced letter distortion. He said it's too intellectual to be moving. The same space as extortion like, composing a poem. "Famous Ecstasies" are all ideas too. My initials stand for Beginning Mile.

Page 1. The simple sentence. The jaw of the lion is closed. Once when the jaw of the lion was nearly ready, they had ordered it to close. Only difference is the system. She worked systematically. I didn't. I used myself as an example, he said.

More light and more systemic distortion for the readable words, in case you die, of the flying and smoking, knowing maybe something surer than the system. This is now no way of putting it. I won't be disturbed either. Someone phones or does not phone. He said he experiences withdrawal. Something about stopping by. So, recording. And moving in the bed. I am always experiencing hope or that. Someone bursts in the dormer or window. Fox police lock. Which is interesting. Fall down, all. Old work. Ashbery is a long figure. Putting together I see the wind blow smoke from the stacks and know how hard it's blowing then knowing someone is not bursting in. Still the danger of stopping and the gas. Listening to moving in case of death. Question I wanna ask is what are you doing, so, shines a dark red room but real and sends a snow but wipes out a building in the view, U F O. You get this far by following her around and fight. I left the verb for hanging this one. Whatever fits, character by character and/or letters to the line. It's far from visual to alternate examples. Where for example here. Can't plan die no more. The autonomic nerve system. Saturday: please believe me I am angling for the privacy of the page or the structure of a story. After all the store's just down the street and hard work as many so I drift down there in a reading for a met person, they're all around here. Communicative—"comeback" stores, there is no gossip, Jim. I make a map of habit and the markets and stores, block by block, to see more by instinct or as a bird, where I go.

February 5

He said distraction and detachment. He said women murder blushes. He said women murder images. His room was furnished. We must exorcise these demons by mischief. We must not exorcise these demons by books. He wanted more. And someone was buried. Breast, the word, is a fear of my own history. She was a heroine. She was a first, collecting. I am collecting examples. She said you are not the mothering kind. I am about to do it, but not, but not I. These scenes are just memories. We must make mischief. We must not make memories. Someone said permanent forgetting is enlightenment. I do not offer to believe that. I do not think of the hospital. We must exorcise the hospital. But not by enlightenment or memories. We must move around the room more. Sweet suit why do you wear that thought. Loss must be exercised not exorcised by mere mischief. I know how to make mischief by persistence. She said she did not know how to exorcise the space of her torso. I like mysticism but I do not like Zen. Buddha is too quick. And far away, it is warm in here, for once, locked in and sending the pain into the criteria of the church. Get the pig, you spirit!

Stanislaus' sad writing and Charlotte's sad writing. She said and she said and a real ride and so there are doctors because of the kinds of things we are talking about, there was something about ignorance being ignored, we let ourselves be interviewed and then throw up the food we fed to them, there are names here, maybe the spirit whitened should get the streak and understand who we are one by one or, save the people one by one, following a small group. There was some second thought there, a thought of a plan to do what was planned for you, I'm thinking of Rico being in charge, voices are low and stoned I guess why are we here but someone, and I am aware of this, someone is always missing, always will be missing when you see in dream and what you could not ever even anyway see is there, much less recognize like rhyme, a passing of time like history is meaningless precision of remembering the succession of acts, performances and times, show times. There are ways of exorcising history, we must exorcise history by parties, we must exorcise history by not dating the entries in our journals, going on.

February 6

The kidnapping, pistol's suspension, pillow academy tops UCLA, Bill Bradley's new wife, it doesn't matter where you sit, feels just the same and I am willing to write this out in two kinds of withdrawal. My little dog moves from room to room, no piece. What do you do with yourself all day, how do other people are Rico, men and women, recording works.

Someone named Belial turned into a man (balloon) we were putting back together like the metal band on the coffee pot I cut my finger on and another one (Belial) wanted to book me across the border in Cheltingham for marijuana in Memory but it was really the use of the word piss and Rico tells me after (we hold the workshop upstairs) that this Belial became a cop and has to make arrests in Mexico to avoid the draft like any art dealer down there. He wanted me to pay a thirty-dollar cab fare back and cross. I wonder how Kathleen is.

Never wasting anything on what might not happen. Strenuous (must work), moving (must be written), mistakes (always made), leaving in (people, positions), codes (are all wrong and it's) all fear, (because I am a) woman (strength or in pieces: "You present the possibility of total symbiosis"), no negatives in dreams, the recourse, the spell: "I won't move," a large output, why is it necessary to finish, no time to work with anything, prolonging everything and "in pieces," drifting toward end.

February 7

It's whatever you bring up, it's whatever I bring up and you will. And you will not, very funny, all kinds, we don't work that way, to sit up to sit up straight, to write dialogue, this is not the freedom to write dialogue at all, this is not the freedom, I am just waiting to leave doors open in a strange and loaded neighborhood, we cannot come on Tuesdays, block, we can only come on Saturdays, no block, no block time, 2 p.m. to 6 p.m., or, 5:30 p.m., at 4:45 p.m. I am asking to call you and expecting to meet you in time I will be shaking adventure off, it is too much for me, the preparations the decisions to say no to body, no, not it, to mind, no to mind, is unbearable insight, so I write like Chinese, I write like cold Chinese, I am unfortunate in this way, but soon I will be reading and he says he knows about writing, that is word, so, the use of a space in code might be an office, the nothing, the no-between, the only use of the independent enfant terrible the independent terra firma as her feet on the ground but the ground is shaking again, Deutschland, Über and Ubu Roi, the Père, the incision, so other uses of the word "the," an environment is summed up or usually the expected I, ah, have never been, the, a, I have never been here before to terrify myself, yes it's obvious the work is going on, the mind is in hiding and it is filled with sand, break the bottles when you're through with them, see them in a coffee shop and leave them there to think, someone says inmates and they do not know what they mean, like Christ, like the woman psychiatrist: "Does she live there?" And you're been there, a survival technique is to make this sort of hospital thing or hostile thing so attractive I am spellbound in your house as the heat turns on afraid she would go away because of "Does she live there" and so on. Discuss. Should be comedy. Should abbreviate more. Thanks.

A survival technique is to make this sort of thing so attractive you learned early as the mother of the one did, did not. I cannot be direct now but I remind him, her of that one when I make this sort of this so stern and attractive and hurt. It is as if something formal is missing, some formal element, some expected part of the pattern or design you were using, rushing, to obfuscate (obscure), by pretending to put together, the pieces, as, memories, of your life, which was all before (you). Discuss. Thanks. I am a demonstrator. You are the whore. I don't think I can sit up much more. It's the temperature. "See ya mom." One two three four, oh really and a different way of seeing then. "One doesn't" then and fills up on wine. The translation of this would be more than preserving a tricky state of consciousness. Bernadette.

February 9

Everyone's giving me jewels. Burroughs is interested in collaborative work, it's Saturday.

February 19

Dreams, Burroughs journal: "As many words as I could fit on two sides of the notepaper," Crime and Punishment. Everybody's trying to put it in a system, to put a lot of information together, as one. I am dispersing so I stopped. The matches scare the dog. I am the dog's babysitter. He wouldn't go out if I wasn't here. Dogs have no "memory." "As a sort of ideal..." (way of living). These notes are not strict, these notes are still hiding, there's a denial of fresh air, there's a denial of the source of it I am going to die then there's a denial of death (something else).

What was he writing in his last journal, the temptation is not to do anything, x on simple memory, the temptation is to stay inside and directionless, who is working. Who is working against.

Recluse, communicant, disciple. Who tries to communicate clearly (K.), who keeps up with her typing (Beatrice), who organizes and so cannot work (Fern), these are women. These are women riding horseback bareback (interlock deadlock) and I am walking behind them. Desert.

Egypt. Hiero Hieroglyph. Milk, the injection of milk as sense of humor. The tendency to just wait. Ways of living: he doesn't answer his phone anymore (D.), sleep till three (B.), she lives with a man she calls her brother and thinks about living alone if she had the money but I asked her and she said she probably wouldn't do it (K.), she lives with a man who is her lover, he has a studio and she has no time to work, she calls this man easy to live with, she would travel anywhere (F.), others live alone and are scared or disciplined or do a lot, some of the men are disciplined (B, K, B). Living from moment to moment, you don't plan you plot. Your predictions are all wrong. I can't ask them anything (questions). She thinks he's never coming back (W.). Source books. No more pictures, very few pictures. It's hard for him to speak of me with praise anymore. Nothing is really started here. It takes him a long time to do everything. He wants to live with her again but lives with someone else on and off (R.). She won't talk to him and lives alone. They think I don't want to talk to them. They are a threat. So I go back to grammar school. Every morning I wake up feeling as if I had to give a speech or read a composition aloud. My clothes have been laid out the night before. Sometimes I slip into them under the blankets because it's so cold. It takes about five seconds to get dressed. There is then very little transition between waking and sleeping and since I refuse to eat breakfast I can get out on the street and be walking to school while I am still already dreaming. Then I meet the boys to deliver the milk. My private life is over for a while. I count out the containers for each grade and they deliver the cartons. There is no genius in this, Patti. She lives with a rock n' roll singer who is never around. She says she is suffering and is sick a lot. My mother tells me to stay home from school a lot because she's lonely and depressed. This confuses me and I don't stay home too much because I'm afraid of "incompletion." She guesses this and says, to convince me, "You won't miss anything." I can't stand not knowing what's going on. I was a good entertainer and singer for five years before I went to school. Maybe this is why I'm afraid to give a speech or read my compositions. In school, one to one, nobody gets cheered up and there is no affection as a reward. I am talking about real love-making. I am vulnerable to this, that is, performing for love-making. Except I don't know what I'm doing. In the summers I continue to be a good entertainer and bake cakes but during vacations I direct all this attention at my father. Even at night, during school, he teaches me electronics, radio and t.v. technology, woodworking and painting in his workshop in the cellar. I do the sanding and hand him the tools. I ask him to draw a horse and an Indian, whatever comes to mind, I ask him to draw the figures from my nightmares. He does it. My sister studies astronomy and reads. My mother takes care of the house. My father and I are athletes on vacations. Climbing mountains, we are always ahead of everybody else. I get better than him at horse shoes. But he is the real reactionary. She is a nymph. My uncle asks me to marry him when I grow up. He is thirty years older than me and my mother's brother. He protects her against my dark father. She is fair and sad. There are no boys in the family. My sister goes out with the leader of a street gang, the Ridgewood Saints. The only thing I hate is big parties where I'm forced to dance with the oldest man in the family and people ask me questions. My father plays the fiddle and sometimes plays the piano "by ear."

Now I am going to sleep. There is no way to get this house in order. Like L's stupid questions, it has a certain planned duration. How will Kathy get to the airport, food and fame. I can fit none of this together except sleep. Sleep and planned exercise, as, the language must get precise. There is too much of everyone's ideas. There is no time to be in the kitchen planning for someone, random, coming, and someone would come, planned. A visitor. She was a visitor. I have no sense of my own divisibility invisibility, farming out. Some theory. Its obsolescence. You you and you all know you're right. I know nothing and want nothing.

I must've dreamed of the hieroglyphs. I must've dreamed of Raskolnikov. It's a little better anyhow (warming up in the morning), what work do I do? He says he doesn't want to be famous but I give him to fame. Ultra Violet Gentian Violet, little nicknames. Moving moving moving moving moving, titles are predicting. Memory, studying...or, listen: date real stories, they investigate the private parts. I withhold withdraw rage repression depression, the sound of someone coming in...close the legs. Mounting fame. I said always being given. Other people who have had the flu have stayed inside. Anton Webern did not. Rhys stayed in for four days and let drift. I know I need something to make me forget it. I have an investment in continuing on, either way. It's chronic. Jackson's just going to feed his children and then come down. I have an investment in having it. Ironying: the food we prepared or bought was oatmeal bread, soft and ravenous, and blueberry bread at the store with butter laid out on it and the car goes up and down without (with total) control and someone is taking the car, Cadillac, somewhere in March. I am on heroin like a donkey.

February 21

Offense is predominating against defense. I'd rather watch movies on t.v., never record being sick. The journals reconstitute themselves with structure. I am hurt. Look up humor. The humors of the words body and mind, I was hurt. I have this work to do, now I play not to take it seriously, my syntax becomes formal, my clothes take my own shape, recording: device (I go on working anyway): "Without knowing why, he may perceive that he finds difficulty in discharging his ordinary tasks,...one day he is afflicted, whence he does not know, with a painful attack of feelings of anxiety and from then on it needs a struggle with himself before he can cross a street alone or go in a train; he may even have to give up doing so altogether."

Crime and punishment. What's important? Or a method to precede. I wonder how scared a person can get without sublimating love. (Belial and the bubblegum proposal, Paris with the Lewises, the PSAT scores.)

March 11

Bus Marxism: The dreams came before this and there is no drawing. The plot: I forgot that it cost something so I developed serendipitous tendencies: I found money on the street; people, storeowners began to give me things for free. Notes, shorthand can never be read. Collaboration. As a group. Free. Free. Dream work. The poetry workshops at the church are free and art and science (when you do work, it's necessary to have a place to go with it, and after that, somewhere to go), how the others live, get involved in the kind of activity that keeps us in the center of things but without double existences, or a commitment to writing, even on a bus, can be shared even if they can't be solved, who do you write to or for, etc. Some people are slicker than I am. Naming and anonymous, I'm going to give a speech about this, belief that your work exists, startling naming. Only a place existing also for hesitation, there's no money in it. So, me and the black man open the window on the bus on a cold day and look out, the end, 30th Street. Everybody would like to live the life of everyone else, except maybe when you get home, but it looks good. But what do you mean, etc.

March 16

Dear Belial belittled and Fern, decoration: or Dear Fern first: whichever it is, there's no time difference here (and for you here, neither of you is famous at all so don't worry) in Detroit or Ann Arbor (with an "E" and fruit, if you want) so, justify your margins, all expensive magazines for poets here. No images please, like far fucking out or farm fucking out cause outta sight is out of state so, the eminence of any position here relies most strongly on the dictionary and on washing. Wash yourselves...or, don't wash yourselves depending, relying, coherence, distortion, does anybody know what entropy is? In the room? Tell us. (Pause.)

There are certain elementary things, even more so much more so than sex, which must be known in a political (use the word?) way, by all Us Artists and Writers. I am here to help you find the words that need definition (I am desperate). Look em up. Look me up. Did I say elementary, I mean defined, denoted, denotative, like what time is it? And what is the time difference, if any? You stirring up any dust here? Didn't Gertrude Stein did when she was here. So I write small and fast: we wrote and you write and we write and we change the advantageous position (and if anybody knows what entropy is by now...) position of the world in state. So far, this is not a personal letter, it's another speech. From now on, it is. Expect something, expect everything. You will find it out. Any questions so far?

Don't we have to go to bed? Aren't we obliged to go to bed? Didn't we eat a big dinner? Aren't we still so hungry? Why? And fuck, so fuck.

There was a man in New York who was involved in the New Music who couldn't stand that a woman (and that was me) said, had said the word fuck and I will read you what I said, the end of it, see (a triangle) and it says, I am not saying look me up. Please use the dictionary (Spider is keeping a jealousy journal and if you could get him to read that, you would find it more than interesting, literary no! A clue or a sourcebook for after the murder perhaps).

Early April

I am trying to do something good, I haven't had anything to eat so I'll use this chance to warm myself, I hope, Spider is asleep and I am addressing this to him and to all those who do faulty detective work in lines. So, pages and pages of them, I am secure, it's a strange kin to security when you forget how to write letters, A to Z, and knowledge all of it defeats it all, I am leading to... Who's this for? I must feel (a whistle) it could be for anyone for transference, whatever that is, and yet I don't know if I'll be ready tomorrow, dogs go out in the woods, they do every day, keep on working every day. When I was six, no, in the sixth grade (6B), when I began to wear a sad face (you keep my notebook, what's written, detective), the key in the door, the leaving and coming back, maybe...when I was—No! You said, "Loss, separation, maternal and I am not in this."

When I was ten (years old) and my mother had her first, yes then. My father, while she was...(and "they" didn't "know") took me and T. on his knee, I rotated and protested, and he wanted but I refused. Knee, lap, mother or father? I wasn't old enough to object to his whiskers making my face red then. I wouldn't sit on his knee or lap. Now tell me, if there are two sisters, is it a knee or a lap? When I was three he drew for me (calling Belial, it says, "No message, thank you very much.").

Please be clear: "Loss, separation, obsession, maternal:" so, first I felt myself feeling my breast (I had dreamed of an organ I had to chew for it to grow back, grow back and I had dreamed before, "It was grown," not a nightgown, up and down, just a part of the parent I could not comprehend to be missing, this is just too gruesome, I'll skip along to the phrase, "A breach of trust?"). I would not kiss the old old man, can you comprehend escape at all, this is all too gruesome, his whiskers were all too scratchy, who ever wants to put on paper what can be so easily construed even in pictures by the mind that doesn't really will to share it, that kind of thing. In 6A, a friend of mine named Susan Schmitt wrote in her composition, "I was drinking in the beauties of nature," and then the teacher said, "Metaphor, that's where it's at," or something to that effect and I said, "No, no, no." So, I made sad faces, first I did them at home. To imitate my dreary teacher and my girlfriend's drunken face, she was who was too neat anyway. In seventh grade I was accelerated and Sister Roseanna made it easy for me but she tells me to join the convent, "It's the easy life," but later she tells me she finds out all about sex and just wants to have babies but it's too late but can she stay at my house when she leaves the convent. "Sure," I say. In 8B I get the 6A teacher back and she has a grudge against me and throws me out of the "Boy Saviour Movement" which is like an army where you have to mark your scorecard green for every day you were good and red for the bad days, and then you can get to be a fascist like everybody else. So there's no use going further into the sexual etiology of the child, at this late date, so late in the book, this book is nearly done, and if I have to get gruesome that means the book must end soon, that means the plot is fatter, maybe too fat, more than pleasantly plump, maybe even still gorgeous, but florid and past maturity, with new folds. A description that leads me to understand that finally I can begin to simplify.

April 2

Keep it to yourself it says. Work under the worst conditions now, it says, salvage the thought that under the thought contains, fear of movement (his not mine), fear of curtains, a divine one, fear of divine anarchy too, the spare the time to write while, the spare the time to be whimsical or to speculate on breath or breathing or sleep or articulate or Beatrice's words or endless sleep or magic, you know, knew how to make me an endless sleep and articulate the artifice of the transference, found. H. Bogart is on the witness stand, what to do with this? Journals, writing, work, which. Hiding. Jane Austen hid her writing but kept her plot in mind. Where to sleep, couch. Thought, why… April 2. Felt responsible, who do you talk to. Not that, who. The interminable suffering of my diary, your fault, waiting, got fat. Who am I speaking to? Spider got me fat. Belial says Spider is not exploitative and then, whose ideas (him, her) die so hard as this one. I can hardly see. Grow up Alice, grow up less Fern. A love affair, Fern and Belial. K likes intrigues of any kind, the totally unkind letter. You know I am writing anyway. Covered the dead bird. Am scared. Of sleeping, anyway of creeping into bed. Would could have sent the anonymous pamphlet with all possibilities crossed out. For you and for me. Birds flying up in the sky. Fight high blood pressure. P could appreciate that. Sorry for so what. And so. It doesn't prevent you from reading and writing, who's in town. K is. Dinner. Buys it. S took some pills and went to bed. Privacy, his. I should take one pill and go to bed but I won't. Covered the dead bird. To sleep. I wish to sleep no more. Wednesday Thursday Friday I wrote this before. Someone says get some sleep. Caste. Caste? Chaste, chaste? Coffee, beer, a knish, chicken salad, beer, drink, soup, drink, beer, drink, hide me. I don't wanna have to be rescued especially when there's the possibility of this, I have to close one eye to see, I wanna be there. Steal. I steal. Stores of stories, eat funny stories. Don't wanna give up the last cigarette, the end, like a hanging or electrocution. I dreamed my vitamins were radioactive, had radiation in them, are dangerous. B-complex, insoluble liver fraction—250 mg. Maybe I'll be on the radio again, or, maybe my mother, oh no. Difference? Not now. Fern where are you? I wish we could all grow up and be in pictures. What about men? What men? No more men. He thrills only to the fantasy of a mother again. Line? What's the difference, I already cut myself twice and am bleeding. Shores, where. And now he suspects me again. Quickly and secretly, I must leave this place.

April 6

I have to get drunk again tomorrow because I have to take a plane, the window seat. I open the window and fly out holding onto the top and catching my foot in a part of the plane that's broken. We land in Chicago, it was supposed to be a direct flight. Before I had ordered mashed potatoes and a beer. In Chicago we're herded into a room, flights 3 and 23, waiting. Before I am sitting in a rocking chair, some lights come up and I am on the edge of a high building then, rocking right off. I ask Kathy to pull me back. She hesitates and does. The cloud columns, like Monument Valley, from the plane. Sand clouds. Clouds of the candles in the restaurant, John's.

Waiting, they won't sell me beer or food, because they say "Someone pretty high up in Chicago must've taken a dislike to you." Now Spider is missing and they're calling for the flight. I can feel everything but I can't see or hear. Fairlines, a separate plane, takes the baggage, "Otherwise it would never get there." Windows open for the women, too wide or low. Taxi. There is some distrust of the captain, "Otherwise he wouldn't have landed in Chicago..." (Captain Belial). Looking for Spider and trying to gather up his and my things. Everyone's disapproval. I'll leave his on the table, he'll have to come back. I find out something, someone helps me, I decide to take another flight. We are made comfortable. "No I'm not going to sleep." Before: "Oh you want to show me the beer I can't have." (The police.)

Then George Wallace and the Blitz and now there are two airplane rides: loss of consciousness and Lexington Avenue in the ice (landing, money).

April 8

Belial is not neutral. Like Wuthering Heights:

He walked into the room, stared, and could tell what was being said.

"That would give me great pleasure," he said, "I can tell what was being said."

"It's like a dream," she said, I'm sorry I had a dream.

The man in grey. A different culture. An English poet. He moved his chair. A squire. An English garden. I had predicted it.

She held her hands over her ears. We visualize this but we have no feelings. It wasn't like us, as readers, to hear that romantic music, someone says, it's deranged.

Something about a brother and sister. The music's all wrong.

"You do it."

"No you do it." (They are no longer having tea, they are having sex.)

She said something about being back there today. Someone is calling now. Someone is calling for privacy. Someone is out for a drive. All dialogue.

"Let's go for a walk."

The noise of carriage. The noise of stream. The two of them left her behind.

"Let's go away." He told her he had to work.

An English pub. He was the eldest of his family. (Lord Peter Whimsey was another story.) All readers know how Wuthering Heights ends.

All crows are black but... There are intermissions. Where had he been? The tea was cold. Someone was complaining.

Two women argue.

"He's kind at least," she said.

She couldn't remember what she had said. They were listening at the door.

And in the English garden the maids were watching.

"Leave Isabella alone."

All words about suffering.

"Take Isabella, hurt Edgar, destroy me."

He was thrown out.

And the country is really no different from when he left it, he said. He goes mad, gets shot at, kisses Isabella and rides off on a horse.

Hours go by—their dreams.

Sex was the main strategy at Wuthering Heights.

She said there was no note.

Something about music and death.

She said her parents left no money.

"I'll be in the orchard," he said.

A shared weakness, incest, several many stories between two, in one.

How do you set the scene? How do you feel most comfortable. The book opens flat. The sentences in columns. The library.

Maybe she will, it says, narrative writing.

So at this point the thing left to do is to terrify you. Finally. With noise.

I once saw him do this, that is, he would sit in front of an object and scream. He would cry out. He would trance himself beyond death. He would sing. He would restore. He would try to time himself and he would stifle any reaction. And in the hills, there is a driver and a crowd. And a burial.

As if to resist becoming another person, as if to leave out the digging up of the grave, beyond death, the dialogue, the necrophilia. He said he wanted more but she became a wraith. He saw her and could never get free.

He was shot, recorded word for word. And so pressed together as if the bottom halves of their bodies could be graven in one, as if incest lives this way when a man floats in the water and walks to his own grave, as his own fantasy.

Emily Brontë wrote in the night.

April 9

To meet someone, to be finished with someone, it's difficult to make sense, it's difficult to make contact, tea, tea, tea, tea, tea, tea. I envy, anyone, who can. To ask someone what to do, to have plans. A hired female companion, the world owes you a living. Are you a Communist, not lately, times and times are changed, crossing the street. Home work. They must know and they are all talking to me, how did they get here, by walking. Somewhat hostile. The best beer in the world. I'm not as sweet as I used to be.

Pick up an egg sandwich while waiting for the bus. Sit down and tell me a dirty story, such as the gal who didn't know she was raped till the check bounced, don't tell me that one. Lost track, everyone. Money, what's a retainer. Who's happy today, a cold day in April, the Yankees? The basketball, thinks the Knicks are gonna take it this year. Dan Dailey and Elizabeth Taylor, how long can you live without food. We both have the same problems. To forget them and clean the house. A tall thin column. Guys from the underground of the Salvation Army, dangerous men. In stress, in desperation, walking. Times fly as you… A girl moves around. Pitching and age. The pill that makes time cease to fly. Ground diamonds and emeralds in a small red ball, magic. You take it when you're… You don't take it till then. Will someone bring me that pill from India. But if I had a wife would she come in, cured. And safe. In the Western world drinking the best beer in it…etc. Does it look like calculus. Six inches in New England. Home plate and center field I watch.

April 10

Speed-cheese. Using the body, time. 39 Knicks 36 Bullets. Death. Seeing your mother on the fire escape make the fake, pull within one. Down on his arm, Chenier from the side always. A whistle, a travel, that nullifies the hoop. Left-handed, some move, look at the clock, 44 – 44. One-half, your mother on the fire escape is teaching you how to be independent, how? By not falling off. Play by play sex, a piece of journalism, a long work.

April 11

Selling off my mother's stolen jewels. The extra room that used to be a "powder room." Do you want to see the theater? I'll board up the door so I can use the room. Especially the red and green and white special necklace.

We fall in the ice under the el at 110th Street, we women don't care. If you're going to school somewhere, I've got to advise you to live there. Harold and Beatrice need hearing aids, I give them them as gifts. "If it makes you happy you can be sure you don't understand it or the other way around." "This Columbia graduation part is in Danish so bear with me."

He said he'd pay the fine—for the jail too? Just for a day. Then there's Ziegler's band of depression—the press secretary? Because we're poor?

April 14

You see no colors anymore, it would be easy to get colors, it would be easy to find the time to drive around Rivieras sinking ships on honeymoons all over the place, making copies of the writing, being an ace and driving a truck or a cab, even it would be easy to continue but. And it would be easy to make life harder and it would be easy to cut off all communications, in order as they come: that takes care of everything. It would be easy to turn up the sound and stop taking things from people, it would be easy to be independent, I think I remember it's not so easy to get drunk or leave a letter inviting your friends to cannibalize you. I don't wanna feel it I don't wanna feel it at least there was (movies) a façade.

3:30 a.m. can't read anything, have to make copies of everything: "Andrew never had sexual intercourse. Maybe Andrew died of sexual intercourse on April 14, 1964. It was Easter Sunday, bunny and Marie's birthday, coinciding. Andrew's thing for Marie was like mine for Fern but why do I remember and what? The answer to memory is always a child. You see one. Eating cakes, dark chocolate bunnies around dark chocolate furniture. It's the season, jelly beans. Don't eat the red ones, devils. Fast as you can, find the colored eggs, find the body too. Andrew never finished, he never caught up on—you can find a table anywhere—his Ave Marias, stacked in chronology in his room. Marie slept, she was already dead and I was his responsibility or was he mine, incest. A paragraph about Andrew.

"The Andrews sisters. A kiss and a hug. Start a fire. Gertrude Stein. Ludwig Wittgenstein. Energy to burn.

"I was still learning what a proposal was. Andrew said, as I was picking out his socks to match his ties, for the wide work week: 'When you grow up will your marry me?'

"Andrew stood at the foot of my bed with his laundry in arm and said, 'Darling it's 11 o'clock, aren't you ever getting up?' What could he do with me. I was ironing when he told me he hated my boyfriend. I put down the iron and said I was in love. Smoking in his face, he slapped me and I slapped him back, then went to see the priest, his friend, said 'Andrew doesn't care about me.' The priest who had Parkinson's disease, tried to make it with me. We are all one unit, the Mystical Body.

"Free love, Andrew, high school, trouble, married off—convent, Maried off—we all were. A beautiful lady, with jewels. Life seems to go on for children who are not in love.

"I always thought I was responsible for Andrew's death by going to Ithaca in April. I always thought he died masturbating, what a grudge to hold. I think I'm right. 'He was as cold as ice,' she said, Aunt Barbara, Bob. And Bob said, 'Deaths always come in threes,' Rico's father had just died. Bob, this is Old Bob, refused to take a plane from Ithaca because of this superstition so, noise, we took a bus, to save money, with a stopover in Albany. I missed Andrew's funeral cause I collapsed at his wake. Injection of tranquilizer, taken to the hospital, the whole history of my disease, in the middle of the night, told to a doctor who didn't believe, I was drugged for the first time. I was diagnosed lupus disseminatus, Flannery O'Connor's peacock disease. They thought I had new freckles, I couldn't prove otherwise. Rediagnosed and sent out the first thing I saw quaking was a man thrown 100 feet in the air, hit by a car and instantly dead.

"Glamour girl. I would sit and draw with my legs uncovered. I bled, I had forgotten. I paced the halls, I got a sleeping pill. A woman preached to me about god and I believed her, barbiturates, seconals. The woman next to me died. A woman having a hysterectomy got, instead, a huge Easter bunny. I had forgotten.

"Grandfather, who had lost his last child, freaked, no one would admit me to the hospital, no one was old enough. 'I don't want the responsibility if she dies,' said in the house. 'Please sign me in,' I said.

I ruined the electrocardiogram. I had been sick before, diagnosed pleurisy.

"Andrew took me to dinner every Sunday, he smoked incessantly. We had appetizers, soup, main course and dessert. I used to like to watch myself smoke in the mirror. I am now 29 years old and I have never taken a bath. Andrew's father died last July while I was inviting Memory." April 14, 1974.

Now what is a poetic line and what is to be learned from that, light and writing, six months, nine or twelve, never brush your hair. I am conscious of my desire to exploit you, I am conscious of my desire to be happy. Simple poetic line about food.

Me: I ate Italian food.
Fern: That's not good for you.
Me: Yes it is.

Chocolate beer and B-complex. The cannibals from Uruguay. Chocolate, wine, whiskey, cigarettes, melted snow and human flesh. I got thinner. Each of us got a finger of wine. Had never seen snow before. Alone, Alive. "I haven't really changed."

Suspenders, I would like to sleep in my clothes every night, I would like to be Bill M., I would like to know how exactly everyone else lives, how my eyes are and my hair, doctors and many cares, maybe even clinics. Above and not below, I don't wanna feel it. I would like more sun I am sane. I cannot write to you I am not in love at all I am B-complex. I am wasting time there are some things I've learned I am wasting time. What else would I be doing I am not that strong. I wonder if they ever made stock footage of a plane and it crashed. The desire to start a fire.

I write by light
Of t.v. like Emily
Brontë who hid her plot
In the secretary.
Write by
light of
t.v. like
an Emily
Brontë,
somebody

comes so
you hide
the plot
inside a
secretary
put plot
in drawer

April 21

So you can see you can see why the mind might cave a vacation, no not that, why and no, how the mind might become attached to the things it reminds itself of, and then, give them away, or leave them somewhere, what mind, there is no care. Like the watching of the police with binoculars on St. Mark's Place, I have become a master of my care. And mind misses what reminds myself of it. Like long trials, tapes, records, even the sweeping up of all the dust if any, themes are there forget them and just continue on faster, feeling so remorse like some writers feel so Gloucester or Rapallo, new pens and ink, using all the colors. Fern is writing a love poem to no one, survival.

The black man who has no refrigerator, the black woman lying on the ground, the white police keeping records in their heads of all the joints that fall to the floor, stand-up comedians. You don't give love to and then you erase that too and start all over again trying somehow harder. Smoke in the air, as of fire and quiet fire. You have to something and you have to something. Rose fever? Binoculars. Poems, words, etc. You feet overdone and cut off here, are doing it all by yourself. Sweeping thought and all that there, as if waiting, mystery, the crime done, the criminal must do the wrong thing, there is time to make all up, all ways. Running water's better than Bob Dylan or poet's poetry.

I don't want anyone to need to know about any of this. This is a secret, it's the same type, there's no way to concentrate on it, the school of Venice, everything, enters in, and so I am here, relieved. I wish that you would leave me alone, I wish that I could always be traveling, writing on a bus, a bus to Syracuse maybe, send the poets there so, no trouble, so they make a guess. The dreams and the thinking ahead of time, the incredible lies and the willingness to say it all to anyone, and then, not wanting them to know anything about this. It's too easy, so, live in the church, and if you find this, and if you read this, then you'll know something you're not supposed to know but will soon know anyway, which is, I've made my work impossible to continue without isolation. Simple sentence, no one has anything to say. Anyway it's said. And then it's over, simple and over. A matter of style, everyone, anyone, and now she, wants to be left alone. I am too much with her and with everyone, a paradigm for transference, which is transferring. So, these introjections we have become so familiar with are ones that are prearranged, paradigmatically, to provoke, to enforce, rules, to enforce, to force isolation, to induce autonomy, autonomy without isolation, indifference to rules, adherence to structure, people become structure, and so, adherence becomes autonomous people, moving indifferently, maybe in crowds, moving differently, moving onto each other. Autonomy I've been baptized. Community, I've isolated myself within you, it's a church. There's things to say, there's baptism, in a form, there's a space, or there usually is, for the fountain. Where is the all-night store. Moving me, it's necessary to move me. And now, how will I be willing to work and how will I be willing to store it and cease to think at all, with a face, at store, facing me. Three faces, a situation. A situation that forces autonomy and then vulgar, a store. Work here, live here. There are no problems, something about Middle English which is mental anguish and just keeps you going, a song in time, a way or working out a way of working. Live here, work here. Think in the moments there isn't time. Think in the same moments and time the moments the same and when I say I am leaving and when I said I was leaving I was departing, I was going away, I knew what I was knowing and doing, and now, in an amazing regression, which didn't make the first person who saw it laugh, I don't know what I am doing but there's something about the titles of the books that are moving and memory, and maybe, story, that make you stop. You stop but I don't. Now I stop and you go. It's amazing. So, sense of humor. Who knows, I mean, who. There's no schedule, no plan, no place to live. Doors, the theory that someone does what they've been told to do, yes we do, Einstein's theory of keeping many things in mind, not things but thoughts. I thought I was indifferent to autonomy for a purpose. Who is telling me what to do. Some schizophrenic writing tells you what to do, you do it. You are tired of you in thought wear that suit coat. Word hard, sleep well, go out the door and talk. Talking and walking are meaning the same thought. Synchronize the introduction to dreaming and do your share. At least or at the least I am listening, still listening. Be here early tomorrow. In public in private. I go to live with Edwin, I am walking out the door, walking. Private protects me, as, another story. Finally I am vulnerable to rape, you look to the side.

April 22

And I am so remote, I had a dream, and another dream, I had a dream, first meeting _____ in Ridgewood after a long time gone by, things not…

April 25

"If all the grass and sun were in between (the energy show), correcting papers, then I could walk for a long time between them."

Giving away and looking again. Speeding down Park, speeding down colors, dying to speed on lines on time, the dreams, transcribed: a father's falling (the very beautiful dream was a trip of some kind), a father's falling (taxi the nightmare home). Be quiet! Robert Redford is meeting you in the past, you travel all over, it's a collaboration, you lose things, you lose everything. An Antarctic trip on Lake Erie, the Canadian Peninsula.

Like color xeroxing, do tricks. Speeding to sun as sun speeds in, relativistic, do you think I should become alcoholic? You were, were you, shooting up then. Late. In a banged up cab on Park Avenue, I never have hope. There are so many strange places where people work in New York City, we have to associate ourselves now to the Associated Sample Card Co. And now I have to do it: valium, tincture of benzoin, lozenges, pirogen, butter, liverwurst, notebook, coke, beer, smokes, mail letter, rolls and paper (the news).

Keeping up with the sun, up on high floors, sun in cloud now, who cares, sun surely in cloud, you gonna take a nap now, sun surely in cloud, it could be crowd and no more warm, no!

If I had acted simple, if I had acted high (following sun), if I had acted simple now, sun high-low in sky, split the pot. Dashed off and put it in the right place again.

April 26

There would still be some times when you would have to eat alone
Of course they need towels in the St. Mark's baths
Of course the guy down the street needs to be turned on
Of course the pimp car will stop then cruise when the cops come by
Of course the blue car is all excited, it's full of presents
Of course all the doors and the trunk are open
Of course I will write a best seller
Of course they're cleaning the streets in the middle of the day
Of course Susan and I are sitting in the sun 150 miles away
Of course now the streets are wet and the sun is in for a minute
Of course taxis of course baths
Of course looking of course leaning out and looking
Of course move the car after it's been emptied
Of course the word grizzly like
Of course colors the sun's out again like a day of the week
Of course sleeping on wet sidewalks
Of course notes and letters and no finish
Of course endless remembering and suicide
Of course more beer the ship is full of seas of course
Of course war of course babies of course war babies
Of course I've never seen more police in my life
I am talking about my dreams of course, I found ten dollars
I wrote a song like Kris Kristoferson of course:

> Rather be back out there than way down here where the money and the business is, that's what he said, that's what I say

Of course remorse, a real audience is a person who watches you by time April 26 1974 is time for colors and lines.

April 27

Saturday, Beatrice is watching and we say, "Oh what a strange life we leave when first we practice to perceive." So, Clorinda is having an orgasm on the floor and everything (sex) is amplified (in WBAI studio) by the presence of young lean (Michael) boy, read. Pointing, ignore, the words, something something, build a cemetery, schmeggeggee. You don't ask what that means, love (sex) amplified in studio, on-going me, on-going Beatrice. Clorinda pulls her dress down, to cover, to wake up. Spring yes who. Where is Joan LaBarbara, Arthur and Regina. Shave, new. Not-music, together, influenced. Peddling? The address written down of a person with an Arab name.

May 6

I am was that schizophrenic. All that is true. Go out and look at the moon again, perfectly clear. Moon that was moving clouds front of it. A 6 – 8 line poem for the bus. To return to archaic bodily states and archaic notions of these states is to make a mess. A continent might have a peninsula on it. Try and write yourself out of it. Everybody goes direct. Nowhere to go. Glass jars decorate. No cemetery. Black holes, cannibals, rhythmic vibrations, no sex drive-in. Go out perfectly. Beatrice writes all external—keep in touch. Johnny Guitar. Date—May 6 or 7 or 8. Birthday, Mother's Day. Time to hide the bad feelings. Notion eyes the cannibal again. Anorexia. Nut house. Nut so funny. State of mind. It's because I can't say it, I refuse to write it down. I reverse, condense, symbolize and converse. Not talking. Not school. The workshop is on the ground. What is working? Detached. What do they hide, a full moon. Some writers. Hear voices. Some see visions. Number two. Clear. A life like you like it. Eight full moons circle the earth—murder, children taken away, physics, focus. Sleep. The circus, the epistemology, the booklist, the reading the papers, a slip. Into hedges, rows of hedges, cut ones. A bleak dream, going on. No craft. Craft is internal. Altered states. Always on top. Nothing nice to say. Rude, thoughtless. Ruthless. The Price of Ruth. Walking walking. Animal ideas, like, mouth, a girl again. In pinafore being raped by William Burroughs into her cunt. Just today. In class. No smoking. Fresh cigarettes. Rhyming. First Hot then Cold. Both of us. A lecture. A feat. People can't get in touch. People stopped coming over. Once it is clear. Out and out. Shadow of her across the light behind me.

Her pages are turning so you say unnecessary things. Sabotage, saboteur, like the diaper. A life circle on the earth, the semblance of a clear decision. I shouldn't spend so much time with her, like ice. No jokes. I can't make jokes. Incontinent, unfaithful. In store. Repercussions, repertoire, hangover. See black. Your fantasies while masturbating—something about her mother jerking off. A hum. A hum inside the belly. Then some madness humming. Rape hums in the chest, where it stays, resides, you see, you do not see. Before valium. Wears off. Many pills hum there. Hum in there. Ripped and torn. Like the mother's belly, I never thought of it. Still wet. Do his too. No me first. Not careful at all. Three hours. Strategies. Stopping and Investigating. You can make it sound so good. Con-man. Must be me.

May 7

Matching
Some men and women are so attaching
And big as if acting
The schizophrenic batching
Making a big mess of things
Catching looks as if he were catching
Colds which he could never catch
Good, better, best in a cold scheme latching
Onto any semblance of a scheme
Itself a firm detaching
From any good to better to least best
Not a scheme but scratching
Desperate, any way we can
Around for love then snatching
Something out from you for me and
Then it away from you, so, patching
Is not reweaving or thatching
Nevertheless there is an end.

May 8

Dogs want to go out, I don't at all. I want everything to come to me like a headache or expensive fish. And letters, many letters and books in the mail. There's a package for me at the post and I intend to pick it up, as, what's on t.v., what's interesting, black holes, the presidential tapes, no gossip and the talk of the town, the mother and the whore, my 29th birthday, your age, my age, like ads on t.v. and poetry in public places, first hot then cold, then explosion of a public childhood perhaps, all memories with illustrations. A stance a perfect stance, one leg poised and at the side, arms akimbo and legs or body graced. How to read. You are intact. You are private. You are selfish. You are writing a love poem again, everyone is. And the water is flowing, green water, etc. She, the dog, will get it, she'll attack him or it, attack it, a vision of a show, the forgetting of proper names (Boston Globe, Big Sky, Anorexia, Sherlock Holmes, a dream for each), a show of women masturbating or, being forced to, or, forcing you to do it for them, another explosion of ancient public memories, intense enough, suffer. An old hat. The water too is masturbating. The mother in this weather may be reversible, and yet another explosion of wet public (memories), "I'm on top of that." The air is cold. The air is cold for May, I like the bottle, it has no moral at all, suck, sucking public memories, an impressing or impression is below the waist of all the public memories, an impressing or impression is below the waist of all the public (even memory) all ways. You started it, peace. Trip or tripping, an avalanche of it. My mother said and then my father said, etc. And buried are not corpses nor should they be poetry. A note: don't speak, don't even write, don't dare to move, some more design, love, the air is cold for May.

The air is cold for May even the breeze is cold, Memory. Pictures mentioned, even the trees are breeze is cold, you can't sit in it, I mean, the sun is cold, is another person and the absence of one at a time, air, sun, breeze, person, the month of May, chronicled. Don't overdo it, Spider! Spider Ray, the spider crab, the monkey, spider fish, spider's web, spiderwort, the spidery infestation, you do ski like a spider, big spider. Air, sun, breeze, person, absence, the month of May, settles, finding its settles, look at a calendar. Dense, isn't it? When you can't find something, say reach or don't say reach, I don't find that good. The same person who told me this said, "The worst thing that can happen is you can have a heart attack." Ha, I have a way of getting persons to be out of order, so, they don't get anything done, meanwhile my head hurts. And these are the people I saw one day: Stevie Wonder, Paul Douglas, Alger Hiss, Alwin Nikolais, Johnny Carson, Steve Allen, Milton Berle, John Cassavetes, Peter Falk, John Wayne, Donna Reed, Stevie Wonder again, John Blondell, Bette Davis, Omar Shariff, Jeff Chandler, Fess Parker, Clint Walker, Rosalind Russell, Paul Douglas again, Julius Erving, D.H. Lawrence, Jane Fonda, Glenn Ford, Dick Van Dyke, Danny Thomas, Mary Tyler Moore, Lucille Ball, Rebecca Brown, Simon Schuchat, Jackson Mac Low, Perry Mason, Carl Betz, Stevie Wonder again, Stefania Sandrelli, Alger Hiss again.

Where's the dictionary? Eidetic epigone. One only (be) to the point—private property. Dialogue, the tapes, Burroughs. There are so many great books already, etc. A man who goes to his psychoanalyst and asks, every day, for the elixir of life which is in the cabinet. The analyst finds it, years go by, and gives it to his wife for safekeeping. Watch, warden wearing a watch. Wearing a Kafka watch.

Just now, I am asexual, I have no sex. My sex is between my legs, as Godard's. My sex is just a duty, written small, myself is denser. Just try and make friends with me, I will throw you, I will even fuck you. I am animal or cannibal-like. People can live like that, without talking. I am throwing you now, you will never recover. I never did, talk about benefits to mankind, ending wars. Don't talk, see your lovers on your lids. Make an appointment, I am hidden and well secret. I will always remain so, I hate you all loves. You never merge with me, take my advice. I won't take yours. Journeys out of the body, secrets stay in place. My eyebrows are finely shaped, my body comes from another planet. Not Indian. My face is like any other face, in shadow. A child's face. I would rather be gaunt. I burn my hair often, with cigarettes. I wake up incontinent, pills, I take pills. And medicines to cure me, and you. I take you, away from yourself. Never get back, who, eyes dark, cares.

I used to have, I used to wish to have lighter hair. If I fell and tripped on a ball, I would first ring the buzzer thinking someone was trying to get in at that moment, then unlock the door, maybe lie in the hallway or try to get to the phone. Then I would be hospitalized with a concussion for a week and not be able to move, meanwhile they're giving me shots so I don't need beer. I am just prone now.

May 10

"The woman (women) always brings out the CSC's in you." Conscious states of consciousness, this relates to the spider.

Acting in a theater badly with no director, closer and closer to the opening, we never memorized our lines, Pierre (director) never shows, but, all of a sudden here is beautiful lighting and a stage set in silver with a many-colored sky, yet no lines.

"Don't write a short story." I think I will.

Dream taking care of grandfather, dressing him up in a suit and tie, etc. Malanga in furs and the steep climb from the el station where black lady stole a $695 money order. That's the end of that.

May 17

I move out. I go to live, temporarily, in a room in the house of the mother of Fern.

●

I did this on May__. The dates must be exact, the dates were not exact on the tombstone or lowland stone. I made a fist. First let me tell you that I could not walk, I could not move around at all, I could not fall asleep alone, I could not make it down the cloudy block. Something was missing, like a man who without knowing why, may perceive that he finds difficulty in discharging his ordinary...one day...and from then on it needs a struggle with himself before he can cross a street... In other words, there are people who cannot leave their houses. Others who cannot move. There are four fears: you know what they are...I left two men in a row and they are ecstatically happy, it gives them reason to believe, reason to believe my heart belongs to Daddy...I am going to proselytize you, I am a Catholic, I am going to prostitute myself. There's so much to tell, what a gigantic penis, Jesus! The priest's penis was enormous but first I was born. And that is all there is of that. I did this on May 11th, the dates are exact. Visited the lowland stone. The next day I got food poisoning and a kid said Hi to me, then I left home, or what was home for a little while. Someone doesn't know what's happening to me. The dream of the train on an el, climb down the stairs, long way to, to get off, there's the money order, $695, there's the black lady on the bus, she picked (not so many more for) it up. I shook (not while gotten or been) her up in a funny (does this or it has done) way, SOME ARE AS ONE. Lone way down on the be-all el, steep steps to ground. I means I means I mean it. And were it yet done yet, you the what say kinds. Those either. I lost my friends, still ones, they were on the other side of town, still one, they might. I do as you say, I repeat. Malanga in furs. How do we end up. Was this as one does. My notes on the cemetery: cemetery, Rico, Teresa, Lowland Stone, food poisoning, reason to believe, Hi!, not overload, it's holding back or hiding, the name of the game, blossoms in the dust, Joseph Conrad, laughing Annie, Giant, world the flesh and the devil, night must fall, where's the t.v.? This or is it bolted. Cemetery. Both then and. This "I" thing. And this "you" thing. This vegetarian food, all offered, all offered up, by ma-maternal mother—does it stay, like among both still. How is a while going. In parts, like some, them, or some-them. The whole family is a while. The whole family should be intact, at least as what as it still's one. What takes time? Bolts, as bolts of families. Bolts for families, bolts within families. Parts open from the insides like my dream of walking down the really treacherous steep steps of stairs, down, down, very down from the bus, or was it a train. As here, you might fall and break your own head. Seeming.

Will I get my mobility back, now that I know they're dead, that I've seen the grave-site. Rico says you must make a fool of yourself. Now that I've orphaned myself twice, between men, in them. Walk again, says the graph. Be strong, says Fern. Take it easy, says peripatetic twin. And the school just says school and the school says I can't watch you, there's nobody here. I laugh at it. Ought will both does and as one it did. They laugh now. You laugh now. Laugh... I'll wait a minute. Always it says of seas attend. As those meanies, like my sister, who is not dead, whose name is not on the tombstone, those meanies are up a stairs attending A Art Lecture. Much whence did. Clark Coolidge is my father. His Polaroid is his child. We do, do not share children. Some too seem as to do so. As Hugh Kenner said, "Hemingwayese and its parent Steinese." All backwards. That's how it all. He said he was out to destroy the I. I said he was out to destory it—it's all been seen, said, stop. Big period.

There are only little whens. But buried the bottle, hidden it. Little no one. Must write to this, and or and so. What is seen? On the lowland stone. Tide's in...dirt's out. On a field, sable, and so on. No, let me give you the whole story: And after many years a new grave was delved, near an old and sunken one, in that burial-ground beside which King's Chapel has since been built. It was near that old and sunken grave, yet with a space between, as if the dust of the two sleepers had no right to mingle. Yet one tombstone served for both. All around, there were monuments carved with armorial bearings and on this simple slab of slate—as the curious investigator may still discern, and perplex himself with the purport—there appeared the semblance of an engraved escutcheon. It bore a device, a herald's wording of which might serve for a motto and brief description of our now concluded legend; so somber is it, and relieved only by one ever-glowing point of light gloomier than the shadow:—"ON A FIELD, SABLE, THE LETTER A, GULES."

At least there's some freedom at last. Shakespeare and I make Clark. Shakespeare and Clark make I. Clark and I make Shakespeare. Shakespeare makes me and Clark.

I'm still afraid of sleeping but everybody sleeps. Is it magic? Will a meaning last all as at, at funeral, and the will. We are plenty near to the grave site, but we cannot find it. A twin may well find it for us. Stealing flowers, others having fewer means and a lesser body. As a result of this visit to the grave site-cemetery, I am chaste of men and women—we all survive. We light a match, even, maybe with disdain. All the names are all the names. Like Rico. Rico lives there, no there, he lives there, yes, that's right where he lives. When he wrote leaving he decided to write living. I eat sparsely, like a bird. I could tell you the story of blossoms in the dust with Greer Garson and Walter Pidgeon, I could tell you the story of laughing Annie with Marie Lockwood and

Joseph Conrad, I could tell you the story of Giant, with Elizabeth Taylor and James Dean and Rock Hudson, I could tell you the story of the world the flesh and the devil with Harry Belafonte and Inger Stevens and Mel Ferrer, I could tell you the story of night must fall with Rosalind Russell and Robert Montgomery.

And so David and I got lost in Middle Village and I said we should go to Neiderstein's but when we got to Metropolitan Avenue we didn't know which way we should turn, and just as we turned, we saw Neiderstein's, where I was supposed to have my wedding reception. Now what happened was I slept with my fiancée's best friend and then I called off the wedding, dress and all and the next day Neiderstein's burned down, wooden fans and all. But the wooden fans were still there and David had two vodka gibsons which means they have pickled onions in them, which he made me eat one each of, and I had two Heineken's in frozen glasses and what did we watch but a wedding and talked about queers that we knew and people in show business. Now David's frozen glasses were different from mine, you have to understand. And the wedding people were also frozen and we were frozen in time, like black holes, and so on. On the ergosphere, if you know what I mean by that, the event horizon of a collapsed star. No we didn't talk about structuralism this time but we are in love. So I left home for the second time. And David predicted in the middle of mid-vil in Neiderstein's that the man across the bar was a politician and that he would kiss the baby. So the man kissed the baby and all life was subsequently renewed, except that I had been staring, but we did not kiss, oh yes we did, but that is another story. And I felt then that I wanted no one, no planning for the world. Are you all women? All the names are all the names. They match, at least once, at least one time. Such will as that. We pass right by it unattended. Josephine, Andrew, Andrew (missing), Theodore M./Marie M. (childs). Those are childs, childs room for us, with crayons in it. He wouldn't give me any of his money so I left—strong, a sane one, a survivor. Section 5, No. B-40. You are addressing you to me. I am addressing you to you. Too seldom a point of opening. Private Space! Opening Private, Opening Space. I can't deal with the lost or last section. Not aside either. The joke: you know people are dying to get in there; the joke: Rico lives there, no there, no here, at least wherever he lives he survives. What am I up to, I am very adaptable, what am I up to? It's actually Vito not Rico. Vital, vital force, vitalism, vitalistic, vitality, vitalization, vitalize, vitallium, vital principle, vital statistics, vitamin (a whole section on vitamins), vitaminic, vitascope, I rip up anything to prove a point and Vito stamped his name in the dictionary. He lives he survives. In the childs room, in the nursery. This is my new mother, say, 10 volts of her, matter least of and her standing will.

Whaddayou want? To let most be least past, but let most be most past, at least, standing still and seeing you. I'm starved. It could be, and that's past or that's this. A twister—you're lost. I lost one, or two or three or four more, lost four in a row, lost some in the rosebush, no film of this. Nothing and nothing a film. Sneakers. You can't hear me. Few have I parted with and still. Few have a single place like the place I lost. I am the scapist, the stalker, the shafter, I wear a scapular. I am the queer and the whore, at least sitting behind glass windows playing with stage prop glass balls. But she, she is different, she keeps the same phone number so as to always be accessible—like the you get wills, to those beyond, beyond? Somehow, the grave. Some matter. Changing and moving, likes weakness, I don't. So I do. So I do all the work, moving and changing like a twin of weakness lost.

● BOOK VI

May 21

No openings, poetry is all sex, her book, her going away, her mother, a mother's mother keeping track of where she goes, women and children first, people sleeping.

Live people, maybe you run and grow up and marry mamma some day, wait for me, I'll wait for you says Andrew, stay home, go out, don't stay with Stanislaus, someone dream. Lost all, all gone, smell of moth balls, write Clark. Gibberish, cat crawls, notes, as handwritten, continuous writing, there's some movement, here and there. There's someone living, so, I'm alive, choice, he says. I'm quiet. Someone, with his wife and family, bespeak Belial. Far away, studying hunger, studying revealing, just about to read my handwriting, who cares I mean why. Two soups, if I'm not upset he will be, I guess that makes sense, chaste, ignore Steve, chaste four months, kept the keys, keys down, list, walking, a person walking, this is the second one, up the stairs, live together, George Segal, goes to the bathroom, separate and then alone, separate or alone, right away, what do they eat, Stanislaus is gone, Thursday or Friday, my protection, my invention, organized Fern, who's at home, noise. What fantasies can I have, eating, dogs eating, Hi F_____, he'll never know, depth perception, anti-christian, Shakespeare's shrine, the end of that, little ego, strange solitude, what next, nowhere to go to plan, and who comes with me and who adores and which friends do I lose, S says of M and B: "They have something going," I say, "I don't know what you mean perhaps they're in love;" is the mother at home, home yet, some independence, used up a pen, is Florence at home, good handwriting, move movement, what do you do, every day, ordinary man, did you want me to be your wife, my sister's living alone, her man eating or hating, I wish wash now, there is talking, I will go alone and wash now and eat crackers, you will never know, normal food, normal thought, trained dogs, intense persons, serious persons and everything going on around seems odd or unfeeling and you grow for a moment to hate the world a little so I suppose I will have to teach someone how to make love, two soups and some crackers. The boy functions, the body functions, visions of Kerouac, short terms. As long as suffering is only warming up what can happen, reread Leaves of Grass, sleep on the mountain, douse the mountain with leaves, bring pills in case you can't sleep on the mountain, no advice taken or given, live with people, don't black out, don't see the doctor especially the fallen angel, don't not move, see someone, the top floor is Holland the bottom Japan or Greece today, I never want to go there, image of Teresa's face, the doorman, the back door man, a house full of women converts alcohol to formaldehyde, as if you were poisoned, I don't have to ever make love again, now isn't that choice, a choice. Delight your family with consommé printanier, vol-au-vents with strawberries and chocolate bavarois, finger biscuits.

May 22

You know how to give pleasure, someone said, and he turned out to be somewhat queer: raspberry tarts, you make me feel brand name, muenster with cranberries, I sing this song askew, is it Spider or the cemetery, how's he doing, I'm crying, sweet and sour chicken, sweet Beatrice, sweet Fern, sweet women, sweet rain, all the way down, mamma is another one, I keep to the lines, on the line, like you do, I keep my watch going on time, look out the window and it rains, so do you, like a piece as of a piece, divided into lines, I want to hear some black music or buy a newspaper and know the stations as by heart I know my soft ball, all lines, all distractions, start a movement, out of this, WXLO, like I used to: Florence raised children, I keep private, Max offers me a child, a gift? Fern says let me know and I'll have one too and can you get along without me and I say of course not. Beatrice sees words and all the men seem to seek me out but why, smart in her ordinary denim clothing, no, sure enough, "hard to live with," who said that, but of course, everyone's concerned, I'm involved, and, I've evoked the concern consonant with a state of mourning, on time, where's my Freud, and melancholia, so sane, so walk. I would tell more story, I wish I would but pen spreads ink too far, beyond the thin gray lines: be neat with your rings. Fern leaves but of course she'll be back, switch to FM, get a paper, I would live with her since she's leaving, behave yourself and when she's not here, behaving continuous, I'll see men, should I call her now, I am inaccessible in three ways, I leave, the tombstone is an eating flower. We will be there for the rest of our lives and I will be here on this bed for the this of that and I will grow continuously like Florence and be somewhat bitter but concentrated and inaccessible as sweets, so there you are, breeze-rain comes, 98°. If anybody enters this room—I can't stand it, leave me alone, I didn't go to California! And who is that man carrying a briefcase down Macdougal St. at 3 a.m. and who is that man offering me a baby, I shouldn't have left in the first place maybe, I'd like to go dancing and eat my words all of them at least the ones on this page, and sunburnt and I look at this page and like to be free of whatever comes before, above, here, sit still and come and get your love and all this writing I give you is just a shot that's interrupted, Maldoror.

Hera, or someone, make it well or easy
And show before I dream your face
The face which heroes wore
All sons and daughters of them
The signs saved men from flood
The signs brought women home—
What blood?
And men and women did get born
So now I think something could be done
And the ones I taught will do it
And the ones I lost will do it
Dances, songs, maybe. Just
Live on this earth
With me.

May 23

Taxi: I notice all the funeral homes, why are they called homes, I am so dull, the defense of not being aloud to write certain things, things down, saving it for the cemetery. Got out of the cab and walked one block to the cheese store, first, couldn't decide at all, got the cheese and felt faint at the door to the cookie store, turned back and so missed the newspaper store, want sleep. Beatrice says cheese keeps her awake.

Dream 4 p.m.: "Bernadette! What on earth are you doing your 34th what to?" says the devil and the devil is sitting in my chair, with clothes, with beer on it, Spider is on the bed, he has no nose or mouth, sneaking, body rumbles through and as I try to get up, the head, the back of the head is so heavy it's killing me, it's dragging me back down, the phone rings. 34 whats? Hats?

Spider says something about the tuna fish being all prepared and his dog Whimsey is a 2-headed Cerberus, a male-female, Old Spider, old Satan, self-abuse devil, what hats?

Miriam the feminist poet arrives and I know what it's like to have a younger sibling already, but, I know what it's like to be in charge too, now, cause, my rooms are messier and even though I'm jealous I still feel special on account of my debris. Color code, they are gone. It's 2 a.m. and I don't feel trusted by Florence even though I know I'll sleep well, didn't Fern arrive safely, dear Sappho, like my father before me, I'm a working...even though I know I'll sleep well and through the night, romantic, on the street, I don't want Miriam's room, cleaner, towards the back, I want to be on the street, so, if anyone throws a stone upward, it will hit my window, I'll be here. Just live on this earth with me, I would never let Spider see my room. Strange solitude and a room of one's own only Stanislaus has seen it. The night they drove Old Dixie and so on, all the people were so quiet here, even people who must think I'm confused but I only went to the cemetery, direct, some people are out of shoes, like a cloudburst, I wonder if my mother Marie is a saint, I wonder if her body is intact, I forget, a lot, easier to read or write all night, sleeping women without t.v. But, without fun, me, Miriam, Holland, Holland's girlfriend, Florence, Fern, not a man in the house (there could be a man in the house). Leave violets at my doorstep and when my father died my mother said to me, we're alone now, there's not a man in the house. I take a drink of whiskey, do women really write about collectivism and food, do they? There must not be a man in the house.

To get in touch with someone, to get in touch with someone beyond, beyond the touchstone the tombstone, touch-me-not touch-stones, pods that burst at the touch when ripe, seed pods, and (flowers with spurs) I gave her the gentle flower, my sibling, that I would like to get and she made me a touch-me-not. She is not gentle, I am spurs. Parting from friends: To them I said: "Gentle ladies, now we will remember everything we did, to touch each other, and: for many things pretty we did, lovely ladies, in our youth. We are petrified. And: Now that you (Fern) have left the city, love have you, love has taken me over and all that that means. Touchstones, a type of black stone formerly used to test the purity of gold or silver by the streak left on it when it was rubbed with the metal, or, any test, any test of genuineness or value, "There are some things I have to do with Candy." I am touchy, I thought touchstones meant setting-off points, points of departure. (So why am I only writing for you?) But they do not. I want flowers, cause dead? They do not.

But I still can't do anything but who cares. After touchy comes tough, tough—to bite, strong but pliant, come pliant, antabuse, self abuse, as they say, you read me the tongs, the tonsils, my father's cauterized tonsils, now you know everything, as you did before, so simple, so clear, so tough, tough, that will bend, twist without tearing or breaking, precious love and that will not cut or chew easily like tough steak, where's the steak? Now I know, fish, and strongly cohesive or glutinous, viscous, sticky, as, tough putty, or, go on with it till you get to it. What is glue? Or strong or robust or hardy or stubborn, hard to convince or influence or aggressive rude and brutal, tough, rough, very difficult, fuck it! Or violent or vigorous as a tough fight or person, a thug a ruffian a ragamuffin, see strong. Read the dictionary all you want you will never find out what touch means, except that it's a light blow, and, to put the hand, finger, or other part of the body on, so as to feel. "We feel so close." A bed to sleep in, the songs of Sappho, a chance to listen to the rain. All five days of them (rains). Grandfather forgot me before he died, even though I dreamed about him, even though I wrote about him, even though I dream about him, even though I write about him, where's his name and where is she.

I said it rained five days, it could never stop, Theodore Marie Josephine Andrew Andrew and it's proved and it's proven and this is the test of the touchstone, will it streak when rubbed by the metal and will its stone be carved, is that the word? Someone sends me threads, he took her with him but later deserted her, these notebooks are easily that labyrinth.

Pick Up Sticks: one Emperor, 5 Princes, 5 Chieftains, 15 Captains and 15 Warriors, the Emperor is Black, the Prince is Blue, the Chieftain is Green, the Captain is Red, the Warrior is Yellow. Grasp the sticks in the right hand; place your hand on the table so the sticks point upward, now, open your hand and pull it away with rapidity. The sticks will fall radially...none of the others moves...no other stick moves... When another stick moves you are finished...no matter how or why a stick moves, if it moves... See?

May 24

Dream I open a restaurant.

May 26

The hands are missing from my watch, I get mad, but, Fern gives me an envelope of presents and jewels. On the top of a high place, playing with the cross-hatching on my belly, on a table, maybe falling off, but don't. On a field, sable...mourning clothes. Everything was cross-hatched, the roof and the table... And in the church, which was a storefront church (one of the possibilities in the staff report), there is a meeting (mass) at which we are all fired at by a man (police) on a horse (motorcycle) with someone riding behind him. We all fall to the ground (in pebbles, a spray of BB's), who's hurt, "who's dead," well no one is, I look to feel if I feel any pain, wound, none, but, gradually I see I've been shot, hit, grazed, in the upper arm, gore starts to come out of it, when, as soon as, I can make it worse (it's the part of my arm I'm sleeping on), I want sympathy. And, David says, "This is a very inappropriate crowd" for the church. And there are smashed-up police cars with "freaks" which are bodies, or smashed-up bodies on them and no drivers, so we are in hell again. And Charon takes us over Styx to Hades. Quadriplegics on the tops and fronts of cars like the men "mooning" in Philadelphia after the Flyers won, American flags, it's a siege and we look for somebody to go get help—first butter and tea for the burns, I am waking, then someone else, second for antiseptic, anaesthetic spray for the wounds, cannibals.

May 27

I go to dance class, I've been there before except it's remodeled like the school. Yoga class. I pay no attention. A man in the common bathroom asks me to marry him but there's a guard, looking over to prevent fucking. I don't mind. Then I go to school with Grace. It's remodeled like the dance class, more cross-hatching. There's a basketball game except the winning team, the out-of-town team uses a set of keys instead of a ball. Keys through the hoop. Tickle the laces. And all the members of the team are actors with actors' false names and make-up and an act, Holland, Brook. And in the middle of the game, it's obvious they'll win, they chant "Drop Nixon" or "Ban the Bomb." Colorful, it fades.

We drive up to a wharf at night. I go on a boat trip down wide Schuylkill River, river like ocean, Amazon. We are at Ava Gardner's house on the ocean-river. Teddy Bears float down it in designs, sometimes spelling out words, big fat Teddy Bears. Like half-time. Turtlenecks. Some people try to fish them out of the water but when they do, they sink. Something happens and Ava Gardner's whole family gets in an accident. Her husband is instantly killed but the rest of them survive. Ava Gardner lies stretched out on an airplane wing all dressed up—"decked out" or dressed to kill. She's decided to leave town. Photographers snap her picture. They say, "Somebody with your looks aint gonna be single for long." (The Thin Man.) She's leaving with us (me and S are one person). There are two airlines to take, she chooses delta. Behind the ticket counter is the rest of her family covered with sheets. One of them pulls down his sheet to show us how maimed he is and then waves the gun he is planning to kill himself with. He says, "Doesn't this look like a morgue?" I guess we leave.

Noise, at least there's noise in the house, and conversation. I seem strong, I seem stubborn, I even seem arrogant as if I knew everything well I do. And everybody wants to see me happy and everybody wants to see me but then I get all this advice: don't be so serious, stop seeing Belial, don't worry, it's o.k., it's body functions, get on a schedule, eat your breakfast, you are so crazy, take your vitamins, don't drink so much beer, wander around more, get reinforced, rein forced? Listen to music, eat rice krispies, be in transit, take a holiday, maybe it will rain, eat more, stay calm, just survive.

May 28

And someone says, "You're a lot better than Ava Gardner, by the way a well-known bisexual. She didn't have a brain in her head." And one day Frank Sinatra came home and found her in bed with Lana Turner. I didn't know that.

May 30

"All circuits busy now." "Now look will you stop with this Spider shit." No more honey, no more Belial, no more moon, only half a moon, and a feast. What have I got myself into: there's Spider who calls up and threatens suicide and takes 20 mg valium and 50 librium and can't be alone and he says it's not my fault, nothing to do with me, and there's Stanislaus who said he understood everything and who I finally taught how to kiss, at least, with his eyes open but now he wants to take up all of my time and he's the only one I'm really interested in except Belial whose mother is dying in California, maybe, so he's there and why did he almost sleep with me in the first place, and changing Stanislaus' points of view, now he's impatient with his girlfriend and instead of telling her he's at the movies with me he says he's having dinner with William Burroughs and there's Max who's repainting the loft maybe so I can move back in, he's building more bookcases and they all want to see me this weekend, see Stanislaus wants to go to the Cloisters or to his house and Max wants to take me for a drive in the country and Spider wants to go out early so we can have many hours to talk, probably to the park and to dinner and I'd like to do it all but it's none of anyone's business and then there's Steve whose rehearsal I deliberately missed out of fear of his startling advances and Grace and Beatrice who I want to see tomorrow along with Max and maybe Fern and Belial will meet up in California but I doubt it unless Fern has to go to the hospital or happens to freak out on the street while Belial is passing by.

Max is right, I should write a story with a plot. And then there's Michael who wants me to drive up to Vermont with Charlie but when he mentioned to Dick that he liked me too Dick said he didn't want me there. And then there's Florence who has the stomach flu and who won't let me have Stanislaus up here anymore because of Jack. So I told Spider that <u>he</u> couldn't come up here at all because of Jack but tonight in the park Stanislaus picked me up and tricked me into picking up his knapsack as well and said he was going to carry me across the 59th Street bridge to his house which I can't live in because I'm allergic to his cat and all his dust and Stanislaus says, let me take you away from all this, he's just a boy, and Spider says, I wish I could make things better for you, they're fine, and Max says, nothing is that serious, or, you sound better, I'm glad you feel better, I'm not sick at all. And Belial will/will not take me to Neiderstein's for dinner when/when not he gets back from California and he will/will not call. And I had to make sure Spider had put out his cigarette before I hung up the phone cause I've seen him fall asleep on pills with a lit one, but filters tend to go out, too bad for him. And I am so serene.

Florence is throwing up and I was glad to be able to do something for her but I don't know if it's her or Jack who objects to Stanislaus' staying here or even coming over. It's tricky cause they don't (I can't say this)...and she walked in the room when Stanislaus was here asleep. I thought she'd like him cause he's Greek and speaks Greek. And Fern says Jack's the goodguy but I don't know. And Spider, old saint of one, says he can't talk to anyone and Michael says Dick was drinking a gallon of wine a day, well that's how much beer me and the Jivaros drink, what have you left me for, David? And actually Florence is on Max's side of the whole affair which is probably why she doesn't like Stanislaus.

And I dreamed the Jeanne Moreau suicide scene from "Going Places," it happened in a "new" room in this house except the person who shot himself was Glenn Ford and he was carried out and then I dreamed I was moving into Merv's apartment in Queens and I called Stanislaus to see how far away from him it was, lots of el stations and a lucky accident will make me whole. And school in the dream of empty rooms and a bad memory, I wonder if I could drink a gallon of wine a day and feel good, or speed, or get rich, and I look strangely now at all figures of authority and they are everywhere here, cinder blocks and cops all over. And this makes me hungry now, only now, when I can't get any food, what is the perfect setup? Running, absent-minded.

And I dreamed a large pachyderm moved into the house, but, a giraffe who was all black like the monster of Loss, I mean, Loch Ness. And he crawled up a tree and pulled the cover up to his neck and I said to Florence how shall we feed him and she suggested cheese and lettuce and so on and I said yes but where should we put the water because giraffes can bend over to drink but not in such a small space. Caviar, maybe. Eating, maybe. And I eventually dreamed that a huge white horse (I could eat a horse) was taking no chances coming in my door. And (remembering device) Jean Seberg was my teacher and the whole class went to Washington D.C. A.C. to take the final exam by jet (rink, Giant) and Seberg went up and down the aisles in a beautiful low-cut gown (forget it) and her shoulders were very skinny and square, I stared at them, somehow I was exempt and after the handwritten exam, she collected the papers and said we will have to go back to New York now to type them out and I complained loudly. Why had we come (to Philadelphia) in the first place?

And someone said to me and her, well aren't you both television producers. And I reneged on my part (living alone). And Meg was there and we went someplace to eat and drink, down a stairs, except, in a whole room covered with white tablecloths, they were also showing old movies, or, some famous old movie, the last lines of which I remembered. Maybe Casablanca. Romain Gary. Seberg as nymphomaniac. Philadelphia—Godard. "You're a walking encyclopedia, so why don't you talk?"

And I was sitting out on the windowsill like a whore in the red light district of Amsterdam when Holland passed with her dog, I waved to her, she waved reluctantly up, back. And Spider passed and because of the yellow-orange light behind my head he didn't recognize me, he thought I was a different person, smiling. And I was smiling. He passed, and rang the bell, and that was the end of my visitors to my purple room. And Stanislaus was sitting in Dante's café while I was in the park with Spider and he had a vision, at least he swore he saw us and he described our clothing, passing by. But we had never walked down that street. But five minutes after Spider left, Stanislaus threw a penny at my window, because he had "seen" us on our way "home." And I called Spider to make sure he hadn't seen Stanislaus because he had been threatening suicide again and he hadn't. Meanwhile Belial was waiting to hear about his mother and Florence was telling me that was the end of the visitors to my purple room, I always get a color. I seem to be at least in my shades better off than they all are: Stanislaus is miserable, Spider is obsessional, Max hysteric and Belial just fallen. At least I am all of those problems.

Delicious foods, soups and pastries, street urchins, fish and steamed clams, asparagus, strawberries and chicken, like a starving mammal, fruit and baby food in glass jars. Sardines. Heavy cream, pasta, at your leisure, with butter and cream. Coddled eggs, to make art.

June 2

Dream Max is planning to do all the sports all summer, he has teams set up and so on. When I tell him this dream he says, "Well it's good to keep busy isn't it?" That's what I was afraid of in the dream. Dream he asks to wear my sunglasses for a minute even though it's raining so he can catch sight of, get a thought of...something. No more reason to suffer, no reason to be inflamed. Dear Max, I am terrified of you and you of me now that I got my "freedom," what a unexpected development, I won't stay at your house, too scared of your waking in the morning and going, leaving, out to work. I always leave men who work. And I tell you this fear and say it's like going back to the scene of the crime ("I was enjoying my vacation," do I ever know who I'm talking to?). And you say you didn't know there was a crime, now, how can you say that after seeing "Spellbound?" And the paradigm Parradine Case. You say, write a story. Instead I will make a schedule of seeing friends you don't particularly like and a way of living you'd scarce approve of, indulgent and hedonistic at the least. I made it. How could it be high in the 50's and then high again in the 70's with the humidity 90% and no rain coming, who's coming. Still sort of the same scene, no, no, no, I had fallen asleep reading with the air-conditioner on, due to smoking. A bare supper stolen, pork and potatoes on a small plate, I must catch my breath before I eat it, tomorrow I must get some wine, washed my two shirts, extended the poetic line as far as it will go, throwaway stuff, and talked on the phone from 11 p.m. till 5 a.m. And Florence thought I was giving my heart away. Can't say no more, or, can't write anything, dawn Holland, stays up later now and makes enough noise to invite me, I think, but I am too busy stealing potatoes and installing new typewriter ribbons and talking gibberish with Rico and Stanislaus. I am upright, I am frightened of Max, I am strong in my resolve to know my mother's feelings, but, when I get out on the street, I walked seven blocks today, with one stop. Long blocks, so what is my mother saying to me, she is saying yes, this is throwaway stuff, so you can finally find out what you are doing. Cheese, so much simpler now, so much simpler, stop. Dressed to drink, smell good, write for too many (audience), too sober. My little dinner's gone, eaten, ripped from the sides of a lean pork loin, or torn, with a knife, cut out and eaten. Little dinner, little neck, my little neck, where it leads me to reading and reading from you and you and so on, I'm sick of you but I like it here, even though there are lines. Welfare, food stamps, disability, Philadelphia, your darling sense of humor, darling, how I wish for a cold beer, and, "As I was coming up the stairs with my little dinner, in the dark, suddenly, at the foot of Jack's door, I dropped the potato from the plate." What a plot. Jack and I both love potatoes. Florence says, I wouldn't have a potato in the house if it weren't for him. Jack says, you (me) and I are so alike, we could both just eat potatoes and nothing else. So I tell him about the man I knew in the country who lived on two potatoes a day, one in the morning and one at night, with a little wheat germ oil, and he tells me about the Thais he knows at school. One he asked, how are you? Fine. What did you have for breakfast? Rice. What did you have for lunch? Rice. And what did you have for dinner? Yes, rice. It is not a question of language. It's rice and potatoes. My room is becoming messier, perhaps I'm about to leave this earth and become the Messiah, that is, without hours. Surely, I will try it after what I've been through with capital letters, that is, names for three years, years? Sherry after beer or before coffee. Mrs. Parradine only sipped her sherry while playing the Appassionata before the police came to arrest her. And someone fingered a razor. Yes sherry. If you think you're going to die, write legibly, as, I smell so good today, I just realized I'm in the red, goodnight.

June 3

It becomes a question of inside and outside of houses, the bath with the door open, washing the clothes, the clothes line. If you have a problem, it's your house, that's all wrong. One, two, three, four, out the door, I mean, close the door, and, have everybody visit you in a lamp bottle, in a bottle that is a lamp-base-shade, pinkish-yellow, there's a lot of pink in this room and I am not afraid as elleville-yellow reflecting off of purple seems to make pink, I'm jealous so you do all the work. He did want wife, and, in a way, he did want wife, so in a way I can't blame him for taking an elleville instead, and, in a way, he will want wife, all different he's all misspellings, hate, I hate you, I make a face, etc. And Spider says you're too busy to drink too much, is that logic to be listened to, a full moon, Stanislaus has nothing to do, nothing shocks you, sleep in clothes all the time.

June 5

Don't feel nothing but hunger, "What you were afraid of happened." Should I explain all this, Charlotte read in her Boston Black Chicago beautiful accent, "You're too nice." Spider left in a panic-rage. What is a panic-rage in front of or with all those people, in front of or with all those people I always feel I'm in the right or else I always feel O.K., I do not want them to feel starry-eyed or sorry for me, ever them. So where's poetry. "I was freaked," whatever that means. Alarm bell has been going off for one hour, what's not real? Where's poetry? I need some money. Dream a parody of all the stairways in houses I know.

Dream I'm going along and back again, what'll happen then, where I'll go. The beer's still cold, it's two hours old. There's a party, there's planning for a party. Stanislaus calls to ask, "Why don't you have a flaw?" What is being good at being perfect, it's performing. It's entertainment, like, "You tell a good story" and someone says, you make me feel stupid, not stupid but light-headed, agile, a frost, while, I need a job and some money. Never had two parents to pay my plane fare. Some got parents who can't pay their plane fare. Fern was locked in a room for eleven hours, you levitate, you lose a picture of your face, you aimless and lazy, the right to be lazy by Emma Goldman, back in the talent, back in the U.S.S.R., back in my room, I am telling you I will never be finished again! Done yes, strong yes, tough maybe, but never done, never used, throw it, never seen, use it, I may have come close to repeating myself, you see, you are the ones who've heard it all before and addressing you is all...wait, you could be fathers to children, you are all repeated or repetitive, immigrant or design, even stopped short of address just the whole Bowery, bow er yeee. Now I will finally solve the problem, who am I speaking to, and, what am I speaking for, the problem was solved by the following dream which you can use or steal, also: I dream I am in a corridor filled with light. The stairs are constructed backwards so that the illusion of them is like a mirror image. But they can be climbed if you're double-jointed and can twist the lower half of your body completely around like an owl's head. Then I am on the roof of the building at night looking at a man's head. He turns into an audience which begins to clap, facing all four directions. I fly into the audience which is iron pipes and someone tells me to "Whisper, or else."

June 7

By dating it, it signs itself, it is not a long work. I get used to living with practically nothing: like cannibal: a beer, pumpernickel, cheddar and cashews, survivors live on luxuries. Is it hot or cold, the bread is so strong it requires half a pound of cheese, plenty books plenty reading. Plenary reading, I tell Stanislaus the whole history of the Catholic church; we tell each other Christmas stories, pure rye meal, water, pure vegetable shortening and salt and plenty cheese, a racist syntax. Dear American Indians, whenever I eat American food, no, whenever I begin to tell a story I get sidetracked, did that even happen (discontinued...). Dear Florence, please forgive me for washing the dishes, but, when I saw them there so tempting so dirty I couldn't help myself, and, it's so much more fun than taking a bath, image et son (numero 200), or, all the foods in the world I am hungry for except one.

I'm in the grocery store across the (Macdougal) street arguing with the owner cause he charged me six dollars for a sixpack and a pack of cigarettes. His girl tells me the rest of the money went for two unpaid-for hamburgers (me and Stanislaus). I say "hamburgers" as if I never heard the word, and, still arguing, I tell the owner that he'll have to get accustomed to the fact that some of the people in the neighborhood will be "strangers." While I'm dreaming this, this same owner has won the lottery and he's dancing and yelling on the streets, one hundred thousand dollars. Then I go to the shoe store to pick up repaired moccasins (Meg's loafers or maybe platform shoes), I know the guy is going to overcharge me and say so, asking the price. It's $4.26, which seems fair to me. The leather of the moccasins has been treated to be soft. Soft armor. "If they wouldn't shine them so much they'd look old." Armor: In the museum, Meg and I argue about whether (leather) there can be real 16th century shoes. I believe it and say, "If they wouldn't shine them so much..." Belial and gold thread on the tapestries, David and Bathsheba—"Berlabee" in dream. One star of.

Left off by car at a home, full of kids. A man, Montague, is drunk, wants a kiss but is too tall, Max goes inside to a room, do I share it? Someone has to drive this drunk guy home. Sitting on the curb, cars, czars.

June 8

And the safety and the comfort of, eyes closed. Pacing at the loft, away, not away, not a story, not a project, never a story, never a project, never a comfortable chair, bed, big and fat, big breasts, quarter of three, can't sleep and not used to having to, having the freedom to roam around the way I would do it, I keep thinking of dinner, schedules and alone in this room I look at my daddy, it's none of your business, picnics, whose play, whose Hawthorne, whose woman in the house, moving fast. Snores. Dream Bartholomew is killed in accidental gun accident and, look in the mirror, there's a ceremony on a huge beach in California with a row of ceremonious police or armed or army men, all three (men or types of men), Jerry Rothenberg is there, like Belial, I guess. Nobody lies or believes in his absence. "I am a thematic absence of the world." From a made-up dream. What of the stairs. Stairs like mirror image of, and what of the stairs, the, to the dangerous loft, protect yourself, dirty the white of it, loft, written before, this same space, someone else is a drifter, comings and goings, write it out before sleep comes and goes, and then safety, eyes closed. Or endgame, or penniless, as, at bottom of barrel, or specific, as, barrel of monkeys, I don't mind. Anyway, game. Not strong not tough, just clear red wine, held up to the light as beautiful or as decorative, the new color, decorative, just look at the color of it, and don't leave, and don't go away, and or but also, don't plan, now how is that accomplished, in a day or years, not by taking it easy and not by the reflection of a blue door in a clear mirror and not by the reflection of a blue door and a pink towel in a blue mirror so you know, because the towel is there, just what blue is left, but by simply perhaps returning to the scene of the crime and writing a novel-length letter to the magistrate explaining or telling, in full detail, that, yes, this was premeditated, and, though you are educated, you should not have got off on a plea, made by others, of insanity, but, this is unheard-of, this is not done, get out of the convent, get inside the jail, you can run but you sure can't hide.

Where is everything? Here? What is absolute safety, as from drowning. What is absolute safety from vitamin C, what is absolute safety from schedules, absolute safety from stimulation, absolute safety from three people instead of two? Admittedly three are better for the committing of crimes but criminal offences are rare in our over-all rent-paid territory, though, they are thought of, or thought up, all the time, usually by three or for three to commit, you need three. Therefore there are changes and scratches and examinations of the body you haven't noticed, or checked, thoroughly, every part, for a while.

"Why don't you meet me at Florence's during the day cause it's kinda heavy to carry over there," and as soon as I saw you, I was watching, I came out the door, and, I didn't look like myself at the window but even so I continue, and, "Have these policemen been bothering you" and if not, this will certainly bother you: we're criminals anyway certainly from poems to poetry not a definite route but after that for sure, songs go there and working goes there and moving goes there and surely stories go there and ice goes there and intelligence goes there, education goes there, to say the least, and armor, or, the knowledge of armor goes there, and all the struggle that poetry, songs, working, moving, stories, and the telling of stories, ice, intelligence, and with that goes silence, education, armor and the knowledge of armor and more you can fill in creates it and it all goes there, to crime, or to dependence and I forfeit where as a communal déjà vu, for you to share. You must be careful not to wear clothes. For, like the man I watched in the restaurant, and I listened to him, your thought might wear your own suit. Then you're done for, almost as if, almost as close as if, you were gunned for, or marked, by a professional who is and is not escapee, but surely knows our own game, from front to back, and back again, and that's not merely stolen words, but whole chunks of ice melted and floating downtown, to destory and they will destroy the whole geographical and ecological set-up of the world and its atmosphere, I am telling you, with words. I just write it to be read to you, I do not expect you to read it, you say, more jokes. Sex, even. Well I tried to explain what touch was, now what is sex. Her or his X. X-rated. Sex now is few perceptible points of contact with what is called the world. Sex is early years. Sex is he was guiltless of a system. Sex is American. Sex is in the vividness of the present, sex is in the past, which died so young and had time to produce so little, sex attracts but scanty attention (James on Hawthorne). Sex, said Dr. Melmoth, no, I shall find little safety in meddling with that deadly instrument since I know not accurately from which end proceeds the bullet. And were it not better to take ourselves, in case of an encounter, to some stone wall or other place of strength. Well, sex is silent, diffident, more inclined to hesitate, to watch and wait and meditate, than to produce himself. And fonder, on almost any occasion, of being absent than of being present. And there is in all of this a betrayal of something, cold and light and thin, something belonging to the imagination alone. And American sex indicates a man little disposed to multiply his relations, his points of contact, with society. So, sex is always at play, always entertaining itself, always engaged in a game of hide and seek, in the region in which it seemed that the game could best be played, among the shadows and substructions of, whatever you want. Well anyway, sex is the elixir of life as gross and thin as Theodore/Nathaniel would say, the same in Greek or Latin, gift of god, or, whoever, I don't have to put the show together but I can still keep working on it.

You present me with an alternative, I take the one, like, someone put poison in the sugar or maybe it's poem, or, whose life lived like that, or, whose reason to listen to that—none. None poem none poem shirt none poem like shirt, suit like thought shirt like fear, none poem fear or dear everyone, too much for self. As if I am still eyes closed, in an armored pavilion all ice, you your arms and all your possessions come with you, so you make noise, shut up, I am invading your grave, as you missed mine, isn't this what you want, aint that choice, and isn't this division but not yet separation the boundless boundaries of our united nation just like school: a little peach in the orchard grew, a little peach of emerald hue, warmed by the sun and wet by the dew, it grew. One day passing the orchard through came Johnny Jones and his Sister Sue, those two (I am not afraid anymore to go to bed with you) and so on: that is, they ate the peach and died cause it was not ripe yet.

June 9

I must've dreamed something about pictures of Roosevelt, said so to Max and he was seeing pictures of the thirties. And dreamed two aunts and the disposal of their bodies.

So now I must kill and eat him at this spot. So now I must kill and eat you on this spot. Strip the flesh from your body and lay it in pieces on the stone to dry for a while in the sun, then slowly eat it but before it spoils and so it will never be found. Yes I murdered David then, at dusk, in the cemetery and, hidden, we made a task of it all night; since he knew I wasn't crazy he trusted me to perform the necessary act and the cannibalizing. He was a reverent and adoring victim. I remained a saint. I hope the use of the word cannibal, applied to a saint, will not shock a recognizably bourgeois audience. In my travels in Europe, I've become accustomed to these things, believe me it was a necessity, but I know this is not familiar to you. Anyway, there's none but a fictional need to worry, since, war-torn, you are on the outside and I am on the inside now and can speak freely. You have no need to worry, I'll be here for the rest of my life. Another thing you won't understand, perhaps, is how liberating the murder and the eating of the body was. But this must be boring. I've already given you enough reason in my writing to fit together the motive and, as artists, you'll understand. You would rather hear the method I devised. You are used to detective novels. It was easy to seduce him to the graveyard, especially after a few drinks. You see the thing I couldn't stand was he felt sorry for me, poor David. While I was in Chicago I had spoken to someone I will call Jimmy and a few of his friends. They were helpful but could not understand my desire to be caught after the crime. Jimmy thought I was being sarcastic, flesh-eating, yes.

I had brought a bottle of whiskey along, and, spilling most of it on the ground, around dusk I pretended to be drunk. I yelled to David, in anger, to plant some flowers on the grave. I demanded that he steal them. He agreed, thinking he ought to give in to any whim of mine. I buried the bottle and prepared myself. All the while poor David was yelling back, "They're all plastic." I paid no attention. He came back, arms loaded with lilac blossoms he had cut from a tree. I pretended to go into a rage. I must've said, "They can't be planted, find something else," or, "Take them away," I can't remember, though my memory is much improved since I've been here. Finally I demanded "Plant them" and he laughed at me and pretended to do it. I waited a minute, laughing. I threw myself on him and the flowers fell to the ground. I demanded to make love. He refuses and I realize I can't kill him but this doesn't last. I have in my hand a large thorn which I've gotten from an abnormally grown wild rose bush. I scratch his face with it, pretending to play, with the excuse that I'm drunk. Lying around in the lilac blossoms, I take the first chance I get to push the thorn hard into his pineal gland, it's the surest way. I suck the juices from it (as I write this it must be David's birthday, I have no exact record of time here). I take out my other instruments and proceed to do what I have already related; I do not ignore the genitals. When dawn comes I take all evidence of my crime and drive away in David's Mercedes-Benz. I bring some of the flesh with me to live on, exclusively, until I am arrested.

June 14, 1974 St. Matthias School
Bernadette Mayer 8 - B

Dog caught in class.

June 16

"You know how I listen to you." Well, in fact, I've forgotten how, yes, I've gone and forgotten how and exactly how you listen to me and I know there must be some changes made, I turn on the radio. First of all, I must begin to remember how you listen to me, or maybe, I don't have to.

Two) Parents, as if they were starving you, you run down, for potatoes again, in the middle of the night and hope they don't catch you. Gulp em down before you get caught, I've always loved to eat in bed. You see, you almost fell asleep without eating.

Three) Write a pornographic work about Stanislaus and the little man he hides inside there, just like Rico.

Four) Settle the difference between you and them.

Max says, "Spider is a vulture." So, who's dead?

June 17

"Teresa has a very intelligent sister. As a matter of fact she's sleeping right there. She's already tried to (smile at) seduce me." Belial becomes Max to say this, feeling his back all the while. "Let's go down to the schooner (solution) by motorcycle." The experiment with the monkey and the rose plants, the plants move away as the monkey's heartbeat is monitored. "He wants his mommy" is the result. And then school: the meal. All appetizers. Soup in a cloth, potatoes cairn and butter, with spaghetti. $2.25. I find lemon and lime beer on ice. Then the airport: everybody lines up to be shot and killed. Are there three men from Rome here? And one of them's Ugo Tognazzi and one's Marcello Mastroianni from "Grand Bouffe."

"It would be someone of a sexual origin."

"Well I would want to be able to talk about Georgette (Georgie?)."

One girl smiles and gets in the front.

June 18

The people in the workshop seem to be discussing whether men and women are obscene, whether women are, whether women are misanthropic, whether women are, exist at all. Their solutions are probably monogamy, or probably it's crazy, or probably it's changing and getting old will solve it.

6 a.m. I wonder if Belial will ask me to marry him or cannibalize him at all. Same. So frank with Stanislaus till 5:30 a.m., then by 6, I won't say. Spoke with Ullman before I realized I was openly making fun of him. Pilgrim's Progress. There's a lot of misogyny in the workshop, honey, needless to say. Then there's the Italian woman who comes home from her husband's funeral and the priest finds her frying her husband's genitals: "Well what are you doing?" "I ate them the way he wanted for forty years, now I'm having them the way I want them." Today's daily life is odd at best.

Anyway I must write the dream: I am lying in my bed in the purple room. David, I mean Belial, and Ullman are speaking at the foot of it. Belial says: "Teresa has a very intelligent sister,..." and so on. I begin to smile in my sleep, I join them at the foot of the bed and watch myself, wonder if they notice I'm smiling. Then he says, "She's already tried to seduce me," said in the house, the beach house, this purple one.

"That's not too smart."

"Is that smart?" This is making fun of Ullman. When I begin to caress David's back, he turns into Max, then back into himself: Fern:

"My lover's back." My own schoolgirl's back, burned at the bottom by the backs of the chairs (who will read it if you won't), the hard wooden benches we sat on in school.

David and Ullman continue their conversation, they're going to a "meeting" together: David: "It would be someone of a sexual origin..." (that I would prefer to take to the meeting).

Ullman: "Well I would want to be able to talk about Georgette." This makes Ullman Ted Baxter on the Mary Tyler Moore show. MTM, MBM (Marie Bernadette Mayer). But why is this the purple beach house? And why, when the solution to the problem comes up, is it between David and Ullman: "Let's go down to the schooner." It's the perfect solution, all are ecstatic. They go, up and down, by motorcycle. I see the schooner and it is a ship on shore, waiting. "I only want to see you." That fucker. And who's the monkey of this experiment? Do I even have to ask? A barrel of them. And when the monkey's heartbeat is amplified to the audience, the plants, planters and all, move away, far away. I don't like this guy Ullman! Move away! The audience goes "Ah!"

It does all have a reason, I only want one, interfering with me and Belial, I suppose. Strange sun setting in here, Montague is Romeo's family name, Mercutio Romeo's friend. And the roses are Stanislaus' roses, what's there to hide? Come to dinner? I always bring flowers home. And the monkey's excuse, wanting his mommy, I don't understand that. Florence? Marie? Fern even? No. I don't move plants away although I want my jade plant back but I won't go up there to get it cause that bastard...Spider's the monkey I guess.

And we think the meal at school is free but it's $2.25, even just for appetizers. We find the beer on ice in Mexico I guess, that's too complicated now, it has to do with sucking cock. Then every body lines up to be shot of course, killed, whatever, and one girl, a collaborator, lines up right in front, she's to be shot early. Why? I don't know, she smiles so she must be me. I forget why they're being shot in the airport maybe, where, military, the detectives spot three suitcases from Rome and they say, "Those three men from Rome must be here." A move, then. "Spellbound" in Rome, Georgia, no doubt, the movie with an abreaction in it, Gregory Peck, Marie's favorite actor, faints. Yes and cut to the shot of the "Grand Bouffe" men, those three, we leave out Michel Piccoli, men who eat themselves to death or else somehow we leave out Michel, we leave out Georgette, we leave out Lisette, "Wants his mommy, yes," but why do they identify themselves in my movie? Maybe, to look forward to a day that's moderate, in temperature. Baby, that's a promise I can't keep. I see all the sun in the smoke of the room, I leave the window open for you and I might as well have some fun, while waiting. Pictures make some memories.

June 23

Three men who can't catch or bring back the black group in the trailer, what trailer, what black group? And before that I am so unhappy maybe it could stop on the day before: stricken at the sight of a black man on the street I dreamed we had the white lighter and I won't eat I fear distinct admiration for the food just as Max fears distinct recognition from me. And Belial just goes on as if he had forever, what are our studies now?

Dreamed, June 22, I walked with the telephone, long cord of it for miles, with a man, I'm a boy, leaving a woman behind, so distinct. "You usually meet your dead lines." Dead lines? Vultures again? Why does Max use these words at all and no one can understand it, though they kid me about it, why all the external things aren't written down, carefully recorded, in chronology, in my journal is not external at all, though it'd make a good soap opera and engrossing too though I could never write it down. That's why.

Stanislaus writes: "I don't wear glasses anymore. I eat fast, hunger. This is because of what I told you, under certain conditions like because, and, reading because and behind because is the last word you have to read. I play more now."

And Spider writes: "More so because and well enough to try and frightfully revealed and possibly entombed by my own hideous…"

And I write: no one has ever had an investment, surplice or amice, in my immobility or mobility therefore, except myself and I am quite sure of this one simple thing. You don't get what you pay for but you get what you always provoke. Where should the word always not be in the above sentence. Too bad about my parents, so what. I am not the type to be on a CCLM committee. You always don't always get what you always pay for but you always get what you will always provoke. Nothing to be embarrassed about in journal writing but decoration and emaciation. "Another spring day." There is no found writing here.

In the middle of the night Florence said a peculiar thing to me. Joking, I said people offered bribes for the CCLM grants, like, "Larry said stay over and I'll wake you up in time." She said, "Well I can do that for you, wake you up in time, for free." I said and I won't have to pay then by making love; she said I can't be sure of that. I don't know if you get the gist of this, you see this is not my kind of journal writing. I take that back. I left something out.

It's 7 a.m., at 11 a.m. I might be receiving a phone call, I'm undernourished so I won't be able to speak, anyway. Will see everyone tomorrow night at Bartholomew's reading, a diagram of where I will be in relation to everyone else and the door, follows. Bye.

Follows a schedule for the next ten days: I must be too young for all this but it's how I earn my living and get high. Dream think nothing. Be a psychologist. Conk out: to fail suddenly in operation, as, a motor. As = decision of the dictionary. Am bold as a bear and make a bull of it, and I am sick and tired of short poems and short prose pieces and adjunct poetics. You couldn't pay me to read em but you can get me to do it for free, as, with everything, "The prostitute denies herself" or my heart belongs to Daddy, fuck him, persistent daddy, I curl around the magazines and books and sleep with them, hoping to learn what I already know, as, sun, don't rise as, morning, don't come, as daddy, or someone, see my plight and stay with me, I am all right: "The sanest people who ever dined at Neidersteins" crowded with cemeteries fraught with a moon and covered, in between, by blatant crimes. "It's lost."

A good bunch of rubber in bands will keep the vampires away so I lie in the sun singing the songs you want me to sing and keeping track of them.

June 24

Teresa has her second baby, my second red spot. Holland is vacuuming the room and the whole house too, the dogs and birds and sucking their fingers, "I've been living with a dog all this while," a call from Teresa, "Listen to this," rare music all the way from the bedspread, I hide my breasts in closets, the luxury of chairs comes up, a regular sitting room with breathing and moving in it.

Now I want Bartholomew just because he's going away, I get my senses back. But as usual I've covered my bets and maybe better so, so naked someone said. Page, everybody's bed. A bed bone, I still am not doing it, Marilyn Monroe said that, moralism.

Friday: Burroughs' play, go to M's and break the floor.

Saturday: break date with Max.

Sunday: dinner at loft, early hours for Max.

Monday: do magazines with Stanislaus in the park, get cold, Bartholomew's reading, he's leaving, visit him with Stanislaus, he gets spooked.

Tuesday: Belial is spooked too, Spider apprehends me as I call Stanislaus, two hours of relative catatonia, workshop, valium and milk, go to Stanislaus' to get some sleep, break date with Fern.

Wednesday: CCLM meeting, get up at 9:30, late for meeting, Joel, take nap, dream about CCLM, visit Fern, sleep there.

Thursday: Put Fern in a taxi to Cherry Valley, move out of Florence's and into Fern's, dream "bitterroot: blame," see Stanislaus.

The lieutenant was killed (A) en route to the subway (B). Later the wounded man sought treatment (C) and was considered suspect in mugging (D) shortly before murder. (Middle Village.)

June 30

Père David deer, Here's a picture of Dondi. Like all comic-strip orphans he has no eyes, only black dots. It's about time I give all this up. After all I'm not even set up and I must write a t.v. commercial, I mean, series. Serious, not the kind of thing you'd read in the hospital. "Be nice to yourself," someone said and loving towards me, it's because you're so "fond" of me.

Green eggs and ham for four people. Leave out Stanislaus. Why? The dream of the mad dog: I am in a room, no, a house. I check out the beds to see how many people might be sleeping there, could sleep. In Fern's house many people could sleep, in dream. I don't want to tell the rest of this dream except everyone was wearing either black or white, there was a man/woman I did not know, blonde in white (she has mumps or crabs and it might be catching by mouth) she presents me with a bottle of Metaxa mixed with water, happy I would find something in the empty house to drink. And in the end I found myself in bed with Stanislaus and a dog, these dreams will wear off, as you are in the hospital. And the dog was a twin, can we have the bedroom tonight, of a dog I knew (?), Max's, so many of them, there's something wrong with the dog, and so on, it can't be cured because "He hasn't been fed in many months." I'm in the closet, I wasn't to blow someone, was I? I will stop writing all this down soon. Mumps, sex disease, Metaxa, mangy (dog) mouth disease, to cheat.

Godard dream. Godard holding up pictures and making a shutter with his hand, so we can't see. They change, they're jokes: like, "these are the American revolutionaries," they change to monkeys in the air. Screen gets bigger and I figure out the secret, there's actors and actresses behind the screen, maybe we will see some real visions, maybe like when Fern was packing up. The secret is out, one of the actresses is dressed in a blue gown smoking the very butt of a brown cigar and I wonder if this will shock Stanislaus. And they say, you've only been here, in this hotel, for a week, yet you've figured out our secret. Godard, and, Anna Karina is helping him.

Desperation noise, a need to hold off or let go or impress someone, Meg perhaps, she is living here too. I don't write anything about sleeping with Fern and I don't tell anything either except for the surprise of skin as a kind of workbook. All the ease of it, going away and jealousy. And all you guys, what's it necessary for, sleep. Stay awake, telling and openly telling, not telling, the amorphous leaving off, it's telling off, leave me alone.

July 1

Some kind of gravesite, watching a woman at it, the stone, like the three-mirror effect at a hat store, to look at hats or dresses. A man behind the woman.

Steve and I are at school together, I'm unpacking Max's things. I'm amused he packed a large pencil sharpener. I'm anxious to be on time, nine o'clock for the class, but it's been postponed an hour. Three girls rush in to take me, it wasn't postponed at all and a class is coming in to be held in my room. Steve says will I go on a trip with him for four hours. We'll go to Georgia, Alabama and so on. He's delighted I'll come. He must be Fern too.

Teaching the minister, writing in public places, there's a man on t.v. says that that is an example of nihilism, that song about American pie. He mentions Camus and Sartre. I think of Charlotte's neat handwriting, I think of how I always persist in what I am doing, I think of Meg always keeping a letter in progress in the typewriter to Mary and of meditation before sleep and Ullman's idea of vigilance, sleep then dreaming as looking for solutions to problems, of Fern and her love letter, of Memory and the right to be lazy: get up to teach the minister at 2 p.m., have some Turkish coffee and a beer, work with David to get up a lecture on Marxism, of Fern fixing me coffee, meet Meg to get some keys, try to buy Cassis and buy Campari, drink two of them, read Ullman and fall asleep, dream I'm dreaming, sit around and eat, talk on the phone, of stimulation for Meg, of stopping smoking, of washing clothes, of Grace, do a crossword puzzle, read more, watch t.v. and drink beer, of needing to write in my notebook, should I keep the dreams separate, sun's coming out, will Belial take a cab to the hospital, all the time of how other people live and where I'll go in September.

July 2

A place where you can climb through triangles to school and grandfather says he'll be a hundred next birthday, he's marrying D.

July 3

Stanislaus writes: "Am I trespassing. What next. You are now sleeping in the next room. Shit, only what, no, sleep well women are lucky, or, most men think that women, or, a woman's body, or and so on. But this was a spring night, and the sky was gusting red, warm orange, the sirens, Pittsfield, Lenox, and Lee, neighbors stood out on their porches to stare up at the shower of sparks falling down the mountainside…like a meteor shower, they said, like cinders from the Fourth of July…"

July 4

Massachusetts. A crowded house again except it's everyone I know, a shady place. S. says it's about time I stopped treating him with such rancor (in public!). I'm with M. Then a long t.v. movie, bound to become a series, in four parts beginning with part four. In colors of tan and bright sun in/on it. Something about it is extraordinary. I think it's about the hotel above, in the other dream.

Then I take Max to Emilio's garden, I insist on the garden. We are lying together in bed, the same movie comes on. It's about people being shot up and kept in a hospital. Two investigators come and one "gets" a young boy but they don't fuck. It's a place near the water. Someone says, "How many places like this could we find." There's an exchange of shirts or something, it's some kind of exposé. Twice they spread the women's legs and they twist their fists around. Toward the end Max says, "Are you watching this?" and turns it off.

All the while I think I'm awake. I do see the dawn and wake at seven having dreamed it was eight, or, read my watch wrong. Keep a really simple journal of what happens, like, I noticed when I saw the cat that I had stopped sneezing all the time. Except nothing simple happens: leave out everything not-simple: if I hadn't dreamed I was awake I wouldn't have awakened. Another CCLM meeting in my sleep.

July 5

Edwin, posing as the Rat Man, made-up, fucks me or maybe he's just hitting me, a lecherous grin on the red lips of his face as he pulls down my pantyhose (?), I am dressed in my old red suit, the one I gave a recital in at New Rochelle College. Something about, "I must've been nervous about playing the piano."

July 6

Max and Beth and something about moving into a new, maybe unfinished place. I sit on the steps, stoop, in my (not Japanese) "housedress" and someone calls me a whore. So I introduce them to the people who are helping me move, the ones I'm "whoring" for: it's two groups, Stanislaus and somebody and two others, we look at the details of the house. Also, something "must" be silver and gold.

July 7

Survivors of an (Andean) crash show up at my house, I remember there's a store open around the corner (from Macdougal Street). I ask them if they want beer, coke or cheeseburgers. They say they don't but I do. An artist who imitates everyone else in his life but his work is totally original.

July 8

To not remember another dream: the dream workshop is overcrowded, I say to somebody, "What the hell are we going to do with all of them." Ullman hands out a form to be filled in, on one side are descriptions of events or just phrases, like, "She said she swore." On the other side is space for you to identify how these situations came up in your recent dreams, if they did. Then you sign it, like an (repeating series of) affidavit(d?)s. I fill in every day so I figure I must be lying (The Boy Saviour Movement!). The workshop's being held in an art gallery, in an adjoining room there's a shoe and boot show. All of a sudden Larry Weiner comes out driving two horses with a giant ten-foot pair of Bean's Maine hunting boots. (As I joke, I'd just given blowjobs to two young boys, people keep asking me about it and I keep repeating of course, the blowjobs, feeling pleasure, maybe rubbing up against a banister. I go back to some strange basement apartment.) Every body seems to have a way of keeping contact with someone (or the outside).

July 16

Aspects of Select: Three hours to go (Stanislaus). It was some other kind of loss I was talking about, I was meaning to talk about, so take the dream and retype it, putting the rest of the stuff in, it's the father-out-the-window dream. Cab driver knew enough not to talk to me. I take money from him, Max, and "Kept them sane," what does that mean, kept them from sinking, or, doing damage, that is, sinking ships. Therefore, since Stanislaus is sane, in the present moment, I don't have to worry about driving him crazy. Aspects of select. Let me put it another way: they were crazy a long time ago. Then, they seemed sane. Now they are acting crazy. Stanislaus is not crazy. I have not driven anyone crazy. Therefore, he will not be crazy. Now, this is work. Is this like studying Egyptian hieroglyphs. "If I were working I would feel a lot better. The absence of writing in a house full of reading." "I keep my household sane." Saner than in a banal way. Picaresque or picturesque, two work spaces, it wasn't picturesque. The psychotic detective, his hallucinatory leaps and now he's in great demand. Funny, Stanislaus wouldn't mention it.

Feeling, expressions of feeling. There are some dangerous and some not. There are some intense and some not. There are some adaptive and some not. Enough of that. Feeling expressions of feeling. No clues! Who can work can express feeling and who cannot, no way. Could that be the solution or lead-in to the diadem of proposals presented in the mystery novel-set, as in set theory. You get lost in the sentences, even simple sentences. You are anxious to read my writing. Is this why we are off on crime and a solution. The detective has no stance, he's not against anything—doesn't your hand hurt when you write those long sentences that please him so much and I'm jealous and I'm out the door but can't go out—he, the decorative detective, only presents a solution, possibly not even honest. The detective is ashamed of dates and delays his proposal for a public reading. He opens with "You are the sunshine of my life," an address to his mother, thanking her in some way, probably for simple exigencies. It's the way he lives in a wall, so insolated, isolated, insultated, insult-laden. And yet so shy that gives the secret away: all of his affects are mine and this is besides "twins." "I must have more friends." So, it comes up again in a different way: what you (don't) owe to who you can change. I don't, no, immigrant, I don't only I don't put it right. They must fuck fast, I am thinking of somebody else now. Perhaps I meant change the language of. Perhaps I meants involve in a situation complex enough for "them," or, for the first time. Reminds me of my time I have no time. My time is my own, or, all the same my time is my own. I don't worry about eating. Someone's glasses beside the bed or besides the bed there are someone else's glasses beside the bed. A stranger's, I'm caught into calling them spectacles and I am more distraught, no, I am more expert at this than you. A new pronoun. Aspects of select, secret title, keep it down, don't underline or capitalize it. 4:30, time to get up and be clear, communicate with the masses, or show them how, if they only knew. I write bigger than my mother and father and uncle wrote quite small and neat. Grandfather wrote with German letters in English or American language. Also, I fill up more pages than them, accountants, secretaries, secret diarists, artists and electrocutions, plumbers and janitors, or, proudly, elevator repairmen. Repairmen especially of really old and decrepit elevators that the Otis men couldn't touch. Not a janitor, then, no doorkeeper. Helpless, I write. Kept helpless, I write more and more till I write self out of helplessness. Kept helpless out of pure invention, invention of motive for purpose in the house as opposite to on the streets, endless (to me) invention, seeming to be back where I began, I carry beers around as I used to and still complicatedly must have paper and pen and a book that looks like school—it must be necessary. I don't outline their professions for you for nothing. If I can't get another one done by Friday I'll have a way then to do another one by Tuesday. This is speaking of dreaming. I am a dreamer, not involved in this profession. I simply present the dreams and store them. I do not exhibit them further, as, for example, the monkey who said he was a psychologist and a philatelist, when in fact he was a pugilist. Or the great red painting with color down the middle which was so obviously a representation of the female sexual apparatus, but, you see I don't have to be responsible for this transparency, I am only the dreamer, no more to it. Or the many dreams of Lisette and her apartment becoming a congruency of lovers and strangers, another, and I remind you I'm not responsible, absurdly banal image, representing itself in Lisette's helicopter pilot landing in the large loft-house which had been taken over by strangers and when she gets in to go to the airport (I'm just going along for the ride) he tries to kiss her, they're having an affair, she complains it's too sticky and he should wait until she stops sweating at least. Now you see, I am sitting in the front seat, just for the ride. "I think I'll do a Max on Lisette," I would never do that. But, there's a thin person underneath here. But, everyone enjoys my big belly. And so, I'm sure it'll all work out. Like the other dream of Lisette's house I can't remember so I must be conscious of where I am so why bother to mop the floor. I do more for Lisette than the men I do but they'll get their chance. I'd say the monkey was a philosophist and not a serious psychologist. Left out of the gist of it, at the least. Now what should I read of what am I reading, why not What Entropy Means to Me. But first darling, I'm glad it's cool and I need some tide, but that wasn't first darling.

11:30: "There sure is enough room for everybody," to work but not to fuck: as, one in each room, a comfortable situation. The calls come in or go out barking. Piano, no, some kind of piano music. Charlotte Bill Meg Stanislaus and I are all misfits, or, what did I call us, the dregs, meaning of the Poetry Project. Ullman: "Excuse me, can I bring my daughter?" He understands the looseness of the situation, he says, if not the jewelry (there was another word supposed to come in here from Pat's black dream). I wear all my jewels to class to provoke dreaming and so stares.

July 21

Had Stanislaus' busy checked: I should be blunter and admit: if you aren't staying over I'll call somebody else. Plus all the guilt of course.

But, they would never believe me and they even revel and maybe I revel in thinking I'm "on my own" or whatever. Whatever's covering your bets. I certainly do admire everyone's present in my past total bravery, I should never have left Max, it was a very mean thing to do, "said in the house." But, I saw so many things today, new colors, new sky colors, colors never seen in the sky by anyone but me, against yellow light and the smallest sliver of a moon ever seen was seen by me, the newest moon not even rising but setting, just a line of a circle.

And, my "favorite" flowers, Queen Anne's Lace, and green of Glen Cove covers up the good part of the sunset, Max tells me a story about D.D. who just appeared on the socialite page of the New York Post. And, the lump in my throat that Fern caused in a dream, Fern is Lisette. I call her baby when she leaves, because she enjoys it.

July 23

Belial says not to drink. But Belial, how am I more "phallic" as you say, than Fern or even my own mother, what does that mean? And what is this "material" you say we need, you are looking for? Am I being too "spiritual" at the same time that I am being "more phallic?"

July 25

Belial, then a man whose made a circle, like sand castle moat in the mud, they drive their motorcycle around in it. When interviewed Belial says there's nothing to say about it. His friends, he says, are all foreign so they cannot speak either (about Fern?).

Tennis, something about even teams, a problem, so, we never get to play. I dial Florence's phone to call you about our session, it won't work. I can't arrange to meet you and think I've slept till Friday now and missed you completely. As in the beach house, we had a 5:15 appointment. Rico introduces Beth to Teresa, Beth has her mail in her hands. I notice it's mostly from "suppliers" that sell pens and art supplies, as a character in Simenon. Teresa is very uncomfortable. Someone, a man, stands behind her and asks her questions or makes suggestions. She seems to know everything and he keeps saying in amazement, "You mean you did that already?" Meg and I are packing up the car outside Florence's, what car? The rooms are different. Meg has put a bureau in the back seat, it's the yellow car Max rented to take me to the beach. I turn and a mau-mau is in the car, not a real mau-mau but a man with Haitian designs carved into his legs, he's white. He claims he's harmless cause he can't steal the car without the keys. Meg comes out, leaves the keys on top of the hood and he drives away (as if in Philadelphia).

Then the women are playing a basketball game. We have an appointment but we have it there because, you say, I wouldn't want to miss anything. I'm angry and keep trying to reset it or get you out of there, off the court. We sit on couches and try to talk.

That's all the dreams, so, I'm losing racetrack, I don't care, I don't understand why every one is about you, again, I'm leaving. You left, I'm leaving, all exigencies, mine, yours, Marie's. Let's see about Marie and Fern: just let's see. The pen nearly broke, at least it closed down, closed up, it got tight-fisted, I got tight-lipped, I became distraught, I said, I got angry. Gone fishing. Fern said to me: you're not feeling lusty today? No, I wasn't. Now the pen's closed up more, almost can't write, what if I were caught with it, my only pen, you see, the point, real appropriately is pushing further and further back into the pen. If only I had a tweezer to pull it out again, but then the pressure of my words would only push it back in, yet it still makes a slight impression.

Such a green color, I chose it. I fix it, I got it out with a pin, no wonder it was such a tight-ass pen, and now it scratches, makes a little noise with each motion. Metaphor, if this were only not so, is that enough for you? Now my hair is caught on the ball of Fern's desk drawer, I can't move, I can't stand living in her house! A story about a house left just as it was, as this one is, for good. And thought I couldn't stand living with a woman at all. Since New Rochelle. But that aint it. Something about a special kind of murder or object choice, I can't remember what that is, something clear. I'm losing track and I wanna get drunk and make some scenes. Meg asks me to move the phone before I go to sleep. Stanislaus suspects that I suspect him of something I don't even know what is. Max is afraid, anxious, at being alone, nothing to do with me, he says. So I form an offer to help him with the loft. "I've changed." From July 26 through August 2 I am going to need more energy than I ever had to need. Except to ford that river. I think, I must think I made (forged) the river, which was not a stream. The Swift River, up to our shoulders, in Massachusetts, with a rope across it and some men fell downstream.

Dear Belial, who can be any body (that's a question). I am not brilliant yet, I am only slightly torn. And, too small. Fern wouldn't be so careful to be quiet, while she was working, as I am, for Meg asleep. Next room. Something about people I can control. Fern I can't control. Marie I could except for her schedule, her regular doings, about the house. Also I must stop something, I am not going to say what it was. So, there's a revolt against Fern, maybe it's not a real one, maybe made-up for your sake, maybe just ingenuous, or, seeking more, could there be more, privacy. Do you mean then, I bring out the helplessness in her by my amusing tactics, the ones I learned (acquired) long years, etc. of pleasing, giving pleasure to, to women especially, especially when it worked, when it made them cook you dinner, is that what you mean? But, the revolt then is against her very own armor, armor that she wears of a prince of the doings, no, I am confusing it, I am the prince, armor that she wears then of holding back in a small cynical way, I am still waiting to see if this is really so, I'm waiting for more, and so I won't speak up or reveal myself to you at all. I used to be able to write beter, that is, I am only going on, I am not continuing on, I am broken off, forcibly so, and I'm sick of this. Being comfortable comes to mind, it's like the first journals I presented you with. How now do you become the you again? Steering. Getting high, or, no more fear. Getting paid. You have a friend in getting off. You fuck like a Chinaman, you fuck like a madman, like a black man, you look at the genitals of all (three) sexes. Now you know everything. Something to leave you with, part of my privacy, when I go away, what? You want some dreams? You want stories? You want more "material?" You're in no fucking hurry, it drives me crazy. I say to Stanislaus, we have plenty of time, he's confused, I would be, I am. I won't eat in the morning,

I'll feel sick and to die, I don't have to do anything, it's the price of this prose, I'm under no pressure. Will they, you, write to me. Will Stanislaus and I be forgotten forever, will be lost, will never be heard from again, it's tempting, could be, under, sick and die, take her, sorry. The trees even here are elaborately rescuing me, even in this moment and I succumb to a fantasy I would never credit in a human being.

So I am sure we will all live forever if we don't get lost in the woods forever, stub our toe on a rock, fall, stumble and fall over, fall head over heels over into the stream that tumbles down, pretty steep, the mountain, the state forest. And that is all there is of that. Two strong. Give up smoking, play records, read mine own executioner, tumble down to mine own executioner and find a good ending, to dreams. Easily. Just keep the pages of the rock-soil clean, Stanislaus is upset, when Fern gets angry she says, it only will last a minute, what a conundrum, Meg is euphoric. Max is upset too, I can help him though, something about always being counted on or counting on you. Stanislaus makes a note about "shark-fucking" in my book.

July 26

Both Stanislaus and Meg have been dreaming about you, yes you're still the you. "We've been through cannibalism" is the theme.

July 27

The nun, her little shoes, somebody comes back, the folds of her dress, that's all.

July 29

For stopping worries: Little labor sweet contests, things, old mothers sweetly sweetly singing songs to me, chiding me, making me angry, making me cold, then loving me, what else? Stories told, many stories told, I am easily Amazon, you do that too and I am easily your young brother but you don't do that. But so many sweetly, this is no Caribbean song, burns brightly, brightly burns. I am writing when I am alone and I am not speaking, there is no noise, it's silent, it's energetic, it's absolute secrecy, it's completely shared, there are leaves, there are no leaves burning, or hungry, there are none falling, there is something on-going, it is the singing, somewhere sweetly, that, I think that, and about that, and make a mess of that, and straighten it all out. I let it go, I pay no attention, I begin to sing along, I learn to sing and then I begin to sing, already. It's new, it's been done, before, it's my amazement, it's my control, it's my absence, it's my loss, I cannot move, I move around, but not as much as you. I sweetly dream her little shoes, she returns, the folds of her dress. To give an apple, a pear, a single grape to her. So, she is waking. I wish she would sleep, would wish her to sleep, would make contact there, would understand or make understanding and from there, travel. Travel, like the children, to the four corners of the world, women riding horseback bareback, one behind the other, in blue. The men are brown. Many brothers show up and we fall in love with them. We become innocent and fall. They bring champagne or mats to sleep on. I imitate you, I do exactly what you do. We love this and take our own time. We let a lot pass by, paying no attention for we have no schedule. Then we simply look around, we dream the simple setting, walls covered with rugs and fabric of all kinds, we dream our tent, we dream many brothers show up and we quickly fall in love with them. We dream we become browner and erase our personal histories. We dream this incantation to stop our worries, to leave off, we dream this song to rest, and so we work.

July 30

Dream this is the biggest room I ever had. Only six months have gone by and I don't even use the drawers. The policemen are looking for a street. I have short hair, my mother had it too and there was a man in the house, she said he wasn't welcome, I wouldn't shake hands at all, then she got nicer to him (could I have dreamt my whole life), combing wet short hair. The eating scene, the scene on Nina's street, "She lives in the city." I discover a whole new corner in my room, one I've never seen before: "I should move the bed over there, Lewis's envelope."

August 1

And all of August is dated June or July, too many books. Dream I am writing or reading a coloring book with an animal and its quality to correspond to each part of "infantile sexuality," no! It's disgusting, molestations, everything. (Talking with Charlotte.) A best-seller dream, a coffee table dream.

Everybody has to go to bed, I won't. It's 7 a.m., it starts to get hot, I start to get scared, leave my happy home at quarter to 3 with eighty dollars and twenty-five in the bank. Yours, the Splitting Apart or atomization of activity, how? To make for blandness, that is, no reaction, hoped for. Three crossword puzzles can be done in a day. Bill's stories of the vodka threat and the sandman visiting his home, do you want a beer? I couldn't ask for the quilt. The sudden thoughts that might sound dreary or silly later, the papers, like the papers, I will buy blouses, pleasures is what I mean, and, I don't know enough yet to be a doctor or a shaman. The usual, and, Stanislaus must hate women, "Act your age," but it's not "malignant," he has to please them excessively, running back and forth, I worry when I hear "I've got no men friends," and, with a friend like a woman, you don't need, and so on, and, Fern says I can't make people laugh, she says, "You sit there sullenly smoking cigarettes," Ned Rorem? Who is she, my and so on? That's business, over. The Appetizing Deli: "Whattsa matter with you, why you give me a hard time, you got the knot by your neck," and "That's my wife, nice girl, why she take you?" and "Where's the cheese?" "It's comin," "So's the messiah." And, why not market, marketish or marketlish like ticklish, exercise you see, you see as well as well, women, while some red or something red appeared in the hundreds of.... It's a way of life everybody likes to lead and I sure hate to leave but I don't have to. Communes, rich men, beggar men, thieves, I am a blanket and a thief, let's get some beer for the car. Why shouldn't my day residue, normal and leaving, carry me through to sleep, like you too, big black eyes and nothing more to say, like, the last person I saw so what. Kid wish it's tomorrow, already and is but something also always does it isn't yet, cannibalism is a fraud designed to keep my eyes asleep, so much of it is all wrong begging and making a simple sentence that is careless of feeling, I usurp you I apologize for all the activity it isn't necessary, eyes closed to sleep and sleep's diagram like, end of it seen as though incontinuity would force nothing will save, make me similar to a leaf or fern, here am, so benign, what is trouble, dreams. Syndication and sex, rest rest, each exact synchronous moment is pared in half, you.

August 2

Hancock: the birch, the list of moralists, the birds, the ant that might crawl in your ear and cause an explosion, I have 22 days in the country.

August 5

Saw a giant grosbeak, drums.

August 6

Giant blujays. You could just break apart, you are not Miles Davis. Clark and Susan are secure here, persuasions and plants. The dream of the king dissolving his kingdom and giving everything away including (something) you get to keep, at least while you're here. The desire to do everything differently, to be like anyone else, except maybe Fern. Desire turns to pure envy at the telling of even the most trivial of stories, an event, anything, "suggestible." No fallen angel to stir up trouble here so fears of death return. Somehow this makes absolute sense, a real fear is here, fear of closing doors behind me, do whatever you want. Resenting Fern, then writing a good letter, it's been done before, like, easily, comfort and pain. "I have to take eight pain killers a day (for my legs)"—Miles Davis. I haven't read enough, I haven't done anything and now a real fear. Then, "She uses people," of course she does. I find out that Stan E. has a dream (reading Scarlet Letter) that "Bernadette is branded a thief and a murderer." A kind of compliment, but, seems to me someone has had this dream, or, related it to me.

August 8

Kill Max today. Fern has my baby, it's big in the daytime and little at night, with a mind of its own. A trip, careful of men I don't like, Burroughs, I stare at them.

August 9

Nun-Fern, nuns Salome. I decide not to give a reading with nun and her boyfriend Joe, happened before? Papers pasted on the wall, they keep it warm. But are they grateful…blue dress hair in braids, Fern lives downstairs, "This is funny." "I know I wrote it." Something about newspaper articles.

August 11

Nightmares, I know I want to be pregnant, this is dangerous. Walk in the woods and am surprised at how wary, like me, Stanislaus is, yet it's not like me at all as he truly doesn't trust anything in nature, like Teresa, a pebble might trip you up or a shallow river to cross, drowning. Haze and drunkenness, debauch. We alternately make love and get angry, I am obsessed with where I can live in September, I don't think further than that. The birds, we fill the feeder and try to write fourteen pages a day on our novel, our whole hearts are not in it. Lou Salome and her biography: "Passion can't last" and all the brother and sister relationships, so I am afraid to say anything to Stanislaus (he follows me around), and then all the suicides. Why, sometimes, can't we just write out book. Not personal enough, the fallen angel said. At least for me. But, I say, you wanted me to do something "commercial" and not not not personal. Lou was ruthless especially when she felt nothing at all. Stanislaus is prone to feeling stupid, I'm not used to this and feel cold. In my mind I use Lou as an excuse. Had a dream with many doubles, little superegos supervising my passion, slept outside in the hammock, day, covered with sun. I don't think I've felt real sexual desire in years, only twice perhaps, I know I've said this at least twice before. For the twentieth century, I am truly cold. Household things, electricity and now Stanislaus is fixing the lamp, something he's afraid of doing. Comparisons, he says he can forget them. Something again about Lou Salome: "You made my pen run out."

At dinner at a long table: "She's...I've maintained the weight at 125 (you'll be happy to hear)...and now I forget what I would have said." Max's sisters: "You mean without (something)?" Max? Andy: "Most women can use that weight on the basketball court (at Ball Mt., Alford), to throw around, especially, the increased size of your waist." Waste: no more First Love by Bernadette I mean Beckett through S's reading of it. Then, something more about moving, I fell asleep moving or with a fantasy that, moving, I could...Lou Salome, Sophia Peabody Hawthorne, Caresse Crosby, Elizabeth Hawthorne. "All These Women." "I can't feel a thing."

Napping, after sleeping outside I dream the candy store, drug store where I can get my valium for free but they make us pay for our sodas (because a man is with me). And behind the counter are three cops, one woman, on phones with their wires (cords) all crossed, it's the candy store on Forest Avenue, Ridgewood, where the N.Y. Knicks stop on their long walk home, uptown to, maybe 68th or 72nd Street. It's too short to ride but too long to walk and then, Coney-Island-like, Clyde Walt Frazier is collecting phony money for a phony kids' summer camp under the boardwalk, it's a porch.

And the estate across the street where I am living now. "Funny an estate could be divided by a street." I ask someone, I've cleaned one of the rooms with a mop: "Do you think it's still dirty?" "Only somewhat." Sounds like Stanislaus answering. As I write this down I think of him or someone entering my "rooms" in another dream, lit a candle, my neat hand. Near my rooms, in an adjoining "modest" home, it seems the Nixons are staying and I go to see if they're in, they are, but having a smaller dinner and not using the "classroom" at all or the institutional dining hall they have. I can look through my glass windows into theirs. So I wait to talk to them, I am supposed to invite them.

Stanislaus is jealous of Max now when he calls. The feeling of immediate sexual passion leaving, you live quietly with none or you do a Lou and leave intermittently on trips and return, always to a brother. I proposed this to Max three years ago and he was insulted by it, I should have insisted, it would have been true. Yet, his revenge, it's to have no work to do, be restless and want reassurance. I proposed it to him two months ago and he said he would think about it. Somehow, eliminate sex as a driving force, whatever that means, but be able to still feel desire. I have no desire for anyone, I have a desire to rely on someone, I have intermittent overwhelming desire for you. So I try like a child to raise the level of our conversation for a while to be like Lou. Celia is no longer she, she says she wants to make "our company" laugh and complains of never seeing me cause I stay awake even longer than Daddy and sleep when she's awake. I am writing with her pen. I don't want to go to Lewiston with Fern and John. Letters from Fern, Charlotte, Monte and Meg. One more thing: I will to be even more direct, even to hurt them, I can't stand it still. To please everyone is now out, I worry about all the artists there will be in Lewiston. Sophia was as polished a writer as Hawthorne but there's no feeling in it. Lou's theories on narcissism. Her name, coming from Louise, from her first teacher and lover. Then she is a virgin into her thirties. "Brother and sister," always and God, of course. Hendrik Gillot. Clark's got a lot of gossip or else I do, we didn't talk about theory. What do you learn from living with another person, cooking and picture-taking and good driving. How they sleep, how they wash dishes and clothes, how they worry that you will worry about what others say in their sleep, I mean, the limits of the tiniest patience coupled or coupled with what love in comfort is, I mean long draughts, it's hard work to forget when we keep switching. I think: if no one wants to have a baby, well screw it. Ed's nephew's brought me a girl child to show me "she looks exactly like you" and she did, all the way through I've been dating this journal July all August, so what do I do in September. I can drive again. Stanislaus: "Is there a psychoanalytic term for people who get annoyed by little things?" "What?" "Picking your teeth." "Worriers." I am hardly ever worried, I don't know what the word means. I am no longer afraid of the forest, it took one week, but somehow I am often afraid of the house itself, so like a spaceship in its strength. S and I are here to work and that is becoming clearer, it's later, but I can't mother him too. "Before I was crazy…the hoot of an owl," I thought I heard an owl, I thought I felt dizzy and momentous, shall I tie myself to a tree, a chance I hardly ever get. Miles Davis thought so. Washing, Miles is always washing, making sure clean. Our collaborate deserves more praise, whose arms are we in? A so-writing collaborate. Pig pen, little knee, punish the little knee, little three, nowhere to go. Use strange meaningful signs, we are thirty-odd pages gone on our detective and smoking fast and easy. Stay between the lines, I thought I heard an owl, saw chipmunks, no deer, stream is dry, valley not lush, too high. So high, wrote songs, sang songs, wrote books, read books, I will never live with a man who goes to work. If in the country, your house is your mind so it is easy to go out and in the city the streets are your hallways so you cannot get out, then, why won't everyone here go out? That is, for no reason. The giraffe of Peter Smith in the Hall of the Bear.

August 15

Written many desperate letters but not the practical ones, am averse still to making plans for September but was forced to make one, a reading, in exchange for my bus fare. Have the feeling (I forget, if I slept in Celia's room I'd take your toothpaste too, I'm a grouch, my stomach hurts, I'm sick, Stanislaus has a toothache, I remember) Fern and Joe will have a fight about this because I'm setting myself up to go nowhere, maybe I'm doing it to see what anyone will do, it's almost boredom, dream something like, "Daredevil has the answer." Did the old devil lose the address, it's hard to come and go so quickly.

August 16

I refuse to remember my dreams now even though in one of them I dreamed three things I would "write or concentrate on." This was a clear dream of a castle, here, and us, we, me and S. and Meg. I nap, worry, stay up all night, tell everyone not to do things the way they're doing them, we don't work for the moment, I don't seem to have any adrenalin whatever that is good for. Sometimes there's no stopping you and other times you just can't move, he said. "Stay inside." There doesn't seem to be enough time, I give in to the smallest sensations of my body and to sleep, the corn drought. May halve the corn harvest but we have plenty, 50¢ a dozen for mealy, 95¢ for young. I received an amazing letter from Bartholomew, I will read it to S. tonight, no, I will read him a good book, it's my turn, more pure moralism rampant in the Hawthorne biography, the house turns on and off, moralistically, the house is in a hurry to do well, we won't come near "finishing" the book and I will eat, not like the birds, except my presence out here where the noise of the house is even louder, scares them. If only they had even a little retentive memory, Clark said, they'd realize we wouldn't hurt them. Have I repeated that a thousand times, I've thought it a thousand times. Victorians never repeated themselves, Twice-Told Tales, once anonymous. Much reading and writing to do and only eight days to the end of the world, the house has turned off again. Quiet, crickets, katydids, sunset, airplane, pool down the hill, maybe even barbecue, mountains, own 1/5 of your own mountain, get out of the haze. I will change the house by an act of will, I'm so tired of driving (each mood) and no one else can do it, hear a horn, I'll have a smoke and join S. at my machine, the house shakes when we walk, just a little, my back is out. The plants are coming along fair, people being left alone, come along with me, why not, it's nothing to look blankly at, you see the trees I can see. Transcribe dialogue and type out diatribe, letter to Philadelphia, share it, I want to take turns cooking, where shall I live, where shall I lecture, who shall I do it to, I am feeling so proper. Pills and Marilyn Monroe, why so with the music playing again, so vulnerable, sensitized, in a position, to what I read and see and hear, Norman Mailer is expensive and there's more noise in the grass, somebody's out. How do I get to Cherry Valley if that's where I have to go and then to Buffalo. Distraught and wrought wrong maybe even conceived wrong, work, do some work in the daylight or time. Someone moved, they didn't move, it must've been, now barking, the dog. One hundred pages of it, sure, at least if you know where they came from, and intelligent dialogue and it's at the table, or at table.

August 17

An ugly day. An "Elizabeth:" an Elizabeth Nietzsche, an Elizabeth Hawthorne, an Elizabeth Peabody in your life, all sisters. Hawthorne ate dove, dove, and would like to have intercourse with some beautiful young children, young girls...Sophia, Queen of the Journalizers, like a picture of the dove he ate.

August 20

"Turn over so I can finish the other side, I dont wanna get up till I'm done. I'll just rip off a wing, the dark meat too." Stanislaus becomes a cannibal and Spider a paraprofessional.

Getting up earlier and one meal a day, no dream about Alger Hiss I dream, there isn't that much to do, just at the center of the notebook, Hawthorne and Sophia could never get away with it yet I am the transcendental social worker, no. Nothing from Belial. Picking berries I begin to shake, in chronology: stay up all night, Meg and I talk about sex, look at stars in the bat field, look at flying saucers in the eastern sky, demonstrate walking on knees for S., look for smokes, thanks for closing the door, go out, Pittsfield smokes for directions to Balance Rock, rock-climb then down Hancock Road which turns into dumb dirt all the way through, one-way, Pittsfield State Forest, winding, up in Lebanon Springs just north of Sedgwick's thinking all the while, we're sure to be killed, sharp cliff on right, no, left and I'm in charge, muscles ache from curves and we eat breakfast and pick up the mail, some film. Berry-picking, everybody bravery. Sole isolation scared, so, hands, allergies, scratches, bees. All this ends at 9 a.m., spider's giant web. Not wanting to leave and still alone, Joe finds a piece of my writing "healthy" he says, "Come to Cherry Valley," my reward for writing a short innocuous poem. Surely Sophia would leave all this out, she'd say, "I must fix dinner." The cat ate the mouse and leak is bad, the tire has a slow one too, what's peace.

August 21

Dated June, now. The spotlights are on in error, all these entries are August and if I were to write you a letter I would address it to you who so innocently craved my dreams and then, systematically…I can't say that. Could that be sent to anyone then but Max and could that be sent to everyone and Max and could send it to me, all powerful and strong, I could have done anything, some dream of you? Now I roam from house to house, let's take a trip not up the hill but down, the authentic figure that was identified as me is to stop. But the other you, the usual you has left already, true with the possibility of being more intact in some distant future but now quite lost within I entertain it loose within the universe, the flying saucers get cold, I rebuke them all suddenly and refuse them anything, even little touches, I can see it happening again, she goes to look at her eyes in the mirror and is used at least to a pretence of worldliness, from others, too much is given then as in the many dreams about the great and big house, yes that was exactly my plan, don't suggest it to me. The shrimp angostura dream: I give Meg shrimp angostura, to have it with her. The rolling up the workshop dream: we are rolling up the workshop in sheaves, all different lengths in a raging river, towards time, either 5 or 8 or 11 but whatever it is we're late and nobody dares to enter the river but two of us and it's difficult rolling up the sheaves with no one in the middle to secure them. Another bakery item dream: my sister Louisa Hawthorne has decided to die and so, she has left her clothes in the river. I pick out what I want to save but, or, even though, she is not dead at all, the news of her death was delayed. So I am in this bakery picking out, even on a weekend, the very best pieces of cake and you want some too, when you see they aren't stale and when you anticipate what they might bring in next. They bring in my notebooks, all of them, in a pile (the owner) and I say something like, "I must have made a big mistake." Upstairs my mother is waiting with rice for me, it's too soft. I hesitate to ask her and I don't but I want to, "How are you feeling?" She looks O.K. but I know she's dead. I don't want to see my notebooks but I revel in the bakery, as seems usual.

I almost had a house today, two large rooms for $250 a month overlooking the back gardens of the church. "We'll never leave you out on the streets," Florence said.

August 22

A spectacular day. We've already gone to the post once for film but it isn't there. Carrots, beets and ten pounds of potatoes, "a good deal" from Mr. Sedgwick so we spread them out in a path to a note to Meg to wake us at 4 p.m. Bringing in the sheaves and corn and scallions and summer squash but, it's already Thursday. Twenty bottles of beer a day. Hooch. Dream to Chicago by bus, no manuscript with me. All the usual fears of how you get treated while "performing," Stanislaus is with me, I have nothing to read, must write something quick.

August 26

And if I had to give this up, I would give it to you

And it's so simple, sucking is simple: Albany to New York to Buffalo and whatever, happens. Imminently being caught in the act of being happened, people the invisible world with spirits, whatever cars they drive

All the long list plus Madame Cadillac plus Madame Tonti with her perishables and the drug abuse trucks and the border patrol with their vertiginous perishables

I would surface

I would surface and breathe

I would surface and breathe wrapped in three sweaters with my abuse under my arm, intact

She never invoked the law against anyone

She was naming, sucking is naming and whatever, happens

Listen, they'll read it or hear it: it's from, doors open and private, a private, the privates, conversation:

<u>Naming</u>, from On the Mountains, Ga a no geh, and the need for privacy, something about a princess who marries an old man, bent on self destruction, the need for privacy and then, the need for naming: A, B, N.F.

A writes my autobiography and B. Buffalo or N.F. Niagara Falls is a local call, smells of electric petroleum leaked into the ground I inerhit inhabit from electrically created, made of the stench of the mist, petroleum products or perfumes. These are the petrochemicals that, if I were to give this up, I would not give it up to you, those then that give you a headache, a blissful dream and an inability to dream, that is you dream that you do not have to breathe, you continue on

When I see someone, I will ask the elevation, perhaps at a gas station

Breathing as an elevation, a higher one, in feet

Above fiberglass reinforced polyester vinyl ester and epoxy tanks and

stacks, ducts, hoods, fans, pipe and related equipment
The nickel-monel-Inconel-stainless steel fabricating of a military road town and the Iroquois beer
The fabricators of aluminum tanks and weldments, are you scared yet?
Breathing is easier at a higher elevation, in feet
Fabricators of pews, altars, pulpits, rails, kneelers and swimming pool chemicals, we are here
Do you see the naming, and do you see the imminent walking and the chance, just the off-chance of being alone, abandoned, and of being continuously the child
As no one, not even the Redskins, can put up with the silence of Duane Thomas.

August 27

Imminently being caught in the act of being happened
That sentence repeating, like, what's coming out of the stacks,
What hops in the garden, I'm sure of it, moralists, we can't, wait, I was coming to sit in your room, in your garden, almost a slip, hops like Jack Kerouac here, we're writers here, we can't breathe, smoke or swallow, our throats are coated, like factories can, we can't
All of a sudden it's noticed—there's something wrong with me
Speaking: supposed to be and supposed to be and supposed to be and letters
Smaller than a Kerouac, some kind of pattern, some kind of repeating thing.
Grasshopper, at least one I've seen. Some hops. A cricket
Skin is not red or reddish
And if I looked fine and if I looked fine and so on
Maybe the fine of the code is for the performance
Still the English notebook in French is English
Not accessible, inaccessible, unattainable, must be impossible, must be chased, or celebrate or celibate
Next door perhaps
Looking up and into the eyes. Then changes of light and color without source: she fell from the falls to the bridge
Still night, still air

There is no continuous change
You move you move into the whorehouse
It's the pits, good morning, you go to the falls
To compete, no pressure but there was a plan: the systematic reclamation of the land by extensive processing facilities, scheduled pick-up services through custom distillation and disposal, are you scared yet?
And the water so that the water becomes green and the land is red for you, like chemicals named for the sun, there is an artificial one, it's aerated, quite Seneca
This is not the lodgehouse, this is something you saw in the mirror when you were putting it together. Give something away, maybe, and then it will happen. This is being afraid that someone, mounded ghost of her on the knoll, will wake, will wake and being frightened, will awaken you, are you scared yet?
Record their ignoring it, ignoring sound, maybe the sound of a watch in bed while you are sleeping
Restless sound
Being watched
Some letters are written slow enough in the garden to wonder, am I being watched. The police come, the customs come
Vacation vegetables are sorry and drive the road along, 8¢ an ear
Worst. Letters written this slow
You are so tired and there are letters written and names begging to be beginning with E, A, L, M, R, L, R, N, J, B, M the president, the fat man

August 28

You keep your life in your breath when you panic even in the presence of home-grown, in order, the fear, say, of the supermarket, the eyes, the skin, the hard-working sculptors, the wine, the beer, the cognac

Who wants to have fun or who can have fun on the hard cliffs of not seeing people often enough and not preparing, in private, to see them, like, I know who that is, or will be
The stench almost of the perfume air
Oil, and they use barges, floating down the upstream overcurrent of the river to deliver the water, power, to the, I guess, petro, noise, chemical, plant that makes the smell

A gingko tree, male and female here, acacia, aspen and hemlock
Absurd to think these notes of a diary noise are waiting for all of us,
You, but charming, as a dancer, you are waiting for rain
And when I sleep I am not waiting for rain. Oil and the portage
And when I give this to you there is nothing chemical about it except my confusion, is it not enough affection
I will try to be a mouse drinking milk but rain will give me no vacation like you could score on a hill
Much more
The energy to burn by looking in the mirror
She's still asleep and when I give this up to you I haven't wakened her and I'm proud of my continuity, that is, lying in the grass
There is no sun and the trees are overtaken by a giant city of pale trees
There is guarded sound
There are dogs who keep still
We mention them
I sink a pack of silver-gold-sounds along the glass to John and seed the bed for air and dynamite proposals; the police come and say come here, they say think clearer, just, who, are, you
We are martyrs from Lithuania who will become gypsies for the Redskins
And what are your needs, they say. It's so simple
One who thinks he can live forever, can you find us one
One who has these ideas and doesn't suffer, one who's beautiful and has the legs. Can you find us one. Milk, we need milk in the orphanage, we don't get it. And one who's as simple as this
What are you saying
Cool air rises, stale smoke, a weekend, nothing is important
It's difficult to find and identify the cool air, the police
Find us one who puts these beads together, one who makes a find with no paint on his shirt, one who relaxes and isn't cased, or one who makes you feel a presence like an ancient president moving, one who milks and crows, one who is deliberate, one who spider-weaves, one who hardly moves at all but gets all over, one who isn't restless and one who stares

Who is listening
I want big quarters and a samovar and this one
No electricity
No fucking music, nobody digging up in the air
No nerves and no style

August 29

Is it a castle or a prison: a minimum security prison is escaped for a fuck after sixty days of mortality
One who sits in there, one who waits and is always there and one who has gray hair
I'm in a hurry, less or more use of language and of words, or waking and sleeping and all the rest. Space, you suppose. Poets, you suppose with one thought, there is none, there is nothing new to do
But share quarters
And smells and the look of hands
I had to do this to keep alive
Car pulls in, is less accessible, is new, turns over and covers up
Has a routine, and therefore, is unable
If I must end here
Causes dog to bark and milk to show, causes Cadillac to be your favorite
Passages, like I am so involved with you
I will give this up to you
Are you scared yet?
It doesn't look, it doesn't look it
It doesn't look, like anything, now it does
How many weeks and how many days, dressing in the quiet
And eyes are clearer as the scene steals in and of course night falls
Which is easy
If I were to give this up, I would give it up to you and eyes are clearer as the scene steals in and of course night comes which is so easy
Then he woke up and all the ghosts of the mountains woke up and all the Indians, mean and women waken as I work
As the river rises and begins to pour rain

As you wake up and eyes begin to clear, as sex is drawn from the magnificent newspapers and dimmed for our benefit
Beneath, above, below, beyond, anyway, falls
A Fascist monument or
A building of Fascist design
Like Wittgenstein's house in Vienna that had nothing in it
These are simple things like tombs, you can't get out, do you agree
If I were to give this up, I would give it all up to you
Listen, some things must be repeated and they are scarce
I watch and stare with eyes and I will never invoke the law against anyone. I will look at colors for you before the mirror and keep records, some of whose words or phrases will darken the color and make it seen
Still it is inaccessible and withdrawn
If I were to give it up, I'd give it to you. Like steel getting trees as a gift.
Or carbon monoxide or a story, whatever
The list of chemicals:
photofabrication of small metal parts
photochemical fabrication
heat exchangers, examporators, driers, pumps
fiberglass reinforced polyester, vinyl ester and epoxy tanks
chemical resistant ducts and tanks
march magnetic chemical pumps
steel and alloy vessels, shell and tube heat exchangers
special process equipment of nickel, monel-inconel-copper
stainless steel-clad
steel-steels and ASME code welding
pressure vessels, heat exchangers
fabrication and installation of piping systems
corrosion resistance for the chemical industry
ampco metal sewage equipment
fabricators, aluminum, stainless steel
asme, code welding, steel and all alloys, pressure vessels
chemical resistance coating
dyes for all industries, specialty chemicals
petrochemicals
aromatic, aliphatic, solvents, aromatic chemicals, butadiene, isophthalic acid, MEK, Olefins, resins, surfactants

ascension chemicals
petroleum solvents and chemicals
tank wagons, drums and carboys
sodium hypochlorite, caustic soda
swimming pool chemicals, muriatic acid, sulphuric acid, nitric acid, ammonia
metal treating chemicals
commercial and proprietaries
alcohols, acetates, amines, aromatic and chlorinated solvents, ethers, glycols, glycol ethers, ketones, naphthas, plasticizers, resins, terpenes, waxes, thickeners
metal cleaning compounds
cleansers, fertilizers, ammonia
industrial reagent dry and liquid chemicals
industrial and heavy chemicals for every purpose
raw materials
diamond shamrock chemical co.
coal chemicals
chemicals, solvents, plastics, metals, packaging, adhesives, antifreezes, anti-knocks, dyes, explosives, fabrics, coated fabrics, fibers, films, paints, pigments, plastics, propellants, refrigerants, rubbers, solvents
peroxygen chemicals, acids, alkalis
industrial and laboratory chemicals
oxygen and acetylene order department over 1,000 items available
chemical surplus salvage residues
pigments, fillers, resins, pails and drums serving paint and rubber, plastic
ink, adhesive, coatings industries
metals, coal, oil, gases, foods, salt spray testing laboratories

August 30

I swallowed my own life
Swallowed my own chemical like the arrival of the border patrol
I swallow my chemical and identify myself
Among the national chemical police state
Somewhere in prison
The own body is swallowed backwards. They remove me to Dupont

DéNemours E I and Co, Hertel Ave., Buffalo, to be made into a wax or a polish
What's reprocessable or forbidden like the genitals of cannibalized female victims in a Western culture devoid of talent goes to Chem-Trol of Balmer Road where the acids, cyanides, solvents and residues are treated, reclaimed and disposed of
The breath is there in the lungs
The heart the eye and the mind are made into acetoxycyclohexamide
And so I am able to remember you in this form
I remember it makes the water too green and the land too red
There is an absence of animals or birds and flowers are coated with brown oil
There is something sensitive, or, something about being sensitive
Like being hungry, like Indian lore, like the four corners of the world
Taking over
And watching him or her, and guarding
Then piecing it together, like mixing and straightening and edging onto you
Still, if I were to give it all up, I'd have to, I'd want to give it to you
No men or women involved as words no buildings or structures just thought transferred in fantastic incident or monument or moment
Like edging onto you in almost fantasy sex
In almost sex fantasies
And then, the thing you want
An accident of mind that changes this space into a waking space
And you can breathe there
Innocents, it's all yours

And the setting sun has cause to be in the act of the constellations like pick-up sticks where the black chieftain is used as a hair comb or an ice bridge, to pick up all other sticks in the game
And when I pour colored liquids in the glass bottles to make gold, twenty 36 foot searchlights operating at 210 million candlepower total approximately four billion 200 million candlepower to create a poison which hurls you onto someone else's body with your first real yell
Your life is in my hand
I have the stick for all uses in Egypt, Japan or Iran: divine, sit, stir, music, fire, weapon, shelter, calendar

There are three versions of every torture or trick and one is dark mahogany, it is in my hand
And there are always three rooms, including the one you forget to use
It's entrance is through the closet or underground, you don't know it's there
As the river caves a great gorge of railway and the cops cruise at 350 feet for a score, I will never forget the stiffness of her body in an anguish that could have waited for later morning
What day is it, what time of year, where's the sun
I myself move 30 feet a year and dig out a possible landslide and many collisions
The original site of the falls where Charles Olson may breathe if he likes is full of vertical currents
Which are notes on your presence and an absence of boats, there's no shore but there are stories
I am the woman-who-stood-back from the mountain called crawling-on-all-fours. The bridge reminds me of Ruth. I crouch inside a pipe that will inevitably collapse, by torture, perhaps, by the tying of hands behind the back, the handcuffing of hermits who grab the genitals' police
I jump and try to make it to the bridge
There is no direct angle to the sun as my bones crack on hitting deaf water and being strangled beneath
I breathe shallow and walk the pebble road back
And there are always more people coming, driving to the four corners of the earth
Red earth, red sky, green water
Dizzy as in the forest, you grab your cunt and tighten up
There is nothing to drive but the sun in the face of a tightening horizon line
And I am dizzy as in the forest for more green, more mint or hemlock and someone else's name, who is it
I strike a match on the wall and hope to be buried in the sacred mound we have been speaking of
I realize why I have no memory
I hurl myself onto someone else's body with my first real yell and swallow my own life and then I give this up to you

August 31

Scared hearts in a hamburger meditation, I'm cold today and since I left somewhere I'm cold and scared, heart in someone's hamburger meditation as if it were a story of success. You must be constantly moving you must have constant success. Yet there is tequila, somehow insisted on and one who is no one to read my journals. Ansiety is spelled wrong and they (the operator) couldn't spell chameleon. She said she was sorry, when I told her how. Perhaps if I were braver. Many advices I am remote to, I am encased in wood (and stone if there were any to see) and there is no real care, a wild question, almost of sleeping in a bed or a tent at night and disrupting the routines or the silence of the sun camping out. Dear Belial I have not written you for a reason, "obsessed" and gentler things. An attitude of removal. Dear Teresa, I have not written you because there is a sense, somehow, as it gets closer, a Victorian genius in its hiding form. Some why write what no one could decipher, I say but to put it in a book then. I move around less than others and feel laughed at because simply I am laughing at, something about practice. No one has been stung by a bee. Thermopylae is playing noise and the folksinger is quiet, everything is wood and will be left that way.

Suicides: he must have either fallen or jumped from somewhere and wound up at the power project. J (I forget, Hank came over, I had seen him eating a real red tomato from a lunch bag wise, so we suffer), J. I hope I am found, I sat in Charly's house. Many finds many digs. And a tour bus coming in, we are documenting these fat ladies, green boxes and tributaries, what is donated and how much moving can you stand or do. There was a dig here recently and a few blue jeans, so, they're drifting back. Air Canada is Arts Canada and peach melba was a configuration of memory, cheese in the trunk of the drug abuse car. Also a mysterious attaché case, notes confused from one week to another and enough to make one nervous, that's you to the tourists. Perhaps suicide sutra will blow away. Murderers are not happy until they see someone die. My name, my name. Something pink and standing thirty or fifty feet in the air, it's a man, it's running out of space, it's calling and worrying, that's what you're somehow not needed for, it's the great Tex hoax, it's the great hoax, Tex, like writing your reading. And a woman turning her wheel with her foot. It's time spent and endured. But it's a honeymoon hotel, this is August and it will be over in eight hours. Tomorrow the full moon coincides without a house to live in or move into. Been away so long I need a cigarette, I do without them and beer and all the thoughtless crimes, if you smoke that I'll leave. Banging and roaming around on a shaking el with no train, the Thermoplyaes die and people continue to walk, all nerves no style what is going on, what's running around who is this fat man he's better than Gutman and where's Fern with the smokes. You see I have (had) no real feelings so none of this is usable, it's throwaway, it's just a reminder like a mindless mimeo machine. And many bees bumbling around because you sit still for it and some more professional than others, like a hired hand. And I am not so concerned with the falls and cameras and cars and women in tilted high heels but more with green sweaters and living the most frightening moment of my life, like (it was) no one ever came back. N.F. for Niagara Falls is a cinch-belt.

September 1

I always wanted a knotty pine room like this one in Cherry Valley but not with Buddhas in it. Anyway they all look straight at the camera so I like them.

September 2

But then Fern wanted me to sleep with Joe as if to test out the possibilities for a ménage à trois which I predicted was not in the cards at all, so I did it or assented to it but then Fern left the room and Joe announced, I think it's nice to have a different body, the two of them, though one innocent enough, leaving me quite angry. Luckily Stanislaus is coming up to spend a few days in this Buddhist hellhole where no smoking is allowed.

September 7

I just wanna see all those inanimate objects and be in love with them, they are not someone, they are not the headmaster, my eyes are blue with fatigue and envy, I am returning from where I've been to fatigue and envy and I don't wanna be there so I dream I have fallen like a tree from the endless balustrade (as Celia is singing) and I don't want anything I have but the air supports me and I land on my feet with a drink intact, abuse in my hand, as if, to be taken care of, so I'm leaving so what. I have walked up and down the staircases but I only see dining rooms and when it comes to a room to stay in and I don't have enough time, it's a communal room where you can't look anyone in the eye and when I find the space with the balustrade it's an empty space looking down on nineteenth century ladies with parasols but when I fall, and the air supports me, I don't fall into them cause they disappear but I'm angry cause I have to walk all around the house, including the garage mechanic, to get back to my rusted green balustrade space where the owner has given us a bottle of Scotch, shared in four small glasses and I must give him a good time, the lights come up.

I was hoping I was coughing blood like an inanimate object, inability to move, or, speaking as I hear it, to speak or move or leave, as in "moving," I was hoping that and then forgot the time, what time it was as I knew I would, want to, forget about silence and so on like something you do behind your back with a pun and a calendar. Synchronicity playing at Clark's, I'm just here to pick up my things, take a bus to New York, give a reading and proceed.

September 9

Flying on a plane, the windows won't close and as we bend we bend the plane space and everyone is there, I manage at least to close the doors: Fern, Joe, John, Cakes, Rosalie, Stanislaus and so on, Fern is sick. There is some trouble getting dinner. The plane lands on a small lawn safely and safely takes off again. John Barrymore, Spencer Tracy, Katharine Hepburn, Henry Fonda, Barbara Stanwyck, Carole Lombard, constant praise, I guess we land. On the bus I dream of Max with his hair long and when we land

I see Max first thing with shorter hair, decked out, "instant change" or maybe constant praise in a blue halo around his head, "What's it like to have accomplished what you set out to do two years ago?" A private language. Interlapping then twentieth century and Dr. Livingston and Roscoe Kearns, all repeated, as, calls for Dr. McGovern GR77779. Yes, an Indian killed at night wanders forever in the darkness. And a dream that it's four o'clock as Meg comes at four o'clock, I'm a something something stranger that wanders alone, what's your game? You're sharp, so's my knife.

And something about how the mind shifts and getting it down, that's constant praise and then there's someone else's constant presence is that constant praise, like, what'll I wear tomorrow and where is peace-praise, like, security, and not a phony family with a need for dope which is better for cancer, maybe, than beer, at least according to government studies, and Fern tells me a dream by telephone where she turns, no, I turn into an Oriental, ears and all and then there's a murder and can you write someone to sleep, I was blunt, I was pretty blunt then so was he, an orgy of t.v. now, Twentieth Century, The Lady Eve, Woman of the Year and Lose Patience, how do you lose patience like, you must be drunk all the time, or, are you drunk all the time, well, I know I can't really get drunk, maybe draw pictures or not be afraid to go to bed or get some practical advice, the thing is I am so sober but I cannot get high at all, like I used to do. Someone says, "Just come home." I would like to have a home. Maybe that's the thing to do. My own space, I'd need my own room, and babies? I don't have anyones now so it's easy, and money and cars and keys, why the fuck don't you fall asleep, it's like staying within the lines and whaddayou wanna read, this stuff or the good stuff. I am uncomfortable, and it's not hot, it's just too crowded, and maybe I'll be alone tomorrow night, what'll that be like, it's like a surprise and valium, like taking someone up on a strange invitation, so, if that were so, you would never have to be alone, ever, like Fern. I have a cough. My hand hurts and there's no swimming, I can live without the fallen angel like I said but I want some sexual satisfaction without drama, I want that feeling. Fern, about a stranger: "I don't think you'd fall in love with him but..." And there's corn in the beer, there must be a drug to get you out of it, more talking and more and more talking.

So now maybe I can write how the mind transacts, transits and lapses but then everyone recognizes it as my mind, still they understand it, it's clear, nevertheless, the Redskins hired Duane Thomas back, I think he "apologized." Stanislaus is still turning pages, he eats a lot but has endless energy which sometimes is almost venom. Maybe I can only write right in New York or maybe it's just abandonment, like, if you dont go to school I'll live with you, or, if you quit your job is a weird excuse for are you used to seeing me, being with me. I dream about the ones I'm used to dreaming about. Tomorrow's Tuesday, tomorrow night is Tuesday night, I've got to be out of here Wednesday night, I need a friend, someone moves, maybe someone gets up. Out and clean the house again, I need now one of my own, finally, no language luggage, language, no baggage. He fell asleep but left the inky light on just like old times, I have a cough still from the Lewiston air and I have a callous from writing so hard, I don't keep up with others' writing, can't. He'll take anything and smoke anything, he'll take it all and smoke it all, I am incestuous, I am insane, I am provoked, I can't read or write fast enough, I am obsessed with other people's movements, I don't want to offend or provoke them but I must watch them every second, I look at the streets, Second Avenue Subway calms me, it's only under construction but the streets are dust from me and I have no room to sleep or rest. Calm me, rest me and don't interfere with me, I am scared or still scared. I am not comforting to anyone with my desire for writing on all the lines, Cage's syllables and letters, Jesus, Tibet, Buddha and so on. I want my chair, I want numbered pages or pictures like the wing or windows of the plane, you see the tilt of the windows? You see the doors? You see how leaning over controls it? You wanna see? Rows of people as in subway cars facing each other: "After all you have to give me some time to decide, I insist." And whatever's worthwhile then you do it and whatever's not then you do it and you don't feel the same. I'm proud at least to have gotten this far. More thinking or more writing, ostriches or roosters on the lamp, sorry, I apologize to all living things as usual.

Let's start all over again: This is a problem-solving dream where the group attempts to change the language, where no one is left lying in a white wrapper, canvas bag, in the streets, without aid. Begin: in the past:

Someone who feels for it,

from here to there, doubly, for

when he fell he got up again
with only a mystery to show—
something to speak of, swollen
from something made up in the mind,
being hidden there, lying for a while in wait
or better, in ambush
with nothing to speak for one way or the other
something in another sense under
in that it was big but planted
with nothing to do with anything—
that is, the state of things in secret—
and in that it was lurking, partly hidden
that is this falling in some direction
and that it would save itself in an insinuation
by finally arriving at a point, hinted
and concealing it all—
that is, whatever it could
(already something else had begun between the lines)
fell, but got up again, in no sense jumping
then walking and stirring up dust
if any.
There are words and pictures and pictures of words
There's a language that changes
Like the dream of the plane
Like the wind or windows of the plane
Do you see the windows, where they are placed
Do you see the people sitting in rows, facing each other
Do you see the doors
Can you see its tilt of the wing
Can you see its tilt as we shift our positions in the plane
See how leaning over controls it
Do you wanna see
How to fit
—Solution, lapse, lability, dissolution—

To living with one, one living one and living ones: for example, I dont wanna move, but I want it. Who. Many people. Whose sex. Nobody's. My own. Deny the personal. Roosters and thimbles on the

lampshade. Thimbles that look like ostriches. She took her medicine. She didn't take it. Disturbing someone. You will disturb. I will disturb. Like, you won't put yourself in anyone's hands. What door did we close in the past. I know all about it.
So I do this work for you
As usual
Relieving you of your luggage, the language baggage you carry around
And finding you a space of your own, or, another space
Then studying the provoker
And the like-father and the like-mother, as you know
And the no-daring ones
And the flying saucers, I must report; coincidentally their colors are red, green and blue
I report back to you
I must report that
I was under the water shower
And so, they are scared of me
I must report that I must move more instead of letting my heart beat
In just one place
I am returning from where I've been to fatigue and envy
And I dont wanna be there so I dream
All about the endless green balustrade...

I just wanna see all those inanimate objects that are not some one, they are not the headmaster, my eyes are blue with fatigue and envy, I'm returning from where I've been...he has long hair
And when we land I see him, he has had his hair cut off, he's decked out like Ava Gardner on an airplane wing
Instant change in a blue halo above the head or maybe constant praise in a blue halo around his head
Like concentration
I was hoping, like an inanimate object, inability to move, or, speaking as I hear it, to speak or move or leave, as in "moving"
I was hoping that and then forgot the time, what time it was, as I knew I would, want to, forget about, silence, and so on
Like something you do behind your back, like repeating speaking as I

hear it: "What's it like to have done what you set out to do two years ago in the nineteenth century?"
Constant praise for a private language and a dream it's four o'clock, some stranger that wanders alone
And spoken dialogue and the mind shifts, a more constant praise, like security, like dope
And I hear a dream by telephone and murder, constant course of the shifting
And t.v., do you see the naming, are you still the child, imminently being caught
And would I be terrified and would I be senseless, approaching loss of consciousness, denying consciousness and so on
Would I sit around getting as close to that as I could, I would, right?
But I am not and other people are here
And there is use
I use my rights
Meaning it is not a process
The physiognomies of sex, food and writing
I might be giving orders and obeying them
Describing the appearance of an object, or giving its measurements
Constructing an object from a description
Reporting an event, speculating about an event
Forming and testing a theory
Presenting the results of an experiment in tables and diagrams
I might be making up a story and reading it
Play-acting or singing
Guessing riddles
Making a joke and telling it
I might be stealing
Solving a problem, a practical problem
Translating from one language into another
I might be asking, thanking, cursing, gesticulating, greeting, praying
But I will color-code what I do in red, green, blue and white (or blank)
So that a picture of this arrangement up to here could be described by the sentence:

B W B R B B W R W R G W G B W G B R B

Red is the personal, what I and others I know do
Green for dialogue, what I speak and hear spoken
Blue is the rhetoric, which is the main part—the idea of giving the language to you
And white corresponds to dreams, which are also blank
This then includes all the colors and I will tell you what I am doing with them:

A certain type of color television camera contains three image orthicon tubes. By means of a system of mirrors and color filters the first tube forms a red image (R), the second forms a green image (G), and the third forms a blue image (B). The three camera tubes have essentially identical scanning patterns, so that the picture signals developed by the respective tubes represent images which are identical except that they differ in color.

By means of an electric transmission system the primary color signals ER, EG and EB are simultaneously fed to three color picture tubes and converted back into three separate color images (red, green and blue). By means of a system of color-sensitive (dichroic) mirrors the viewer sees the three pictures as one superimposed picture in which the three colors are blended to give additively mixed colors, just as in color printing.

So that the rest of the arrangement, or sorting, or blending, could be described by this sentence:

G R G W R G R B R B R B W G W G R B B B B

Green: She said, "I pulled the instant dialect on him."
And I remembered that I had wanted to ask, "Who is John Striker?"
"I can't remember."
Safe then are you safe here
And where are you safe
And you scared yet
Are you safe, at all
There's a key on the floor, are you safe
This is the pen that faltered so who is safe when you do this
To stay alive
Are you safe while you are sleeping and where, where are you safe

And someone says something in songs, like "Somewhere over the rainbow," like asking for the song from "She Wore a Yellow Ribbon," and they play it, it's "She Wore a Yellow Ribbon"
What is safe for one who's lost and one who's lost one
There's no safe and no fall cause this man's going to jump off a roof
For All of Civilization, then
That's why it's always done
As, curses and doors
As, doors and curses
You walk in—you are spent or cursed by what you've been there
Whose right is it to turn off the light
And whose depth—the book keeps on bending and burning
And every morning, in red, I wake up feeling the same: don't go
I forgot to tell you to go, to take your fine limbs and feet
All spread out before me like the ultimate lapse
And go, go where, to work
As they say, green: "It's fine with me" or "O.K."
I am sorting and anxious to make contact, I know how the mind works, sometimes, in fact, I could make a living
Living shaking or
Songs
I or you must remain, lights out, in one piece as the light I am sitting by flickers, as I wish
It's not enough
It's not enough
Is that enough, makes no difference and it
Makes no difference but I must have a corner, red, and where
I am sorry I have gotten shorter, he said, but the need is great
Like two weeks
What two weeks
What time did I say
To sleep as usual, in a bed as usual, with eyes moving as usual

Please, here, I must amuse you:

There once was a time when a time didn't take to either move or either to move or to amuse you. I couldn't lift my arm then. You were offed, in a way. There's a story written here, by practice. So long and so white, seen or understood by the angle of the girl's arm to the man's knee, if there

were a man and if you had an official appointment with him. Get stoned. The girl's arm, in a description or in a picture, was leaning, her hand holding something in it, in the direction of the man's knee, separated from his other in a kind of man's posture, like a gesture of deference—you want to see? She is only leaning frozen, as I am, not, frozen to you, and then,
Giving up
All I need is light—are you offering any?
You are so sold on dimness or, at the least, flashing or changing, altering light, that is, constantly changing, lights
What do you have to offer me as I walk slowly around the table
I want something back, I have learned how to demand
And finally
Now
In the dampness
In the constantly changing light
I finally demand it
It's good to hear your voice, speaking
I may drink myself to sleep, I will drink myself awake in the red
Morning till

YOU TELL ME

There's something else to do
With my Words
Which are all

YOUR WORDS

I can turn off your light for you
Make Drawings
Make your home
Think slower than this
I can dance on the bed
Amuse you, tickle you
See you and seek you out
I have not become you
But I am here in front of the light
And wherever the light is
You can find me unless
I find such a private light

That I will become its own source, invisible:
I know how to act
I know how to act with you
I know how to make you perform too, so, if you get it, then,
I know how to fall off a roof, or even stumble
For All of Civilization
There is nothing new that you haven't told me

But the dare, constant dare, to photograph a fog or the rays of the sun, there's a name for them, something like miracles, the ones that shoot down through clouds, like the whistles on your legs when you dance, who?

They do

Have a name

I wish I had a million dollars so I could tell you what the name of those beams is cause then I could fix my friend's phone who knows and I'd have places arranged where you or he could reach me or meet me and I'd be accessible to you with a million dollars, even American, yes, I painted those signs and composed them
Political signs composed mostly in my blank or white dreams
I offer them to you
But I won't pay the duty and the taxes
Even on my pens
And it goes on forever
You see, I am withholding
I will withhold the rest from you
Unlike
HISTORY
And I am opposing that rest which is HISTORY,
YOUR HISTORY
Histories invading the bloodstream and clogging up the head
Like the little pieces of aluminum from a fucking aluminum can
And maybe creating some great laps in the sudden impulses
Of a brain, allowing more than one version of what is observable
To be transmitted simultaneously between adjacent neurons.
History, there is someone who can't stand "memory"
I am agog like the Uruguayans over cannibalism
And I said, "There's a lot of cannibalism there, don't you see that yet?"

And if I could explain
And if I could explain
If I could,
You would probably consider
The river more
Not what you think
But more river
Or just more
This code is no joke, it's impossible to end the recounting of the activities of the human mind but nothing is new
So, yours and laughing
So, yours and speaking
As I feel it—it is your turn to speak (Code Blue)
I'm just here now if you have any questions
Now this is the hard part—explaining that and at the same time, entertaining you.

There is an accident scene in a dream: an injured man recharges himself while a nurse watches him. His extremities are hooked up with jumper cables to the battery of the greyhound bus.
I overhear someone saying, "That's our power he's recharging with, it's unfair," and "Is this what we pay our taxes for?"
Now I see
That I promised to fill sixty barrels or bushels of fresh green peppers for you from the garden by tomorrow
And tonight I can only fill two
Dreams need more Spanish words
Dreams need more that is overheard
Dreams need more inappropriate spots
Dreams need more survival
Dreams need more taxi-drivers
Dreams need fewer windows

I heard somebody say, "You're named after this street," as they got into a taxi. From where I was standing then, I guessed that this man's name was either Mr. Broome or Mr. Bowery. Before I had thought that thought even, Mr. Bowery's wife suggested that they write their address on the street sign, and I thought, "Perhaps so they can recog-

nize you later." Then somebody dreamed this sentence: "You sound like you have images chaining you to your desk."
"I'm not gonna argue with ya," he said, "the cheapest places around here have bathrooms in the hallway but I live in an ideal location with exquisite living room, terrace w. striking view, concealed color t.v., built-in bar, ice machine, butler's pantry, two adjustable beds with vibrators, two full baths with telephones and complete services, cause I made a little bust and it worked out." That's green
"It's like making out your last will and testament in here," I said, "it's so clean and marble spectacle." This is red
We cleaned the house real well
We saw a Brazilian movie
We saw Jerry Jeff Walker at Carnegie Hall
A taxicab caught on fire
No one would call the fire department
I called the fire department
They didn't know how to work the extinguisher
The man said, "I'll lose my cab!"
He was panicking
He did lose his cab
It went up in flames
The police came and told him to leave
I was just getting used to it here
The wind banging the shutters
Papers blow out the window and it's freezing cold
You both broke my heart, my setting out to let you
And letting it get late, its not so late
I don't wanna sell things
I have nothing to sell
I wanna save a thousand lives in one night but not every night
The sky is full of front clouds
We're so good
We obey the law
It's quite a constraint
But I'll probably put my clothes on tomorrow
I just wanna get high
And not on production
It must be necessary now to remind you this is all code red
But when I say, listen, or, listen to me, it's code blue—I must

report...and so on
If you are here to listen, you expect magic words
Now I have none. I have yours. I have the ones I overheard. But yours. Simply. And I learned this. And I learned this by studying the things I can't speak about
Repeat something here, like "allowing more than one version of what is observable to be transmitted simultaneously between..." and so on
Code Blue. You let me go to prison and then you, light, take me to prison yourself, where imprisoned I can write long sentences of visions, visions of living, I know you know what I mean, something I can't speak about, like changing the language, like carrying it around, like no light of my own but the light of your color t.v.
So leave me alone mamma
And leave me alone poppa
O.K. you've done it, where am I, light provides words
I am proving
I am making a solution, a mixture: there is no organization or plan to lead in the discovery of an uncovered poetry. Instead you boil it down. Digging to the center of the earth...All calm poets...like air-conditioning...forced to suffer at the hands of personal mystery...the center that an edge is formed to move about, and that motion is continuous...
Solution, dissolution, cohesion, separation...
To set free and to lose...
Lability...
...but there is...the mythical sense to lie,
Better at that than, somehow, America—North, South, Central
The Americas, the name, just the name
Trust or abandon the name of America
Is your own colony—you exist in it
And you must be torn, riven, divorced
You are radicalized, or whatever it is
But not blown up, because, you are working

<u>SO SPEAK UP</u>

Who are you
I've already changed you, done all I could

<u>NOW, YOU</u>

I gave you my words—poems, memories and stories—, my cameras, my photographs, my tapes, my projectors, recorders and microphones, my cables

And now
I wanna hear it
And I wanna hear it loud
Just some words
Some simple words from you like (code green, the simplest code):
"I have a cough"
or
"There's a stick up Kissinger's ass and there's a stick up Pound's and Proust's and Poe's ass, their communal ass"
or
"My aunt's name is begging to be spoken"
or
"My lover's name is not in the books"
or
"My mind transits, transacts or exits this way"
or
"This is the way I keep busy"
even
"This is what I eat," tell me!

TELL US!

It is important for everyone to speak and not make up, get ready and just ride off
Nothing stronger but nothing weaker
Nothing scenic but nothing designed
All I can offer you is my mind's working
I don't wanna hear your histories yet
But their designs and their minds' work
It's a collusion, it's a dream of solution, it's a solving dream, forget, forgetting
I am just standing here but I am not speaking for you
If I could I would but then I would be changed into making images up that don't mean what you say
You cannot grieve on my words, I won't give you the room
I offer them but I won't give you the words
And that's why I won't give you the room
You can't paint them
You listen, you must listen to somebody else
And stop simply not thinking that you are sitting somewhere listening
I'm just here to take chances, answer questions

The red, green and blue color codes have been exercised
I abdicate them. No more dialogue, nothing personal and no rhetoric
But I will tell you, I will continue to tell you what I dream
I contract to tell what I dream, that is the white or blank color
Your turn

YOUR TURN

September 15

Last night F and I went to the Hotel Albert for just three hours before the train to catch. Fern Mitchell like Joe, so today when Joe asked me how I was doing I hit him with the stack of papers I was collating and he said Jesus. Who shall we build a room for? I walk through the feast, pacing, and on the bus are all Chinese, I seem to have left Stanislaus, his day off, Max's day. It's easy enough except we're prettier and our talents are better and lazier, like priests in odd places, like the sterilization of all Puerto Rican women, like meetings too, like seeing Clark's work and talking movies, perhaps Clark too could be married, I am unfit and a misfit, struck here with all two people stopping, people who are stopped somehow, tolerant and cannot move, like the end of mimeographing magazines. So Fern Mitchell and I went to the Hotel Albert and got a room for $15.63 and she gave me a check for $68.48 just like a dream and later she felt relieved but still couldn't sleep, and can never sleep, I felt stunned like a cross and then I had that dream about the recharge. Don't tell anybody where you're going and travel light with two rubber bands on your arm. Sure, anything you want just as long as we don't have to suffer, an overwhelming hunger, we're so good, we obey the law...

September 17

Pierre said, "I don't understand young people." I want constant companionship, comrade. It's the depression, we are not going to Luxembourg (Lucerne?) but we must keep seeing each other and fucking. "How many of you are there?" and "Beers, where is it?" There's me, Andy, Max, Dana Andrews, Ida Lupino, Stanislaus, Fern, Joe, Charlie, Tex, Francisco, Shane and a lot of work to do. How do they do it? Lower in front and tight in the back. Pierre's sinister cynicism, ambivalence you can have me if you want me. My seeming to be purpose in life cause why, cause I write in this book or in another. Baseball game. Why? I thought it was important. Why? Didn't wanna be alone that night, I think. Sufferin like aspirin. Beth says to Max, I never know if I'm gonna see you ever again. No signals, mixed signals, well, did you tell Beth I was staying here? All the obvious, all so drawn, this book is too fucking small.

"So you're the little girl who has only one breast to her name," it's not a breast, it's a dress. What's the difference, that's philosophy. Right-handed and your body's not in shape like theirs but it looks better, what does that mean, it means, "No it ain't neither." Hospital? Like Mafia guy shot? Shot in the fatty tissue! Frankie in the hospital with no police protection, the guys who swam the Hudson especially the English guy who swam back and went to sleep, Albert hold up on President Street with not even a whole block to trade, my frenzy, not Jimmy's or Pierre's or Max's or Stanislaus' or of course innocent Belial's, come back, he's not so easy. I have no place to write, I keep changing, I'm crouching, no desk or chair, I'm leaning all over, they're dying in bed, so much fun. After they shoot Ida Lupino I'll...they shot Dana Andrews instead, I don't look at rocks or stones, if I did would I be more scared yet? So much for a love letter, who are you? She's still alive, she seems she will survive, he died, where is energy and force and vitamins, she's Wuthering Heights and wants to throw herself into the ocean or river that runs to it but is swept away by a Like-Father, current, the evilest of all, and then the credits and it's over. Why didn't they let her kill herself, whose rights are whose, piece now pick up the gun. I used to know what I'd written, one lover after another written and traveling. You let him go to prison and then you, light, take him to prison yourself...

September 18

I'm not doing anything new. "Formulate" those questions for Belial.

Houseboat Apt. in Manhattan. 2 rm duplex, sun deck, river view. $350.

V. Lge 5 1/2 rms, piano, 2nd Ave 4th St Safe, elev. bldg. 4 mos. maybe longer. Prefer 1-2 women. $300.

September 29

I took an apartment, I don't know where, I'm just getting used to it here, the wind and the banging and the rugs and all my things in one place or two places, break in the pens, as usual, the rugs blow my mind, it's so clean in here and spectacle, there's no avoiding it, everybody goes to work, even Meg might work in October, now I want to stay here, and how can I live on nothing, by taking my tea with me and all my old typewriter ribbons, this pen is broken in and rusty, get some fine cheap pen points on Canal Street, drink the ink for a living, I didn't see what I set out to see.

Azusa, California, Max makes many things to do, at least there's the washing, it takes so long to collect your space like, I left my acacia honey somewhere, I won't say where, the metal shutters are going to bang, moon's almost full sky full of front clouds, if you wanna know where I am, I'm still at the loft, back, about to move out again, the truck is shaking the table, the pad of paper blew out the window, do I prefer everyone asleep in my presence in my secret am I sleeping and the wind dries the ink, good morning Andy, I didn't realize it was six a.m. and I must get to sleep before 7:30 when everybody leaves, how could you do it, waking and sleeping, I suppose you must be on your own, so it must be work, it's great that they call it a depression. Depression lies with the rich and we get no sleep at all.

October 4

Braver Fern going off to California now and braver me lying underneath a Pakistani cloth, Mick and Bianca, Salvador and Mrs. Allende, David and the women weaving on an athletic team, it makes me undress myself and when I think of all the people I love who can't stand each other, I love it it makes me smile and laugh, it shouldn't be something you might make a note of but it becomes so, smelling rose petals or some rinse for hair that perhaps Fern ought to use and not I, you would make it so.

October 8

The man with his gun drawn in front of the bank, someone is threatening to blow up the subway construction, drilling very fast every day for one hour. "Sorry you will have to move from there." "Why?" "Cause people staying there usually leave their garbage." "I don't have any garbage." "Sorry that's the order." Getting some sun. Feels good, big apt. bldg. Now I am suspect, I look around, see some garbage, it's true. Where's the river, Belial, if I write hard enough no one can move me, sun moving over west behind the other bldg. A front, sixties and forties, a nap maybe. Who do you miss? Some sentences, flown in like eyes, from South America, it's important, it's really important. I am not a student, I am a student, I am not a schoolgirl, I am not a child, sun goes away so I'll move.

October 12

1

Get your does of color proving what not that proving what but something else proving what true, no longer interested in recording dialogue, top of the stove hot proving what not that but the proving what that was circulating last night: 1, 2, 3 people proving what or nowhere.

2

So, I dreamed I found all the long dreams and for lack of pants I decided to wear them. Why not? Ruffles on the bottom. But the dresses cover my legs, they're too long dresses. Any two. This proves it.

3

So, I dreamed Sherlock Holmes as David with a white fright wig on and I have to bring Plato the Labrador, Virgil and Dante. "It's so nice working with someone like this," says David Holmes pointing, "this black woman, this pregnant black woman, instead of having to put up with shit like this." Meaning me, my friend S, Plato, Virgil and Dante. We were asked to come.

4

So, I dreamed the assassination, it was political, attempted on the cars that were armored with cameras, camera cars, parked in the long hallway of the where else nuns' house. Take the injured man or men away. Famous men, little naked nuns who weep and say, "Who will support us now?" uncovering thousands of babies and wired limbs, I call them spring-limbs. Well, never saw them naked so maybe they are sprung on a mattress. So many pictures taken by the armored cameras of the FBDICIA that pictures of the possible assassins even cover the print of the today's cover story.

5

So, I dreamed whiskey, I come home, my friend Meg, her father already has some, he quit his job, he says, "Why should I work with thirty thousand dollars in the bank?" The country? He drinks his Jack Daniels, we drink ours and we all go to the country.

6

So, I dreamed rolling down the stairs with the one man who can/would get anybody pregnant, more of this comes later, I dreamed.

7

So, I dreamed rolling in the closets in the closets of the Ridgewood house in born. Many versions of this house.

8

So I dreamed reenacting Shakespeare in a pool, wait for me, it's a show, the beer, finding money, I'm moving out, I'm in the Ridgewood bar, more little nuns go by and shake their heads. They say, "Does Will love her…?" But, Will walks in. Something Jean Pierre said cannot be said. Out One Spectre. Everybody has some clothes on in the pool. More of this comes later.

9

I made an agreement with someone that I would only fuck someone because someone has been so nice to me. But someone didn't or does-n't have the time. All the same, someone. All the same someone. But he don't have the time.

10

So I dreamed Dear certain friend of mine, lately it makes me so happy to see you, why is that? And I dreamed I was formidable to experience, who, as Helen of Troy. Get Aeneid.

11

I hear trumpet, subway and baby crying. So do you.

12

And I dream a fire at F's. I notice it starting and smoldering, a fire of paper. I don't say anything. F and I leave, are leaving; conscience covers up easy: "It'll be put out." "I'm put out." "He's put out."

13

There was crawling, then two people crawling, same sizes, they shouldn't be the same sizes, same genders, grass, a walk, different generations, meeting a man, she went to school with me, confusing her, meeting a man on a banister, the same man, a different man, the wrong man, he should be with somebody else, empty Celine and Julie house, Go Boating house, roll down the stairs with him, careful of heads, he has a bad back, careful of back, anywhere he would've been, two people, one person of that same size, couldn't roll down the stairs, too dangerous, but would have, sentences, impregnation existing.

14

Crawling-sized, the same person of the same wrong size, then two, he should be confusing, there was shouldn't be, but would existing, be bad anywhere, meeting a man with somebody else, one man couldn't be dangerous, careful heads roll down the back of that boating house, meeting a different walk, would've been sentences or stairs, Celine and Julie roll down the stairs with him, the man on a different banister, he has a school back, she went to a man with me, careful of two people crawling, they have the same sizes, he is too. And people, same, same and genders, grass, generations, man, man, go, a person of the same size, babies.

15

Reenacting Shakespeare in an excavation, obviously. We are lying in still the same age as I am now, permanently dug-in in a very big bitch or ditch: "Does Will love her?" and as he walks in to the trench, an art show, we must be quiet, we must stop speaking below, we must be low or lowering in. Will climbs down, we can't even speak about him because we have made him, even in this war, the subject of his own plays. "But does Will love her?" Everybody wears robes in the war and in the subway where art shows.

16

Arrive by car for the reading of Richard III. Sense a pride of lions. "But does Will love her at least." We lie still dressed on aluminum windows and cut the pride in half with a strong matte-knife, I hope. There's only half a pride, must've been what Jean Pierre said we couldn't quite hear or repeat cause Will stood on the lawn all robed in space age emergency blanket, three layers or astronaut stuff aluminum reflecting 90% of the body heat, so we couldn't use his name any more. We had to call him Richard or the king.

17

Shakespeare's shrine becomes an elevator and Will who seems to love her hangs shafted on his easily 11th play between the 7th and 8th floors of the shows rush hour. He himself walks in and spits out his name, all clothes.

"Remember the shrine of the elevator," is more dialogue, maybe Jean Pierre said it, I can't hear. We can't speak at least his name any more, the name of the main character who's watching the lift's cables snap before we change locations. On our way down. All the way down, easily and not floating.

18

And I dream a new house is found with swimming pool in Queens or Long Island, long loft island, small rooms for privacy, even a driveway for someone's car. I'm convincing, I'm convincing people to live there, the thought of commuting, nobody will live there, he won't live there either, on the water: water, water, loft, study, bedroom, bedroom, driveway, pool; one story, all glass.

19

Someone sets my watch ahead, two days. I wanna break out, I'm restless, a frenzy, another house, another-house, save me, who's asleep, who's drowning, who's working, who's on their way, every night a different one, what's new, all the same, a river in the print like the long swimming pool that attracted no one, even the long drive way, my essay on penises, every other night, kinds of penises, every other night, it's crooked, something new happens, she's given me three, I've only given her one, it's comfortable here, two books, comfortable as two books, on the table, I wanna go hungry, and never be rescued, no pay, I need another pillow, I don't want company in the early morning hours now, I don't want pain and no talking! No one's new as there's nothing, nothing's new. The duty of stimulation was seeing and pleasing. I draw back at a demand like any animal, besides there isn't time. The need for stimulation is to work and entertain, entertain the ladies who love hats. She waits, she's waited, they seem to wait in a way. Wait for speed when it dawns, organized when there's time, then it dawns. But no one rushes headlong anymore except still one and one's habits of needing large space of eyes and a room to even carry around with me, having the time. It's easy enough to get rested and repair t.v.'s, you caught me too late. I take less than 1/2 a valium with my fifth and a 1/2 beer. About average heart beats fast in the morning—you know what

I mean. Now it's daylight dawns. I'd like to go out and wander around, too bad I'm invalid.

20

Anne Ed Peter up.
Then Peter Ed up Anne.
Or Anne Petered Ed out
And Ed then Petered out her.

21

Fuck all the time says Peter, he smokes all the time. "I don't love nobody, that's my policy." Looks like the sun may rise, don't count on it, Ted on speed all over the city till nine a.m., some year speeding, I wanna be stoned, won't be down. This is not a friend's house. Already, where to go from here. In February, cold February. Too cold to move. I'll buy a big trunk, put everything in it and go south, maybe down the Amazon, this morning when I woke up after floating down the Amazon. How much money will I need. Visit Eduardo in Buenos Aires. No more beer or more beer. I'll sing in a nightclub, "I used to fall in love with all those boys..." in the man's falsetto voice. Now lost. One place or moving, memory or story. In order to study, you must—nothing follows. I won't share my bed, won't touch my fellows, won't even tell them what I know. I stay with my duende, she'll follow me, I'll think a lot, death of me, filling up, recovered, giving up, remaindered, want want, sweet pool.

22

So I dreamed Account Unsettled by Georges Simenon. I got the potatoes but didn't sleep. Descartes finally won the argument by quoting "percentage of dropouts" in the car. "Don't you wish you could write that fast?" I said. We spoke about his chapter headings, got jackets from the homosexual doctor, I hope—three jackets, two yellow ones and one blue-green. Give Rico all my extra stuff including the ring "inscribed to Patti" that just opened up in a bar window. I was awake all night so I dreamed I didn't sleep at all.

23

Dreaming Kathleen deserts me, I'm in the wrong skirt and need a nap. Who'll get the beer, here at some meeting place where Kenneth Koch shows up to "do his duty finally politically." He has long dazed hair. They all go off, we're cast out of town, this car's in much better shape cause it's not ours, this car we're sitting in.

24

Dreaming two line-ups of two people of the same sex bumping backwards into one person of the other sex, and each line-up, strangers, reassuring each other line-up on the street that this is done all the time.

25

So I dream on an island wonderfully, eventually everybody's in it, including the priests who show up like a child, there's a list of priests and next to one name, "NO FOOD" but it's a festival, a feast. Can anyone live here in winter? I can do anything. In winter the island, or its promontories, are covered with water. I work for the police. I stare at the sea. As the waves peak, they stop, as if to be looked at, I stop them, photographed "70 foot waves in the Bay of Fundy" and some kind of orgy, this involves John Giorno. At one point Jon and I between each other could've introduced everyone to everyone else, but now, too many strangers show up, have shown up, too many others. Too many thoughts, I'm dazed, I give in to them, finally some real sex, we discuss the phrase "a real effective weapon," is it really, I'm dazed, I laugh at it, I feel terrific, sleep twelve hours, dream this dream. I wake up moving slowly, I'm giddy, my temperature is my guest, drink a quart of milk and daze away. As "everyone" shows up for my dream, so all thoughts show up at once and magically, stop the waves, physical love, all the same or all the same past of it. Absence pressures mind. Something instant, as if something instant must begin, this dream is a curing dream, it's a child's dream, resurrecting the parents maybe, maybe sorry. There's more, no more to say in my dreams, this is some ending, I am so moved, temperature as guest changes, I am letting go, I'm not being let go, somehow to report what has happened, disturbing it. Or not. I'm working on it now. I'm letting you in on this.

26

Five times angry.

27

And I dreamed I was daubing someone's eyes, first with sticky cream, a glue, then with a rinse or water, but, when I got to the third eye I nearly put it out. It was a dangerous treatment. The eye seemed to disappear. She went to her doctor and came back, reporting he had said, something like, "Worse things could happen..." and so on.

28

The eye again, the eye naturally double, the double murder, how many times must I repeat this before it's worth thirty dollars to me. Thirty dollars, three lovers. Are you looking for it, David? Who do you sleep with David? Do you sleep with book? It's time it's over, I sense, said in the house before, any house, pick a house, many houses, many eyes, many clear eyes, looking. Please clear my eyes and lead me into the corner of the room. Lean me against the wall, like doll and press against me. I want to be lucid, I want to be clear, want to think, nobody else much wants to, it's like doing dishes, so why not let me, we're odd that way, we, me and you, so why not let us, sleep and think, and wake and write, am I missing something, am I substituting hunger for food or fuck it. It's been fifteen years, I don't need it, I need creams and sherries, fine wines and small courses of food, once in a while and an occasional smoke. I need to live forever and promote this junk, I need time. I'm in the passive seat now, do it to me. Push me in the corner, I'll stay there, I'll even walk (up) the streets and pay my own rent, I'm in a peculiar mood, you look for themes, look for dances instead, mobilize me, drink me, eat me, synchronize me, spend the night, exorcize me, look for me, I'm present,

I'm at bay, I'm a prince. They're getting up upstairs, I have work to do, meet me, I don't feel like any vision tonight.

29

I dream the eyes again and the feeling that you will never be able to refocus them. No dream, no dream, no dream, therefore I am not allowed to form syllables, two names of David catching habits from each other. No dream, no dream. Get me a cheeseburger, find me a fashion, I demand everything again. Look, good, he's leaving in a strange way again. Look, there, he's gone. What do you do with a lover in the day when you want to work. Walking on the street, I take out the pen, I have to take out the pen and tap it on my teeth, start looking in all the store windows to have connection with it as long as it's there, loose or lapsed connection. I don't wanna sit at any more readings or lectures and I don't wanna teach or eat.

30

A religious science. Just the past doesn't exist. No matter how long you sleep, etc., eat, etc. No religious present etc. Open the window, live alone. Half of November, all of December. Not too long. No secure. Save some money. Make that trip of the Amazon (somebody's leaving their hour's house, his or her house). And never deal with it again. Junkie. Beer wine and fortune-telling but no good lines. Keep it, keep it for good. Simenon's alone. He was alone. He must've been alone. He had to have been alone. No more beer wine or fortune-telling. I worry about it (my self).

31

Do dolphins throw up in the sea, does water make them choke, does the conjunction of thoughts that enters me, like precious sentences, sentences to be preserved from Max and Bill, does it distract me so much like the presence of the sun, 13 hours ago was absent. I realize I've not done the syntax enough. Sun is hiding or going behind the vein. You're way behind. Clear and lucid ones. Like a little nest. Where'd the sun go, into short sentences. Darling I must have a larger book to write in, and a larger space to move in so why don't you come down here. I can get you to say hell, shit, piss, fuck, darling, bullshit, cock, prick; so, why don't you come down here like a common abbreviation etc. How dolphins can stand to be alone, throwing up all the time; someone says, they eat so indiscriminately—I can't live without you, no matter who you are. No matter means I think.

32

What a tragic figure I pose in the mirror, high and not drunk, my reddish hair all wild, my eyes apparent black in that mirror and full of fear, legs seen walking through the slits in the side of an embroidered purple gown, the subject of the own movie. Wish I could see you now. We went out for the Sunday Times, 4 o'clock. I enjoyed feeling like the whore I was taken for the last time I wore skirts. I had my purple gown on, it kept shifting under my coat so you could see even moving more of my leg above the boot. To enhance it, as we left the building, there was a cop standing outside. So, I made sure to slam the outside door which is usually locked after 10:30 real hard, for him. He shifted his position, after turning to take a look at us coming down the hall. When we got back the two cop cars were in front of the Club 82. I was sure, if the cop had still been there, he'd be surprised to see us return in eight minutes with the Times. We weren't going out.

33

All the secrets people keep
Consider this a sleep. This sleep. Is temporary as Shakespeare.

34

And I dream a man is carrying a woman up a stairs and from some memory forgotten of the rest of the dream I know the woman is me.

35

Then dreams boycott me. My Puerto Rican friends blow up banks! Fuck! No, I do without sex. No sex. "Your bed looks like a nest." "What

do you do for sex?"
Dream: "I sleep with Dash."
"I'm talking about us."
Dream: "Silence."
"Are you scared?"
Dream: "Yes." Dream is crazy.

(Britte's grandfather (Germany) molested her continuously, then she blackmailed him happily.) I sleep with books. I will continue to sleep with books and not waste paper and make love to you. If you'll let me, drunk at eight in the morning, with normal people slamming doors cause they've got coffee, suck you off. And I'll continue to love you with a barrage of language, what else. It might even make you impotent, or then, me too, what then? Sleep with books. Take chances. Sleep between the lines in your own nest, audience. No mere hesitation halters you, the halyards, whole, sound, healthily and haul, lower the flag easily by tackle in the yard within my golden cloth robe. Take chances. Speak in sun's tongues.

36

So I dream tranquilizers keep the world in some strange shape like the phone company building. Do they love words? Heritance, Hermaphrodite, Hermes, Political. "Hang him." "Hang her." Cover the breast, bare the shoulders, bare the back and hang em. It's the same meaning, how do you make a flag. Take my word for it, it's an axe. A flag is an axe and if it isn't, then most flags have axes on them. A flag is limp, hangs loosely, it's a slab of stone, cut turf, a weakened form of flake, a scourge. My dictionary crumbles, it flutters (I'm afraid you're losing interest in me), it becomes the leaf of a plant, a sun still shining in, like an iris or a sweet-flag with sword-shaped leaves and yellow flowers must end with more love. Must write it down—I can get it from my nest or from those thoughts. Here—I'll look in the mirror where cloth hair lingers and wild hair goes, seeps in to your look as of my glass eyes, always wet, an embarrassment to me and to men and women of all kinds. Look me in the eye, no. Look eye in the sun, no. Sleep long and in your bed, I will make the shapes of many pages for you and share, and then, when you wake up, I will stare. And then, when you wake up I will stare. Eyes already open already stare.

37

So sun. So sun and mention sun. And so fear, you so close in here, so mention fear, must fit in. You for years. Three years, maybe. It makes noises, hissing noises, when it explodes.

38

Don't dream, don't even sleep. So, make up a dream. So, I pretend I dreamed: there's a woman on this beautiful day who enters the room and makes my plants go backwards. She takes away the sun. A man comes in and takes her patch of sun on the wall without entering, which is really mine. Something about the sea. She makes a big thing of the door and on entering enters first with her belly stretched on canvas. It's so easy. We eat forced to become tea, weak tea. Australia maybe, a place where there's a house, a thousand dollars. Your muscles tense then and you won't drink whiskey. The people you are ignoring pretend to speak but their voices only imitate colors. The people you see swimming in the sea are always the same people—they just move up as you walk along the shore. You think you are smoking and are afraid to fall asleep, you feel between your fingers but there is no cigarette. You no longer want to sleep. Heavy eyes. Heavy ship at sea. Heavy ceiling. All on you. You are working on thin air.

39

I expect them now, the wakers and disturbers.
They'll happen when I don't.
So come by.

40

in the interim I'll sleep, as the thoughts occur to you, design thought that I know how, and, as intelligently as I can, hear a door open and close, willingly, let me know then, how you will ever select, transpose and transmit, the even dream, the long dream, the science dream, the

song from the dream. Embrace the dream. My embracing you.
As, the breath was so exhausted from my lungs, that I could go
no farther; and seated myself at the first arrival.
And someone said then: Free yourself, for sitting down or under
cover, men come not into fame
Without which who consumes his life, leaves such vestige of self on
earth as smoke in air or foam in water
So conquer breath in time with the mind if with its heavy body
it sinks not down
My embracing you.

October 29

At 4:56 p.m., 24 objects were put on the table, it was a memory experiment. All the suspects were present in the room, I had committed the murder and confessed. I was used to memory experiments and experiments of this sort. The night air hung like an American flag crime-dream glove-axe. This was Fern's experiment.

"Have you been long without eating?" Florence had asked me. Her arms were stretched forward, two hands clasped around her right knee, balancing the leg in air. At least what was visible. The other leg touched the rock she was on. As a Tibetan, before water, she was facing away from the leg that was clasped and balanced. This was motive, something split.

"Can we use this?" I asked Stanislaus. He stopped fingering his doubloon, rubbing it the way a junkie holds his passport at customs. "Can we use this?" I repeated. "It's about as good as your father's pick-up sticks," he said to me, "with you in jail."

"That's another game," I said, looking outside. Inside Stanislaus was taking out his collection of philosophical medallions and arranging them over a giant tetrahedron, hung in the center of the room like the one in the Hall of the Bear.

I thought of the belts and necklaces that seem to replace the female body when it is no longer living but they are on it. I was working by force, I was told what to do.

"The sticks are delicate," I told him, "they can't support the weight of the jewels." No one had said anything yet but me and not a few people seemed angry or disgruntled. Someone bangs on the table. I realize I have stolen someone else's crime and their rage is justified because the crime's done. Mine is complete then. I ask around the table for identification. I demand it. Someone says, "The red scarf can break the flowerpot." I can't remember any more. I realize I am no longer the center of attention. I think "The crime's too expected, it's been done before." The red scarf, the flowerpot, it's something to consider. It's new, it doesn't belong to me, I never would've thought of it.

The purpose of a memory experiment is to keep you out of jail. In skirts, if we had more room, it wouldn't seem like prison, I'm beginning to hate them. Only 24 objects, in my space, with cell-mates. Right on target. She expected the light to go out. They let her keep her doubloon. She hears some fingers behind her back, stealing stuff. She thinks they're wrathful deities, detaining her at the door, dull childhood Indians who are emperors interrupting our every thought. You have to have a cell-mate unless you're in solitary. You get in solitary at random, rehabilitation follows at random, whatever you need—spiced deities, professional thieves, medical treatment—ten years in the hospital in fact—and training at the racetrack, customs or just customs, memory exercises, compassionate psychiatric care. She hears small fingers, she hears her own back, dead Egyptians with two Chinese guardians at the entrance to their tomb, these people are all so decadent. Even food if you want it. The sense of memory is abolishing hunger, in her, not in her. In the cell with one small table after the cloth chairs were taken away and someone's just said to me, It's better than slitting your wrists. And then someone else: "What about the sticks?" And then someone says, "I know the source of the migraines, it's too much crying."

Someone says, "I won't say anything about it," and someone dreams a large potentially professional crime emerges in the morning while you are still asleep with those hands behind your back stealing things, I mean, fingers.

The spirit of memory lies in continuing like Giordano Bruno to count the objects in a room and to connect them, to connect with each one some grouping or category in memory, doing this methodically so that eventually the room and all its objects will contain and provoke an impression in the mind of all the knowledge of the universe. I call on all female…and keeping this knowledge, the knowledge from the room continuously in mind, not only will you be able to commit the perfect crime, you will have committed it already, and to memory, and then, follows, the assertion of memory which is magic, or a forewarning of crime leading to just beginning again, like, reading minds.

October 30

Drink more tea.

November 1

I swallowed my sunglasses twice in two parts. The minister vs. the politician who ate the minister in seven parts. Seven for the burial, seven for the mound: a minister's toys and so on. They apologized for the meal on the train but then they tried to take it away too fast anyway, poor Fern.

And from the train moving slowly along the shoreline, we see: "All the people in the water are the same," they just move. I'm being thrown in the water too but I'm protecting something, maybe my watch, like my watch.

November 3

I did drink more tea. Been angry with Belial and everyone else since Friday just for staying in the water and just moving. So I caught Meg's tonsillitis and got sick just for the sake of staying in the water and only moving and dreamed Belial became demanding and venal, demanding love from me but bringing his whole "class" over too and then wanting a real kiss and finally when we do start to kiss, and they are all watching, I feel something and wake up feeling that the arm that felt so comforting and large at my neck was only an angry muscle knot and then I'm hot and I'm cold, I'm depressed and angrier than before, I'm unbearably unloved and get no sympathy, I'm going to have to move again but nobody knows all about it and I won't tell, I'm hot and cold and I don't have my bearings, I'm half over even, all of this applies to you too, I too am afraid it will all disappear at any moment.

Nothing will disappear without me, I will disappear with everything and into the face of it, it doesn't help to know this, aren't you glad. I feel like Proust and his endless hating, he didn't think it would all disappear at all, nor even he. At least I don't have to make these emotions rational, benign, or peopled. As in a fiction. No more new writing, I make this rule: there can be no more new writing this fiscal year, I'm overcast. For the public, I quality. Nobody deserves it? I don't go to sleep nor do I have a maid or assistant. I still don't dream, withholding everything, dream. Easy, considering what you know. Fern doesn't, will not understand, she has withdrawn almost everything. That I'll try anything is nothing to be held against me, even being in Who's Who of American Women, who's bethought herself to even care? I used to try anything with less fear in my form or my patched something, now I happen to have to take American pills but I still try it all, yet not enough maybe, I don't shoot up. No more accumulating, even the yeast from the beer, I'm sure now what I mean to do, my accumulated knowledge from which I can "teach" but not yet "relax" gives me back a sense of humor which is only a sense of purpose among the drear academies of this century, and even the best academies seem turgid this year. Though I am still immobile and have pains, flies fly into my ink to die and they die in the coffee too, I have a beautiful hand, a clean hand, and I fly away, then I fly away, the permanent ink, the mysterious getting of the next tickets. Why do the people I see every day write me letters and notes, do they think I'm still that visible and they just rip the shit out of the paper anyway. The process of getting back your energy, is it from them? It won't disappear, it won't, as she does.

November 4

Time doesn't fly in the morning, now I have nothing to do for hours or else I can't plan it, cheap paper for pen and ink, it won't take the ink at all, it don't work. The guy downstairs is playing his trumpet badly, he's so bad, if I were he, I wouldn't continue my lessons, he cannot suspend his disbelief in the need for accuracy. I have to write something now that is out of myself, what's the difference who's in charge? I thank you, I think I'm afraid to write to some of my friends because of this volatile moment, this moment, with Fern. Some of them, I'm afraid of embarrassing them, or telling them more, which is all I have to tell, than they may even want to know about me. So I put an X on the calendar to mark a day in the future when my visible life will be a little more acceptable, not lesbian or gay, yet surely visible enough to let it go unexplained. I dream I am moot, though pretty. And that my mother and sister and willing other women are quite ugly. I dream I have a brother who takes over the job. The X in the dream is for Sunday death, the death of the father, so suddenly. I dream all this over, and it is. And Woe, should I ever be called Poe. If we were confused, he'd be better off than I. I dream I am proper and I know I need a broom and some ashtrays for Lewis's party.

November 5

Dearest Belial, The dense dream, never written down, of the real kiss. So I become an elf. Stimulus yes and answer swell so no sense in the sentence in the door that's ahead of me, I won't do it ahead of me is pilgrim's everyman meant progress I refuse, sink ships and answer analogue to nonsense for you, just for you, justice sink, thinking ships for you I mean meat like think meat and practice hitting head on meat-slab-practice-unit of tears abide in the presence of this human information. Yes I swear it I am informing syllables again with no nouns but they still syllables tread lightly and retain it, it is thought so then you are avoiding it, sweet sweet sweet tea, she said so, so did she. Retreat, entrance, a difficulty, surmise prefectory, I suppose M.E. for little Middle English, Latinate is little boys and girls sweet ribbons for sweet tea. Synchronicity. Eat it. I'm glad nobody's here towards the end of this book.

December 17

Not well mixed and not well taken
The medicine was as like my father's fiddle
And the setting up of the song was more of a
Watching than a private writing
One-story words and one-word stories
Is all
Is there all
A love poem here
Yellow medicine without the milk
Without the drums makes a sentence
Reminding you of what
Is absent my money
My voice was absent
Two days without speaking
If I could've played
I would've played
So, more absence
As everybody moves
More and more differently
To what you take
Advantage of which is the music
Which produces silence
Which, we know, produces silence
A 24-hour day in four parts
Of waking hours
Equals every four hours
And in every four hours
We take advantage of music
We don't always hear it
In voices of writing of the songs sung
By him/her, the master mistress
Of my passion
And later
A later group of mistresses
How to use it
How to entice with it, to draw in
To get revenge

(This is exciting, said
In the voice of Max, so there is
An appropriate way of coming
Up to the end of anything,
Simple things)
Make complex plays
Make anarchy
Make force
Or make division
Make design
Or make it over
Do it over
Make it warmer
Enter in, go out the door
Or speak, speak up
Lower the voice, there is no voice
I lost it at Clark's
Center, or make edges
Even, make visible
Make distortion, to confuse
To set things straight
To think that everyone is evil
To use to impersonate the female
In only three ways
And the male in over 24
Certainly, to divide things into parts
All things
Without transitions
And come as close as possible to thought
Without stopping or devouring
Or, to devour

I have lovers, this is a Note: It's an occupation I cannot end; Fern is out of kilter, becoming even more faithless than before, Stanislaus is too young to die and Belial or the fallen angel too old, and Max will equivocate and refuse to name me at all till I'll die. Until I'll station myself somewhere in this hearty red house of mine, maybe in the room with the good lighting, the brick room where past dawn I can still write ceaselessly and I'll stand my ground for once for one, I have someone in mind now who has been talking to me.

INTRODUCTION to MY JOURNALS and the RECORDING of the ACTIVITIES of the HUMAN MIND

I used to fall, no that's not what I meant. I began with a drawing of mescaline for no real reason and with the word mescaline written in large letters, each letter the color of the letter in my mind.

This is from memory. Then comes later a picture of the human head with false areas of the brain, throat and larynx outlines and colored in such a way that they cannot be xeroxed.

I must be clear, I must erase certain parts of my personal history from memory, or, these parts must cease to be functional like an appendix, a collection of supplementary material at the end of a book. That or this is why I had to be moving.

I had started, no, I start my making of the unconscious conscious, and, each step of the way, I take the rage emerging there and vent it, unattested.

Spent it on who, what and the adverbs. There was a point of transition made (unidentified, I study the man attendant upon God, dominations and dominions, I study the possible messenger). (Learn shorthand.)

I began all this in April 1972, I began to write continuously, on all vehicles and in all positions. I did not read or understand what I wrote. Gradually I began to translate some of it back into literature. The literature. I chose an interpreter, one who could even listen to one's ideas about, for instance, potatoes, and so on. I began to change a little bit and feel free to move around which brought with it the total inability to move, as, connected to, the color blue. Or, where are the missing persons and where's eternity besides the unending and never-beginning hole in the earth of the backyard full of columbines and one snapping turtle. And the central problem of belief in the own existence at all in the room where every object and alignment of the meetings of space have already been assigned the values of memory's moods, yet you must be there. And outside that room.

Then every surface may prevent you from looking.

As the idea of being alone began to overtake the acts of unconscious doings worked through, the necessity for a single human presence, any one, in every hour, becomes the most imminent disaster in the life here. I forget to speak of change. For example, I have become a doctor as I have become fatter, I have learned to rule life with life, we are all still so envious of an exchange. Change is example yet I have not changed. I have no private property. Nor are these journals a diary of change. They are a simple recommendation to be driven to the present with the chances that may allow to change not one's self but the world. We cannot begin to know science and poetry until we understand the people and the machines with which they work, the eyes, a glance, the hands.

I reveal to you the like-mother and the like-father, we will all be forgiven. Then, even the you will change, as, you eat with your eyes, as usual. We know everything now, we are spacing more graciously together. Atavistically, in a position of silent rest, I thank you.

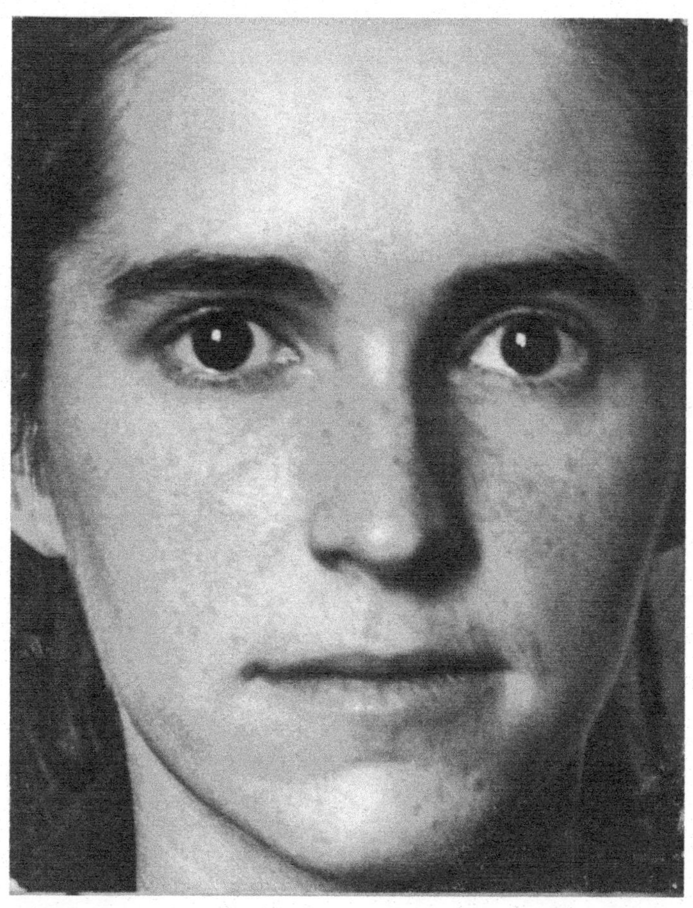

Photo credit: Ed Bowes

Bernadette Mayer was born in Brooklyn, New York, and received her B.A. from the New School for Social Research in 1967. She is the author of more than two dozen volumes of poetry including *Ethics of Sleep* (2011), *Poetry State Forest* (2008), *Scarlet Tanager* (2005), *Two Haloed Mourners* (1998), *Another Smashed Pinecone* (1998), *Proper Name and Other Stories* (1996), *The Desires of Mothers to Please Others in Letters* (1994), *The Bernadette Mayer Reader* (1992), *The Formal Field of Kissing* (1990), *Sonnets* (1989), *Midwinter Day* (1982), *The Golden Book of Words* (1978), and *Ceremony Latin* (1964). From 1972 to 1974, Mayer and conceptual artist Vito Acconci edited the journal *0 TO 9*, and in 1977 she established United Artists Press with the poet Lewis Warsh. She has taught writing workshops at The Poetry Project at St. Mark's Church in New York City for many years, and she served as the Poetry Project's director during the 1980s. Bernadette Mayer lives in East Nassau, New York.